MW00790738

A Season of Inquiry
Revisited

A Season of Inquiry Revisited

The Church Committee Confronts America's Spy Agencies

Loch K. Johnson

University Press of Kansas

Published by the University Press of Kansas (Lawrence,
Kansas 66045), which was organized by the Kansas
Board of Regents and is operated and funded by
Emporia State University, Fort Hays State University,
Kansas State University, Pittsburg State University, the
University of Kansas, and Wichita State University

Library of Congress Cataloging-in-Publication Data

Johnson, Loch K., 1942–
A season of inquiry revisited : the Church committee
confronts America's spy agencies / Loch K. Johnson.
pages cm
Includes index.
ISBN 978-0-7006-2147-7 (hardback)
ISBN 978-0-7006-2154-5 (ebook)
1. Intelligence service—United States. 2. Governmental
investigations—United States. 3. Legislative
oversight—United States. I. Title.
JK468.I6J64 2015
327.1273—dc23

                        2015026513

British Library Cataloguing-in-Publication Data is
available.

Printed in the United States of America

10 9 8 7 6 5 4 3 2 1

To Leena, with love and devotion

This renewed publication of Season of Inquiry
is dedicated with admiration to
Senator Frank Church and Vice President Walter Mondale

You see, the way a free government works, there's got to be a housecleaning every now and then.

   Harry S. Truman

Contents

List of Tables   xi

Foreword to the 2015 Edition   xiii

Preface   xix

1. The End of an Affair   1

2. A Committee Is Formed   8

3. Establishing an Agenda   22

4. Assassination Plots   41

5. Rogue Elephant   50

6. The Cave of Bugs   59

7. Sinister Forces   75

8. Adrift   87

9. Bombarded   99

10. Orwellian Nightmares   110

11. Resistance   129

12. Covert Action   143

13. Tragedy   157

14. From Abuses to Reform   165

15. Backlash   174

16. The Big Leak   185

17. White House Counteroffensive   194

18. The Late, Late Strategy   206

19. The Committee Reports   215

20. The Oversight Bill   231

21. Victory—And Defeat   243

22. Aftermath   258

23. Reflections   272

Postscript to the 2015 Edition   285

Chronology   293

Appendix 1. US Intelligence Leadership, 1947–2015   299

Appendix 2. Organization of the US Intelligence
   Community   301

Appendix 3. Text of Relevant Intelligence Amendments
   and Acts   303

Notes   307

Index   333

List of Tables

1. Church Committee Membership Profile, 1975 13
2. Key Amendments to Senate Resolution 400 238
3. Intelligence Oversight on Capitol Hill 264

Foreword to the 2015 Edition

The first iteration of *Season of Inquiry* (this being the second) was published in 1985, a decade after its subject—the US Senate investigation of America's secret agencies in 1975—had come to a close. I had served on the investigative committee as special assistant or designee to the chairman, a Democrat from Idaho by the name of Frank Church, one of the Senate's foremost experts on foreign policy. My intention in writing the book was to provide the public with a glimpse into how a congressional investigation works, warts and all, and to help inform my fellow citizens about key issues related to the hidden side of our government, the nation's espionage agencies. The investigation proved necessary because the Central Intelligence Agency (CIA or "The Agency") had been charged by the *New York Times* in 1974 of spying at home, against the very people it had been mandated to protect in its founding document, the National Security Act of 1947.

The allegations of domestic spying sent a shock wave through the political establishment in Washington, DC, and across the nation. Fears of a gestapo inside the United States—a concern raised by some in 1947 during the debate over the wisdom of creating a CIA—suddenly seemed less far-fetched. This uneasiness about the secret powers of the intelligence agencies was fueled by the public's recent experiences with the Watergate scandal, in which a president had lied to the American people in an attempt to cover up a late-night GOP break-in to the Democratic presidential campaign headquarters, located in a suite at the Watergate Hotel in Washington, DC. The scandal drove Richard M. Nixon from the presidency in 1973, rather than face an impeachment vote in the Senate which he was likely to lose. Moreover, the nation had just gone through the Vietnam War, the most wrenching combat experience for America since the Civil War. The conflict in Vietnam had divided the nation into hawks and doves—pro- and antiwar factions. Even those moderates in between remained concerned over allegations that presidents Lyndon B. Johnson and Nixon had been less than forthcoming with the public regarding the progress of the war. In 1971, the controversial leaking to the *New York Times* of the Pentagon Papers, comprising extracts from a then top secret Department of Defense study of the war, reinforced the widespread sense that neither president had been fully truthful with the American people about setbacks in the jungles of Vietnam.

Coming on the heels of these deep rifts in the country, the notion of Big Brother spying against citizens captured the headlines of the nation's newspapers and was enough to move lawmakers and the White House (now led by President Gerald R. Ford) toward a major probe into the dark side of government, heretofore a security domain left largely to itself. In January 1975, both the

House of Representatives and the Senate rushed to assemble panels to examine the allegations published in the *Times;* and the White House, wishing to avoid being accused of whitewashing a spy scandal, followed suit by creating a special investigative commission of its own, chaired by Vice President Nelson Rockefeller.

The House panel floundered at first under weak leadership but rallied under a new chairman—Otis Pike (D-NY), who met on Capitol Hill with his Senate counterpart, Frank Church, to divide up the investigative work rather than duplicate efforts. The Pike committee would focus mainly on analytic mistakes made by the CIA—that is, its errors in understanding and forecasting world affairs; the Church committee would take on the question of illegal CIA spying at home, along with the topic of whether or not other agencies in the nation's intelligence committee had engaged in operations that transgressed the law.

Both realms of inquiry were important. The focus of the Church committee, however, was certainly a hotter potato to handle. Violation of the fundamental charters of the espionage agencies, which domestic spying would have entailed, was a matter of utmost seriousness in a democracy based on the rule of law. The very survival of the CIA and its companion secret services might be at stake, had they proved to be impervious to the nation's legal boundaries. The Rockefeller Commission was never part of the Church–Pike accord to divide up the investigative terrain, as one might expect in a government based constitutionally on a doctrine of separate institutions (the Congress, the presidency, and the judiciary); the White House went its own way, choosing to concentrate on the charges of illegal domestic spying—an overlap with the Church committee. Even on Capitol Hill, the Church–Pike accord was general and vague, and the Church panel ended up assigning some of its staff to look at intelligence analysis too. The Church committee, with its 150 staff members, dwarfed the size of the Rockefeller and Pike staffs and was able to take on a wider array of investigative topics.

As it turned out, the Rockefeller Commission completed its work within a few months by directing its attention mainly to the subject of illegal CIA mail opening. It issued a report that was much more hard-hitting than critics had anticipated, sharply chastising the Agency for its domestic espionage activities (even though some of this spying, but not all, had been at the behest of the Johnson and Nixon administrations). The Pike committee, riven by ideological and managerial disputes, lasted a few months longer into 1975, but eventually self-destructed. Critics accused the panel of being biased against the CIA from the start, incompetent in its handling of classified materials, and confrontational in its methods of inquiry. However talented Pike and several of his colleagues were, the chairman proved unable to guide his committee toward a successful public reporting. At the eleventh hour, the full House voted to bottle up the Pike committee's top-secret draft report, which in February of 1976 leaked to the *Village Voice*, a New York City newspaper. The perpetrator was never found, despite an intensive investigation by the Federal Bureau of Investigation (FBI). Some observers on and outside the committee wondered if the CIA had leaked the draft report as a way of further denigrating Representative Pike and his committee.

On the other side of the Hill, the Church committee moved inexorably forward with its investigation, which had enlarged beyond its original focus on the Agency to include possible improprieties committed by America's other intelligence agencies: the FBI, the National Security Agency (NSA), and a host of other primarily military espionage services, as well as—speaking of hot topics—CIA assassination plots around the world. The Church committee had greater success than its House counterpart in negotiating with the executive branch over access to documents, witnesses for hearings, and the declassification of papers the panel hoped to use in its final report to the public. The differences lie chiefly in the willingness of Senator Church and his co-chair, John Tower (R-TX), to exercise patience in dialogues with the White House and the intelligence agencies in pursuing the information the committee needed to have.

These negotiations did not always succeed; gaining access to documents on CIA covert actions to manipulate foreign governments was a major sticking point, and the panel decided to back away from some requests. Moreover, at times the Church committee, too, seemed on the verge of collapsing over disputes with the executive branch or its own sometimes heated internal disagreements. Nevertheless, less ideologically smitten than the Pike panel and guided by leaders of national stature—Church, Tower, Philip A. Hart (D-MI), Barry Goldwater (R-AZ), Howard H. Baker Jr. (R-TN), and Charles McC. Mathias Jr. (D-MD), for example—the Church committee managed to carry on. Eventually, it produced an avalanche of reports that laid out in great detail the domestic abuses committed by the intelligence agencies, along with an in-depth examination of the CIA's use of covert action against Chile and several of the Agency's assassination plots, along with many other topics.

The Church committee discovered that the *New York Times* articles had only scratched the surface of abuses by the intelligence agencies. The panel's reports chronicled a litany of disquieting operations carried out against American citizens, including the CIA's Operation CHAOS to spy on Vietnam War dissenters and—in some ways the most chilling finding of all—the FBI's Operation COINTELPRO. The Bureau operations involved not only spying against Americans but also secret efforts to destroy the jobs, marriages, and reputations of individuals whose only sin had been to engage in activities protected by the First Amendment, such as protesting against the war in Vietnam or joining the civil rights movement. Troubling, too, were the covert actions against the Allende regime in Chile, which had been democratically elected by the voters of that nation, and the assassination plots, which had been aimed at leaders of poor nations in Africa and Latin America.

The Church committee recommended almost a hundred reforms for the intelligence community, most designed to keep these veiled agencies within the boundaries of the law and American values. A sea change in attitudes had occurred. No longer would the espionage services reside outside the Madisonian framework of checks and balances, fashioned by the constitutional framers in 1787. Henceforth, they would be as much a part of the US government as the departments of agriculture and commerce, subject in the same way to close and regular budget reviews, periodic hearings (even if most would have to be in executive or closed session, because of the sensitivity of intelligence tradecraft), on-site inspections, and all the other tools of accountability—or oversight, to use an awkward political science term.

Initiatives drafted by the Church committee soon became law, such as the setting of a ceiling of ten years on how long an FBI director could serve (J. Edgar Hoover, the enabler of COINTELPRO and other dubious operations, served in that office for forty-eight years); and the Foreign Intelligence Surveillance Act of 1978, which required warrants for national security surveillance against Americans (telephone wiretapping and home searches, for instance)—operations that before could be carried out at the whim of a president or one of his aides. Sometimes in the past warrantless wiretaps had been used for political purposes, as incumbent presidents attempted to learn more about the strategies and tactics of the opposition party.

Both chambers of Congress also created standing oversight panels for intelligence: the Senate Select Committee on Intelligence (SSCI) and the House Permanent Select Committee on Intelligence (HPSCI). With these entities in place, the hope was that no longer would intelligence accountability be as lax and episodic as it had been in earlier days. (For an appraisal of that hope today, see the postscript at the end of this book.)

This is the story told in *Season of Inquiry*: a time in which the United States, in an unprecedented experiment, attempted to bring at least some degree of democracy into the shadowy world of espionage. Soon thereafter, in a ripple effect, other democracies—among them those of the United Kingdom, Canada, Australia, and New Zealand—would move to improve the level of accountability over their own spy services.

The work of the Church committee has been widely heralded as a success. The most extensive scholarly study of official inquiries conducted by the government of the United States since 1945 is Paul Light's 2014 *Government by Investigation*. Light offers special commendation for the Church committee. In his words, "It is impossible to single out one investigation in this book as the best of the best, but

I often return to the Church committee's 1975 investigation of intelligence abuses as a model of the high-impact investigation."[1]

Others, though, have seen this experiment in intelligence reform quite differently, including national security adviser Robert C. McFarland; the writer of spy thrillers Tom Clancy; and even the distinguished former president George H. W. Bush, head of the CIA at the time of the so-called intelligence wars (as some in the CIA remember 1975). They look upon the Year of Intelligence as a disastrous intrusion into the vital, delicate operations of the spy agencies that were so critical to America's defense against communism during the Cold War and now against terrorists and rogue regimes. Some critics have gone so far as to suggest that the terrorist attacks against the United States in 2001 were a result of the Church committee's crippling of the nation's intelligence community twenty-six years before this horrific event.

In truth, Frank Church and his colleagues sought to strengthen intelligence, not weaken it. As a former Army intelligence officer in World War II, and at the time a senior member of the Senate Foreign Relations Committee (which he would soon chair), Church understood the global dangers facing the United States and therefore the importance of good intelligence. His most important speech during the investigation addressed the question of improving intelligence analysis.[2] What he and his colleagues could not abide—nor should any citizen—was lawlessness by the secret agencies.

Whether the Church committee was of value to the nation, or a liability, is a matter for the reader qua citizen to decide. I would only note here that each of the nation's spymasters, with the exception of William J. Casey of the Reagan presidency, has endorsed and even praised the "new oversight." They see the post–Church committee rules as an opportunity for the intelligence agencies to understand better what their operational boundaries are; and the nation's intelligence chiefs have been glad to share their heavy responsibilities with lawmakers and the courts. For instance, the highly regarded former director of central intelligence Robert M. Gates has written: "Some awfully crazy schemes might well have been approved had everyone present not known and expected hard questions, debate, and criticism from the Hill. And when, on occasion, Congress was kept in the dark, and such schemes did proceed, it was nearly always to the lasting regret of the Presidents involved."[3]

I am proud this book, my first, is being published again. The Church committee experiences are worth remembering. The University Press of Kansas has kept the original volume intact, rather than tinker with revisions that might undermine the primary virtue of a study like this: a recording of the mood and essence of a significant government inquiry. The only changes have been to add this foreword and a new postscript, to update the chronology and the list of intelligence leaders in appendix 1, and to provide a chart of the current structure of the US intelligence community in appendix 2. The drawings and photographs that appeared in the original edition have been dropped, along with the now-dated "Bibliographical Note."[4]

I want to thank the University Press of Kansas, so ably led by Director Charles T. Myers and Editor In Chief Michael Briggs, for taking up this initiative. Mike has a long interest in intelligence and we have been discussing the topic for years, so it has been a special privilege to work with him on this project. Heart-felt thanks as well go to senators Howard Baker, Gary Hart, and Walter Mondale for their retrospective conversations with me about the Church committee; to the late James Angleton and William F. Colby for also sharing their retrospective thoughts; and to several of my mates on the Church committee staff, with whom I have had many helpful discussions about the Year of Intelligence: the late Georgetown University law professor Barry Carter; Washington, DC, political consultant Peter Fenn; ambassador Karl F. Inderfurth; DC attorney and author James Johnston; the former Church committee staff director and diplomat William G. Miller; the former Church committee chief counsel and author Frederick A. O. Schwarz Jr.; and the chairman of the National Intelligence Council, Gregory F. Treverton. As well, I express my appreciation to Professor David M. Barrett of Villanova and to John Prados, two of the nation's leading experts on intelligence, as well as to Donald A. Ritchie, an expert on Congress, for their endorsement of this republication project; to Karen Hellekson for outstanding copy editing; and to Leena S. Johnson, my darling wife and peerless in-house editor for forty-seven years.

Loch K. Johnson
Athens, Georgia

Preface

This is a book about the United States Senate. Its purpose is to provide the citizen with a look at how this institution works (or sometimes fails to work)—not in its ordinary, day-to-day business of helping constituents, debating policy, and passing bills, but rather in the extraordinary conduct of a major investigation.

The focus for the study is the 1975 Senate probe into alleged abuses of the Central Intelligence Agency (CIA), the Federal Bureau of Investigation (FBI), and several other federal agencies known collectively as the intelligence community (see appendix 2). This investigation lasted sixteen months. Hundreds of witnesses were cross-examined; thousands of pages of sworn testimony were gathered; several volumes of reports were published; and ninety-six proposals for reform were recommended.

The Senate inquiry (and companion investigations by the House of Representatives and a presidential commission) rocked the intelligence bureaucracy like nothing before, even overshadowing the humiliating defeat suffered by the CIA during the Bay of Pigs invasion of Cuba in 1961. Its leaders spoke darkly of a struggle for survival and warred among themselves (and with the White House) over appropriate tactics of self-defense.

As events unfolded and the White House realized it faced a serious investigation, the bounds of comity between the presidency and Congress—always strained—grew steadily more taut, soon frayed, and then threatened to snap. In Congress itself, disagreements over how to proceed led to a deep schism in the Senate investigating committee and sent the full House of Representatives into a tailspin of acrimony and self-recrimination. With these institutional conflicts came the further complication of personal ambition, as individuals involved in the investigations positioned themselves for the 1976 presidential sweepstakes or otherwise moved to advance their careers and reputations.

The story in these pages is about rulers at work. It examines the tangled lines of conflict and cooperation that stretch between the executive branch and Congress. It underscores how jealousy, friendship, suspicion, pique, ambition, fatigue, and other human traits intervene in human affairs to alter the anticipated course of events. It shows the difficulty of achieving any change whatsoever in a government where power is fragmented among a large number of people within the executive branch, the Senate, and the House; where individual policy makers respond to different constituencies and hold divergent conceptions of the common good, conflicting career aspirations, and varying time frames for the achievement of goals. It demonstrates the enormously frustrating task, always faced by Congress, of prying information loose from the executive bureaucracy—particularly one under siege.

Despite such handicaps, the intelligence investigation of 1975 succeeded. Though flawed, the inquiry satisfied the primary standard by which a legislature must be judged in a democracy: it enhanced the freedom and well-being of the citizens. The overarching thesis of this study is a reaffirmation of James Madison's view that fragmentation of power—despite its frustrations—provides a critical defense against abuse by individual power holders. This is both the paradox and the genius of our government. Congressional investigations, when fairly conducted, have evolved into a vital part of the safeguards wisely prescribed by the nation's founders to restrain executive power.

This thesis will have its detractors. Some believe the Senate intelligence investigation had just the opposite effect: that it was an unwarranted exercise in self-flagellation, a witch hunt leading to the destruction of the very intelligence capabilities designed to protect us from foreign and domestic threats. In this view, therefore, the end result was a decline in the freedom and well-being of our citizens.

Readers will have to draw their own conclusions. My objective is not one of advocacy. Rather, I seek to lay out the events of this inquiry as carefully as I can, with all the inevitable limitations involved in such a task. As John Updike has put it (in "The Blessed Man of Boston"), "from the dew of the few flakes that melt on our faces we cannot reconstruct the snowstorm." A more definitive account of the intelligence investigation will be written only decades from now. This is an interim report, with the shortcomings that that implies. I can only hope the study has some compensating virtues, especially freshness of impression, closeness of observation, and honesty of record. I would also hope that it might contribute to the continuing national debate on intelligence policy.

My observation post for these events was as a Senate staff assistant, on leave from university teaching. The investigation was a rare chance for me, as a political scientist, to compare the textbooks on Congress with the real thing. During the inquiry, I served both as an investigator for the committee and as an aide to the chairman, Senator Frank Church, Democrat of Idaho. The latter position provided a unique perspective, though it obviously raises questions about my capacity to evaluate the chairman and his committee objectively; I can only say that I have striven for scholarly detachment. After the investigation, I served as staff director for the Subcommittee on Intelligence Oversight, US House of Representatives; this gave me an opportunity to view the new oversight at close hand.

In the interests of readability, I present this study in the first person, and except for the beginning and concluding chapters, I employ a chronological style. The use of first-person narrative emphasizes the personal nature of this odyssey, for here in essence is the saga of a journey I had the opportunity to take with Congress into the largely uncharted waters of the CIA and other intelligence agencies. We were swept along on a river of fortune that would prove to be as exciting, treacherous, and capricious as the one carrying Huckleberry Finn and Jim toward freedom. Just as Huck's raft was an uncertain and precarious structure, so was the Senate investigating committee, similarly buffeted about and thrown off course by the unpredictable vagaries of forces swirling around it.

Chapter 1 provides a brief history of executive–legislative relations in the field of intelligence; chapter 2 introduces the membership of the Church committee; with chapter 3, the investigation begins to unfold. The rest of the book traces the efforts of the Senate to examine the charges against the intelligence agencies and to construct a more vigorous approach toward monitoring intelligence policy in the future. To place the Senate investigation in context, the narrative occasionally considers the parallel efforts of the House investigation, as well as the response of the executive branch to both. The next two chapters offer an appraisal of this era and explore its effects on the country today.

The descriptions of events in this book draw on interviews with members and key staff aides on the Senate and House investigating committees; a review of notes (unclassified) kept by some participants, including my own extensive jottings on the political interactions of Senate committee members; accounts of the inquiry published in the press; the public papers of the Church committee; and, especially, my own observations and recollections. My discussion of committee meetings will sometimes appear thin; this is because most of these meetings were devoted to an examination of secret intelligence operations. My interest is with politics and process, not with a whistle-blowing critique of intelligence operations, so I have carefully steered clear of such materials and have had the manuscript read by a government publication review board to avoid inadvertent disclosure of classified information.

This book has been a long time in the making, and along the way many people have been helpful. I am pleased to thank them here.

Several staff aides on the Church committee read the complete manuscript (at twice the present length) and offered valuable comments. Special thanks to Peter Fenn, Rick Inderfurth, and F. A. O. Schwarz Jr. I extend my appreciation as well to the staff of the Ribicoff committee for opening their files to me.

Professor Harry Howe Ransom of Vanderbilt University, the sage of scholars on questions touching intelligence and democracy, kindly read the entire first draft too, and made thoughtful suggestions. He and his excellent work have been a source of inspiration for my own more humble efforts. An anonymous reviewer for the University Press of Kentucky also provided helpful ideas. Richard J. Storrs read the manuscript in its early stages and gave me a useful student's perspective.

From 1975 to 1984, I interviewed hundreds of intelligence officials, members of Congress, and legislative staffers about the problems associated with secret intelligence agencies in a democracy. My appreciation for their willingness to help me explore this subject is great. For this book, I am most grateful to the legislators and staff on the Church and Pike committees who took time out from busy schedules for interviews and who gave me access to their own files from 1975 to 1976. William G. Miller, staff director of the Church committee, was especially gracious in allowing me to review his detailed notes and memoranda from this period; the recollections of John T. Elliff, leader of the committee's FBI Task Force, were also of great value.

I owe a debt of gratitude as well to the Department of Government at Ohio University for granting me a leave to join the Senate investigation, and to the Department of Political Science at the University of Georgia for financial support and encouragement during the preparation of this study. Encouragement came to me also from Alan Gates and Peter Shepard. The editor of *Polity* kindly allowed me to draw upon my Spring 1985 article for portions of this study.

The preparation of this book was made much easier by a happy writing environment. I thank Kathleen and Roland Johnson for their unbending confidence, Leena S. Johnson for her patience, support, and skillful proofreading, and Kristin E. Johnson for a steady supply of leaven.

I thank Randy Austin, Bob Bolin, and Miriam Kerley for research assistance, and Suzanne E. Overby, Kim Kelley, Jeannine Hall, and Pamela Smith for page after page of neat typing. Naturally, none of the good people acknowledged here is to blame for any errors of fact or judgment that I may have made.

1

The End of an Affair

Two young men stood on either side of an easel that supported oversized charts, expertly drawn. One man braced the charts while the other occasionally moved a pointed marker along rows of figures or up and down the slopes of trend lines.

Seated near them, a stout man in his fifties read from a typed statement. He spoke precisely, seldom looking up. His words fell in a dry monotone on the table before him. A gray ribbon of cigarette smoke curled slowly toward the high ceiling from an ashtray on the table. All three men wore white shirts with buttoned-down collars; they might well have been marketing experts tracing annual sales for a board of directors.

The "Board," however, showed remarkably little interest in whatever profits or losses the charts revealed. Nor was the room anything one would expect to find in corporate headquarters. It was elegant, even stately. Doric pillars, carved from wood, embellished the rich walnut paneling. A grand chandelier hung from the center of the ceiling. Through the windows, draped in deep purple, a courtyard was visible; at its center a fountain spewed a column of water into the morning air.

Dominating the room was a U-shaped bench that rose high above the floor. Its prongs faced the three men, as if holding them in a magnetic field. Within the concave space of the bench sat a stenotypist, her fingertips dancing lightly on the keys of a machine.

Two elderly men sat behind the far curve of the bench, each a United States senator and a member of the secretive Subcommittee on Intelligence. The senators listened as the man at the table droned through his prepared statement on paramilitary, or warlike, activities of the Central Intelligence Agency (CIA). As deputy director of the Agency, he was expected to present an occasional report to Congress. One of the senators rested his head on his arms and soon fell asleep, punctuating the briefing with periodic grunts. The other senator, the subcommittee chairman, stared blankly at the CIA official, nodded once in a while, and discreetly examined his wristwatch.

The deputy director had seen the distant look in the eyes of senators before and had grown accustomed to it. He momentarily raised his voice, more to relieve his own boredom than to attract attention: "*Paramilitary* activities have been an important part of our program since the beginning of the Cold War."

The new inflection awoke the slumbering senator with a start. "*Parliamentary activity!*" he bellowed. "You fellows can't go messin' round with parliaments. I won't have it!"

A silence fell over the room. The stenotypist's fingers stopped their dance. The deputy director pursed his lips and looked at the subcommittee chairman.

"Senator, this briefing is on paramilitary, not parliamentary, activity," the chairman said softly.

"Oh, well, uhruumph," said the senator, clearing his throat. He paused and tugged at his ear. "Okay, but you stay away from parliaments," he admonished, and shuffled out of the room.

At a nod from the chairman, the deputy director resumed his statement. He could hardly wait to return to headquarters; his colleagues would enjoy this latest episode in congressional oversight. The legislative watchdog not only lacked teeth; it was sound asleep.

While this incident supposedly occurred three decades ago, the story is still told with relish by officials in the CIA—a favorite response to outsiders seeking an Agency assessment of congressional oversight in the intelligence field. (In the congressional context, the awkward word "oversight" has come to mean the monitoring of executive branch conduct by Congress.[1]) Behind anecdotes like this one lies a stark conclusion: legislative oversight of the American intelligence agencies has been ineffective.

Congressman Les Aspin (D-WI) remembers asking William Colby (director of the CIA, 1973–1976) what had happened in the past when House oversight committees objected to a CIA operation. "He was stunned," says Aspin. "The question had never come up before. The committees preferred not to get involved."[2] This attitude was shared by the Senate. "I remember when I first came to the Senate," Frank Church (D-ID) once recalled, "some of those senior senators who did have this so-called watchdog committee were known to say in effect: 'We don't watch the dog. We don't know what's going on, and furthermore, we don't want to know.'"[3]

Even if the overseers had wanted to know, they might have failed to obtain the full story. Former CIA director Allen W. Dulles (1953–1961) told the Warren Commission that when he was at the Agency's helm, he felt obliged to tell the truth only to one person: the president.[4] On another occasion, in a remark to a colleague, he widened the circle by one. "I'll fudge the truth to the oversight committee," he said, "but I'll tell the chairman the truth—that is, if he wants to know."[5]

Nor was the National Security Council (NSC) brimming with details on CIA activities. As former secretary of state Dean Rusk remembers, "I never saw a budget of the CIA, for example, although I was a statutory member of the National Security Council. The CIA's budget apparently went to two or three specially cleared people in the Bureau of the Budget, then was run briefly by the President, turned over to Senator [Richard] Russell [D-Ga.], and that was the end of it. He would lose the CIA budget in the defense budget, and he wouldn't let anybody question it. There were no public hearings on it. So again, his judgment, his word on that was the last word."[6]

Congressional supervision of the CIA was ostensibly the duty of four subcommittees. Both the Senate and the House armed services committees had a CIA Oversight Subcommittee, as did the Senate and House appropriations committees. The subcommittees seldom convened. As one member of the House Armed Services Subcommittee remembers, "We met annually—one time a year, for a period of 2 hours in which we accomplished virtually nothing."[7] This was during the 1950s; later, in a burst of vigor, the subcommittee began to meet five times a year for a couple of hours each session.[8]

A comparable languor settled over the Senate subcommittees. According to Senator Leverett Saltonstall (R-MA), the Armed Services Subcommittee met during the 1950s "at least twice a year" and the Appropriations Subcommittee "at least once a year."[9] Since their membership overlapped substantially anyway, these two Senate subcommittees were combined in the 1960s, with Richard Russell as chairman. Ten members served on this panel (five from each committee). The Russell overseers met with blue-moon frequency, seldom more than six times a year and often only three. Their hearings—or, more accurately, briefings—normally lasted three hours or less and were sparsely attended.[10]

In short, the CIA, with its thousands of employees, large budget, and risky operations spanning the globe, was subjected to roughly twenty-four hours of legislative "probing" in both chambers over an entire year.

The failures of congressional oversight have stemmed in part from the paralyzing awe engendered by the sheer size and complexity of the intelligence community, with its more than forty agencies and multibillion-dollar expenditures.[11] Legislators have also been reluctant to become involved in its tribal disputes. Concern over the possibility of inadvertent breaches of security has played a role too. A CIA overseer in the Senate once observed, "The difficulty in connection with asking questions and obtaining information is that we might obtain information which I personally would rather not have, unless it was essential for me as a member of Congress to have it."[12] John Stennis (D-MS), then chairman of the Senate subcommittee for CIA oversight, said in 1971, "You have to make up your mind that you are going to have an intelligence agency and protect it as such, and shut your eyes some and take what is coming."[13] William Colby adds, "The old tradition was that you don't ask. It was a consensus that intelligence was apart from the rules . . . that was the reason we did step over the line in a few cases, largely because no one was watching. No one was there to say don't do that."[14]

This same tradition led members of Congress to the conclusion that leaders of the intelligence agencies were honorable men who could be relied on to do the right thing, without the meddlesome interference of outsiders uninitiated in the esoteric arts of espionage. As one senior intelligence officer has said, "Men like Richard Helms [CIA director, 1966–1973] are the cream of the crop in our society. If we can't trust them to do what's right, we can't trust anyone."[15]

This view was heartily endorsed by intelligence officials. During his tenure as CIA director, Helms told newspaper editors that "the nation must, to a degree, take it on faith that we . . . are honorable men devoted to her service."[16] Colby entitled his own memoirs *Honorable Men*.[17] For the most part, the adjective is amply deserved, but the faith produced a careless form of oversight and was ultimately harmful to the country.

Another reason that members of Congress avoided digging too deeply was sheer lack of time and interest. As every observer of Congress has concluded, its members are harried individuals. They have more meetings to attend and people to see than they can manage, so they must establish priorities. In the middle of a Senate hearing on secret CIA operations in Chile, Senator Hubert H. Humphrey (D-MN) once declared, "I have to go now. I am trying to get jobs for 400 people in Minnesota today. That is a great deal more important to me right now than Chile."[18]

Usually highest in priority are those people and places that can enhance re-election opportunities for legislators. Intelligence briefings fail to meet this basic requirement; in fact, legislators are unable even to talk about their good work in this field, since much of the information is sensitive and classified. President John F. Kennedy once told a group of CIA professionals, "Your successes are unheralded—your failures are trumpeted."[19] This is not the kind of public service equation that politicians find appealing. As one student of Congress has concluded, "In general, members intervene effectively in the bureaucracy on matters where they can claim credit for intervention."[20]

Finally, and perhaps most important, legislators have no doubt usually preferred to avoid responsibility for often controversial intelligence operations. It has been politically safer to look the other way.

This is not to say that the history of congressional oversight in the intelligence field has been completely lethargic; occasional flaps have sired narrow investigations.[21] A comprehensive evaluation of legislative oversight, however, must be sharply negative. Few would disagree with Professor Harry Ransom's judgment: "Formal congressional surveillance of the CIA over the years has been sporadic, spotty and essentially uncritical."[22] A political cartoonist captured the nature of the relationship; it was obviously an affair.

A few members of Congress have struggled to correct this constitutional imbalance. From 1947 through 1974, over two hundred resolutions were introduced calling for improvements in congressional oversight.[23] Few managed to make it out of committee, and none was approved by Congress. Indeed, from among these largely feckless efforts at reform, only four represented serious initiatives. In 1956 and again in 1966, a small band of senators tried to create an intelligence oversight committee that would go beyond the small and inactive CIA oversight subcommittees already in existence in each chamber. In both instances, the measure lost by a wide margin. Then in October 1974, a few senators, led by gadfly James Abourezk (D-SD), introduced a bill to prohibit CIA involvement in covert action (that is, those secret operations designed to influence events in other lands); henceforth, the CIA would be engaged strictly in intelligence gathering and counterintelligence. This Abourezk Amendment, too, lost by a lopsided margin.[24]

Those persons seeking reform lacked the sine qua non for success: a strongly aroused public. Occasionally, sharp questioning of intelligence activities came from the press, as in the case of the 1967 *Ramparts* magazine exposé of clandestine ties between the CIA and the National Students Association;[25] but even this significant revelation caused only a ripple on the passive sea of public concern over intelligence matters. As is frequently the case in the American political system, a truly major event was required to stir the public toward demands for reform, in turn stimulating Congress to act.

Such an event occurred in December 1974. Reporter Seymour M. Hersh of the *New York Times* captured the attention of the public in a series of articles, beginning on December 22, 1974, which accused the CIA of "massive" spying and illegal intelligence operations directed against antiwar activists and other American dissidents. According to Hersh's sources in the CIA, files on over ten thousand American citizens had been compiled by the Agency, despite the language of the 1947 act that barred the CIA from any security or police function within the United States.[26]

A select few CIA insiders immediately recognized the Hersh disclosures as part of a highly secret compilation of questionable activities that had been gathered by CIA director James Schlesinger (1973).[27] In May 1973, Schlesinger had sent a memorandum to all Agency employees requesting them to forward to his office any activities known to them that seemed to fall "outside the CIA's charter." The new director was well aware of the public charges implicating the CIA and his predecessor, Richard Helms, in aspects of the Watergate episode; Schlesinger prudently decided to begin his tenure with a clean slate. To his surprise, the list of possible abuses grew like a malignant cancer, soon totaling 693 items spanning the Agency's history. Operation CHAOS, the domestic skulduggery unearthed by Hersh after two years of digging (and with the friendly assistance of factions within the CIA who were willing to blow the whistle on bureaucratic rivals), represented just part of the full listing (dubbed the "Family Jewels" by those in the CIA with access to the lengthy document).

Within the next several weeks, stories of other startling CIA operations came tumbling out of newspapers and television reports. The coincidental firing of CIA chief of counterintelligence James Jesus Angleton heightened public interest; his ill-timed departure was wrongly perceived as an admission of guilt for Operation CHAOS. (In fact, Angleton had been dismissed over a professional disagreement regarding the Middle East.[28]) William Colby, Schlesinger's successor and director at the time of the Hersh blockbuster, remembers that "a press and political firestorm immediately erupted."[29]

On the heels of Watergate, the new revelations provided the next news sensation of the year and brought quick reaction. Letters and telegrams poured into congressional offices calling for an investigation into spying against American citizens by the CIA and other government agencies. Senator Humphrey, former vice president and an influential leader in the Senate, quickly announced that he would introduce legislation, as soon as Congress reconvened in January, to create a permanent Joint Committee on National Security to oversee intelligence operations. "The time has come," he said, "for Congress to face up to a responsibility it has shirked for too many years."[30]

No one knew this truth better than long-suffering Mike Mansfield (D-MT), a champion of intelligence oversight reform for two decades. He had risen through the power lattice of the Senate to the highest perch, succeeding Lyndon Johnson as majority leader in 1960. Now he set his staff to work drafting a resolution calling for a Senate investigation of the intelligence agencies. In another indication of legislative determination to act, Congress passed the Hughes–Ryan Amendment during the last days of 1974.[31] This statute, which required the president to approve and report to Congress all important covert actions, represented the first successful effort by legislators to place controls over the CIA since its creation.

Not to be outdone, the Republican administration led by President Gerald R. Ford rapidly established a presidential commission to examine the charges against the CIA—a move widely interpreted as an attempt to preempt the field and render unnecessary a more hostile probe by Congress. (In 1967, a full-scale inquiry into CIA ties with the nation's educational, labor, and cultural organizations was purposefully headed off by President Johnson through the appointment of a presidential commission chaired by Undersecretary of State Nicholas Katzenbach.[32])

In part, the extraordinary outburst on Capitol Hill in response to the Hersh disclosures was a matter of timing. The Vietnam War had raised the specter of an imperial presidency, and if Vietnam failed to impress upon Americans the dangers of excessive discretion and secrecy in the executive branch, the Watergate crisis emphasized the point. It also brought about an interest in investigative journalism unparalleled since the days of Upton Sinclair and the muckrakers. Much of the Watergate story was broken by then unknown *Washington Post* reporters Carl Bernstein and Bob Woodward. Their success and subsequent fame were an inspiration for untold real and would-be journalists around the country. When Hersh drew CIA blood, every self-respecting reporter with a national security beat swarmed over intelligence sources for fresh leads.

Watergate not only whetted the appetite of investigative reporters but also spawned a pervasive attitude of suspicion on Capitol Hill. The newly elected members of Congress in 1974 (the aggressive post-Watergate class) included a large number who had won office by campaigning against the imperial presidency of Richard Nixon and promising a new morality in government. At the first hint of CIA domestic abuses—hardly a month after their election—these new members rose together in loud indignation, demanding a full inquiry. Probably not even Richard Russell (who died in 1971) could have withstood so thunderous a roar from the back benches. "Surely the most important factor in all the furor," reflects then CIA director Colby, the immediate focus of the outcry, "was the radically altered nature of the Congress."[33]

A still deeper cause was the profound change in United States relations with the Soviet Union, symbolized by the term détente. In the words of John M. Crewdson, a *New York Times* political analyst, "As the hostility between the West and East that had marked the nineteen-fifties began to fade, so did the public's acceptance of the CIA and its appointed mission of guarding against the Communist peril."[34]

All of these forces combined to usher in a new season of inquiry, one that would go far beyond the gentle probes that now and then had visited the intelligence agencies in the past. On 4 January 1975, President Ford established the Commission on CIA Activities within the United States, chaired by Vice President Nelson A. Rockefeller (which became known as the Rockefeller Commission). On January 27, the Senate voted eighty-two to four to establish a special committee to conduct a nine-month, $750,000 investigation of American intelligence operations. The Year of Intelligence had begun.

"All the tensions and suspicions and hostilities that had been building about the CIA since the Bay of Pigs, and had risen to a combustible level during the Vietnam and Watergate years, now exploded," remembers Colby.[35] The long affair between Congress and the CIA had come to an abrupt end.

2

A Committee Is Formed

With the following words, on January 21, 1975, Senator John O. Pastore (D-RI) introduced Senate Resolution 21 to establish the investigating committee:

> In recent weeks and in recent months there have been charges and counter charges spelled out on the front page of every newspaper in this country. The matter has been discussed over television and radio. The people of America are confused. They are asking themselves, "What is actually happening to these organizations which are essential for the security and the survival of our great Nation?"
>
> In order to clear the air, in order to cleanse whatever abuses there have been in the past, so that we can recite, once and for all, the proper parameters within which they can function, I am afraid we will do irreparable harm to the security and survival of the country unless we do this [sic].[1]

For him, the "big question" was, "To whom are the intelligence agencies responsible?" Further, Pastore wanted to know: "Who got us into Cambodia? Who got us into Laos? Who got us into the Bay of Pigs? Who got us into Chile? Who got us into all over the world, and under whose authority, and why was not the Congress told?"

Senator Barry Goldwater (R-AZ) was the first member of the minority party to speak in the debate. He sounded a note of caution that seemed to echo down from three decades of congressional attitudes toward intelligence oversight: "There are many times . . . when we are confronted with testimony that we do not want to hear. It is of such a highly classified nature, I do not think, frankly, anyone outside of the intelligence community should hear it." Goldwater appeared to have collared the culprit even before the investigating committee was formed: "Who is responsible for the military to go to Vietnam? It was not the Pentagon; it was the President of the United States, who was the only man who could do it. Who is responsible for the CIA, FBI, and DIA [Defense Intelligence Agency] and others getting into fields I have a feeling they did not want to get into? The President of the United States." The prospect of leaks on the committee also troubled Goldwater. "The Watergate [committee] leaked like an old sieve," he said, "and we sure do not want that to happen in an area as sensitive as intelligence."

The second (and last) day of debate on the resolution occurred almost a week later. Early in the morning, before the Senate convened, the GOP caucus selected its five members for the proposed eleven-person committee, endorsing those senators recommended by minority leader Hugh Scott of Pennsylvania. Senator John Tower (Texas), one of the five and later chosen as vice chairman by the Republicans on the committee, said the selection was an "acceptance of the inevitable."[2] The other GOP senators were Goldwater, Charles "Mac" Mathias (Maryland), Richard S. Schweiker (Pennsylvania), and Howard H. Baker Jr. (Tennessee).

"The important thing here is to restore public confidence so that these agencies, in the final analysis, will be responsive. That is what this is all about," said Senator Pastore as debate resumed. While Goldwater had seemed convinced that presidents were to blame for intelligence agency excesses, a different theory nagged at the mind of his colleague Senator Baker.

"We ought to find out not whether the CIA, for instance, was engaged in domestic surveillance, but whether somebody was running the show," said Baker. "I know Congress was not running the show; and I want to be relieved of that shuddering fear I have that the White House was not, either." He alluded to the desirability of contacting former president Nixon as a witness "to determine if the president of the United States knows what is going on."

As the debate ended, Senator Robert Packwood (R-OR) read an editorial into the *Congressional Record* chiding the Ford White House for failing to see that "far more is needed than a narrow blue-ribbon commission [a reference to the Rockefeller Commission] studying a very narrow set of allegations." Pastore asked for the yeas and nays and, following the slow litany of a Senate roll-call vote, the result was announced: yeas, eighty-two; nays, four. Four Southern conservatives voted against the creation of the panel: Jesse A. Helms (North Carolina), William L. Scott (Virginia), Strom Thurmond (South Carolina)—all Republicans—and Herman E. Talmadge (Georgia), the only Democrat.

With the Senate Select Committee on Intelligence Activities now a reality, majority leader Mansfield introduced into the *Record* a letter that he would subsequently send to the intelligence agencies: "We are writing to request that you do not destroy, remove from your possession or control, or otherwise dispose or permit the disposal of any records or documents which might have a bearing on the subjects under investigation, including but not limited to all records or documents pertaining in any way to the matters set out in section 2 of S. Res. 21."[3] Then he announced the names of the six Democrats who would serve on the committee: Frank Church (Idaho), Philip A. Hart (Michigan), Walter F. Mondale (Minnesota), Walter D. Huddleston (Kentucky), Robert Morgan (North Carolina), and Gary Hart (Colorado).

Philip Hart had been Mansfield's initial choice for the chairmanship, but failing health led him to turn down the job. While Hart was making up his mind, Church went to see Mansfield to express his own interest. "When it began to surface in the press that there was evidence of serious abuses on the part of the CIA," Church later recalled, "I had a natural desire to do something about this."[4] According to one acquaintance, "he almost knocked down Mansfield's door to get it."[5]

In asking Mansfield to consider him, Church emphasized that he had been in the Senate for a long time (nineteen years) and had yet to be chairman of a major committee. "I thought this was an investigation of major importance and that my time had come to take hold of a responsibility of this kind," he recalled.[6] Mansfield listened to Church's request in typically laconic fashion, without indicating one way or the other what he would do. Church never even knew he was on the committee until Mansfield announced the list of senators on the floor.

Church immediately found himself surrounded by the press outside the Senate chambers following the vote on Senate Resolution 21. The press corps was unaware of Mansfield's initial offer of the chairmanship to Philip Hart or Hart's refusal; they simply assumed that Church had always been the choice because he outranked the others in seniority. (The next day, in a brief organizational meeting of the committee's Democratic members, Church was officially chosen chairman upon being nominated by Philip Hart.)

"I would not see this inquiry as any type of television extravaganza. It's much too serious to be a sideshow," Church told the crowd of reporters, adding that the objective would be to "safeguard the legitimate security interests of the country" while uncovering abuses of power and finding ways to forestall future abuses "lest we slip into the practices of a police state." He saw no threat to the CIA, "only an effort to see whether agencies are adhering strictly to the law."[7]

Pastore, the father of the resolution, felt that the intelligence investigation would be far less dramatic than the Watergate inquiry. Later that day in his office, he told a reporter that "this investigation, because of the very nature of it, will have to be in executive session" (that is, closed to the public).[8]

It soon became clear, though, that the chairman had a different conception. Appearing on the show *Face the Nation* the following Sunday, Church promised to hold as much of the investigation as possible in public. He also reaffirmed that his "ultimate objective is not to wreck" the intelligence agencies "but, if necessary, to reform them."[9]

The Senators

By chance, I arrived in Washington on a research trip soon after Church's appointment as chairman of the investigative committee. I had worked with him as an American Political Science Association Congressional Fellow in 1970, and now dropped by his office to wish him well on his assignment.

We spoke of the opportunities and the dangers, and of the immediate plans for the committee. The staff director would be William G. Miller, a gentle individual in his forties with years of experience as a Foreign Service officer and later as a staff aide in the Senate. Most recently, Miller had served as top aide for the ad hoc Committee on Emergency Powers, cochaired by senators Church and Mathias. He was a Republican, but he had earned a reputation for bipartisanship; he had an ability to work with senators of various ideological persuasions, a tactfulness derived perhaps from his training as a diplomat. Strongly recommended for the position by Mathias and already known by Church, Miller was acceptable and available, knew the Senate well, and could move into the position quickly. He was the proverbial right man in the right place at the right time.

No other staff members had yet been chosen. Acting on an impulse, I indicated to Church an interest in working with him on this important enterprise, though I reminded him that I knew virtually nothing about the CIA or any other intelligence agency. He picked up the telephone and asked Miller to consider me for one of the staff positions.

The next evening I took a taxi to Bethesda, Maryland, where the Churches lived in a modest split-level home. Among the guests were Carl Burke, Church's closest friend in high school and the campaign manager for all four of his Senate elections since the first in 1956, and a campaign fund raiser from San Francisco. For the past year, these two men had taken soundings around the country to see whether Church had a chance in the Democratic Party for the 1976 presidential nomination. The results were encouraging. Now, though, the investigation brought these plans to a grinding halt; the Church for President movement would have to wait.

After dinner, the conversation shifted ineluctably to the approaching investigation. A guest asked Church what had gone wrong with the CIA. "For twenty years now, the activities of the CIA have gone unwatched," he answered, between sips of coffee. "Also of the FBI. And during that long period of inattention, there has been an open invitation to a series of presidents to use these powerful police agencies in wrongful ways."

A guest asked about the doctrine of executive privilege, whereby presidents sometimes refuse to provide information to Congress. Church acknowledged that problems could arise over questions of executive privilege if, for example, the committee sought detailed information about ties between the CIA and the National Security Council. He expressed hope that the committee could proceed in a way that would persuade President Ford to give the Senate a maximum of cooperation. If the committee failed to get cooperation, it would resort to all the legal devices. Doing so would be time-consuming and difficult, however, and could well lead to litigation in the courts. Church wanted to avoid that direction, if possible.

Another guest wondered if, like former Senator Estes Kefauver (D-TN), who had achieved national prominence in the 1950s as chairman of a special committee investigating crime, Church could use his chairmanship to gain voter popularity nationwide. With the committee's work scheduled to end in September 1975, several months would still remain to mount a presidential campaign.

Church pushed thick black hair back from his forehead and replied, "I think that is very questionable. In the first place, if we conduct a nonpartisan and judicious investigation, it will greatly reduce the publicity. In the second place, I'm not at all sure the political climate is such as to give this investigation any appeal. In a period of recession, when the minds of the people necessarily turn to the recovery and control of inflation and increased employment, it may well be that an investigation of this kind will seem irrelevant. This is a serious danger. I think there is as much chance that the investigation could backfire politically as there is that it would benefit those who are members of the committee. This remains to be seen."

The question of internal unity among the investigators arose when someone observed that the committee's membership reflected great ideological diversity—including some men whose sole purpose could be to protect the intelligence agencies. "There are no guarantees that public fireworks can be avoided," Church agreed. "I can only say that I hope to build a confidence among all the members of the committee in such a way as to reduce internal dissension as much as possible."

The composition of the committee had been an issue during Senate debate. Senator Huddleston had argued persuasively in the Democratic caucus for an eleven-person committee to allow a broad representation, rather than the smaller committee that some desired for security purposes. Later during the floor debate, he stressed that the committee membership "must touch upon the various ages, views, geographical areas and philosophies which are a part of the Senate and our nation-at-large. To structure it otherwise would diminish not only the acceptance of any findings and recommendations but also the possibility of reconciling contrasting views and theories which must be accommodated."[10] Mansfield remembered giving "a good deal of thought to the selection of the Democratic members. . . . What I tried to do was bring about a mix based on philosophy, geography, and the like."[11]

Table 1. Church Committee Membership Profile, 1975

Member	Age	Region	Lawyer	Seniority	Reelection	Vote Index[a]
	Characteristic					
Democrat						
Church	51	West	Yes	19 years	1980	75%
P. Hart	63	Midwest	Yes	17 years	1976	97%
Mondale	47	Midwest	Yes	11 years	1978	97%
Huddleston	49	South	No	3 years	1978	70%
Morgan	50	South	Yes	1 years	1980	35%
G. Hart	38	West	Yes	1 years	1980	80%
Republican						
Tower	50	South	No	14 years	1978	20%
Baker	50	South	Yes	9 years	1978	40%
Goldwater	66	West	No	7 years[b]	1980	0%
Mathias	53	Northeast	Yes	7 years	1980	70%
Schweiker	49	Northeast	No	7 years	1980	70%

[a] Based on the voting scale developed by the Americans for Democratic Action (ADA), a liberal group that follows and evaluates congressional voting patterns: 100 percent would represent a "perfect" liberal voting pattern on a series of Senate votes; 0 would represent a "perfect" conservative. These indices are from votes takes in 1974, the year before the Church investigation. See the *Congressional Quarterly Weekly Report*, 8 December 1974, 8–9.

[b] Senator Goldwater had actually served a total of 19 years, including 1952–1964. Having left the Senate to run for president in 1964, however, he lost his seniority and had to start over again upon his reelection in 1968.

The final selection did produce a fairly broad representation, with some skews. Gary Hart, for example, was the only genuine youth (table 1)—though admittedly the Senate had few from which to choose. In fact, given an average age in the late fifties for the plenary membership, the committee actually was on the youngish side; Philip Hart and Goldwater were the two oldest. Regionally, the South was overrepresented. Professionally, attorneys were in the majority—a fact true for the Senate as a whole: 64 percent of both the committee members and the Senate itself in 1975 were lawyers. The nonlawyers on the committee were Huddleston (former radio announcer), Goldwater and Schweiker (business executives), and Tower (educator).

Pastore's desire to see "new blood and new faces" on the committee was fulfilled, as the seniority statistics demonstrated. Three members were freshmen in the Senate (Huddleston, Morgan, Gary Hart), and another four had been reelected only once (Mondale, Baker, Mathias, and Schweiker). Only Church, Philip Hart, Tower, and Goldwater were old-timers around Capital Hill, and only the chairman and Goldwater were in their fourth terms.

A key criterion in the selection process was reputed to have been the date that members would be up for reelection—this was a sensitive investigation that could prove to be a political liability. With the exception of Philip Hart, who held the safest seat of any committee member (having won by 67 percent in his last election), every senator had at least a couple of years to recover from the inquiry if it proved unpopular, and most had a breather until 1980.

Of greatest interest to me, though, were the voting records of these men. As one of the guests at Church's dinner party had noted, individuals of disparate ideologies had indeed become members of the new committee. The national Republican Party has long been split into liberal and conservative wings, and this division could be seen clearly in the committee's GOP contingent. On the conservative side were Tower, Goldwater, and (to some extent) Baker—all from the country's southern rim, the Sunbelt. The liberals were Mathias and Schweiker, both from the Northeast.

Baker, however, failed to fit easily into a mold with Tower and Goldwater. He was more moderate: "Like the Tennessee River, he flows right down the middle," his mother once noted.[12] He had also been an archcritic of the CIA during the Watergate investigation. No one had ever established any firm evidence that the Agency knew about the Watergate break-in before it occurred; circumstantial evidence abounded, though, and Baker retained a high level of suspicion concerning the Agency.[13] Under strong attack from liberals in Congress, the CIA reportedly dreaded the possibility that Baker would prove "an implacable conservative Republican foe in the Senate," determined to prove his Watergate suspicions correct and vindicate his reputation.[14] In contrast, Tower and Goldwater seemed protective of the CIA. Both men admitted they would have preferred to see the inquiry left in the hands of the Armed Services Committee, on which they sat. Baker, I had a hunch, might be a swing vote between the conservative and liberal Republicans on the committee.

The voting records of the committee Democrats indicated that they were decidedly more liberal than the Republicans (at least as this philosophical perspective is measured by chartings of the Americans for Democratic Action; table 1). Moreover, all the Democrats except Morgan had opposed the Vietnam policies of the Johnson and Nixon administrations. Morgan seemed to be the only plausible candidate on the Democratic side to join a voting coalition with Tower, Goldwater, and perhaps Baker. Faced by only four possible opponents, I felt confident that Church would have all the votes he needed as the committee made its decisions along the way. Time would prove me dead wrong.

As I looked over the list of committee members, I thought about the impressions they had made on me over the years. Goldwater, a tall, impressive man with white hair and a firm jaw, had been a leading voice of the conservatives in America since 1958. First elected to the Senate in 1952, he soon developed into one of the most popular speakers on the Republican fund-raising circuit, almost as widely sought after as Dwight Eisenhower and Richard Nixon. He had lost badly to Lyndon Johnson in a 1964 presidential bid, but many of the issues he raised in that election continued to be intensely debated, such as the health of the Social Security system.

Tower had been an assistant professor of political science at Midwestern University in Wichita Falls for nine years before becoming in 1961 the first Republican elected to the United States Senate from Texas since 1870. He was short, smoothly mannered, natty, and articulate.

Baker had struck me since the Watergate hearings as the most capable figure in the Republican Party. Having made his million (in real estate transactions) before coming to the Senate at age thirty-eight in 1964, and married to the daughter of the famous Republican minority leader of the 1960s, Senator Everett McKinley Dirksen, Baker was a man of great talent and ambition. His experience as a trial lawyer in Knoxville and a stump politician (no Republican has ever garnered so many votes in modern Tennessee history) had sharpened his debating and oratory skills to a fine point. Both his mother and father had once been members of Congress, and in 1975 many already believed Baker had his sights set on the White House.

Mathias, a graduate of Haverford College in Pennsylvania and the University of Maryland Law School, came to the Senate in 1968 as an antiwar candidate opposing the Vietnam policies of the Johnson administration. Of all the senators I had observed, Mathias was the most professorial. I could imagine him passing through Roman forums, toga flowing, head in the heavens, lost in thought. He was a thinker and a philosopher, but he had a practical side too, derived from his experience as assistant attorney general in Maryland, eight years in the US House of Representatives, and a term in the Senate.

Schweiker also came to the Senate in 1968, and in the same rare way as Mathias: by defeating a well-known incumbent. Schweiker's record was unorthodox. He became the first Republican senator to oppose the war in Vietnam; he voted against President Nixon's controversial Supreme Court nominees, Clement Haynsworth and G. Harold Carswell; he opposed bill after bill introduced into Congress by Nixon and Ford; and he refused to support a single presidential veto exercised by Nixon. In short, he voted a lot like Mathias.

The Democratic faction on the committee posed more of a puzzle, chiefly because Huddleston, Morgan, and Gary Hart were new to the Senate and without an established track record. The Democrat I knew best was the chairman.

As a child, Frank Church had been sickly, suffering from croup as a baby and bronchitis every year as a boy. The wintry north winds blowing off the Rocky Mountains into Boise seemed to linger in his chest through spring, weakening his body and sending him to bed while other youngsters skied and sledded. His mother remembers him often at home and in bed, reading, during this early period.[15] History books were his favorites, followed by political biographies and even political speeches—especially those of William E. Borah, then a popular United States senator from Idaho, a Republican and chairman of the Senate Foreign Relations Committee. Borah's voice often came over the local radio station; Church would lie with his head on a pillow and listen intently to the deep, rich tones and ornate style. From early on, a day rarely passed that young Church did not read the newspaper from front to back—and often aloud, in tones imitative of Borah, to the neighborhood children gathered on his porch.

By the time he was a senior in high school, Church had achieved a statewide reputation as a champion debater ("Boy Orator of the Snake River," said the newspapers). He spent two quarters at Stanford University and then joined the war effort after Pearl Harbor. With illness a thing of the past, Church had grown into a sturdy six-foot-one soldier. He was sent to the Burma–China–India theater, where he served as an intelligence officer and won a Bronze Star. After the war, Church returned to Stanford, coming away with a Phi Beta Kappa key and the Medaille Joffre (Stanford's esteemed debating award).

The summer following graduation, Church married and departed for Boston, where he had been accepted at Harvard Law School. It was a year of disaster. He soon experienced symptoms of deep fatigue and nausea, painfully reminiscent of childhood ailments. The young couple packed their bags at the end of the school year and transferred to Stanford University Law School, where the climate was more hospitable to someone with a history of bronchial infections. Even in the healing warmth of California sunshine, however, Church was no better—indeed, he felt worse, and his lower back began to throb incessantly with pain. Medical examinations at Stanford discovered why. This was no influenza; Frank Church, age twenty-three, had terminal cancer.

The shock was profound. His marriage was just beginning, and there was a new baby. What to do? Perhaps take a last fling in Europe, make the most of the six months of life left to him. Maybe just return home to Boise. Or possibly try a few more doctors to see if any hope existed. In desperation, the Churches turned to other physicians. One—a pathologist—suggested a last-ditch remedy to stop the spreading cancer: extensive surgery, accompanied by a new procedure involving massive x-ray treatment. There was no guarantee that the cure would not kill the patient earlier than the disease, but at this stage Church had little to lose and a life to gain. First came the surgery to excise a swelling tumor and lymph glands, then deep radiation, which produced intense nausea and pushed Church to the edge of death. His face turned gaunt and ghostly pale; the quick laugh had gone; his weight plummeted to ninety pounds. "He was just a crisp," his wife remembers.[16] As Church put it, in understatement, "the issue was in doubt."[17] Then, at the eleventh hour, color returned slowly to his cheeks, his appetite picked up, he felt like looking at his law books. The treatment had worked.

Within two years, Church finished his law degree with honors and returned to Boise in 1950 to practice his profession. In early 1956, he strode into a fellow attorney's office and announced, "I'm going to reach for the moon!"[18] His hat was in the ring for the United States Senate seat held by Republican Herman Welker—who would have all the advantages of incumbency plus the redoubtable coattails of President Eisenhower, America's most popular political figure.

What had emboldened Church? "After that experience [with cancer]," he once told a reporter, "I decided that life itself was the major risk. It could be snatched away at any moment. It has to be lived to the fullest. I had to take big chances. Win or lose, I had to play for high stakes."[19] The young attorney, who still looked like something of a choirboy, had taken on the philosophy of a riverboat gambler. When the cards were dealt, he held four aces: a "sparkling oratory"[20] that brought out the crowds; a handsome television presence; an indefatigable energy that carried him into every corner of the state to shake the hands of seventy-five thousand people; and plain luck—Welker fell desperately ill during the campaign. Church won by more than forty thousand votes, even though Eisenhower carried Idaho by sixty thousand. At thirty-two the fourth youngest person ever elected to the Senate, Church had taken a run at the ladder of success and landed near the top on the first try.

Two years later, Church (temporarily a protégé of then Senate majority leader Lyndon Johnson) won a seat on the prestigious Foreign Relations Committee, the same powerful forum in which William Borah had served from 1924 to 1940. As George F. Will has remarked, it was "the closest thing to apostolic succession in American politics."[21]

Over the course of his two decades in the Senate, Church developed a reputation as a loner. He seemed to stand apart from the clubby, backslapping, logrolling, joke-telling, good-old-boy style of politics characteristic of the Southern members who had ruled the most powerful committees for so long. He was independent, serious minded, courtly mannered, at times distant. Perhaps a psychologist could trace this aloofness to those many hours in bed alone with his books; the individualism of a sparsely populated, mountain-walled state; or the self-realization that his brain was more efficient than most and could act alone.

Certainly, compared to his colleagues—unbookish for the most part—Church was an intellectual, a star debater who brought his cold logic and refined analytic skills to Washington, a man who preferred his own brief because few could prepare one better. To his critics, he was a bit too precious, still too much the boy orator, the choirboy, despite the passing years and the jowls forming below his cheeks; they described him as "too nice," a "sissy," "too painfully honest," a "cross between a boy scout and an old maid," and (the favorite) "pompous."[22] His admirers, though, applauded his brain power; the Senate speeches that sometimes recaptured the great oratory of a century ago; his integrity; and his courage in taking on President Johnson, the multinational corporations, and now the CIA.[23]

The central truth of importance about Church in the Senate, however, was simply that he had been elected young and reelected ever since. This meant a natural rise through the Senate hierarchy; with few exceptions, those who serve long grow powerful as they ascend to committee chairmanships. The process occurred automatically on the standing, or permanent, committees. On the select, or temporary, committees (like the nascent Intelligence Committee), the gold ring of a chairmanship was bestowed by the party leaders. In 1975, Church's time had come. He had paid his dues, and the select committee chairmanship went to him—a temporary, albeit important, honor.

As for the other senators, all were virtually strangers to me, men whom I had passed occasionally in the corridors of Congress, whose faces over the years had stared out from newspapers, whose images had flickered across my television screen. Philip Hart, the father of eight children (and the only member of the Senate with a beard), was like few other senators: soft-spoken, unassuming, humble, a listener. It was often said he was "the gentlest and kindest" man in the Senate.[24] Behind the admirable equanimity was a fast mind; many Capitol Hill correspondents saw him as the brightest Democratic senator (and Mathias the brightest Republican).[25]

Walter Frederick "Fritz" Mondale, the son of a minister of Norwegian ancestry, was the attorney general in Minnesota in 1964 when the state's senior United States Senator, Hubert Humphrey, became vice president. Mondale was appointed by the governor to complete Humphrey's term, and in 1966 he was elected to the Senate in his own right, with a respectable 54 percent of the vote. Mondale was an "all-American boy": athletic, clean-cut, attractive. He would have been perfect behind a pulpit; only the three or four cigars he smoked each day hinted at a different career. He was widely regarded as a rising star in the Senate, his trajectory aided by his mentor, the powerful Senator Humphrey.

The three rookies on the committee—Huddleston, Morgan, and Gary Hart— were the least-known quantities, though Hart's career before his Senate election had been remarkable. He had helped lead the archliberal senator George McGovern (D-SD) to the Democratic presidential nomination in 1972 against heavy favorites like Senator Edmund S. Muskie (D-ME) and Senator Henry Jackson (D-WA); then, only two years later, he himself had won a Senate seat from Colorado—a state previously dominated by the Republican Party. Now he faced a baptism by fire in the Senate: only three weeks a member and he was on a controversial investigative committee. Here was a difficult challenge coming on top of the one he already faced: convincing his legislative colleagues that he was not a "bomb thrower" McGovernite bent on radicalizing the Senate.[26] Which was the real Gary Hart, the McGovern campaign manager or the more conservative person he now seemed to be?

Huddleston (like Mondale and Tower, a minister's son) had been a state legislator and president of the Kentucky Broadcasters Association before winning a Senate seat in 1972. He was burly, mild-mannered, and witty, and he was generally considered far less conservative than most of his Southern colleagues.

Morgan, another Southerner, was the second man on the committee who had served as attorney general in his state. He then went on to fill the seat left vacant by Senator Sam Ervin's retirement in 1974. Short and youthful looking, Morgan had developed a reputation in North Carolina as a consumer advocate. On intelligence and foreign policy issues, though, I expected him to be conservative in the tradition of Carolina senators.

The Staff

From my days as a congressional fellow, I was well aware of the typically chaotic and overcrowded conditions in the Congress, but when I arrived in Washington in mid-March to join the investigation, my office was unlike anything I had ever seen before. Assigned to G-308 of the Dirksen Building, in what had been an auditorium, the Senate Select Committee on Intelligence was guarded around the clock by armed Capitol Hill police. Inside, the auditorium was being divided into various work areas. Pale green partitions cast a greenish hue throughout the huge space, creating a maze of narrow corridors through which new staff members slid by one another sideways.

The place was in a state of anarchy: desks were being moved in, the high ceiling lowered, telephone lines placed, office supplies distributed, and heavy combination safes pushed on rollers to the rear of the auditorium. People scurried through the verdant maze like hungry mice. I followed a staff aide through the turns in the labyrinth until we reached the center of the cavernous room, where Bill Miller was seated in a small area reserved for the staff director.

Along with the chief counsel and the minority counsel, Miller would be responsible for the staff, under the guidance of the senators on the committee. (Who was ultimately in charge, Miller or the chief counsel, was yet unclear.) Below this triumvirate would be four major task forces comprising senior staff professionals. Then would come a support staff of research assistants, press aides, security personnel, and consultants, plus a team of secretaries and clerks. The task forces would deal with military intelligence (the National Security Agency, or NSA, and the Defense Intelligence Agency, or DIA); domestic intelligence (chiefly the FBI and the Internal Revenue Service, or IRS); foreign intelligence (the CIA); and the question of command and control—that is, ties between the White House and the intelligence community (appendix 2).

Miller asked me which task force I wished to join. I thought I had come to investigate the CIA, but after a pause I chose command and control. It sounded intriguing and seemed the best way to gain a broad perspective on the intelligence community.

As the partitioning of the auditorium space neared completion, the perimeters of various staff encampments took on clearer definition. At the epicenter stood the cubicles for the staff director and the chief counsel, guarded by three women who served as assistants. In the center, too, in a separate cubicle, sat the chief press liaison and his assistant. Surrounding these nerve centers and filling the front two-thirds of the auditorium were areas laid out for the four task forces. At the rear of the auditorium was the research center, jammed with researchers, filing cabinets, and vaults for classified materials.

Other pockets of activity sprang up wherever floor space could be found. The minority counsel and his assistants located themselves by the research center; the security force stationed itself near the front doors; the photocopying equipment and its operators were in an isolated corridor; the payroll people were in a cubicle near the front; secretaries typed away at desks throughout the auditorium; and here and there, staffers lodged themselves behind desks hidden in nooks and crannies around the border.

Once these islands filled with people, the result was bedlam—at least for someone accustomed to the quiet cloisters of academe. For the moment, however, only half the staff was in place, and G-308 was merely in a state of disorder.

Soon after I arrived, Miller put a significant organizational arrangement into effect. Eleven designees would be selected from the various task forces, one to work closely with each senator, facilitating the flow of information between the staff and the committee members. These would be important posts, for each designee would be expected to attend every committee meeting and assist "his" senator; the designee would also be responsible for helping the senator prepare for hearings. I became Senator Church's designee.

The organization of the staff soon took on additional wrinkles. First, it was quickly evident that the minority counsel was unwilling to settle for the designee arrangement alone; the Republicans wanted to select a third of all the staff hired. Under pressure from Tower, Baker, and Schweiker, Church bowed to this demand.

When we finally reached our outer limits (135 people), the staff was composed of fifty-three investigators, or professional staff. Like the senators themselves, the committee's professionals were primarily white, male attorneys—Washington's favorite species. The investigation of the CIA was, quipped one Washington cynic, just "another relief act for lawyers."[27]

The chief counsel, of course, was the top lawyer on the committee staff. Shortly after I took up residence in command and control—or, as it came to be called, the White House Task Force—I saw him sitting alone in his cubicle, scribbling furiously on a yellow legal pad. "Fritz Schwarz," he responded with an engaging grin as I introduced myself. I knew from reading a committee press release that the formal name was F. A. O. Schwarz Jr., and from staff gossip that he was a grandson of the well-known New York family of toy manufacturers. Schwarz was a tall, solidly built man, with strong facial features, large hands, and unruly hair. He had crewed at Harvard, graduated from law school there, and joined the prestigious New York law firm of Cravath, Swaine & Moore, rising quickly from associate to partner. In this interval he managed to spend a year in Nigeria assisting that nation to revise its constitution. His relaxed, sometimes rumpled, appearance belied a comfortable means but accurately reflected a lack of interest in the society page; his mind was preoccupied with the careful marshaling and presentation of evidence, not the carrousel of New York's social elite. Schwarz had an active interest in public affairs; he had advised the New York police department in the 1960s on matters related to the use of deadly force and in the 1970s on guidelines for the prudent handling of demonstrations.

The leadership qualities of the chief counsel were immediately apparent. Whereas Miller was reserved and slow to make decisions, Schwarz was aggressive and strongly opinionated. He spoke and acted with the firmness of a battlefield commander, though he was rarely gruff. Schwarz and Miller were men of far different experience and temperament. I wondered how long their dual leadership would remain equal and harmonious.

Minority counsel Curtis R. Smothers came to the staff soon after Schwarz was hired. Within the army and the Department of Defense, Smothers had held a variety of posts from trial attorney to deputy assistant secretary of defense. An associate professor of law at Georgetown University's law school, he was young, black, articulate, self-assured, and fashionably dressed. He was also something of an entrepreneur, teaching law, running a private practice, and serving in a key staff position on a major congressional investigation—all at the same time.

The committee was assembled. Just how well its members and staff would work together was impossible to predict. Strains were already apparent, but no one had time to worry much about them; the investigation was gathering momentum, and we were soon caught up in the tasks before us. Paper warfare with the executive branch was about to begin.

3

Establishing an Agenda

"As with a child, so with a serious congressional inquiry—the first few steps set the eventual course," noted a Washington columnist soon after the creation of the Senate committee.[1] Which direction our first few steps would take us was far from clear at the beginning, though we had no lack of signposts.

The mandate of the committee, spelled out in section 2 of Senate Resolution 21, was extensive.[2] As well as "other matters as the Committee deems necessary," we were charged specifically with a responsibility to probe fourteen major areas—with illegal CIA and FBI operations at the top of the list. Though some of the assignments overlapped, the scope of the inquiry was staggering. The Senate's Watergate committee had taken well over a year to investigate wrongdoings in the single presidential election of 1972; the Church committee was expected to look into a multitude of alleged sins spanning decades—all in eight months.

Fritz Schwarz and Bill Miller were well aware of the time limitations. "I made the judgment very early," Schwarz recalls, "that there were bound to be some abuses we wouldn't cover. The best we could do was to pick out ten, fifteen, maybe even twenty subjects and get really into depth."[3] Miller was primarily interested in "the structure, nature and performances of the intelligence community, both foreign and domestic, the cost of each agency, their missions, and evaluations of the usefulness of the intelligence obtained"—all questions related to the quality of intelligence. As for abuses, Miller recommended that the committee focus on only "a few cases to pursue in depth."[4]

Virtually everyone understood the necessity of selectivity, but from the multitude of possibilities, what should be selected? The resolution would serve as an outline of the prominent features on the terrain to be explored, but the committee would have to fill in the details and chart new courses, if necessary, as the task forces fanned out like search parties in the quest for information.

Discovery

When Schwarz arrived in March, his start-up device was a chronology: a mapping out of who did what and when in the intelligence agencies, with a listing of specific events in one column and precise dates in the adjacent column. Chronologies, chronologies, chronologies—they became the staff preoccupation during March and April; we turned them out like dedicated monks writing scripture. ("Schwarz's chronologies became a holy writ before which everyone genuflected," recalls one staffer.[5]) Drawing from the chronologies, Schwarz had each of the task forces prepare a "discovery plan" for every organization ("entity"), operation, and issue that we had identified as significant. This approach was essentially a strategy for fact finding—the initial responsibility facing the committee.

The strategy comprised four parts. First, we were to draft initial document requests for the White House and the intelligence agencies, concentrating on basic documents related to authorities and procedures relevant to the issues within our legislative mandate. The chronologies helped frame the precise time periods that most interested us. The next step was to draft elaborate follow-up requests for documents, this time delving more deeply into the intricacies of organizational relationships and operational details. We were then to prepare an initial set of questions ("interrogatories") that we thought would be important to ask intelligence officials when we reached the interview stage in our fact-finding mission. In all this work, the investigators were asked to be sensitive to leads ("discovery tips") that might direct the investigation toward important new findings. Finally, Schwarz's strategy required us to make a preliminary listing of key persons to interview.

Early in February, a former CIA official, Harry Rositzke, suggested that the Church committee investigators faced three tasks: "to establish facts, judge their legality or illegality, and recommend executive or legislative remedies if they are needed."[6] He was exactly right, and by April we were well underway in our search for hard facts. Our agenda was beginning to take shape.

In January, Miller had proposed the following schedule of hearings in a memorandum to Senator Church: March—testimony from the heads of agencies and departments (first in executive session, then public hearings); May–June—hearings on key cases (such as the Huston Plan); July–August—hearings on reforms; September—wrap up.[7] One of the items our committee had been unable to requisition from the Senate supply office was a crystal ball; with one, we would have realized how naive these plans were.

The basic problem in our planning was that we were unable to dance alone. Like it or not, our partner was the executive branch, for it had what we needed to conduct the inquiry: information on intelligence activities. We might have been ready to tango straight to the center of our mandate, but the executive branch preferred to waltz.

Occasionally, in the beginning, we managed a few hesitant steps together. First, on 26 February, came a brief but friendly visit with Attorney General Edward H. Levi in Church's office; Levi promised that the Justice Department and the FBI would cooperate fully with the committee.[8]

The next day, Church and Tower met with William Colby (who was director of the CIA throughout most of the investigations). In a spirit of comity, Colby agreed to waive CIA employee secrecy oaths in dealing with our committee, [9] thus removing one of the major obstacles between the committee investigators and information about past intelligence practices. He also promised to provide all CIA organization charts down to the branch level since 1947, as well as all budgetary information and all documents on legal authority.

As part of the bargain with Colby, Church and Tower accepted his request that everyone associated with the committee (senators excepted, as always) sign secrecy agreements promising not to reveal classified information. In the view of the committee's chief attorney, Fritz Schwarz, our willingness to enter into this agreement with the CIA and other agencies "was absolutely vital to our success as a committee." Otherwise we would have gotten "hung up on procedural questions. We needed to get moving."[10]

Soon after we struck this pact with Colby, we reached a similar agreement with the FBI. This understanding included the additional stipulation that the actual names of Bureau informants would be blocked out of all documents. When CIA documents finally began to trickle our way, they too had the names of agents excised. This the committee found understandable and acceptable. "Removing these names was perfectly reasonable," Schwarz concluded. "It didn't hurt us in the slightest, yet they would have fought us forever if we hadn't agreed to this."[11]

Church told reporters he was satisfied that Colby intended to provide all the information the committee needed for its investigation of the CIA. Next, he would seek to gain similar assurances from the president himself.

The committee's delegation to the White House included Church, Tower, Miller, Schwarz, and a couple of other staffers. They were ushered into the Oval Office on the morning of 5 March, where they were greeted by President Ford. With Ford were Henry Kissinger, secretary of state and national security adviser; his deputy, Brent Scowcroft; Donald Rumsfeld, White House chief of staff; Patrick Buchanan, a White House speech writer; and three other staff aides. The presence of top Cabinet members signaled serious business.

The committee was ready for serious business too. Tucked into his coat pocket, Church carried a list of key documents that he intended to request from the president: (1) a Colby report to the president discussing CIA involvement in assassination plots; (2) NSCIDs; (3) classified executive orders; (4) budget studies; (5) NSDMs, NSSMs, and NSAMs; and (6) legal authorities.[12]

The acronyms on the list would be particularly controversial because they referred to National Security Council documents. The NSC (not to be confused with the NSA, a subordinate intelligence-gathering agency—see the diagram of the intelligence community in appendix 2) is the president's primary advisory group for national security policy. Its papers are among the most sensitive in the government. NSCIDs (pronounced "n-skids") were National Security Council Intelligence Directives; NSDMs ("niz-dems"), National Security Decision Memoranda; NSSMs ("niz-sims"), National Security Study Memoranda; and NSAMs ("niz-ams"), National Security Action Memoranda. No congressional committee had ever gained access to these top-secret documents before. Nor were Colby's report or the budget studies likely to be won easily. I envisaged Ford reaching into his own coat pocket, pulling out a large rubber stamp, and emblazoning Church's list with the words EXECUTIVE PRIVILEGE.

Church summarized the mandate of Senate Resolution 21 and ended with the declaration that "Tower and I are in agreement, take comfort in that."

"Indeed an uncommon alliance," Ford responded with a grin.

Church thanked the president for the cooperation shown by the administration so far, referring to the lifting of the CIA secrecy oath, and told him that the committee staff had all accepted the secrecy procedures requested by Colby. "We will not be a wrecking crew," he promised. "There will be no dismantling and no exposing of agents to danger. No sources will be compromised. We, however, do need information." He asked Ford to issue a written directive to all the departments and agencies dealing with intelligence, requesting them to cooperate fully with the committee.

Ford said that he wanted to cooperate but was reluctant to do so in written form, because then he would have to write a similar order as well for the recently established investigative committee in the House of Representatives. This he was disinclined to do. The implication was that we were to be trusted to conduct a fair inquiry, but the House committee was not—a conclusion reached perhaps because the House panel did have a few members with a record of biting criticism against the CIA.

"It's best not to formalize," said the president. "Let's proceed on a case-by-case basis."

"The form of cooperation is unimportant," Church replied. "I only hope the Senate Select Committee and the executive can cooperate and stay out of the courts." He reached into his coat pocket and handed the list of document requests to President Ford. "Here is a list of the information we need."

The president looked at the list as Church continued: "This is not a formal request for the Colby report, but the committee would like to have access to the information Colby has reported to you, both written and oral, regarding assassinations and other matters."

"That's been given to the Rockefeller Commission," interjected one of the White House aides.

"We hope to get all the Rockefeller documents and testimony, too," said Church.

"I will consider the Colby matter when the committee submits a formal request," said the president evasively. He would force the committee to take a formal vote on this topic before considering it further—yet another delay.

"I would like the president to facilitate the work of the Senate Select Committee in the files of various agencies," Church tried again.

Poised like an overweight tiger, Kissinger leaped at this one. "Asking for information is one thing, but going through the files is another. The covert action files are very sensitive."

"Senator Church is not asking for the right to go fishing in the files," said the president, spreading out his hands in a calming gesture. "I am certain all his requests would be relevant to the inquiry." He shook hands with Church and Tower, and said that the executive branch would be "as cooperative as possible." The meeting was obviously over.[13]

Just what the committee had accomplished at this session, if anything, we would find out only (in Ford's words) on a "case-by-case basis." Certainly Kissinger's remarks failed to encourage us. Whether the committee would obtain Colby's document on CIA activities, submitted to the White House in December 1974, remained unclear. On 28 February, CBS correspondent Daniel Schorr had revealed on the *Evening News* that this document contained information on CIA assassination plots. Ever since, the committee considered access to it a high priority.

As the responses in the Oval Office suggested, the attitude of the executive branch toward the Church committee was ambivalent. Colby and Ford showed some signs of cooperation, but it was an uneasy honeymoon.

The CIA, in fact, had raised a cold hand against the committee as early as 20 February, less than a month after the Senate voted in favor of the investigation. Appearing before a House subcommittee, Colby said that criticism of past CIA activities "placed American intelligence in danger" and warned Congress not to "throw the baby out with the bath water." Referring to the allegations by *New York Times* reporter Hersh, Colby observed: "These exaggerations and misrepresentations of CIA activities can do irreparable harm to our national intelligence apparatus and if carried to the extreme could blindfold our country as it looks abroad." "CIA Critics Hinder Work, Colby Warns," read the *Los Angeles Times* headlines the next day.[14]

The Church committee, however, had refused to be a passive suitor. Speaking before the National Press Club on February 27, Church voiced doubts that the White House investigation of CIA activities, headed by Vice President Rockefeller, could resolve the allegations made against the Agency. "The executive branch cannot, with sufficient credibility, investigate itself," he said, and added that he hoped the Rockefeller Commission would complete its work soon "and make its records available, as a starting point, for the more comprehensive congressional investigations to come."[15]

During this early squabbling, the press, the courts, and the public produced a gusher of leads that further shaped our agenda. The biggest press story concerned CIA links to death plots against foreign leaders: Fidel Castro in Cuba, Rafael Trujillo in the Dominican Republic, and Patrice Lumumba in the Congo. One source told a reporter in a telephone interview, for example, that Robert Kennedy (President John Kennedy's brother and attorney general in his administration) had stopped a deal between the CIA and the Mafia to murder Castro.[16]

The Ford administration, it soon became evident, wished to avoid taking on the assassination question, with all the dangers it held for further antagonizing the intelligence community and the conservative wing of the Republican Party. White House press secretary Ron Nessen suggested on 10 March that these allegations might be better dealt with by the Church committee, with its "broader charter."[17]

While Rockefeller himself refused to discuss the assassination matter, he did ask the president—immediately after the death-plot stories broke—for an extension of his commission's deadline for a few weeks. Soon thereafter, in the middle of March, the *New York Times* reported that the assassination controversy had become a "dilemma" for the White House. The Rockefeller Commission would look into the allegations after all; the president had changed his mind "because of increasing concern over the assassination reports."[18]

Senator Church subsequently announced that "we'll look at the evidence and get to the bottom of all these rumors."[19] A Senate investigation of the CIA could hardly ignore what had now become the most talked-about intelligence news in the country.[20] Assassination rumors were rife, inflamed by an admission to the press from Colby on 16 March that the Agency indeed had discussed the possible assassination of foreign leaders. For the first time, the CIA had conceded that such discussions really did take place. Senator Church quickly responded to the admission. "In the absence of war," he said, "no agency of the government can have a license to murder, and the President can't be a 'Godfather.'"[21]

All this talk of assassinations stimulated a renewed interest in the murder of President Kennedy and the possibility of CIA involvement in his death.[22] Press stories and public interest soon added this item to the agendas of both the Senate committee and the Rockefeller Commission. Like flypaper, investigating committees in Washington seem to snare every halfway relevant topic buzzing in the air, for fear of being accused of an incomplete inquiry. On the committee staff, we approached the morning newspapers gingerly, wondering what new revelations would be added to our already weighty mandate.

The intelligence story that received almost as much coverage during the spring as assassination plots was Project Jennifer, the CIA operation to raise part of a sunken Soviet submarine from the floor of the Pacific Ocean.[23] The ship assigned to perform the recovery mission was a deep-ocean mining vessel, the

Glomar Explorer, owned by mysterious millionaire recluse Howard Hughes. The news broke on the morning of 19 March; by midafternoon Senator Church had added this James Bond adventure story to our long list of items to investigate. "If we are prepared to pay Howard Hughes $350 million for an obsolete Russian submarine," Church told the press, "it's little wonder we are broke."[24] His committee colleague Barry Goldwater disagreed. "Frankly," said Goldwater, "if they hadn't gone out and raised that sub, I'd be mad."[25]

Throughout spring, the press kept us hopping—and our agenda bulging—with other leads, some of which were productive for our investigation. Leads poured in from other sources too. Cases before civil and military courts concerning matters of surveillance brought much new information to light on intelligence agency activities. In a New York superior court case, for example, a twenty-six-year-old woman, Mary Jo Cook, described in detail how she spied for the FBI on antiwar groups.[26] Cook eventually became one of our witnesses for hearings on the FBI.

Other committees in Congress were generating new information as well. Testifying before a House Judiciary Subcommittee on March 22, for example, chief postal inspector William J. Cotter said that he had given the CIA a deadline of 15 February 1973 to "get superior approval" for its illegal mail-interception program or discontinue it.[27] The program was finally abandoned, but, said Cotter, not before thousands of pieces of first-class mail, twenty written by Americans, were surreptitiously opened and reproduced during a twenty-year period. Our Domestic Intelligence Task Force immediately began to correlate its mail-opening research with the House Judiciary testimony, searching for corroboration or inconsistencies of evidence.

Additional "discovery tips" for the committee included letters, visits ("walk-ins"), and long-distance calls from the public. Several of these personal testimonies were of the "CIA tried to carry me away in a flying saucer" variety, but others seemed genuine and plausible, and we did our best to check them out. Sometimes they led us on a wild goose chase. One staffer on the Military Intelligence Task Force received a long-distance call from a Western state. The caller insisted he had urgent information on the subject of military surveillance of civilians. Couldn't he relate the information over the telephone or by mail, asked the staffer. No, the information was far too sensitive. The man's credentials were genuine; he had served in a unit known to have been involved in surveillance activities during the 1960s. So the staff investigator made the long plane trip, plus a four-hour drive through desolate countryside. When he finally arrived, though, all the witness had in mind was to show the official off to his golfing pals at the local country club: he was so important that the federal government had come all the way out to a small Western town to see him. The man had no information apart from what was already in the public record from the investigation of army spying conducted by the Senate in 1973. Disgusted, the staffer packed his bags and made the long journey back, vowing never to make the same mistake again.

As spring faded into the collar-soaking humidity of a Washington summer, the committee staff traced the internal workings of the intelligence community, drafted fresh document requests, and sorted out new leads (whose sheer volume threatened to crush us). On 12 March, Church sent letters to Colby and President Ford formally asking for selected intelligence documents. A week later the committee sent its first formal document request to the FBI, through Attorney General Levi.

Also in March, Bill Bader (the Foreign Intelligence, or CIA, Task Force leader) suggested to Miller and Schwarz another approach to the search for documents, perhaps reflecting his training as a historian. He had concluded that the first priority of the committee was "to document and analyze the legislative and organizational history and practice of the CIA."[28] This meant obtaining immediately all the documents the committee could dredge up on the history of the various CIA operations, for only they would provide "the necessary frame work" for the investigation. Before "the guillotine falls," advised Bader in a rosy prognostication, the committee should request as top priority all CIA organizational histories, as well as every NSCID and related classified executive order on intelligence. These papers would allow the committee to trace the evolution of the Agency's operations.

Fritz Schwarz was interested in gathering as many documents as possible, and as quickly as possible, but his perspective was less historical than abuse oriented. Bader, the historian, and Schwarz, the litigator, saw the basic problem in a different light (though their document wish lists overlapped). "The work of the committee wasn't that dissimilar from the IBM [International Business Machines] case on which I worked earlier [while at Cravath, Swaine & Moore]," Schwarz has said. "Both required getting into a new subject that had a lot of documents. The major difference was that on the Senate committee we were not trying to make a case; rather, our objective was to show certain facts and learn certain lessons. We weren't going at it from a predetermined view as to where the bad was."[29]

The difference in epistemology between Bader and Schwarz was of more than academic interest; these two views drove a deep wedge into the staff. For Bader, Schwarz's approach was all too much in the fashion of an IBM suit. "The document requests, under Schwarz's influence, became a grab bag," he recalls. "He wanted *everything*. The requests were unstructured, rambling, unfocused. We didn't know where we were, let alone where we were going. A much more effective discovery process would have been to concentrate on the CIA histories written by their own people. The footnotes alone in these documents contained a wealth of leads."[30]

Schwarz and his assistants, though, were not content to wade through agency histories alone. Gimlet-eyed, tireless, they pursued practically every lead that came along in search of one major objective: dramatic evidence. "Ever since its establishment, the CIA had been relatively free of congressional supervision," states Frederick Baron, Schwarz's top assistant. "To overcome this tremendous inertia, we had to make the case in spades during the investigation. Only dramatic facts lead to changes."[31] In Schwarz's words, "We had to highlight abuses if we were to achieve fundamental, statutory improvements."[32]

Both men thought the attorneys on the staff were best equipped to uncover abuses. "The methodology of lawyers was ideal for digging out what happened," according to Baron. "Miller, Bader, and the others could help interpret the facts, of course, but we had the appropriate training for the basic fact-finding." Few of the nonlawyers on the staff were impressed by this argument.

Miller preferred yet a third approach. For him, the most promising pathway was the interview—and the more civil, the better. He recommended to Senator Church that the committee turn to interviews, given the likelihood of a prolonged struggle over documents. "We will learn more from interviews anyway," he concluded.[33]

"Access to information in the executive branch was a matter of quiet diplomacy, not litigation," recalls Miller. "Treating the investigation like some kind of legal case was detrimental. This approach was viewed in the executive branch as pure harassment, which in turn led to argument and delay. Some of us on the staff had to spend a lot of time in these early months sorting out this disaster and rebuilding bridges destroyed by committee litigators."[34]

"My own experience as a lawyer," counters Schwarz, "had been that words are fine, but people can always slip around oral testimony. There is nothing like the contemporaneous document for establishing facts; indeed, an investigator is probably never going to get really reliable oral testimony."[35] His aides were equally adamant. "Our successes came from dealing with the intelligence officials as witnesses, not as wise men," emphasizes Baron. "Each document we were able to pry loose led to more documents, more questions, more witnesses. It was like pulling back the layers of an onion: each time we thought we had come to the last layer, we discovered another."[36] One staff lawyer remembers that he "enjoyed the repartee on the cosmic scene with Miller and his assistants, but the real case for reform grew out of the detailed evidence marshaled by the attorneys working with Schwarz."[37]

The arguments went back and forth on the appropriate methods for obtaining the information necessary to the inquiry. The end result was that we went forward with all three methodologies. Sometimes the friendly hand of cooperation reached across these disciplinary lines, never in full trust, but at any rate pulling toward the objective of learning whatever we could about the intelligence community in order to propose reasonable reforms.

The incipient divisions on the committee staff were brought to the chairman's attention, gently, by Miller in early April; he suggested to Church in a memorandum that the investigation required "two on-going but relatively different approaches."[38] One would examine "the nature and character of the intelligence agencies—their history, present structures, and principal activities," he wrote, folding together his and Bader's interests. For this portion of the inquiry, Miller recommended "benign interviewing." The second obligation, the investigation of abuses, would implicitly require a less benign approach. For the time being, Church ignored the proposed dichotomy.

Though Miller was pessimistic about the opening of document sluices between the agencies and the committee, he nevertheless joined with Schwarz to lobby the executive branch for access to papers. The first face-to-face session took place on 1 April in the ornate Old Executive Office Building next to the White House.[39] Awaiting the committee staff leaders were three men chosen by President Ford to work with Congress during the intelligence investigations. Miller and Schwarz came quickly to the point: over a fortnight had passed since the committee's first document requests were hand carried to the White House and to the CIA, yet the committee had received nothing beyond a few organizational charts.

The White House aides listened patiently, then presented a problem of their own. The volume of material requested by the Church committee was overwhelming, they lamented, and extraordinarily difficult for them to clear with their small staff. Compliance would take time. They counseled patience. Miller and Schwarz were left unsure whether this was simply a further delaying tactic or a genuine administrative bottleneck that would temporarily slow, but not stop, the flow of documents. Schwarz was inclined to give the White House the benefit of the doubt, for the moment.

At first the benevolence of the chief counsel seemed well placed. Two days later, the White House telephoned to inform Miller and Schwarz that they would soon receive the NSCIDs, NSDMs, and other documents requested in Church's letter. Miller was ecstatic. This is "unprecedented," he told Church, "a major accomplishment" that "narrowed the scope of executive privilege."[40]

Early Scuffling

During the early period of staff preparations, the committee never formally convened. On 9 April the members gathered in a small but elegant room in the

Capitol for their first full-fledged meeting, marking the real beginning of the investigation. A sense of excitement permeated the staff, and the senators also seemed to have buoyed spirits. We were all feeling a little smug too. The House Select Committee on Intelligence had been established in February 1975, just three weeks after our own, but seven weeks later it had still failed to hire a chief counsel or any investigators. The House committee chairman, Lucien Nedzi (D-MI), was drawing serious criticism for the extremely slow pace of his inquiry. A *New York Times* article quoted one House source who speculated that "the question has to arise" whether Nedzi was deliberately delaying action out of some reluctance to set his committee in motion; in contrast, the Church committee was lauded for its progress.[41]

Praise like this appearing in the *Times* is guaranteed to brighten the faces of even the most jaded politicians, and the members of the Senate Intelligence Committee were basking this day in the sunshine of good publicity. Behind this confident scene, however, lay an edge of uneasiness. Committee members and staff grew daily more concerned over whether we would ever obtain the documents we had requested from the White House and the intelligence agencies. Despite the recent telephone call (3 April) promising NSCIDs and the like, nothing important had arrived at the committee premises. A dozen organization and personnel charts were all we had to show for a month of bargaining for papers with the executive branch.

The committee was also aware of a burgeoning counteroffensive from the CIA. On 22 March 1975, for example, chief of CIA Latin American operations David A. Phillips retired from the Agency to rally former intelligence officers as private citizens to defend the organization from outside criticism. Phillips's targets, ostensibly, were former CIA officers who had written critical books and articles on the Agency, but his Association of Retired Intelligence Officers (ARIO) had all the earmarks of a grassroots lobbying effort against any criticism, including that of our committee.[42]

Further, CIA director Colby seemed to be stepping up his public defense of the Agency. On 7 April he told an audience of news executives in New Orleans that covert activities and paramilitary operations abroad were essential parts of the nation's intelligence work. Colby said that he welcomed the current congressional inquiries into the CIA and the concomitant public debate over the Agency's proper scope, but he also reiterated his fears that "a climate of sensationalism" was jeopardizing the Agency's operations. Some foreign nations, he warned, had already stopped cooperating with the CIA or had started to "constrict the information they provide us."[43]

Troubling, too, were various editorials discussing the high probability that intelligence officials would simply lie to the congressional committees rather than tarnish the image of their agencies or take the chance of making revelations that could jeopardize the security of the nation or of agents and informants in the field. Columnist Tom Braden, himself a former CIA officer, reminded readers that Allen Dulles, the Agency's director from 1953 to 1961, had once said he would lie to anyone about intelligence matters if necessary, except the president.[44] William F. Buckley Jr., the conservative columnist, quoted from an article written by Miles Copeland, his favorite author on intelligence matters (both Buckley and Copeland were once in the CIA): "Almost all the Agency people I talked to assured me unashamedly, almost profoundly, 'Of course we are going to lie to the congressional committees.' They felt that as loyal Americans they cannot do otherwise—except in the unlikely event the members of the committees can be held accountable for their leaks, impossible in the present atmosphere."[45] Senator Church, for one, was already firmly convinced that former CIA director Richard Helms had committed perjury in 1973 before his Subcommittee on Multinational Corporations, which examined CIA involvement with American corporate interests in Chile.[46] How could he now trust Helms to be truthful in this investigation, even under oath?

So even though spirits were high as the committee meeting came to order on 9 April, these other considerations lurked in the background—particularly the concern over White House foot-dragging on our document requests. Senator Church welcomed the committee members, their designees, and senior staff; then he turned the meeting over to Miller and Schwarz, who explained the staff organization and its preliminary research endeavors. I looked around at the elaborate chandeliers, the thick carpeting, the ornate mirrors, the senators' expensive suits, and thought of when I had stood with Senator Church in the carnival atmosphere of a county fair during his Idaho reelection campaign in 1974. Then we wore cowboy shirts and handed out campaign balloons. It was a long way from the sawdust and tents to this room of polished mahogany tables, soft lighting, and lofty questions of national security.

Church asked for discussion on the Miller–Schwarz briefing. Goldwater immediately spoke up. The committee should "slow down," he said. He was particularly worried about leaks: "We're in danger here of destroying what little intelligence this country gets, and believe me, it is little compared to what our enemies have."

Suddenly three buzzers rang out in the room, and three white stars above the floor lighted up—the signal for a quorum call. The committee recessed for a vote on the nearby Senate floor. Dashing in and out of meetings for floor votes hardly seemed an efficient way to run a committee, but that was the way the Senate operated.

When the senators returned to the committee room, laughing easily among themselves, they unanimously endorsed the investigative plans suggested in the Miller–Schwarz briefing. Gary Hart urged the committee, though, to be more precise about its agenda. What were the various substantive stages of the investigation? What was the timetable? No one, it was obvious, was yet prepared to answer Hart's basic questions other than to suggest that the timetable depended in part on what documents we were able to obtain and when.

Then the committee turned to the heart of the meeting: our document request. The CIA had been "friendly but not productive," Schwarz observed.

"What is the ultimate recourse if the agencies refuse to cooperate?" asked Huddleston, striking at the core of our worst fears.

"The courts," Church replied, but he pointed out that what we had so far was "essentially a political problem, not a legal one." The committee decided to write another letter to Ford that same day, hoping to expedite the flow of documents.

Outside the doors of the meeting room, the press corps huddled around microphones awaiting a briefing on the session from Church and Tower. The senators soon emerged, and Church told the press he had been authorized in the committee meeting to expedite the flow of documents from the executive branch by writing a letter to President Ford. Church said he still had no reason to think the White House would refuse to give up its documents, but he stressed that the committee saw no reason for further delay.

It was apparent that the committee was ready to take off the gloves over the documents struggle. Church was becoming sensitive to comments that he was being too much of a "Mr. Nice Guy"—emphasizing responsibility to the point where the administration might take advantage of the committee. The chairman faced a difficult balancing act. He wanted to establish a sense of trust and confidence within the executive branch for the committee, and therefore he did not want to push overly hard on the president too soon. At this stage, an excessively aggressive chairman might also alienate the conservative Republicans on the committee. Church, however, had the liberals on the committee to worry about too, and they were becoming visibly restless over the lack of response in the executive branch to our document request. How long would it be before the press grew just as critical of our committee's slowness as it was already of the snail's pace in the House? The 9 April press conference signaled that Church would not tolerate delay much longer.

The rest of April and May saw the tide of battle over documents ebb and flow inconclusively up and down Pennsylvania Avenue. The day after Church's remarks to the press on 9 April, President Ford gave his State of the World address to Congress. "Sensationalized public debate over legitimate intelligence activities is a disservice to this nation and a threat to our intelligence system," he said, adding that "procedures have been altered in a way that makes the protection of vital information next to impossible." The president's references were unclear, but obviously he was in a fighting mood.

Then, less than a week later, the logjam seemed to break. Miller and Schwarz took a taxi to the White House where, at last, they were handed the elusive thirty-nine-page Colby report on assassination plots, as well as a batch of NSDMs, NSAMs, and NSSMs. Hallelujah! Now maybe the committee could find out how these agencies really worked. But the White House had bad news too. The Office of Management and Budget (OMB) examiner's reports on intelligence were off limits to the committee; these were, in the words of a White House aide, "definitely within the realm of executive privilege."[47] While this was debatable, the committee staffers were so pleased to have gotten something that they gathered up their new possessions and departed for the Hill without argument. Euphoria ran high—only to crash as quickly when a search through the documents revealed that most of the items we had requested were still missing.

Now the staff had to go back to Senator Church for still another letter of protest to the executive branch. This time the objection went to William Colby. "The actual amount [of documentary material] received thus far is disappointing," said the letter. "It is now time to move rapidly on the balance."[48]

When the committee gathered for its second meeting, on 23 April, the atmosphere was markedly different from its opening session a fortnight earlier. The joking and feeling of assurance had given way to a mood of concern and seriousness. Church speculated that the Rockefeller Commission, wishing to avoid being upstaged by the senators, was delaying our request for documents. He was highly agitated. "We're not moving along rapidly enough," he said. "The executive branch is setting the pace. We cannot make ourselves subject to their control."

Philip Hart noted that the executive branch had "given us two go-to-hells. What is our response going to be?"

Before anyone could answer, buzzers rang, white stars lighted up, and the committee members disappeared to the Senate floor for a vote. When they returned, Senator Baker proposed that the committee send additional letters to the president and to Colby, stating that we wanted more from them than a narrow, literal interpretation of papers they should forward to us. Church added that the committee needed to be more specific in its requests and to set strict deadlines for the receipt of materials.

Mondale whispered to his designee, David Aaron (who also served as the White House Task Force director), and Aaron went to the telephone at the end of the room. I guessed that Mondale, who had an uncanny instinct for coming up with a reasonable course of action at just the right time, must have thought of something he'd left in his office that would bear upon how to deal with the documents issue. Within minutes, the door to the committee room opened and a messenger appeared. Aaron rose to receive an envelope, which he handed to Mondale. As Church and Tower discussed how to handle the document delay, Mondale opened the envelope carefully and removed a cigar, which he clipped, stuck in his mouth, and lighted; then he sank back into the folds of his leather chair. I looked over at Aaron; he shrugged his shoulders and grinned.

Baker was addressing the problem of documents. "The funny stuff is over," he concluded, and urged the committee to send still stronger letters to Ford and Colby. Church agreed, and suggested that the committee had been "too riveted in on documents; we must go to interrogatories and interviews, too."

Mondale put his cigar in an ashtray and sat up abruptly. "They're going to wait us out," he said calmly. "We ought to tell them we're going to keep getting extensions for the life of this committee until we finish our business." Tower looked at Mondale approvingly and chimed in, "Amen, world without end." Church nodded, and relighted his own cigar.

In a routine dialogue with the press following the committee meeting, Church complained strongly about executive branch delays on document deliveries. He informed reporters that the committee had decided to prod the CIA and the White House for a speedup, and he warned the executive branch, through the medium of the press, that the inquiry would be kept alive "until we get all that is needed."[49]

Tower, who stood next to Church before the microphones, emphasized that he believed the delay was an "institutional" problem rather than deliberate stalling. The White House was doing its best to clear the mountain of classified papers, he argued, but it was a time-consuming task. Church countered that he saw absolutely no excuse for the delay. The faces of the reporters brightened at the prospect of disagreement between the committee chairman and vice chairman. There might be some news here yet. (Later in the day White House spokesmen blamed the great volume of material and "events in Southeast Asia" for the delays.[50])

As requested by the committee, Miller and Schwarz drafted new letters to President Ford and Director Colby. The letters said, identically: "The fact remains that too much material called for in our documents request remains outstanding and the system apparently being employed to clear material for us builds in excessive delays."[51] The administration was asked to streamline this procedure so the committee could move on with its work.

In a progress report to Church, Miller wrote that "various tactical devices of delay" were being used by the White House and the intelligence agencies. He was so enthusiastic over some of the top-secret paper relinquished by the White House, however, that he could not resist literally underlining the importance of the committee successes so far: *This is the first time that these classes of documents, namely: the various NSC directives, NSAMs, NSDMs, NSC Memoranda and reports have been turned over to a congressional committee.* Even though the White House was still being difficult over the transfer of materials (such as the OMB papers and several vital NSC directives), Miller was pleased that executive privilege had been "pushed back to a reasonable basis." For the first time, the "'national security' barrier has been passed."[52]

On 29 April, Miller and Schwarz made another journey to the Executive Office Building. A Ford aide greeted them, and for four hours the three men went painstakingly over the committee's outstanding document requests. The session was "very difficult," Miller noted.[53] The aide had abandoned his early air of cooperation; he was now a tough, skeptical, even intransigent negotiator. The change in attitude seemed to be a result of the Bader-inspired requests for CIA histories. "I think we have hit a critical nerve at CIA," Miller informed Church the next day.[54]

The Bader CIA Task Force had asked for six thousand pages drawn from case studies on covert action—the most sensitive of all CIA programs. "Why does the committee want to go through these old history books?" the CIA liaison people complained to the White House, which in turn complained—at great length—to Miller and Schwarz. To Bader's researchers, who had a glimpse of the details in these histories, this question was like asking an advance party from the ant colony why they wanted in the honey jar.

The CIA soon informed the committee that it would have to limit to no more than five the number of staffers poring over the histories.[55] The materials would also have to be kept at the CIA, and committee researchers could take only summary notes, rather than photocopying whole portions. Finally, any documents spotted in footnotes in the histories (Bader's reason for seeking access to the histories in the first place) and requested by the staff would have to be closely reviewed by the CIA. If overly sensitive, the documents might have to be paraphrased or their contents partially deleted.

The CIA was now beginning to play hardball, as the experienced Hill staffers put it. The limit of five researchers was reasonable, but refusing to let the histories come to our secure quarters, where we could work with them more conveniently (and where busy senators could drop in to read important portions), was questionable. Most troublesome was just how much the CIA planned to paraphrase or delete from the documents. An investigation based on papers that looked like Swiss cheese was hardly promising.

The full Intelligence Committee met again on 7 May, and the members decided to have Church and Tower visit Vice President Rockefeller to ask for access to the documents and testimony gathered by his commission. The next day Church, Tower, Schwarz, and Smothers called on the vice president. Rockefeller greeted them ebulliently and appeared unruffled by Church's request for all the transcripts, evidence, and "raw materials" in the possession of the Rockefeller Commission.

"When we went to see Rockefeller," Church remembers, "it was the most beautiful finesse you ever saw. My, how glad he was to see me. My, how honored he was at my visit. And then when we asked him for all of the transcripts, he understood why we wanted them and agreed it would expedite our hearings."[56] Then came an oblique "no": the president would have to grant access to these papers, not the vice president.

"Rockefeller was absolutely brilliant in ending up not agreeing to give us what we wanted," recalls Schwarz, "but without giving us really anything to complain about. He winked and smiled and said, 'Gee, I want to help you but, of course, I can't—not until we've finished our work and the president approves it.'"[57] Because the president had appointed the commission in the first place, he ultimately would have to decide which of its materials could be transferred to Congress, concluded the vice president, as he beamed broadly and wrung their hands. Within minutes, the legislators were out on the streets again, empty-handed.

On 9 May, the committee assembled for a special session. One reporter observed that the hasty gathering of the members reflected "the atmosphere of confrontation between the senators and the executive branch."[58]

The chairman and vice chairman reviewed the brief talk they had had with Vice President Rockefeller the day before. "We were very skillfully finessed," summed up Tower. "It's back to square one." Gary Hart, wearing a pinstripe suit and black cowboy boots, shook his head slowly, removed a cigar from his mouth, and grimaced.

Church said he believed the committee would get the Rockefeller files eventually, but he emphasized the importance of moving on with our own staff investigations rather than sitting around holding our breath for CIA or White House documents.

The discussion shifted to the immediate agenda. The staff had many case studies in preparation, and each task force had its favorite list of entities, issues, and witnesses to investigate. The important question, though, was what the committee members themselves wanted to explore first. While some senators were naturally more interested in domestic than foreign affairs, the chairman preferred the latter. Church was considered an expert on foreign policy in the Senate and was the only member of the group who also sat on the Foreign Relations Committee. Moreover, he had already said publicly that his investigative committee would examine the question of overseas assassination attempts. Finally, the assassination topic was the hottest item in town since Watergate; it demanded attention. In short, Church leaned heavily toward an agenda that would begin by examining secret interference by the CIA in the affairs of other nations (covert action), including the possible involvement of the Agency in assassination plots.

The Domestic Intelligence Task Force was a long way from readiness for hearings on domestic abuses (the request for documents from the FBI and the IRS had yielded nothing of significance yet); thus, no senator could argue convincingly that the committee was ready to proceed on domestic issues. Moreover, most of the members—like the press and the public—were simultaneously fascinated and repelled by the assassination rumors and wanted to examine the allegations.

In its major decision of the day, therefore—perhaps of the entire inquiry—the committee agreed to proceed the following week with a probe into covert actions in general and the assassination issue in particular. At last the staff knew the senators' top priority and could plan accordingly.

The final item before the committee dealt with the latest counteroffensive of the CIA. Church had made it known in press conferences that the committee would push ahead with its own inquiries, despite the sluggish pace with which the executive branch was yielding documents. This meant that the staff would now enter the next phase of the investigation: intensive interviews with intelligence personnel. Witnesses would be called in for sworn testimony as the tempo of the inquiry was stepped up. The Agency, sensing perhaps that the queen had moved off the back row, sought to bolster its defenses by notifying the committee of a new procedure it wished to follow: henceforth, the intelligence agencies would provide their own "monitors" to accompany any past or present intelligence officials called for questioning. The monitor, a representative of the legal office in the intelligence agency, would "give [the witness] advice if it became necessary," said an intelligence spokesman.[59] The CIA was donning battle armor.

When Church presented this proposal to the committee, Schweiker summed up the feelings of everyone present. "If the committee allowed this," he said, "we'd be the laughing stock of the Hill." Tower moved to repudiate the proposal, and the committee voted unanimously for the motion. Later, Church explained to the press that the members rejected the idea because "there should be no inhibition, or possible inhibition, as the committee proceeds with these interrogations, and the executive departments will be so advised."[60] The staff's new marching orders were clear: move forward on the interviews and formal depositions.

As the orienting phase of the inquiry ended and the interrogation phase began, two events related to our investigation occurred. First, the House Intelligence Committee finally named its staff director on 11 May (after fourteen weeks), a thirty-year-old attorney and former Senate Watergate investigator by the name of A. Serle Fields. His youth and relative inexperience caused one House committee member to observe that "the potential for slaughter is obvious."[61] How we would interact with the House probe (if at all) had not been determined, or even addressed. Second, the Rockefeller Commission, earlier ordered by President Ford to extend its life by two months to investigate the assassination allegations, decided on 25 May to drop this part of its investigation and close shop.

Apparently the administration had found this issue too hot to handle. Perhaps, we hoped, this meant that we would soon obtain the commission's materials.

The day before our first official hearing (with Director Colby on 15 May), reporters gathered around Church in a Senate hallway. They wanted to know more about Colby's appearance the next day.

Q: Is he asking to bring a monitor with him?
A: He is the head monitor. (*Laughter*)
Q: Will he use the general counsel from the CIA?
A: Perhaps the president might come and monitor. (*Laughter*)

The chairman was in a good mood, pleased that his committee was at last going to hold its first investigative hearing. The press probed further into the Committee–White House confrontation over the monitoring issue. Turning serious, Church said that the White House had "not directly responded one way or another. But the practical response is: the investigation is going forward under the rules the committee has set."

I walked back to the auditorium with my office mate, Rick Inderfurth. "So far it's been like two Sumo wrestlers struggling to get their weight into the ring," he said. "Now, we're at the bowing stage." Tomorrow the adversaries would move cautiously toward one another.

4

Assassination Plots

On 15 May 1975, William Colby walked down a long echoing corridor toward S407, the most remote—and eerie—hearing room in the Capitol. Nestled high by the dome, hidden from the crowds of tourists flowing through the building, this former safe haven of the Joint Atomic Energy Committee provided a secure location for the conduct of sensitive hearings. Inside, the Church committee members sat in red leather armchairs around a curved bench that looked out to the table where Colby would take his place as our opening witness. The low ceiling, windowless walls, and heavily insulated silence—disturbed only by the hum of fluorescent lights—gave S407 a bunkerlike atmosphere.

Colby moved with a confident gait and smiled broadly as he entered the hearing room. He was accompanied by two senior aides carrying large chart cases and bulging briefcases. He shook hands with Senator Church and the other members, and Church administered the oath.

Although the committee was primarily interested in learning from the CIA director more about the involvement of his agency in assassination plots, Colby spent this entire first meeting presenting an overview on the subject of covert action—the policy of interfering secretly in the affairs of other countries. This was a reasonable, acceptable starting point, since assassination was a subset of the covert action genre (albeit certainly an extreme form of interference).

The United States had a moral obligation to assist its friends in other nations to resist communist expansion, and covert action was a concealed form of assistance: this was Colby's theme during the hour and a half. The assistance might take the form of money, propaganda materials, help in winning an election, or a variety of other benefits; yes, even a capacity to eliminate their enemies. The bifocaled leader of the intelligence community, turning solemn and scholarly in his long presentation, impressed the members by his willingness to speak with candor as he went through the history and tactics, the successes and failures of covert action. As soon as the CIA delegation departed, the staff sifted through the documents Colby had brought. The results were disappointing; several papers we had expected concerning specific assassination schemes were not there. The next day at a breakfast meeting, Church informed the press that "there are indications of gaps in the records."

Paper Chase

Our struggle for documents was on again—and not just with the CIA. In gearing up the FBI side of our investigation, we were running into similar problems. The interest of the committee in examining "raw" (unevaluated) FBI files that related to domestic counterintelligence programs (COINTELPRO) ran counter to the Bureau's long-standing policy of refusing access to raw files by any "outsider." Our request, suggested one experienced reporter, appeared "to signal the beginning of a confrontation between the senators and Attorney General Edward H. Levi, who has opposed providing such files to Congress."[1]

The attorney general apparently believed that giving raw FBI data to Congress would violate the constitutional right of privacy of those individuals with whom the files dealt. The committee believed, in contrast, that these files had to be examined if Congress was to exercise its constitutional duty to write effective legislation—in this case, laws designed to prevent abuses by counterintelligence officers in the Bureau. "The executive–legislative impasse may be carried to the Supreme Court," speculated the *New York Times*.[2]

Colby returned to S407 on 21 May to answer questions, for over three hours, about the assassination plots themselves. At the end of the session, the major question had been resolved for certain: the CIA had indeed planned murder most foul. As Colby progressed through the cases, eyes widened and eyebrows raised—even among the more experienced senators. When Colby completed his testimony the next day, Church left the hearing visibly agitated. The press awaited him in the hallway. He provided no specifics, but with a tremble that shook his body, he said to reporters in an angry voice: "It is simply intolerable that any agency of the government of the United States may engage in murder."

Cynics at the time, and later, considered the horror expressed publicly by committee members as so much hypocrisy.[3] The shock and disgust conveyed by the senators behind the doors of S407 struck me, however, as entirely genuine. With only themselves, a few staffers, and Colby in the room, theatrics were neither necessary nor apparent.

So began a long parade of witnesses appearing before the committee. Day by day, the pieces of the assassination puzzle began to fit together, though not without troublesome gaps. Colby himself seemed as forthright as a preacher at first. He gained a reputation for being candid and cooperative with Congress—too much so, in the view of Rockefeller, Kissinger, Helms, and untold numbers of intelligence professionals.[4] He was probably more open than Helms would have been in his shoes in 1975.[5]

Himself an attorney, Colby's perspective was ironically comparable to that of his new adversary, Fritz Schwarz. In Colby's words:

I explained to my CIA associates that the investigation we now faced was like a major antitrust action. In those cases, an enormous number of documents are demanded by the prosecution, meticulously examined, and then three or four specific papers are extracted to prove the case. The only real defense in such actions, I pointed out, was not to fight over the investigators' right to obtain the documents, as the courts would almost invariably rule against you, but to come forward with documents and information so as to place in proper context the documents selected by the investigators and to explain that they had another significance than guilt.[6]

Colby remains convinced that this was the proper approach for him to take. "I recently had a conversation with an experienced staffer on the House Appropriations Committee who has worked in the intelligence oversight area for years," he has remarked. "He said to me: 'If you hadn't cooperated, the Congress would have really torn the CIA apart.' I think he's right. The Congress could not have sat still for that."[7] When it came to the assassination plots, though, Colby closed the door on this theory of cooperation. "Looking into that wasn't going to do anybody any good," he has said. "Besides, it probably wasn't illegal."[8]

So we turned to other witnesses. A mass epidemic of amnesia, however, seemed to sweep Washington in the summer of 1975. Witnesses with vaunted reputations for clear minds mysteriously could no longer remember essential details of operations in which they had been intimately involved. Schwarz was in charge of this part of the inquiry (he aggressively sought the job, and Church leaned toward having an attorney head up everything dealing with abuses anyway), and that meant, more than anything, an emphasis on documents—not "soft" interviews. The major purpose of the interviews, from Schwarz's viewpoint, was to lead us toward more precise requests for documents. The all-important preparation of chronologies was on again.

All of this was consistently reinforced, of necessity, by telephone calls to the CIA and to the White House from Schwarz, then Miller (with his soothing diplomacy), Baron, and others—and finally, when the trickle of documents had stopped completely, from the senators themselves. Between these more urgent calls, we sent letters to executive branch officials—letters from Schwarz, from Miller, from Church and Tower, all with the same essential question: "Where are the documents we requested on such-and-such a date?" And always the same result: a couple of documents would be released to us, then nothing; then our letters and telephone calls would resume. And always the same plea from the White House: "Be patient; we're understaffed for this job."

"It wasn't really a matter of understaffing," Colby recalls. "They just didn't want to turn over documents."[9] For this, Colby was grateful when it came to the assassination papers—although, fortunately for the Church committee, the te House eventually changed its mind about these. "While the heat from the rch committee was on the CIA, the White House told us not to cooperate," Colby continues, "but when the heat began to move toward the White House, they began to give up papers."

This transition at the White House from intransigence to cooperation moved with the pace of a glacier. We hoped that 25 May 1975 would mark a turning point in our slowing search for documents, for on that day the Rockefeller Commission retreated from the assassination issue and gave us the responsibility of sifting through the evidence alone. We waited expectantly for the commission's files, promised publicly by the president in a 9 June press conference.

After thirteen days of waiting (punctuated by telephone calls and letters from the committee to the commission), Senator Church fired off another letter. This time the language skipped over diplomatic niceties: "The requests for documents, interviews by staff, and preliminary testimony should be complied with without delay."[10] Whether because of this letter or not, the assassination papers of the Rockefeller Commission were handed over soon thereafter, and without deletions ("unsanitized," in intelligence lingo).

For the committee, access to these documents was equivalent to finding the Rosetta stone: the file on Operation Mongoose meant nothing less to the assassination phase of the investigation. Mongoose was the code name for several covert action schemes directed against Fidel Castro in the wake of the Bay of Pigs fiasco, and the file contained a thousand leads—names, dates, locations. These specifics were our lifeblood: the key to new vaults, new files, new memoranda hidden somewhere within the bowels of the CIA. With this breakthrough, it was only a matter of time and diligent detective work before we could lay out in detail the Castro plots (and others).

The Church committee, in staffer Frederick Baron's words, had "hit pay dirt." "From the cables," he remembers, "we developed facts so dramatic that the CIA had to put them in context. We would get a certain amount of information, then they had to provide the missing link."[11] This game of cat and mouse took several months. As Schwarz recalls, "The CIA and the White House always gave us only what they thought we already knew."[12]

The Plots

The details we pieced together during the summer documented an unhappy truth: the government of the United States did plot, in peacetime, the death of foreign leaders. Of the five major plots examined by the committee, the evidence revealed that American officials actually instigated the plans for murder in two cases: against Castro of Cuba and Lumumba of the Congo (now called Zaire). In neither case, however, was the CIA successful, for Castro was too elusive (and too well protected by a Soviet-trained security force), and Lumumba was killed by Congolese rivals before the Agency scheme got beyond its early stages.

The three other cases involved the murder of Rafael Trujillo of the Dominican Republic, Ngo Dinh Diem of South Vietnam, and General Rene Schneider of Chile; but their deaths came at the hands of local dissidents staging their own coups over which the CIA had little or no control. Even in these cases, though, the facts show plainly that the Agency had been friendly toward the dissidents and their plans to overthrow their governments—and had supplied them with weapons. The precise degree to which the coups were stimulated by American officials, and whether the American-supplied weapons were the actual murder instruments, remained shrouded in the mists of faded history and conflicting testimony.

In two additional cases, the trail of evidence had vanished to the point where the committee was unable to reach a conclusion. In our examination of alleged CIA schemes to assassinate President Sukarno of Indonesia and Francois "Papa Doc" Duvalier of Haiti, we found that the Agency had provided arms to dissidents; however, the key witnesses swore that these weapons were never given for the purpose of murdering either man.

From documents obtained by the committee, it became clear also that the CIA had developed a capability not only for the elimination of individuals by assassination—the "executive action" option—but for their temporary incapacitation through the use of drugs, chemicals, and biological agents. A special group—sometimes referred to within the CIA as the Health Alteration Committee—passed judgment on these proposals. One, in 1960, recommended the use of chemicals to totally disable for at least three months an Iraqi colonel with ties to the Soviet bloc. "We do not consciously seek subject's permanent removal from the scene," the CIA Near East division chief cabled home. "We also do not object should this complication develop."[13] The home office approved the plan, which entailed mailing to the colonel a monogrammed handkerchief containing an incapacitating chemical. Once again, though, the Agency plan was outraced by events: the colonel suffered "a terminal illness" before a Baghdad firing squad and had no need of a handkerchief.

Sifting through the evidence on the assassination plots recalled for me an earlier time when I had studied embryology. Then I used a microscope to explore imperfectly stained slides of animal tissues. In some places the tissues would be revealed in all their astonishing complexity—every vein, artery, nerve, and duct magnified in brilliant colors. Where a fingerprint had smudged the glass or a stain had been ineptly applied, though, the fascinating trail of vessels and tubes would end abruptly in a gray cloud. So, too, the trail of evidence on assassination was at times easily traced, only to disappear completely or, at best, fray rt in a bewildering pattern like the ends of a shattered nerve. Frustratingly, the break would occur most often at the critical synapse between the White House and the CIA.

Most abundant—and gruesome—was the evidence in the Lumumba and Castro plots. With disquieting clarity, CIA officers told the Senate committee of the instruments of murder that were to be used by secret agents against Patrice Lumumba. Sent by diplomatic pouch from the United States to our embassy in the Congo was a most peculiar and deadly package. It contained rubber gloves, gauze masks, a hypodermic syringe, and lethal biological material requisitioned by the CIA from an Army Chemical Corps installation in Maryland. As one CIA officer remembered with dark humor: "I knew it wasn't for somebody to get his polio shot up to date."[14] On the contrary, the toxic material was to be injected into some substance or object that would reach the mouth of the African leader, "whether it was food or a toothbrush."[15] The result would be quick death.

Still more fantastic, requiring a suspension of disbelief few serious novelists would ask of their readers, were the instruments used against Castro. The first CIA designs on the Cuban premier involved assassination not of the person but of the character. The objective: destroy his public image, the magnetic charisma he seemed to exert for the Cuban people. One solution: make Castro's beard fall out. How could he possibly rule without his beard—the symbol of his daring takeover of the Cuban government from out of the rugged Sierra Maestra mountains? He might as well trade in his fatigues for a pinstripe suit. The method: the next time Castro traveled abroad and left his boots outside his hotel room to be polished, simply have an agent tiptoe up to the boots and sprinkle in some thallium salts (a strong depilatory); the next evening Castro would leave his beard on his pillow. The outcome: experiments with thallium salts on animals in the laboratories of the CIA Technical Services Division were successful, but unfortunately for the plotters, Castro's travels abroad were infrequent, unpredictable, and well guarded. The scheme was abandoned.

Other plans to discredit Castro, equally unsuccessful, included attempts to induce temporary disorientation symptoms—ideally during his major public speeches—by impregnating the Cuban leader's cigars with special chemicals or spraying an LSD-like substance into the air of his broadcasting studio. The most fanciful of these harassment schemes was sarcastically described to the Church committee by an intelligence officer:

> This plan consisted of spreading the word that the Second Coming of Christ
> was imminent and that Christ was against Castro [who] was anti-Christ.
> And you would spread this word around Cuba, and then on whatever date
> it was, that there would be a manifestation of this thing. And at that time—
> this is absolutely true—and at that time just over the horizon there would be

an American submarine which would surface off of Cuba and send up some starshells. And this would be the manifestation of the Second Coming and Castro would be overthrown.[16]

The operation, known as "Elimination by Illumination," never got far beyond the drawing boards—for good reason.

As fear mounted in the United States government over the consequences of a communist infection spreading from Cuba throughout the Western Hemisphere, the covert attempts against Castro grew more frequent—and more lethal. The several plots planned at CIA headquarters included treating a box of Castro's favorite cigars with a botulinum toxin so potent that it would cause death immediately upon being placed to the lips; concocting highly poisonous tablets that would work quickly when immersed in just about anything but boiling soup; contaminating a diving suit with a fungus guaranteed to produce a chronic skin disease called Madura foot and, through an intermediary, offering the suit as a gift to Castro; constructing an exotic seashell that could be placed in reefs where Castro often went skin-diving and then exploded at the right moment from a small submarine nearby; and providing an agent with a ballpoint pen that contained a hypodermic needle filled with the deadly poison Black Leaf 40 and had so fine a point it could pierce the skin of the victim without his knowledge.

The CIA had contacts with underworld figures whose criminal talents and Cuban connections (from earlier Havana gambling days) were deemed valuable. As newspaper stories and rumors had alleged, the Agency did ask mobster John Rosselli to go to Florida on its behalf in 1961 and 1962 to assemble assassination teams of Cuban exiles who would infiltrate their homeland and kill Castro. Rosselli in turn called upon two other crime figures: Chicago gangster Sam Giancana and the Cosa Nostra chieftain for Cuba, Santos Trafficante. Giancana's specific role was to locate someone in Castro's entourage who could drop poison pills into the Cuban leader's food; Trafficante would serve as courier to Cuba and, on the island, would help make arrangements for the murder. Rosselli was to be the primary link among the recruited assassins, the syndicate figures, and the CIA.

Along with "mad scientist" gimmickry and Mafioso hit men, the committee came across references to enough guns to arm a battalion. As an alternative to poisoning Lumumba, the CIA station officer in the Congo recommended that the leader be shot, and cabled his request that a weapon be sent via diplomatic pouch: RECOMMEND HQS POUCH SOONEST HIGH POWERED FOREIGN MAKE RIFLE WITH TELESCOPIC SCOPE AND SILENCER. The cable ended cryptically: WOULD KEEP RIFLE IN OFFICE PENDING OPENING OF HUNTING SEASON, which meant (according to testimony before the committee by the CIA's African chief) that the weapon would not be used until final approval had been received from CIA headquarters.

For Castro dissidents, the Agency prepared a cache composed of "a rifle with

,cope and silencer, plus several bombs, concealed either in a suitcase or some :her concealment" that an agent could carry and place next to the Cuban premier. For Trujillo dissidents, the CIA was prepared to airdrop twelve "sterile" (that is, untraceable) rifles with telescopic sights into the Dominican Republic. The drop was never made since the rebels postponed their plans for a coup. Later, various dissident groups requested sundry weapons from CIA agents. In March 1961, for instance, a request was passed for fifty fragmentation grenades, five rapid-fire weapons, and ten 64 mm antitank rockets. Information about the dissidents and their requests traveled through State Department channels disguised as references to a picnic: "The members of our club [dissidents] are now prepared in their minds to have a picnic [coup]. Lately they have developed a plan for the picnic, which just might work if they could find the proper food [weapons]. They have asked us for a few sandwiches [guns]. . . . Last week we were asked to furnish three or four pineapples [fragmentation grenades] for a picnic in the near future."[17] Eventually, three .38-caliber pistols were sent to the CIA station chief in the Dominican Republic, using a diplomatic pouch, and these "sandwiches" were then passed on to dissidents. Later, three .30 caliber M-l carbines stored in the United States consulate were also given to the dissidents.

To opponents of the Allende regime in Chile, the United States passed three .45-caliber submachine guns, ten tear gas grenades, and five hundred rounds of ammunition in October 1970. Various other American-supplied weapons went to opponents of President Sukarno of Indonesia and Duvalier of Haiti.

In no case was an American finger actually on the trigger of these weapons. And even though officials of the United States had clearly initiated assassination plots against Castro and Lumumba, it was technically true—as Richard Helms had claimed[18]—that neither the CIA nor any other agency of the American government had murdered a foreign leader. Through others, however, we had tried, but had been either too inept (the CIA was the real "Gang That Couldn't Shoot Straight," quipped writer Jimmy Breslin)[19] or too late to succeed. In each instance, the object of our machinations had been the nonwhite leader of a small, poor country.

To some, inside and outside the Church committee, the assassination plots were considered the inevitable result of an extreme paranoia about communism; the strongest nation in the world had lost all self-confidence, lashing out at weak foreign leaders, concocting dime-novel intrigues against their lives, and recruiting thugs and racketeers to pursue our foreign policy objectives. Others suggested that these excesses had to be considered in the context of the times. As former CIA director John McCone (1961–1963) put it with reference to Castro:

Here was a man who for a couple of years would seize every opportunity before a microphone or television to berate and criticize the United States in the most violent and unfair and incredible terms. Here was a man that was doing his utmost to use every channel of communication of every Latin American country to win them away from any of the principles that we stood for and drive them into Communism. Here was a man that turned over the sacred soil of Cuba in 1962 to the Soviets to plant nuclear warhead short-range missiles, which could destroy every city east of the Mississippi. This was the climate in which people had to think what to do. And before criticizing anything that was done, whether I knew of it or not—and I did not—I would think a little bit about the conditions of the time.[20]

Whatever one's point of view on the why of what happened, the record of events the committee spent much of the summer gathering was astonishing. And considering that we were reaching back fifteen years into a world of secrecy, the degree of detail in our documentation was high. Yet beneath our investigative microscopes, the lines of authority often blurred. The most expansive patch of fog settled over what became the central focus of the assassination inquiry: the extent of presidential knowledge and involvement in the plots. CIA officials gave the impression that their obedient agency had been pushed into excesses by higher authority; the higher authorities suggested that the Agency must have secretly drawn the various administrations into the plots without proper orders. By July, these two theories led to the first major tug-of-war within the committee itself.

5

Rogue Elephant

To find the assassination issue officially dumped into our lap in May had been a surprise. As President Ford explained at a press conference, "The Rockefeller Commission, on its own, decided that it wanted to conclude its operations on the basis of the original responsibilities given to it"[1]—that is, the investigation of CIA domestic abuses. The president said he agreed with the decision since he planned to have the attorney general analyze the commission's assassination documents "for any further investigation and prosecution" and would provide the Church committee with materials, too. On 11 June the Rockefeller Commission released its report, which criticized the CIA for "unlawful and improper invasions" of constitutional rights and offered thirty recommendations for reform.[2]

Taking on the full burdens of the assassination probe meant a significant delay in our schedule of work. Whispers among staff members that the assassination inquiry was draining the energy of the committee—notably the chairman—soon turned into open grumbles. In June a *New York Times* reporter wrote that "many in Washington wonder whether the fascination with assassination may distract Mr. Church and his colleagues from investigating other covert activities . . . the end of the year gets closer and closer, and to many working on the investigation the job seems to get longer every day."[3] *Newsweek* concluded that "the welter of hazy assassination charges seemed to be diverting ever more attention from the accusations of spying on Americans—in violation of their civil rights—that triggered the CIA flap in the first place."[4]

The Briar Patch

My colleague on the White House Task Force, Greg Treverton, joked over coffee one morning that "the only successful CIA assassination plot has been against the Church committee itself." He hated to see our other work pushed to the back burner for so long, and he strongly suspected this whole issue might be a diversionary tactic used by the CIA to steer us off course. He was not alone in this viewpoint. "The assassination inquiry was a bottomless pit," remembers Burt Wides, a committee staffer. "It became impossible to get the committee to focus on other subjects. We were mired down in the details of various plots, and time was running out. We were at the peak of our powers in January on the day we were established; from that point on, we were losing momentum. We had to act quickly. Instead we plodded along the assassination trail."[5]

"It was a red herring," Bill Miller concludes. "The assassination inquiry went beyond our wildest expectations."[6] Another key staffer thought it was a setup: "The CIA said, 'Oh, please don't throw us in the assassination briar patch!' and that's exactly what we did—to their delight."[7] A senior staffer told a journalist: "By the time we finished the assassination report, we had lost three things—the public's attention, much of our own energy and will power, and our leadership. Quite candidly, we had lost Frank Church."[8]

Many participants, however, saw matters in a different light. "Had we handled [the assassination report] with any less care," says Senator Church, "we would have lost all credibility, since this was by far the most infamous and extreme action taken by the CIA."[9] The eventual report was, in the words of Fritz Schwarz, "extremely valuable outside the limited subject of assassination. It was essential to have a subject which the committee examined in depth. Our detailed findings concerning looseness in the command-and-control structure, and the immorality and brutality of mind in the assassination plots served as a lesson in the subject of controlling covert action generally and showed where covert actions could lead."[10]

Schwarz saw another value, even though it meant postponing public hearings a couple of months: "It was vital to make the politicians and the American people really *believe* that reform was necessary. You couldn't speak in abstractions; you had to have something real and concrete. This the assassination report provided, in memorable, horrifying detail." Mark Gittenstein of the FBI (Domestic Intelligence) Task Force also thinks the assassination phase was helpful, but for a different reason: "It gave us time to sort out our own investigations," he recalls.[11]

The CIA scoffs at the briar patch thesis. "The argument is absurd," says Seymour Bolton, the chief CIA liaison to the committee throughout most of the investigation. "These plots did more to make the CIA look ridiculous than any other disclosures in its history. Why would we do this? Certainly not to divert the committee from other issues, such as covert action, since the committee went after everything else anyway."[12]

A waste of time, a wild goose chase, an important case study—whatever the assassination inquiry amounted to, a majority of the staff had grown to dislike the way it had captured the attention of the senators. What about other projects? What about the mandate of Senate Resolution 21? What about time's winged chariot hurrying near?

Bill Miller sent reminders to the chairman that the committee had additional obligations. "By a chain of circumstances, the Committee has been forced to concentrate initially on assassination," he wrote in July, pointing out that the staff had seventy-five other projects underway. "Following the Assassination Report, we should turn to covert action, of which," Miller emphasized, "assassination is only a small part."[13]

Witnesses caused further complications—first finding them, then getting them to Washington at the right time; preparing questions and briefing books for the senators; finding committee members to administer the oath before testimony could be taken; obtaining good testimony (at around $500 a day in stenographers' fees alone); granting immunity against subsequent prosecution, in some cases, in exchange for candid statements; and fretting over the frequent bouts of amnesia suffered by key witnesses.

The most unsettling witness incident involved Sam Giancana. Just as the committee was trying to locate him because of his alleged involvement in the plots against Castro, Chicago police found the sixty-five-year-old mobster on 19 June 1975, lying dead on his kitchen floor with at least six .22-caliber bullets in his mouth and neck. The committee was shocked and unsure whether the murder had anything to do with our intentions (rumored in the newspaper before the shooting) to call him as a witness. Senator Church asked the FBI to investigate the murder and report to the committee.

To try to finish the assassination inquiry as quickly as possible, Church established a special Subcommittee on Assassination, comprising himself, John Tower, Gary Hart, and a half-dozen staff aides (led by Fritz Schwarz). This group spent hundreds of hours drafting the report on assassination plots; they met frequently each week in a small anteroom off S407. The atmosphere at these subcommittee meetings was, for the most part, cordial and relaxed. "Have a cigar," Church said to Tower during one of the early sessions. "No thanks," replied the diminutive vice chairman, "it may stunt my growth." The two committee leaders, widely divergent in their political views on most issues, developed a cooperative relationship as the weeks passed. They and Gary Hart went line by line through drafts of the report prepared by the staff.

No formal votes took place, although the discussions were prolonged—at times amounting to arguments among staff aides—over what conclusions could be drawn. Unlike many disputes among the staff, however, these were usually constructive and oriented toward the achievement of a solidly written and defensible report. The presence of three senators on the scene helped greatly to keep the exchange at a reasonable level and moving forward.

Slippery Authority

The staff was busily preparing other phases of the investigation, and the FBI Task Force had already encountered the same kind of roadblocks experienced by the group working on the assassination plots. "The Bureau in the early months," Schwarz recalls, "was clearly trying to persuade us—or scare us—into doing a slap-dash job."[14] The FBI presumably thought it could get by our investigation by tossing out a few superficial summaries, then digging in its heels.[15]

At the first meeting with the FBI to discuss the primary topics of interest to the committee, the Bureau regaled the staff with a slide presentation—a classic dog and pony show. The last slide showed a couple of severed black heads lying in pools of blood on the street. This was designed to emphasize the danger loose in the land. The moral: leave the FBI alone to combat the savage forces that produced this and other horrors.

As the withering Washington summer heated up, so did the committee debate over who ordered the assassination plots: the White House or the CIA? On 24 June, Senator Goldwater informed the press that the Senate investigation would show that the CIA "took orders from the top" in carrying out illegal operations.[16] The next day Senator Mondale said to a group of reporters that he had seen no evidence directly or indirectly linking officials outside the CIA to assassination plots.[17] Senator Schweiker soon joined the fray, arguing for presidential authority: "My impression is the presidents not only knew but ordered these policies by and large," he told an interviewer, adding that past presidents have used the CIA as "their secret police force at home and their secret army abroad."[18] The normally loquacious senators, it seemed, could no longer bear their own self-imposed rules against speaking out on these issues; the steam building up in the committee kettle had popped off the lid.

In a lengthy press conference on 10 July, Church explained why the question of chain of command had become so important. He admitted that the committee might not be able to piece together the whole picture "because it's a long time ago." But he thought the committee had to try,

> not for the purpose of nailing anyone's hide on the wall, but rather to determine an exceedingly important question, which is this: Did the orders that involved the CIA in this dirty business come from the top of the government, or was this agency operating loosely on its own? . . . Now that is a terribly important thing to determine, because if the CIA was so loosely controlled that such operations could go on without having ever been clearly communicated to the President or his immediate policymakers at the White House or at the [40] Committee level,[19] then of course we have an agency running wild.

Church remained uncommitted on which theory he believed. Then, on 19 July, following the testimony of John Eisenhower that his brother, President Eisenhower, had known nothing of assassination plots, Church told the press: "The CIA may have been behaving like a rogue elephant on a rampage," conceiving and carrying out plots without the knowledge of anyone else.

Appearing on *Face the Nation* that weekend, Senator Schweiker "emphatically" disagreed with Church: "I don't think we can point to any conclusive evidence that exonerates the presidents either."[20]

When the committee held a special meeting on Monday, the air in S407 was tense. "We're beginning to polarize," warned Senator Tower. The selective leaking of findings on the assassination plots, and the public exchanges between committee members about the CIA as rogue elephant, had irritated the vice chairman. Senator Baker, too, was upset: "We've got to stop making counterstatements." Senator Goldwater complained that "all we've been hearing is protect Kennedy witnesses." The Republicans were up in arms, and the committee appeared on the verge of coming apart at its partisan seams. Church tried to mend matters: he said that he deplored any committee polarization; that he had suggested the rogue elephant theory only as a possibility; that many witnesses from the Eisenhower era, not just the Kennedy years, had testified; and that the longer the committee took to complete its report, the longer it would have problems.

"Let's remove the gag rule altogether," said Baker.

"Someone has to speak to the press," responded Church. "John Tower and I have accepted that responsibility."

"If we all speak out, the press will have a field day," warned Senator Huddleston.

Gary Hart said flatly: "We must exercise restraint. I take the contrary view to Baker: we must all keep our mouths shut. I'll quit this committee if we all start talking out; it will tear us apart."

"Either we all stop making inferences," said Baker, "or we all be allowed to speak."

Morgan stressed that it would be a tragic mistake to try to pinpoint blame for past assassination plots. Yet he rejected the rogue elephant thesis: "Suffice it to say that the CIA was acting on higher authority."

Mondale agreed with the first part of Morgan's statement but not with his conclusion. "The evidence is a shambles," he said, "because that is the way the system is set up. ["Hear, hear," said voices around the committee bench in agreement.] The important thing is to develop accountability."

During the Watergate investigation, Senator Baker had often repeated a question that became famous: "What did the president know, and when did he know it?" As Clark R. Mollenhoff has observed, the Church committee faced a similar "vital question": "What did the President know about the assassination plots, and when did he know it?"[21]

For several reasons, this was an incredibly difficult—and controversial—question to answer with hard facts (speculation was easy). In the first place, three presidents and many of their top aides were no longer alive to speak for themselves. Among the living, memories had faded; testimony conflicted; and some individuals seemed to yield to their sense of presidential loyalty and to instincts of self-protection. High on the list of obstacles between the committee and the truth was the system of decision making itself, notably the doctrine of plausible denial and ambiguous grants of authority.

The objective of plausible denial was to brush away footprints in a covert operation to prevent anyone from following the tracks back to the United States, and particularly to the Oval Office. Above all, the virtue of the nation was to be protected by shielding the reputation of the president. His office was to be disassociated—in memoranda, minutes, or other records—from any dirty deeds that might be necessary in the rough-and-tumble world outside the United States. Should the CIA or other agencies have to discuss an "extralegal" or unsavory operation with the president to obtain his approval, euphemisms and double-talk were to be used; this would leave the chief executive free to deny, plausibly, that he had granted authority for its execution. It was decision making by a wink and a nod.

This effort to escape from potential embarrassment (and responsibility) at the highest level of government led, unfortunately, to vague directives from above and unpredictable responses from below. When high officials said they longed for some way to "get rid of" Castro (a phrase found often in the minutes of Cabinet meetings during the Eisenhower and Kennedy eras), did they mean to encourage Cubans to oust him, or was this a wink and a nod to have the CIA murder him?

Uncertain, too, was how long the authority for a covert action, once so loosely given, could last. The CIA was reluctant to discuss the black arts with the president and other high officials; consequently, authority once received often drifted or floated from year to year and from administration to administration, without explicit renewal—even within the Agency itself. John McCone, successor to Allen Dulles as CIA director, was never told of Agency ties to the Mafia on the grounds that this was unnecessary since Dulles had approved the relationship.

Against such obstacles, the committee marshaled more than a hundred witnesses, almost ten thousand pages of sworn testimony, and the close examination of thousands of secret documents relevant to the assassination plots. Among the witnesses were the brightest stars in the constellations of the Eisenhower, Kennedy, Johnson, and Nixon administrations, as well as central figures at lower levels who were intimately involved in the plots. From their voluminous testimony came three major theories regarding the origins of authority for the assassination plots: (1) the theory of the rogue elephant; (2) the theory of presidential authority; and, (3) the theory of misunderstanding.

In questioning Robert McNamara, Senator Church expressed the growing frustration of the committee as it sought to pin down responsibility for the plots:

> Now, you see what we are faced with is this dilemma. Either the CIA was a rogue elephant rampaging out of control, over which no effective direction was being given in this matter of assassination, or there was some secret channel circumventing the whole structure of command by which the CIA and certain officials in the CIA were authorized to proceed with assassination plots and assassination attempts against Castro. Or, the third and final point that I can think of is that somehow these officials of the CIA who were so engaged misunderstood or misinterpreted their scope of authority.
>
> Now, it is terribly important, if there is any way that we can find out which of these three points represented what actually happened. That is the nature that is the quandary.
>
> Now, is there anything that you can tell us that would assist us in finding an answer to this central question?[22]

The former secretary of defense and top aide to Presidents Kennedy and Johnson rejected the misunderstanding theory directly but was unable to reconcile the remaining possibilities. On the one hand, he firmly believed the CIA was under the control of the president; on the other hand, he had never heard of any assassination attempts approved by the president. Still, the fact remained; plots had been devised, said McNamara, "so I frankly can't reconcile . . . and I understand the contradiction that this carries with respect to the facts."[23] The fog thickened.

The trouble was that evidence seemed to abound for each of the theories. Richard Helms expressed his belief to the committee that the Agency did have presidential authority for its intrigues against Castro—though an authority heavily clothed in ambiguity and the doctrine of plausible denial. The professorial Senator Mathias questioned Helms with an historical analogy:

> *Senator Mathias.* Let me draw an example from history. When Thomas Beckett was proving to be an annoyance, as Castro, the King said, "Who will rid me of this man?" He didn't say, go out and murder him. He said who will rid me of this man, and let it go at that.
> *Mr. Helms.* That is a warming reference to the problem.
> *Senator Mathias.* You feel that spans the generations and the centuries?

Mr. Helms. I think it does, sir.

Senator Mathias. And that is typical of the kind of thing which might be said, which might be taken by the director or by anybody else as presidential authorization to go forward?

Mr. Helms. That is right. But in answer to that, I realize that one sort of grows up in the tradition of the time and I think that any of us would have found it very difficult to discuss assassinations with a president of the US. I just think we all had the feeling that we're hired out to keep those things out of the Oval Office.

Senator Mathias. Yet at the same time you felt that some spark had been transmitted, that that was within the permissible limits.

Mr. Helms. Yes, and if he had disappeared from the scene they would not have been unhappy.[24]

Though Helms admitted he was never told directly by the president to kill Castro, nonetheless, "no member of the Kennedy Administration . . . ever told me that [assassination] was proscribed, [or] ever referred to it in that fashion. . . . Nobody ever said that [assassination] was ruled out."[25]

Yet within the committee, doubts still lingered over the validity of the presidential authority theory. Perhaps Helms and other Agency officials had misinterpreted the signals being sent by Kennedy and his advisers. John McCone, another CIA director, told the committee he too had often heard the Cuban problem discussed in such terms as "dispose of Castro" or "knock off Castro," but McCone interpreted this language to mean the "overthrow of the Communist Government in Cuba," not assassination.[26]

And always, the language and the memories of key witnesses before the committee were frustratingly unclear. Responding to the ambiguous testimony of a CIA official with a central role in the Castro plots, Senator Church fumed: "'Could,' 'would,' 'probably,' 'assume,' 'might,' 'having a feeling'—and we're talking about a matter of such grave importance as assassination! I must say I find this testimony very hard to accept."[27]

Sometimes the evidence seemed to suggest nothing less than the CIA as rogue elephant. Presidential adviser and noted historian Arthur M. Schlesinger Jr. wrote to President Kennedy in 1962: "One of the most shocking things which emerged after the last Cuban episode [the Bay of Pigs] was the weakness of top-level CIA control—the discrepancy between what high CIA officials thought their operatives were saying and doing in the field, and what these operatives were actually saying and doing."[28] All the former presidential advisers testifying before the committee denied under oath any knowledge of White House or Cabinet-level orders to assassinate foreign leaders. At the Agency level, William Harvey, the CIA officer who worked with the Mafia to plan the assassination of Castro, admitted that he failed to tell incoming director McCone about the murder plans.[29] According to Helms, Harvey kept the entire arrangement with the Mafia "pretty much in his back pocket"—that is, hidden from the view of his superiors in the White House and, apparently, in the Agency itself.[30]

An Agency out of control, a wink and a nod, a misunderstanding—where was the truth? Wherever, it was unlikely to be found in writing. "I can't imagine any Cabinet officer wanting to sign off on something like that," Helms told the committee. "I can't imagine anybody wanting something in writing saying I have just charged Mr. Jones to go out and shoot Mr. Smith."[31] Perhaps it was equally implausible that anyone would come before the committee and plead guilty to ordering assassinations.

Unable to learn the truth for certain, the committee simply laid out all the facts it had found and left the matter there, embracing none of the three theories in its report. The choice was left to others, if they wished to choose. Some critics branded us at best as "cautious"[32] (though true caution would have been to bury the report altogether, as the Ford administration and some members of the committee eventually tried to do); from others the verdict was more damning: we were "bubble-heads"[33] and "dimwitted"[34] for failing to acknowledge the simple truth that President Kennedy, and maybe some other presidents, had given assassination orders directly.

Yet given instances of extreme looseness in the CIA command structure (as illustrated by the operations of William Harvey, for example), who knew for certain what plots had hatched outside the White House? "If we had found clear and convincing evidence directly fixing the responsibility in the White House, it would have been our obligation to report this," reflected Senator Church after the investigation. "This was not the case, but it remained our duty to lay out all the evidence that we had discovered as factually as we could."[35]

Some suspected Church and other Democrats of efforts to brush lightly over the Kennedy years, but in fact that administration became the centerpiece of the investigation. At no time did Church, or anyone else, ask the staff to slow down on any of its cases. Even if the pro-Kennedy senators had wanted to do so, it would have been impossible with Senator Tower and other Republicans deeply involved in the proceedings.

The days of June and July passed in a flurry of witnesses and press conferences. The committee now faced its first major decision: what to do with its assassination findings? It soon became evident that the chairman and vice chairman stood on opposite sides of the issue. The cohesion of the Senate Intelligence Committee, which Church had nurtured so assiduously, was clearly in jeopardy.

6

The Cave of Bugs

"We need to decide on some procedures," said John Tower, opening a business meeting of the Senate Intelligence Committee on 23 July. The suggestion sounded reasonable enough, but the Democrats stiffened at Tower's next sentence. "The minority members of this committee have just met for over an hour, and there is a matter we believe must be settled by the full committee. I yield to Senator Baker."

"Senator Tower has yielded to me because I'm the noisiest on this matter," said Baker, with a disarming grin. He came straight to the point: "I strongly favor a single assassination report to be published by the committee at the end of its investigation, not an earlier interim report."

Church quietly stared at Baker as he explained the Republican view, which pivoted on a concern about drawing hasty conclusions before the full investigation was completed. When Baker finished, Church said, "It would be a grave mistake to hold the report off. Events have shown this story will not hold. Precious little will be newsworthy even after the August recess."

"We may learn more about assassination in the hearings on covert action," said Tower.

Senator Mathias sat slouched in his chair, eyes closed. He looked like a well-fed English gentleman at his club, momentarily adrift in dreamland. He had followed the debate closely, however, shutting his eyes but not his mind. "I find Baker's argument compelling," he said, suddenly opening his eyes and sitting up. "Let's not rush to judgment. Let's not be too hasty."

"I don't find myself siding with Senator Tower and Senator Baker very often," confessed Schweiker, "but this time I do."

Senator Mondale came to Church's aid. He said he was upset about the "bits and pieces" coming out in the papers. "Let's get rid of this tarbaby," urged Mondale, holding a draft of the assassination report in the air, "and get on to something more important."

The other Democrats began to rally behind Church and Mondale. "We need an interim report," said Senator Huddleston. "Let's get this behind us, and go on to all our other work."

"We need to get the assassination issue behind us," echoed Senator Morgan. "We've got to get into the covert area."

Philip Hart was less willing to support the Church position without reservation. Looking rather pale, Hart spoke even more softly than usual: "I will only vote for an interim report if it is titled 'Interim.'" Hart did not want to close the chapter on assassination when it was entirely possible that new evidence might arise in the course of the committee's inquiry into CIA covert operations around the world.

Gary Hart listened quietly.

"It's grossly unfair to the principals to hold this report in abeyance," Church stressed, and asked the committee to decide one way or the other on an interim report. On a voice vote, Church declared, "The ayes have it in favor of an interim report." A chorus of nays from the Republican side had been evident during the vote, but Baker knew that a formal tally would have ended in a six-to-five defeat for the minority, and he said, "There is no need for a roll-call vote."

Church relaxed back into his chair. He had won this one. But he was soon jerked forward again.

"I would like a vote on public hearings on assassination," said Baker.

"Do you really want to push that?" asked Church, taken aback.

"I'm sorry, Mr. Chairman, I do wish to pursue this."

"Let's settle this other matter first," said Mondale. He was referring to a parliamentary point that Senator Goldwater had raised earlier: whether or not the committee had the authority to issue a report on its own, without first presenting it to the full Senate.

After conferring sotto voce with Miller and Schwarz, Church said: "Yes, the committee can issue a report; however, to do so while the Senate is in recess would take prior unanimous consent." Under the unanimous consent rule, a procedure normally used to speed the flow of Senate business in noncontroversial matters, a single senator could object and thereby halt a decision. Church seemed to deliver his pronouncement hesitantly, without full conviction that it was correct.

Peering at the chairman over black-rimmed half-glasses, Tower said coldly and precisely: "I want the report reviewed by the entire Senate in closed session."

Church's face blanched. "No one else but the senators on this committee can judge the report based on the evidence," he said.

"We have no right to put ourselves above the Senate," said Baker testily.

"I don't want the Senate to undo the work of the committee," replied Church. I had seldom seen him so upset. He looked imploringly at the Democrats seated to his right; this time, however, no one spoke on his behalf. They knew that if any one senator—Democrat or Republican—felt strongly about an issue, it could never be railroaded through on a unanimous consent procedure. Church, of course, knew this, too; but he continued to hope the Republicans would drop their opposition to an interim report issued directly by the Intelligence Committee.

"I can't conceive of the Senate turning down our report," said Tower, attempting to mollify the chairman.

"Do we have to decide this now?" asked Church, irritation and frustration in his voice. He could feel his base of support slipping away. Even the other Democrats apparently questioned the wisdom of having the committee release the report on its own authority. Baker's warning, "We have no right to put ourselves above the Senate," had touched a nerve on the Democratic side.

Mondale steered the committee away from a formal vote, saving the chairman from possible defeat and the rest of the Democrats from a difficult decision. "What about the rest of the schedule?" he asked.

Before anyone could respond, Baker said: "I want my view noted for the record that I favor carefully controlled public hearings on assassination." No one in either party showed any support for the idea, and Baker did not push for a formal vote.

The meeting had resulted in a partial victory for Church: he would have his report (or, as Philip Hart insisted, interim report). How and when it would be issued, though, remained unresolved. Would it come directly from the committee, or through the Senate? Was this a dilatory tactic by the minority, or did the Republicans genuinely believe that a committee had no right to issue its own report without the review and consent of the parent chamber? Clearly, the Senate route held the possibility of indefinite delay; if even a small group of senators objected to the report, they could prevent its release—by a filibuster, if necessary. The assassination tar baby seemed to have Church firmly in its clutches. It might never let go. The chairman looked troubled as he left the hearing room.

Inward Strife

While the committee smoked, rumbled, and sparked at the top like a volcano coming out of dormancy, tremors of greater intensity—undampened by the traditions of civility normally found among senators—erupted below at the staff level.

In the early stages of the investigation, relations among staff members had been relatively calm, but tensions seemed to rise with the summer heat. Schwarz became more insistent about shifting key responsibilities to a team of lawyers selected by him. A special staff meeting had been called for 26 June. Rumors rapidly circulated that Schwarz planned a showdown between the lawyers and the nonlawyers on the staff.

The committee designees and the top staff leadership crowded into one room. Miller, sitting next to Schwarz on one side of a wide table, turned directly to the topic of Schwarz's group of lawyers. "This will not be an extra layer between the senators and the task forces," the staff director assured the nonlawyers, who accounted for half the people in the room, including each of the task force leaders, David Aaron (White House), Bill Bader (CIA), John Elliff (FBI), and Alton Quanbeck (military). Schwarz had obviously laid the groundwork with Miller before the gathering and had apparently quelled his fears about a takeover by the attorneys. Others were less sanguine.

One Republican staffer argued at length against Schwarz's intentions to form a special group of lawyers. Though an attorney himself, he distrusted Schwarz's motives. The possibilities of turning the central work of the committee staff over to a New York City liberal—lawyer or not—was apparently too much for this conservative to bear. A Southerner, he spoke in honey-laden rhythms. Schwarz stared at the tabletop.

"What Fritz is asking is for slaves," interrupted Bill Miller, "to compile a thorough index of documents." Aaron and Bader exchanged looks of skepticism. Miller resorted to a long monologue about the importance of the inquiry, hoping to rally some esprit de corps. When he finished, a designee asked the task force leaders to express their views on the concept of a new legal task force.

"The new lawyers should provide only a service function," said Bader.

"I'm in total disagreement with the lawyer group," said Quanbeck.

"I have serious reservations," added Aaron.

All eyes turned toward Elliff. "We need Schwarz's eleven-man force to provide uniformity throughout the four original task forces," he said. Elliff and his FBI Task Force—heavily staffed by attorneys, several of whom had already been tapped for Schwarz's new group—had evidently been won over to the Schwarz position before the meeting. This alliance was understandable (though not everyone in the FBI group endorsed the idea), since Schwarz and Elliff were chiefly interested in domestic abuses of the intelligence agencies.

Miller glanced first at the three reluctant task force leaders, then at Schwarz. "Is there anything you have in mind beyond what I have described?"

Before Schwarz could find the right words, the Southerner's honeyed voice broke in again. He was dissatisfied with Schwarz's performance during the assassination phase of the inquiry: "We have been ill-prepared; half the Republicans are grumbling." His arguments centered on the premise that GOP senators did not think Schwarz had performed effectively in moving the staff along on all the various projects before the committee.

Schwarz objected strongly: "If we'd tried to hold hearings on all these other projects in July, we'd have gotten egg all over our faces. The assassination task was a godsend, allowing us to move forward more thoroughly on all fronts."

The Southerner began to dominate the meeting, advancing one argument after another against the chief counsel. Schwarz's face hardened. "Lawyers have the kind of discipline I need," said Schwarz, an edge to his voice. "They do things in a certain way. I require a personal staff if I'm going to get the things done that have to be done."

Aaron could take no more: "This is a natural culmination of Schwarz's statement eight weeks ago about lawyers being the only ones equipped to get this job done," he burst out.

Indeed, in one of the early committee meetings (23 April), Schwarz had said to the senators, "Speaking from my culture—my background as a lawyer—I strongly believe attorneys are best suited for this kind of a project" (at the time, Miller, Aaron, and the other nonlawyers had stiffened in their chairs), and periodically thereafter he had argued for an inquiry led by his own handpicked team of attorneys. Looking back, he remembers feeling "misled":

> I had the clear impression from Senator Church that I was going to be completely running things. Miller was to take care of administrative matters. I was amazed during these early weeks; I couldn't understand who all those other people [nonlawyers] were anyway. I gravitated toward those who were familiar to me, people with whom I could work naturally—the lawyers. As it turned out, some of the non-lawyers—like Rick Inderfurth—could be just as effective as the lawyers, but I did not realize that at the beginning. I simply knew that a certain approach was vital, an approach that says: let's let the facts lead to the conclusions.[1]

Now, Quanbeck spoke gloomily, in support of Aaron: "These lawyers will come down and run the task forces."

"Here's the central fear," replied Curt Smothers, "and it is unfounded." The minority counsel had joined with the chief counsel on this issue.

The Southerner interrupted again, addressing himself to Miller.

"Now repeat, Bill, what Fritz wants . . ."

Schwarz's large hand came smashing down on the table in a sudden explosion of anger. "Oh, come on! You have behaved improperly," he shouted. "You wanted this job and didn't get it. Now all you can do is criticize. I'm not going to sit here and take these accusations." He seemed on the verge of coming across the table. Those who had begun to doze in the summer heat were suddenly wide-eyed.

Recovering himself, Schwarz slid back in his chair, staring with hard eyes at his critic. The Southerner drew his lips together; his cheeks turned pale. The room fell quiet.

Miller finally spoke: "Fritz and Curt both want this, and I'm going to support them." He said the staff had to be flexible and, sounding like a professor of literature, concluded: "Task forces are not a procrustean bed from which one cannot arise."

"To be honest," admitted Schwarz, "these eleven lawyers will not just be filing and indexing materials." It was not the sort of admission Miller wished to hear at that particular moment, after he had just gone out on a limb for the chief counsel.

Miller looked at Schwarz quizzically. "What exactly is the range of activities of these eleven men?" Whatever understanding Miller and Schwarz had reached, its roots were shallow.

Like a tailback downfield, Schwarz went into a series of sidesteps. He remained vague about his plans for the roving teams of lawyers. Nevertheless, Miller concluded, "I think this is worth a try. I will take it before the committee." He stood up and headed for the door. The meeting was over, and so was the facade of a unified staff.

As Schwarz rose, he looked over at David Aaron and said, "For the first three and a half months the task forces were fine, but. . . ." His voice trailed off.

"But now the task forces are not any good," finished Aaron. He turned to Bader. "I guess we better look for another job." Glowering, they left the room.

Consensus continued to elude the committee's upper level as well. At the forty-first meeting, held 30 July, Church asked Miller to report on the latest bout with the CIA over requested documents. "I'm encouraged," said Miller. "The CIA will meet our requests in four days, and will tell us within one day if they have any disagreements with our requests."

Philip Hart, frail of body but stout of heart, interrupted in exasperation: "What are we here for! We're here to investigate an agency. Here it is, the end of July, and we are still bartering with the agency overseeing files!" His thin arms flew up in a gesture of disbelief. "We don't even have the same access as the Rockefeller Commission." He lowered his voice and sank back into his chair. "When is this point going to be made known?"

"We will have such access before this is over," said Church solemnly.

No one said anything for a minute.

"We must get tough with the White House," urged Schweiker. "We can't mince words. I'd like to see a chart—a box score: when we asked for documents, what their status is, et cetera. Let's go to the press and show with the charts how the White House has been delaying documents." More silence.

Church reminded the committee that we were still being denied access to the Nixon administration papers that we wanted to examine. The chief counsel was told to approach the former president's lawyer once more, letting him know that if the committee was not granted access, we would first subpoena the papers and then go to court, if necessary, to get them.

"If we're going to start litigating, we'd better do it along the whole front—not just pick on Nixon," cautioned Baker, "or there will be a public and press reaction."

Philip Hart, the gentlest-looking senator on the committee, was also proving to be the most aggressive, despite his failing health. "Let's give Nixon's lawyer one week—that's all."

"Let's proceed with caution," said Robert Morgan. "If we get in a fight with Nixon, it will divert our whole effort."

Like Philip Hart, Baker was in a fighting mood. He was tired of constant delays from the White House, the CIA, and now Nixon's lawyer. "Let's issue subpoenas immediately to anyone who does not cooperate with this committee," he said.

Everyone knew the committee had one major decision to resolve when it returned from lunch. "When and how to issue the interim assassination report—this is the question still before us," said Church. "Let's agree on September 3rd for releasing the report."

"We'll all be drifting back from the recess that day," said Tower.

"Then the 4th."

"How are we going to report?" said Baker.

"Let's agree on the day first," said Church.

"Not until we agree on how the report is to be made," replied Baker icily.

Church moved uneasily in his chair. He was being forced back to square one: whether to have the report cleared by the full Senate (as the Republicans wanted) or published solely under the authority of the committee itself (as the chairman preferred). The Republicans were obviously willing to fight on this one, and Church was unsure how much support he had among the Democrats. He was not cut in the style of Lyndon Johnson, who made a point of knowing how everyone stood on an issue before the vote. Church believed in individual decisions, and he seldom tried arm-twisting or cajoling. The words of an earlier famous senator, Daniel Webster, could have come from his own lips: "This is a Senate; a Senate of equals; of men of individual honor and personal character, and of absolute independence. We know no masters; we acknowledge no dictators."[2]

Nineteen years of service, though, had given Church a good nose for political winds, and his senses told him now that a solid bloc of six Democratic votes was far from guaranteed on this issue. Church chose to attack on the periphery. "Well, can we at least decide how many copies of the report we will want printed? I suggest ten thousand."

"The Soviets want a thousand," quipped Gary Hart.

"They'll already have copies of the drafts," joked Schweiker. (His comment made me think of Goldwater, who had claimed earlier in the summer that he feared the Congress had been infiltrated by Soviet agents. He had offered no evidence, however, and the FBI told the committee it had found no signs of infiltration.)

Minority counsel Smothers took this opportunity to offer his views on the report. He found its organization faulty, he said, and disagreed with many of the conclusions.

Tense, frustrated, and tired from spending long hours on the report, Church reacted strongly to the criticism—particularly since it came from a staff aide rather than a fellow senator. "I have some prerogatives as chairman," he said, as a ripple of anger raced through his body. Then he caught himself quickly and said with more control, "I think we can go ahead and complete this report." Smothers prudently chose not to venture further into the minefield.

The reticence from the Democratic side of the room signaled clearly that no decision would be made on the fate of the assassination report before the August recess. The minority had tacitly prevailed over the chairman on this issue.

I walked with Church back to his office in the Russell Building. He was deeply disappointed that the publication of the report would face further delays and worried about the potential pitfalls of opening up this sensitive document to what might become a full-fledged debate by the entire Senate. His eyes showed fatigue, and his walk had lost its lilt. I had never seen his spirits so low.

Outward Battles

As summer passed, a new wave of criticism washed over the committee. "The wreckers are getting ready to dismantle the intelligence service again," warned CIA deputy director Vernon Walters.[3] President Ford had an arrow in his quiver too: with reference to communist infiltration in Portugal, he said: "I think it's very tragic that because of the CIA investigation and all the limitations placed on us in the area of covert operations, we aren't able to participate with other Western European countries [in helping the Social Democrats in Portugal]."[4] As if part of a coordinated executive branch counteroffensive, Secretary of Defense James R. Schlesinger also spoke out strongly against the congressional inquiries, stating that the CIA's sources abroad "have been dramatically reduced" as a result of leaks from congressional investigating committees.[5]

An attack came from inside, too: Senator Goldwater claimed that the committee was trying to avoid placing the blame on the Kennedys for the assassination attempts in Cuba. Goldwater referred to friction between "those who want to protect the Kennedys and those who want to tell the truth."[6]

Senator Church did not allow Goldwater's criticism to pass without comment. "I know of no serious split in the committee," said the chairman at a press conference on 12 August. "I am simply at a loss to understand the reason for the senator's observation." Church pointed out that Goldwater had failed to attend any of the drafting sessions held by the Assassination Subcommittee.

Nor did the committee passively accept the attack from the executive branch.

Senator Mathias, himself a Republican, told a press conference in Baltimore that he thought Secretary Schlesinger's statement about congressional leaks was "pure poppycock" and a "loose charge . . . so wrong that it has to be denied, it has to be refuted."[7]

The committee responded to the executive branch counteroffensive with more than words. On 12 August, the members voted (with Goldwater absent) to issue subpoenas to the White House in order to gain access to certain portions of the Nixon presidential papers. Specifically, the committee wanted to examine documents, tapes, and other records from the Nixon era dealing with the Huston Plan (see chapter 7) and with covert operations in Chile. Whatever honeymoon period had existed between the committee and the executive branch—never very amorous at any stage—was clearly over. Subpoenas meant war.

Appearing on NBC's *Meet the Press* on 17 August, Senator Church deplored the attitude of the executive branch in holding back documents: "Sometimes it's been like pulling teeth, but I've tried to avoid confrontations." The chairman went on to explain:

> As the confidence in the committee has built because of the lack of any leaks
> . . . and the great care we've taken with sensitive information, we have been
> able to obtain more data from the executive than has ever been the case
> in any congressional investigation in the past. . . . But from the beginning
> I faced a decision: whether to try and negotiate for this information as
> confidence in the committee built, or whether immediately to stand upon
> the constitutional prerogative of the committee, invite a confrontation, and
> go into the courts. . . . I think we've taken the right course.

The approach irritated several people involved in the investigation who thought Church was failing to push the intelligence community hard enough. "It was as if we were on trial—not the CIA," remembers a committee staffer.[8] Still, in light of what would soon happen to the House committee, which did pursue a strategy of confrontation, the wisdom of Church's method became persuasive.

Robert Novak, a member of the *Meet the Press* panel, zeroed in on the irrepressible rogue elephant theory and on Church's presidential aspirations.

> *Novak.* Do you want to let the characterization of the CIA as a rogue
> elephant operating independently stand, or do you think you'd rather
> change it at this time?
> *Church.* I would stand on my former statement, because I think that there is
> some evidence—much evidence—that the statement will be borne out
> when the evidence is fully disclosed in the [assassination] report.[9]
> *Novak.* Do you think there's a conflict of interest between your running

this very important investigation and in being considered as a possible presidential candidate?

Church. . . . I have called off any effort on my behalf for the presidency. I've made it clear that this investigation will not be mixed with presidential politics. . . .

Novak. Couldn't you stop questions like mine if you made a statement like Senator [Edward] Kennedy's, taking yourself out totally for 1976, including after the investigation is over?

Church. This investigation will be over by the end of the year. Many people have pressed me on the presidency. I've said, "Lay off. I'm not interested in getting involved until this investigation is over." I don't know what the future will hold. . . .

Novak. But the door is still open as far as you're concerned?

Church. By the time I come out of this investigation, maybe the door will be sealed and locked. How can I know?

During the program, Church turned somber about the dangers of tyranny in the United States. "If this government ever became a tyranny there would be no place to hide," he said, "and no way to fight back, because the most careful effort to combine together in resistance to the government—no matter how privately it was done—is within the reach of the government." Church added that he now knew the capacity of the government to make tyranny total in America. "We must see to it that all agencies which possess this technology operate within the law and under proper supervision so that we never cross over that abyss. That's the abyss from which there is no return."

The Ford White House, however, saw the work of the Church committee in a different light. In a nationally televised speech on 19 August before the American Legion's national convention, the president warned that "any reckless congressional action to cripple the effectiveness of our intelligence services in legitimate operations would be catastrophic."[10]

First Public Hearings

"We must focus on abuses," Church remarked to me on 4 September as we walked to the first committee meeting since the August recess. "That's what this committee is for: to investigate wrongdoing. We need to begin hearings with something dramatic."

Within the committee, the search had been on for a case that would meet these criteria, and one that was reasonably well prepared for public presentation. But beyond the assassination report—which only Senator Baker wished to examine in public hearings—the cupboard looked bare. There were excellent cases on the drawing boards, particularly on covert action, but they still lacked thorough research.

Fortunately, a gift (or so it seemed at first) fell into the hands of the chairman—from the CIA itself. In late August, the Agency reported that it had discovered a hidden cache of deadly poisons in its possession. Colby told Church and Tower that he intended to conduct an immediate internal investigation to discover why these poisons had failed to be destroyed when President Nixon had ordered the disposal of such materials five years earlier. He asked the committee leaders to delay their own inquiry into the matter until he had reported back on his own findings. They agreed, for Colby promised to act quickly. The chairman had this case in the back of his mind as a possible opener, though, if nothing better was ready.

The committee meeting began with happy news. President Ford's counsel said that the White House had worked out an arrangement between Senator Tower and former president Nixon's lawyer to meet our subpoena for materials from the Nixon papers. The committee was relieved; it would not have to go to court—yet.

Following the departure of the White House counsel, Church told the committee he thought public hearings should begin 9 September with an examination of why the CIA had failed to destroy its storehouse of dangerous chemicals as required by presidential orders. The committee members concurred, though without enthusiasm. To some the topic seemed ad hoc and relatively unimportant. A few staffers I talked with later, however, thought the matter significant and spoke ominously of how these substances could have leaked out of their containers—or even exploded—and killed thousands of people.

The meeting came to an end, and the GOP members went down the hallway to a room nearby to hold a caucus. The Democrats remained behind. Both party factions were meeting to discuss the status of the assassination report. In the Democratic caucus, where I sat, the members complained about the delays in finishing and issuing the report. "Goldwater seems willing to protect the CIA even if it has violated its job," observed Church.

"We have accommodated the Republicans enough," said Gary Hart. "If we go further, I will have to issue my own report."

The chairman was beginning to feel even more intensely the pressure of push from impatient Democrats and pull from reluctant Republicans. Here was a young senator, freshly elected, on the verge of rebellion against his chairman, who had almost two decades of seniority. I could see what Church meant when he once told me that every senator was sovereign.

Not all the Democrats were pushing, however. Senator Morgan was worried about tarnishing the reputation of the United States by blackening the name of the presidency. "We must protect the presidency," he said. This was not a popular argument in the caucus; memories of Vietnam and Watergate were too fresh and the distrust of presidents too strong.

Church promised his colleagues he would do his utmost to get the assassination report behind the committee, and he later told the awaiting press corps that he believed "before the middle of September the report will be issued." His optimism would prove unwarranted.

The next day, the committee met again to receive from the CIA a report on its investigation of the hidden poisons. I was startled by the kinds of lethal chemicals and delivery systems the Agency had developed and stored away. Though small in total volume, the poisons—which included shellfish toxin (saxitoxin) and cobra venom—were deadly enough to destroy the population of a small city.

One delivery system entailed first applying poison to a tiny dart the size of a sewing needle ("a nondiscernible microbioinoculator," as it had been called by an enterprising scientist in the CIA Directorate of Science and Technology), then using an electric dart gun ("noise-free disseminator") resembling a large .45 pistol, with a telescopic sight, to propel the dart silently toward the victim. The gun was reputed in CIA documents to be accurate up to 250 feet. Here was the ultimate murder weapon, able to kill without sound and with barely a trace.

After the meeting, I walked back to the committee offices with Greg Treverton. Given the discovery of biological agents that could produce diseaselike deaths, drugs that could cause disorientation and worse, and the involvement of the Mafia in assassination plots, he suggested we call our final report "Bugs, Drugs, and Thugs." The staff had already dubbed the hidden vault of dangerous biochemicals the "Cave of Bugs," though the official designation for the case was its CIA code name, MKNAOMI.

Now it was up to the staff to prepare the hearings. We had briefing books to write, documents to declassify (in consultation with the CIA), witnesses to interrogate, suggested questions to draft for the senators, evidence to array in a logical order, and a hundred details to deal with—from making sure we had a large hearing room to informing witnesses of their rights and scheduled appearances. A flurry of excitement spread through the committee staff, reviving sagging spirits after the long period of concentration on the assassination report. We certainly needed a new boost. The original thin lines of tension between the committee and the White House had given way to deep fissures, and partisan cracks had opened within the committee itself.

Preparations for the hearings on CIA poisons took longer than Church had hoped. His 9 September date slipped by a week to 16 September. While waiting for our public debut, Church grew alarmed about newspaper leaks from "White House sources" concerning the Cave of Bugs. With the press nibbling away daily at the case, by the time the 16th arrived, nothing would be left but a skeleton.

On 9 September, with major stories on the proposed hearings appearing in the *Washington Post* and the *New York Times*, Church felt he could wait no longer. "I regret to announce," he told the press, "the Senate committee has evidence that quantities of biological toxins of a highly lethal character have been retained by the CIA in contravention of presidential orders that such material should be destroyed."

Church continued: "The real question here that must not be missed is how presidential orders can be disobeyed on a matter of such importance." He complained that the mechanism for control within the Agency was "so loose" that the poisons had been discovered by happenstance; he added that when the assassination report was released later in the month, it would reveal other cases in which top CIA officials were apparently unaware of what lower-level operatives were doing. He seemed to be unchaining the rogue elephant theory again, though without using that phrase. Church concluded by observing that the White House opposed public hearings on this subject, but the committee would hold them anyway.

Sensitive to the possibility (scientifically unwarranted) that talk of shellfish toxin might create a public scare about eating shellfish, Church nodded; "Let it be clear that they ought not to be concerned about the shellfish they buy."

"What about the cobra meat?" cracked a correspondent.

The cat was out of the bag. If it had to happen before 16 September, Church was going to make sure the committee got the credit—not anonymous sources in the White House. But the committee members were less than uniformly pleased about Church's announcement and his efforts to build up the importance of the case. "Frank, what we have here," said Mathias on 11 September, "is a rogue mouse." I later told Treverton of Mathias's observation. "A rogue microbe is more like it," he suggested.

That afternoon I ran into Bill Miller near a Senate elevator. "Church is wrong, and the others are right," he said. "The chairman is too abuse oriented." He told me that some thought this was Fritz Schwarz's influence; others believed Church was "dazzled by the klieg lights" and was going for whatever would attract the cameras. The senators were fed up with the assassination report, Miller told me, and some were beginning to phase themselves out of committee activities; others, particularly Morgan, objected to the publicity. Philip Hart had told Miller that he feared we had lost sight of our objective for a "calm, deliberate investigation."

"Church is in trouble," Miller warned and disappeared into the elevator.

The proposed hearings were causing almost as much trouble within the committee, it seemed, as the factious assassination report. "The Cave of Bugs is a can of worms," Treverton said to me; he wanted to get into "the important cases," such as American interference in the affairs of Chile.

If Church shared the view that the Cave of Bugs was less than momentous, his public statements failed to reveal it. This case illustrated how the CIA had become "the victim of its own secrecy," he said on television, emphasizing its importance.[11] He did not stand completely alone. The discovery of the Cave of Bugs "poses some frightening questions," said a *New York Times* editorial.[12] Columnist Tom Wicker thought that "few incidents could more dramatically disclose the dangers of this many-chambered house [the CIA] of deceit, fear, power, and secrecy."[13]

Good case or bad, we were committed. On the morning of 16 September, as I walked to Church's office, the day was cool and breezy, the sky was lowering, and the leaves in the street seemed to dance in time with the butterflies in my stomach. When I arrived, Church wanted to know if the staff had made sure the CIA was bringing the electric dart gun to the hearing. "I want that gun there!" he said emphatically.

Fritz Schwarz summarized for Church the major points he thought ought to be made that morning, and then we went to the Senate Caucus Room, a large and ornate cavern in Roman Imperial style where, two years earlier, Senator Sam Ervin had conducted the Watergate inquiry. The room was crowded with tourists, newspaper reporters, and television and radio crews (the proceedings were being carried live by public television). At the front of the room was a long table, with chairs for the committee Democrats along one half and Republicans along the other. Those with greater seniority sat toward the middle. Thick briefing books rested on the green baize tabletop, accompanied by neatly arranged pencils, notepads, and glasses of water. Each of the designees was crowded into a seat behind his senator, leaving only a narrow aisle—filled with knees—for individuals to come and go. I sat behind Church, perspiration forming on my forehead within minutes under the hot television lights.

Without ado, Church banged down his gavel to begin the first public hearing of the Senate Intelligence Committee. In the next three days, testimony by Colby, Helms, and several CIA scientists revealed that the Agency had spent $3 million to develop poisons and biochemical weapons during the past eighteen years. Documents disclosed a capability to cause deadly diseases and epidemics (the Agency had stockpiled substances that could induce smallpox, tuberculosis, sleeping sickness, and other diseases), as well as to destroy crops and livestock on a massive scale. The CIA had also diffused through the New York City subway system a "harmless simulant" of a disease-carrying gas to test the dynamics of the gas flow and the vulnerability of an underground system to gaseous attack. Besides the shellfish toxin and cobra venom, the Cave of Bugs (actually a room in a building near the Department of State) held nine other lethal substances, including strychnine and cyanide pills, and a chemical capable of inducing abortions in animals.

On the first day of hearings, Senator Church asked Colby for the dart gun. The senators passed it among themselves, holding it up for reporters to see. Cameras moved in, clucking and whirring like an advancing army of mechanical insects. Here was theater to give life to the hearings, as Church had anticipated.

On the second day, Helms referred to the failure to destroy the poisons as an "odd aberration" unlikely to recur. He had ordered them destroyed (the orders were oral, not written), he said, and his orders had been ignored. A scientist in charge of the program testified that he was aware of President Nixon's order, but he did not regard these materials as falling within the meaning of the order since they were chiefly chemical—rather than biological—agents. Moreover, claimed the scientist, the order seemed to apply to the military, not the CIA. But, as Colby concluded, there was "no question but that . . . the decision [to keep the poisons] was wrong."

Throughout the hearings, designees passed notes to their senators suggesting possible questions; Daniel Schorr and other TV correspondents signaled "roll 'em" (index finger moving in a circle) or "cut" (finger sliding across the throat), depending on their sense of what was newsworthy; and photographers circulated, snapping the shutters of elaborate cameras.

Sometimes the questioning grew rather strained as senators quickly exhausted the limited subject of shellfish toxin. Senator Mondale belabored some obscure symbols that appeared on the label of one bottle of chemicals. After discussing their possible meaning for a quarter of an hour, the committee finally decided the symbols simply referred to a room number in the building where the substance had been stored.

Gary Hart sent a note down the table to Walter Mondale: "In light of these startling discoveries, strongly urge extension these hearings additional week and call label manufacturers, can manufacturers, vault contractor, Public Health Service, and GSA janitors at South laboratory!" Mondale scribbled back that permission was "denied."

Church, too, was capable of poking a little fun at the proceedings. At the end of the three days of hearings, he said that "the committee's investigation into eleven grams of shellfish toxin may have reminded some of H. G. Wells's comment on the American novelist Henry James. He described him as 'a hippopotamus rolling a pea.'"

Church went on to observe, however, that the case illustrated "how elusive the chain of command can be in the intelligence community. It underscores dramatically the necessity for tighter internal controls; for better record-keeping; for greater understanding of code words, compartmentation, and the whole range of secrecy requirements. Above all, it emphasizes the necessity for improved mechanisms of accountability all the way from the White House to the outer branches of the intelligence establishment."

An attempt by the CIA to thwart the will of the president or a simple and insignificant bureaucratic snafu at a middle echelon—rogue elephant or rogue mouse—whichever it was, the Cave of Bugs was behind us.[14] We had a long list of other cases to pull together now, including one I had been given specific responsibility for: the infamous spy plan, concocted during the Nixon years, known as the Huston Plan.

"Your Huston Plan hearings may be next," Schwarz said to me as we left the caucus room. That meant the next week, instead of October as originally scheduled! My mind raced with visions of all the work that would have to be compressed into a few days.

7

Sinister Forces

"Let's don't rush into more hearings," advised Senator Barry Goldwater. The Senate Intelligence Committee had convened on 19 September 1975—the day after the Cave of Bugs hearings—to decide what to do next. "We're in very, very ticklish waters," he added.

Goldwater was concerned about staff recommendations to hold open hearings on the National Security Agency (NSA), the headquarters of our communications intelligence and the most hidden of the American intelligence organizations. I had the feeling that if the committee moved like a centipede with a hundred bad knees, it would still be too fast for Goldwater. Certainly he was correct, though, about the "ticklish" nature of the topics the committee was about to consider.

On 11 September, a few days before our hearings on shellfish toxin, the House Intelligence Committee—now led by Otis Pike (D-NY) after a leadership shakeup in July—held a stormy session on the NSA. Since the Church committee intended soon to launch its own public hearings on this agency, we watched the Pike proceedings closely. The uproar that occurred carried a clear message: the congressional investigating committees were entering a minefield more treacherous than we had anticipated.

The trip wire was the decision of the Pike committee to declassify, on its own authority, passages of selected intelligence documents. One indicated that the intelligence community had been widely off target regarding the outbreak of the 1973 Arab–Israeli war. Within this document were four words that Colby, speaking on behalf of the intelligence community (particularly the NSA), asked to be kept secret. The words suggested, according to intelligence sources quoted by the *Washington Post*, that the United States had the capability of intercepting Egyptian communications, despite security precautions taken in Cairo.[1] The Pike committee members disagreed with Colby that the words warranted suppression, and they voted six to three to release the document. In the view of the *New York Times*, the stage was set for the "most serious constitutional confrontation between the legislative and executive branches since the Watergate scandal."[2]

The difference in approach between Church and Pike was becoming evident. The Church committee followed traditional procedures in attempting to obtain classified documents: negotiating with executive officials over what papers could be received and how they would be handled. In contrast, the Pike committee insisted on receiving any papers it deemed relevant to its inquiry without making promises about the future dispensation of the documents. As Pike put it, "The bottom line is that the Congress has the right to receive classified information without any strings attached to it."[3] The only concession Pike was willing to make was to allow the administration twenty-four hours "to explain their position" as to why a document should remain classified before his committee made a final decision.

According to one experienced observer, the difference between the two approaches was far-reaching: "On the Pike position hangs the whole question of whether Congress can exercise effective oversight of the intelligence community in the future. If a Congressional committee cannot say 'we want X' and get it without negotiating and promising, you open yourself to the charm and the lawyers and the whispering in the ear."[4]

Against the backdrop of the confrontation between the Pike committee and the White House, Goldwater's call for restraint was listened to more attentively than usual. "We need more time to study the NSA matter," he said.

"I'll agree with you," replied Gary Hart, "if you'll set a date [for public hearings]." Goldwater thought that would depend upon the results of the executive session briefings and staff research.

Thick clouds of caution seemed to fill room S407. Communications intelligence was an arcane field, and few senators felt confident about public hearings without further closed-door briefings by NSA officials. Only Church and Schweiker argued for moving forward immediately. Without more supporters, though, the chairman knew this subject would have to be delayed. He suggested that the committee turn next to the Huston Plan for public hearings since it was better understood by the members, and the case was reasonably ready for presentation. Between public hearings on the Huston Plan, the committee could conduct the closed NSA briefings; if things went well, open hearings on the NSA could then follow quickly on the heels of the Huston Plan. The members nodded their approval and adjourned.

Gary Hart shook his head slowly as he left the room. "This is like building your boat as you go out to sea," he said to a staff aide. Hart was close to the mark: we did seem to be rushing into public hearings—ready or not. Our cross-examination of witnesses was still underway.

Those individuals most intimately involved with the Huston Plan were former president Richard M. Nixon; agency directors Richard Helms (CIA), Admiral Noel Gayler (NSA), J. Edgar Hoover (FBI), and General Donald Bennett (DIA); and key staff aides Tom Charles Huston (White House), James Angleton (CIA), and William C. Sullivan (FBI). Among these men, Hoover was deceased and Nixon unwilling to talk with the committee without a legal battle. Of those remaining, William Sullivan turned out to be almost as hard to corner as the former president.

A Wilderness of Mirrors

John Elliff and I had flown to Boston on 10 June to meet Sullivan at Logan Airport. Despite constant interruptions from his attorney, he managed to sketch out the history of the Huston Plan. In 1969, Sullivan had been the FBI's assistant director for domestic activities, a post that included responsibility for counterintelligence (the discovery and destruction of operations conducted by hostile foreign intelligence services). In the summer of that year, a twenty-nine-year-old White House aide, Tom Charles Huston, paid a visit to Sullivan at FBI headquarters. The president, said the youthful Huston brashly, wanted better results from the FBI, including earlier intelligence on potential mass demonstrations. Sullivan had numerous meetings and telephone conversations with Huston, tutoring him in the art of counterintelligence. Their relationship deepened into a working alliance devoted to lowering the barriers to intelligence collection erected by a now more cautious J. Edgar Hoover, reluctant in his old age to risk operations that might drive him from office if discovered.

Then, in June 1970, President Nixon called the intelligence directors to the Oval Office. "We are now confronted with a new and grave crisis in our country," he told Helms, Hoover, Gayler, and Bennett. "Certainly hundreds, perhaps thousands of Americans—mostly under 30—are determined to destroy our society." The president believed the domestic instability could be quieted with more complete intelligence: the government must know more about the activities of such people.[5]

Nixon chastised the directors for failing to provide better information in the past and told them to prepare a report outlining how intelligence collection on radical dissidents could be improved. He introduced Huston (who had prepared the president's notes for this occasion) as the new White House aide responsible for internal security affairs, then dismissed the directors. A chain of events was underway that would culminate in a master spy plan.

Sullivan lapsed into a few moments of candor during our interview: he observed at one point that he and others working on the plan had grown up "topsy-turvy" during World War II, when legal questions were secondary to accomplishing a job against the enemy. But for the most part, the interview was a disappointment. His memory faded at critical junctures, and his lawyer prevented him from speaking at others.

When the time came in September to bring Sullivan to Washington, his attorney told us a trip would be impossible. Sullivan's health was failing, the attorney claimed. With the Huston Plan hearings shifted from October to September, it was clear that one of the major witnesses would be unavailable for public testimony.

The second major witness, Huston himself, had reluctantly agreed to come to Washington on 22 May for a deposition. I had anticipated a grim, sinister-looking individual. Instead, the man for whom the notorious blueprint for domestic espionage was named was a slightly built fellow in his midthirties, with glasses, pale complexion, and wisps of thinning hair combed across his head. He might as well have been the curator at one of the Smithsonian museums.

During staff questioning, Huston displayed an impressive memory and intellect. We moved through the Huston Plan almost line by line, tracing the origins of each option he had recommended to the president. As historian Theodore H. White has observed, the options would have permitted federal authorities to reach "all the way to every mailbox, every college campus, every telephone, every home."[6]

Specifically, Huston's plan—drawn from the recommendations of CIA, FBI, and NSA counterintelligence specialists—gave the intelligence agencies authority to monitor the international cables, telegrams, and mail of American citizens; intensify the electronic surveillance of domestic dissenters and selected establishments; break into specified establishments and into homes of domestic dissenters; and intensify the surveillance of American college students.

Huston urged these options on President Nixon with the argument that current intelligence collection on student radicals was woefully inadequate; besides, he pointed out, each of the options had been used with great productivity in the past—before J. Edgar Hoover grew cautious around 1968. In a memorandum to the president's closest adviser, H. R. Haldeman, Huston wrote that the FBI director was "bull-headed as hell" and "getting old and worried about his legend"; nevertheless, Hoover would "not hesitate to accede to any decision the President makes."[7]

It was a faulty prognosis. Even though the president approved Huston's options (many of them illegal), Hoover "went through the ceiling" (according to Sullivan) when he was informed of the White House decision to support the relaxation of restraints on intelligence collection. The FBI director stalked down the hallway to the office of the attorney general and demanded that John Mitchell squelch the plan. Himself upset that he had been completely bypassed by Huston and the White House on this issue, Mitchell told the president of Hoover's intense opposition and expressed his own reservations. Nixon chose not to be on the opposite side of the fence from Mitchell and, especially, from J. Edgar Hoover; he quickly reversed his decision, less than a week after his initial approval.

The president had buckled under pressure from the director of the FBI. Why?

"This is a very complicated question," Sullivan had told Elliff and me be[fore?] objections from his attorney, "but remember several things: Nixon and H[oover?] went back a long way, socialized together frequently, and considered them-selves close personal friends. And Nixon knew that he owed his reputation as a staunch anti-Communist in the fifties to Hoover." Sullivan paused and smiled. "Hoover had his files, too!" Many politicians in Washington feared that Hoover might have embarrassing information against them in his reputedly voluminous collection of gossip, innuendo, and fact. Had none of these influences deterred the president, Hoover held another ace up his sleeve: he could have leaked the Huston Plan to the press, swiftly aborting the whole enterprise.

When Huston learned of the president's change of mind, he was distraught. "All of us are going to look damn silly in the eyes of Helms, Gayler, Bennett, and the military chiefs," he wrote Haldeman, "if Hoover can unilaterally reverse a presidential decision based on a report that many people worked their asses off to prepare and which, on its merits, was a first-rate, objective job." Huston was appalled that the director of the FBI could put himself "above the President."[8] For several weeks, he tried through Haldeman to have the decision reinstated, but without success. His responsibilities for internal security affairs were shunted over to John Dean, a new White House attorney from the Justice Department and a young favorite of John Mitchell's (they would both be caught up shortly in the Watergate scandal). Discouraged and frustrated, Huston resigned from the White House staff in June 1971.[9]

Putting his pipe down for a moment, Huston told our staff he thought there were two approaches to meeting the problem of violence-prone student dissi-dents: "One is the intelligence-collection approach where you try to keep tabs on what is going on and stop trouble before it happens. The other approach, which is perhaps the only tolerable one in a free society, from a perfectly legitimate point of view, is you have to pay the price of letting a thing happen, and then follow the law and hope you can apprehend the person responsible and pros-ecute him according to the law." In 1970, he had elected to rely on unrestricted intelligence collection as the appropriate response.

By 1975, however, Huston had decided that this approach was dangerous. As he would say in public hearings in September: "The risk was that you would get people who would be susceptible to political considerations as opposed to national security considerations, or would construe political considerations to be national security considerations—to move from the kid with a bomb to the kid with a picket sign, and from the kid with the picket sign to the kid with the bumper sticker of the opposing candidate. And you just keep going down the line." The slide from controlling crime in the street to controlling "crime" in the mind could be swift.

In 1970, chief of CIA counterintelligence (1954–1974) James Angleton had welcomed the efforts of Huston and Sullivan, for the end result might have been presidential approval of a broader intelligence collection net—and official blessings from the White House on methods, such as illegal mail opening, already secretly in use (apparently unbeknownst to the president or his fledgling aide). Angleton could speak with authority on specific operations since among other responsibilities he headed up the CIA mail-opening project (code named HT Lingual) from 1955 until its termination in 1973. Questioning him, however, was like trying to find a new planet through an earthbound telescope: it took constant probing, a sensitivity for nuance, and a willingness to endure vast oceans of silence. Angleton might begin an important story, then let it trail out like a vanishing comet and disappear into a black hole of ambiguity. Perhaps the reason his conversation was so convoluted and difficult to follow was his ingrained habit of trying to deceive Soviet opponents.

In August 1975, Angleton said to me, in typically poetic and elusive language, that the task of the counterintelligence officer was to construct a "wilderness of mirrors" in which the opponent would be forever lost and confused. In 1975, the chief enemy of the CIA was—in the eyes of many CIA officers, including Angleton—the United States Congress. I wondered if Angleton's ploy was to lead the Church committee into his "wilderness," where everything revealed reflected something concealed, and the maddening multiplicity of images spun dizzily in the mind.

Angleton was not the only expert in legerdemain at the CIA. He had his equal in Richard Helms. The director of the Agency at the time of the spy plan, Helms had to be questioned carefully about his role in the proposal.

On 10 September, he arrived at our offices for a deposition. He looked weary after the twenty-four-hour plane trip from Iran, where he was ambassador. As he sat across the table from me, crossed his legs, cocked his head, and waited for the inevitable questions, an air of resignation seemed to settle over him. Then, for what felt like a full day, I listened to a long line of "I don't recall. . . I don't remember . . . I don't know . . ." interrupted only by buzzers signaling votes in the Senate—and an occasional moment when Helms's memory would clear, and he would lean across the table to make his point, jaw squared, eyes blinking, grin confident, as if he had just checkmated an old chess partner. What usually inspired these flashes of clarity were the opportunities I offered him to discuss CIA relations with J. Edgar Hoover; he obviously had little use for the man and relished explaining his shortcomings in the intelligence field. Then it was back to "I don't remember." Whatever was hidden in the abyss of his memory refused to come out.

I asked him to identify a couple of documents related to the Huston Plan. "I may have seen these before," he said, "but I have also seen several million other documents and cannot be expected to remember each one." I tried to refresh his memory, but none of my papers or details from other witnesses chased away the great, gray clouds drifting through Helms's own wilderness of mirrors.

Admiral Noel Gayler's memory was equally foggy; he seemed about as familiar with the Huston Plan as he might have been with the commodity and tariff regulations in the Department of Agriculture. With a shrug of his shoulders, he told me in September that he had little recollection of the entire venture, and estimated that he had spent about three hours on the plan during the three years he served at NSA.

Gayler did remember hoping at the time that the plan might accomplish two objectives: to allow the NSA better access to foreign telecommunications, and to resolve the lengthy dispute between Helms and Hoover over greater FBI cooperation in the collection of intelligence. Beyond these points, he had little to say; his time at NSA had been spent from dawn to dusk trying to absorb the science of signals intelligence and monitoring the vast quantities of data captured by NSA's worldwide network of communications-intercept facilities. "I often felt like a fire hose was held to my mouth," he recalled.

On the chance that Gayler's former top assistant might remember more, I drove to NSA headquarters in Maryland to meet with Dr. Louis Tordella, a long-time scientist there and second in command until his retirement in 1975. Though retired, Tordella had been asked to stay on at NSA as a consultant. To my surprise, he had a relatively clear memory of 1970. Though he recalled practically nothing about Huston, he had known Sullivan fairly well for eighteen years and shared his unhappiness over Hoover's obstinacy on intelligence collection. Tordella likened Hoover in his new caution to "the airplane ace who feels that sooner or later he's going to get shot down."

In 1970, Tordella, like Sullivan, had seen the interest of the White House as a heaven-sent opportunity to resume the occasional "surreptitious entries" (burglaries) and other collection techniques that Hoover had abandoned. Tordella had no desire to violate the rights of Americans, he emphasized; his intention was only to remove the shackles from the NSA and other agencies in their pursuit of information about hostile foreign powers. The scientist suggested another wrinkle to the affairs of 1970: the entire intelligence community was undergoing budget cuts in 1969–1970, and a new mandate from the White House for expanded collection operations would have given the agencies leverage with congressional appropriations committees to reverse the downtrend in intelligence spending.

The only other person on my list of high-priority witnesses was General Bennett. (The committee had given up trying to interview President Nixon directly and decided instead to mail him a list of questions on the Huston Plan and other topics.) I discovered that Bennett now lived in retirement on Hilton Head, the resort off the coast of South Carolina. Life as a Senate investigator was beginning to look up.

I flew to Savannah and drove thirty miles through the wilds of the South Carolina coastlands, crossing a bridge from a forgotten country of jungle and run-down shanties to the island of Hilton Head, with its paradise of palms, pines, lavish homes, tennis clubs, elaborately manicured golf courses, and plush hotels.

Sitting in his living room, Bennett told me that he had been glad to see the president take an interest in intelligence problems but was determined not to allow the military to be again drawn into the field of domestic intelligence collection (as it had been in the 1960s). When I asked him why, then, he had signed the report to the president, he replied that the report was meant to present a range of options—not outright recommendations—to the chief executive. Huston had drawn from the report the most extreme options, some of which were illegal. Bennett admitted that, in retrospect, it seemed questionable to have given the president a checklist including illegal activities, since the implication was that the intelligence community would be ready to carry out whichever of these alternatives the White House selected.

Bennett believed that Huston had become the pawn of the NSA and the CIA in their pursuit of better foreign intelligence collection. He emphasized, though, Sullivan's desire to use Huston as a means to bring pressure on Hoover (through the president) to change FBI intelligence-collection policy. "Everyone," remembered Bennett, "underestimated Hoover's ability to sway the final decision of the president."

I still needed a good FBI witness in case Sullivan was too ill to testify. At the eleventh hour, when it was clear that he would be unable to travel, the FBI Task Force found the right man: Charles "Chick" Brennan, Sullivan's assistant for many years. On the weekend before the hearings, the committee's FBI specialists and I met with Brennan. He had attended most of the staff meetings on the Huston Plan in 1970 and remembered them well. He said that Sullivan, not Huston, had been the "principal figure" behind the events that led to the spy plan. In Brennan's view, "Huston did not have sufficient in-depth background concerning intelligence matters to be able to give that strong direction and guidance."

Huston Plan Hearings

On 23 September 1975, the first day of autumn, the curtain went up on Tom Charles Huston as we began our second set of hearings. He admitted that his plan had been wrong-minded, but he noted that five years ago, "we were talking about bombers, we were talking about assassins, we were talking about snipers. I felt something had to be done." Huston scoffed at the suggestion that he had somehow coerced the intelligence agencies into backing controversial intelligence-collection methods and said that he (and, so far as he knew, the president) "didn't know half the things" the agencies were already doing, such as opening mail and harassing political dissidents.

Huston theorized as to why the agencies concealed such activities from the White House: "If you have got a program going and you are perfectly happy with its results, why take the risk that it might be turned off if the president of the United States decides he does not want to do it; because they had no way of knowing in advance what decision the president might take. . . . The president may say hell no, I don't want you guys opening any mail. Then, if they had admitted it, they would have had to close the thing down."

The agencies concealed their operations not only from the president, said Huston, but also from one another—partly out of "interagency jealousies and rivalries, but also to avoid revealing that they were working on each other's turf." If J. Edgar Hoover had known about CIA domestic spying on student protesters (Operation CHAOS), said Huston, he "would have had an absolute stroke." In part, the duplicity was a form of bureaucratic game playing. Earlier in the year, when the staff first interviewed Huston, he had remarked, "The bureau had its own game going over there. They didn't want us to know; they didn't want the Justice Department to know; they didn't want the CIA to know." And across the Potomac, "the CIA had its own game going. They didn't want the bureau to know." During the hearings, Huston added that if the White House "had known these tools were being used and still not getting any results, it might have changed the whole approach."

Senator Church pointed to evidence indicating that the agencies had conducted illegal options not only before the Huston Plan but also after the president revoked his approval. "The president and Mr. Huston, it appears, were deceived by intelligence officials," Church said; the government's intelligence services had operated as "independent fiefdoms," telling neither the chief executive nor one another of their illicit activities. "As in the case of the shellfish toxin," concluded the chairman, "the decision of the president seemed to matter little."

When the session ended, Church was cornered by a few reporters and chastised for handling Huston, as one said, "with velvet gloves." Columnist Mary McGrory later wrote that the chairman had been "incurably polite," accepting everything Huston said, and suggested that Church was trying once more to "vindicate himself" for the famous rogue elephant remark by showing with this case that the intelligence agencies had operated on their own beyond the authority of the president.[10]

The actual explanation was much simpler: the committee accepted Huston's testimony because he was convincing and sincere (or else he was one of the world's great actors). More importantly, his views corresponded with the documentary record and the statements of other witnesses. He never denied his involvement and seemed genuinely to regret it. What he did deny was knowing how extensively practiced the extreme options of his plan already were, and would continue to be after he left the White House in 1971.

The next day of hearings illustrated incontrovertibly that in Project HT Lingual the CIA had opened and copied mail sent between the United States and communist countries from 1953 to 1973—both before and after discussion of the Huston Plan, with its ironic request for presidential authority to open mail. Angleton was the witness. After thirty years of hidden identity, he looked understandably dazed and uncomfortable before all the lights and cameras. He sat bent over in his chair, a scowl on his face.

Senator Church desperately wanted something to spice up the hearings, as the dart gun had done the week before. Fritz Schwarz came up with an idea only hours before the second day of hearings. Why not use some of the startling findings the FBI Task Force had been gathering for hearings on mail opening, which were scheduled later in the year? The staff aide working on that project objected to having his findings used prematurely, but his protests were overruled. Church opened the session with the announcement (which made bold headlines the next day) that the CIA had opened the mail of Hubert Humphrey, Richard Nixon (when he was in Congress), Linus Pauling, John Steinbeck, the Ford Foundation, Harvard University, the Rockefeller Foundation, and a long list of others. As Church recited the litany of names, the caucus room buzzed with excitement.

Angleton, who had headed the mail-opening program, admitted that it was illegal but steadfastly defended it anyway. "From a counterintelligence point of view," he said, "it was vitally important to know everything possible about contacts between US citizens and Communist countries." The program, he remained convinced, was as logical and sensible as maintaining the nation's military defenses. In our earlier talks during the summer, Angleton had emphasized that the CIA opened the mail of only a small number of letter writers over the years—some 215,000. "That represents about 0.001 percent of the American population, and it included people who were involved in criminal fraternization with the enemy," he said. The list of individuals and organizations read into the record by Church, however, hardly represented hardened criminals or political subversives.

Throughout the hearing, Angleton lamented that "the nature of the threat" posed by the USSR was insufficiently appreciated. A few days earlier he had complained to me on the telephone, "The country is going to hell; there is no interest in national security these days, and your committee is a manifestation of this." A few months later, he would berate the committee publicly for "a type of McCarthyite hearing in which the denigration of the intelligence community was its goal."[11] During the hearings, he said to the committee: "When I look at the map today and see the weakness of power of this country, that is what shocks me."

The former attorney general of North Carolina, Senator Morgan, responded that what shocked him was the violation of individual rights represented by the CIA mail-opening project.

Senator Mondale read from the talking paper President Nixon had used in his meeting with the intelligence directors in 1970. It portrayed the United States as a country under siege by young radicals. The document, said Mondale, revealed an "enormous, unrestricted paranoid fear about the American people."

"It was not, in my view, paranoia," retorted Angleton.

I stared at the witness and thought of all the hours I had spent with him, Huston, and others in the intelligence world. Angleton was not an evil man; nor were Huston, Helms, and the rest; they did have a more pronounced fear of "the enemy," however, than most people I had met. For Huston, the enemy had been the young antiwar protesters with their scraggly hair and tatterdemalion garb. For Angleton, it was the KGB and other hostile intelligence services for whom the Cold War had no end. "It is the idea of the enemy," former attorney general Ramsey Clark once wrote, "the bad man, the sinister force that we use to deny freedom."[12] It was also, perhaps, a matter of thoughtlessness. As Hannah Arendt pointed out, much evil is done less because of venality than because individuals failed to consider the implications of their acts.[13] In his well-intentioned efforts to fight communism, I wondered if Angleton had thought sufficiently about the harm he might inflict upon our own form of government.

Our attention grabber for the last day of hearings came to us from the FBI only the night before. I laughed to myself as I thought of Hart's comment about "building our boat as we go to sea." Here I was, after weeks of research on the Huston Plan, banging new planks into place just hours before the appearance of our last witness. The new information was about "black bag" jobs (yet another FBI euphemism for burglary) carried out by the Bureau from 1942 to 1968 against seventeen "domestic subversive targets."

Brennan, the witness for this day, explained to the committee how Hoover had grown more cautious in his late years, fearing that after he had reached the mandatory retirement age (seventy) in 1965, an embarrassing incident might force him from the directorship.

Brennan testified also that the student radicals of the 1960s and 1970s were middle- and upper-class kids—"credit card revolutionaries"—with money of their own; they received little or no funding from foreign powers. The fears of the Nixon administration, and the Johnson administration before it, that American student uprisings were being incited and financed from afar, were completely unfounded, as the FBI (and the CIA) had often told the White House during this period. It was as if the presidents simply refused to believe that their unpopularity was homegrown; there had to be a sinister force from abroad behind the protests.

Senator Church reached one major conclusion—a reaffirmation of his rogue elephant thesis (though again he avoided the phrase): "It is almost as though, from the state of evidence to date, that the president was really an irrelevancy." He ended his cross-examination of Angleton with biting scorn: "So the commander-in-chief is not the commander-in-chief at all. He is just a problem. You do not want to inform him in the first place, because he might say no. That is the truth of it. When he did say no, you disregarded it. And then you call him the commander-in-chief."

The most urgent matter facing the committee now was the stalemate over NSA hearings. In the House, the Pike committee had run aground on the jagged rocks of this controversy. I feared a similar fate awaited us.

8

Adrift

With the Huston Plan hearings behind me, I felt a great sense of relief. A score of things could have gone wrong, each of which had given me nightmares during the summer. Perhaps at the last moment, with the committee, the public, and the television cameras assembled, a key witness would fail to appear (Angleton seemed like a likely candidate for this scenario). I could hear the squawk of a faulty microphone sending ear-piercing sounds throughout the ornate caucus room. Or perhaps something I or someone else had placed in the thick briefing books would prove to be incorrect, despite all the double checking, and Church or another member would be publicly embarrassed. Maybe what proved to be a central document would fail to be among those we had amassed for the occasion. In one dream, all eleven members of the committee turned in their chairs to glare at me with anger and incredulity; I had ground the hearings to a halt for lack of an "obvious" document that the poorest dimwit would have discovered.

But now the hearings—and the frayed nerves—were past; the committee was well into its public phase and seemed, on the surface, to be organized and prepared to lay out its findings before the American people. Behind the scenes, though, lay a different reality, for in fact, ten months after its creation, the Senate Intelligence Committee was still in search of an agenda.

The lack of direction did not stem from an absence of blueprints. Each of the task forces had laid before the committee detailed outlines of topics to be investigated, a great cornucopia of subjects: counterintelligence, the murders of John F. Kennedy and Martin Luther King Jr. (precisely, what the intelligence agencies had known about their assassins), an astonishing assortment of alleged FBI abuses, the use of informants (the largest source of FBI intelligence), IRS intelligence activities, CIA clandestine involvement around the globe, technical intelligence collection—the possibilities seemed to tumble out in endless profusion.

The problem was essentially one of uncertainty among the senators about which topics would be most fruitful. The senators had devoted most of their energies to the assassination report and, of course, to their several responsibilities as members of other Senate committees. Precious little time had been directed toward the consideration—let alone resolution—of what to do once public hearings began. In this regard, the committee was adrift. While it was preoccupied with navigating the assassination straits, the turbulent seas beyond remained uncharted—at least by the senators themselves.

The IRS Hearing

Their interests became somewhat clearer on 30 September, when the committee gathered for a business meeting. Its purpose was to decide whether the IRS ought to be the focus of the next public hearings; as the session unfolded, however, it became obvious that the members were anxious—at last—to explore the future agenda more broadly. This was the first business meeting from which Church was absent (he had a speaking engagement in San Francisco), and the Democrats seemed more willing to speak openly.

Senator Morgan quickly made it known that he was against too extensive an inquiry. "Let's not drag this thing out," he said. "We have almost enough information now."

Senator Mondale, as acting chairman, was wary of the proposal for IRS hearings. "If we start browbeating a bunch of IRS civil servants, it will look just like that," he warned, and proposed an alternative: "Let's start with COIN-TELPRO and CHAOS." These were codenames for FBI and CIA surveillance programs, which from every indication appeared to have overstepped the bounds of the law. "Here are the key programs," he said, "and here we can pinpoint much of the blame."

Mondale asked Fritz Schwarz to report on the progress of the staff in developing the facts related to COINTELPRO and CHAOS. "We're a prisoner of our own efforts to get the work done," Schwarz explained with a pained expression. "COINTELPRO will not be ready until late October."

A gloom fell over the room. Schwarz elaborated on the difficulties confronting the FBI Task Force in trying to pry documents out of the Bureau's COINTEL-PRO files. Acutely aware of the problems they had experienced in the search for assassination documents, and were still having with respect to CIA documents on Chile,[1] the senators nodded their understanding.

A consensus soon began to emerge: it would be unwise for the committee to lock itself into an unrealistic and unworkable schedule just to hold public hearings for the sake of holding hearings. The committee would proceed only when a subject was adequately researched. I knew Church would disapprove of this approach. I was sure he would have argued strongly for setting a schedule of public hearings and requiring the staff to meet that schedule one way or another. Time was running out for the committee; this was hardly the time for further drift.

Since the IRS project was the only one ready, a decision was made to hold a public session on this topic the following week—but only for one day, instead of

the three recommended by the staff. The senators obviously were bored with t'
IRS; abuses by the CIA and the FBI sounded more intriguing.

As the meeting ended, I walked out with one of the staff aides responsible
for the IRS investigation. "The only kind of hearing this committee is interested
in is pure theater," he said bitterly, "whatever will goose the public best."[2] Greg
Treverton joined us, shaking his head. "A meeting should have been held back
in July to decide what priorities the senators had. This meeting should not have
taken place on September 30th!"

The IRS hearing was held on 2 October. What especially alarmed the committee was evidence that other intelligence agencies, notably the FBI, had made
frequent use of the IRS as a veritable lending library of both tax-related and non-
tax-related information about citizens.

Moreover, as the hearing disclosed, the IRS had maintained for nearly four
years a unit—the Special Services Staff (SSS)—whose purpose was to investigate political activists. The SSS compiled a secret "watch list" of some eleven
thousand individuals and groups classified as extremist or radical. Among the
names on the list were columnist Joseph Alsop (a cotter pin of Washington society); singer and antiwar activist Joan Baez; writers Jimmy Breslin and Norman Mailer; rock star James Brown; performer Sammy Davis Jr.; former United
States senators Charles Goodell (R-NY) and Ernest Gruening (D-AK); civil rights
leaders Jesse Jackson and Coretta Scott King; actress Shirley McLaine; the
American Library Association; the American Civil Liberties Union; the NAACP;
Rolling Stone and *Playboy* magazines; and hundreds of others. During the hearing, Church read a partial list of individuals and groups "politically harassed" by
the SSS. Again, this technique had a dramatic effect.

The hearing revealed two incidents that illustrated how intelligence agencies
had used IRS data for political purposes. The FBI had once planned to disrupt
the fund-raising program of Reverend Martin Luther King Jr. and his Southern
Christian Leadership Conference (SCLC) by obtaining a list of the organization's
financial supporters; then each supporter was to be mailed a forged letter, ostensibly from King, indicating that the SCLC's tax-exempt status was in jeopardy.
The objective was to discourage potential contributors and dry up the financial
base of the SCLC. As Senator Huddleston made clear in the hearing, the FBI obtained the names from the IRS (though evidence as to whether the forged letters
were actually sent was inconclusive).

In the second case, the CIA had urged the IRS to open an investigation into
Ramparts magazine in 1967. The objective was to disrupt a proposed series of
articles on CIA infiltration of the National Student Association. In a secret memorandum from the CIA to the IRS, dated 2 February 1967, an Agency official
said that he wished to avoid a more formal request; otherwise, "the [IRS] Com-
missioner will not be in a position to deny our interest if questioned later by a

member of Congress or other competent authority." Apparently the doctrine of plausible denial had its uses beyond the Oval Office.

An NSA Deadlock

That afternoon, James Schlesinger and General Lew Allen Jr., director of the NSA, sat waiting for the committee to convene in S407. When the members had assembled, Church asked Schlesinger to present his views on how the committee should proceed with its examination of the NSA. With a low voice and somber air, the secretary of defense argued against a public hearing. He sounded like Moses speaking from the mount, engulfed in swirling clouds of pipe smoke. He argued gravely, accompanied by nods from Allen, that NSA technology was so sensitive that any public hearing could accidentally reveal information our enemies could use to block the Agency's interception of their communications. In lieu of public hearings, he suggested, the committee might hold as many executive sessions as it wished, then publish a report on the NSA—carefully reviewed to prevent disclosure of classified information. Or, Schlesinger continued, if the committee felt it absolutely had to have a public hearing, it could first issue a written report cleared by NSA officials and then hold limited hearings on that report.

When Schlesinger and Allen had departed, Church remained unimpressed. "This committee showed remarkable restraint during the shellfish toxin hearings, never once straying into the assassination issue," he observed. "Surely we can exercise the same discipline during a hearing on NSA, staying clear of topics that we know from these briefings are too sensitive for public discussion."

John Tower disagreed. He was clearly awed by the delicate NSA apparatus for intercepting communications around the globe, and he feared that this net might be torn inadvertently if handled by inexpert laymen. As the debate continued, however, the vice chairman slowly began to concede—though only after urging the greatest sense of caution if the committee insisted on examining this agency in public.

As was often the case with the committee, once again, it had taken no votes; a sense of direction had emerged from thorough discussion. Such a consensus was easier to live with than a more formal vote, less jarring on uneasy friendships and fragile alliances, but it was also more susceptible to misunderstandings and to varying degrees of interpretation. It was a fluid compact and, like fluids, could assume many forms—or evaporate altogether, as would be the case in this instance.

With Mondale's important support, Church had won the initial argument over NSA public hearings by appealing to his colleagues' faith in the ability of the committee to keep sensitive secrets. This point, though, lost much of its persuasiveness with committee members as Mondale hit the college lecture circuit over the weekend.

Traveling to pastoral Granville, Ohio, Senator Mondale addressed the students of Denison College on the subject "The American Intelligence Community and the Future of Foreign Policy." The speech accurately portrayed the frustration of the committee over the still-concealed assassination report. "Pinning down responsibility for many of the actions the committee has uncovered," said Mondale, "has been like nailing jello to a wall. Subordinates say they were told to do it; higher officials can't remember it." In the course of his remarks, Mondale revealed previously undisclosed testimony from the assassination report which, by committee agreement, was to have remained secret until officially released.

Senator Church appeared on ABC's *Issues and Answers* after Mondale's speech and was asked to comment on Mondale's references to the assassination report. He did, and perhaps at greater length than necessary.

Members of the committee fumed as they read press accounts of Mondale's speech and watched their chairman on national television; they had understood that no one could discuss the details of the committee findings in public. Now that agreement had been broken—and only a day after the chairman had urged NSA hearings on the grounds that members had proved their responsibility in maintaining secrecy.

Attorney General Edward Levi had made a special request to meet with the committee on the NSA issue, and the senators had agreed to hear him on Tuesday. On Monday morning, the auditorium was alive with rumors about a possible censure vote by the committee against Church and Mondale following Levi's visit.

The attorney general was the next chess piece pushed forward by the administration in a defense of the NSA against public hearings. Only recently appointed, Levi must have burned the midnight oil in an effort to prepare himself to discuss the intricacies of NSA technology. It soon became apparent that he had failed to master his subject.

Seated in a hearing room we sometimes used in the Russell Building, with his hand against his face as if nursing a bad toothache, Senator Church obviously thought this ground had been covered thoroughly already (and by more expert witnesses). He did not bother to conceal his impatience. He asked the attorney general if he thought NSA intercepts of American international communications were illegal.

Levi, who seemed surprisingly arrogant—not the usual posture of executive officials before congressional investigating committees—replied that his department had an investigation into this question underway. "This is not the main point concerning public hearings," he said brusquely. "What is central here is the fact that private enterprise will no longer cooperate with the government."

The NSA, he explained, relied on the cooperation of private international communications businesses to provide access to cables and telegrams into and out of the United States; the agency would then analyze certain messages, using sophisticated computer technology to sift and winnow from thousands of communications those involving "suspicious" individuals and groups on the NSA "watch list." Levi emphasized that public hearings might reveal the relationship between the government and the private companies, damaging their business reputations. The companies might then terminate their cooperation, cutting off the NSA from a valuable intelligence source.

Church stared absently at the high windows, then turned to Mondale and asked, "Do you have any questions?" For the next fifteen minutes, Mondale subjected the attorney general to a withering cross-examination on NSA terminology. Gary Hart followed Mondale with further careful scrutiny of the issues. Levi quickly retreated from this onslaught of detailed questions about the NSA to a more secure fortress: the committee would harm the national security if it held public hearings. Period. The witness had nothing more to say and was excused.

Senator Goldwater, who had missed the meeting the prior week when Church had received tacit committee approval for a public hearing on NSA, spoke immediately following Levi's departure. "We're flirting with real trouble," he observed, and asked for a formal roll-call vote on the question of public hearings.

Baker rose and said he had to depart but would leave his proxy with John Tower. He added that he opposed holding NSA hearings the next day (as scheduled), but he would be willing to reconsider such hearings later, after the committee had discussed the matter further.

"The committee has an educational responsibility," said Senator Mathias, as Baker left. "Maybe we should require those companies to stop and think about whether or not they are doing something illegal."

"Well, we've been through this many times," Church summed up. "I don't see that the issues have changed any."

"I call for a roll-call vote," said Goldwater.

"I support the motion," said Tower.

Mathias looked perplexed: "I'd like to offer an alternative. It looks like we've hit a sensitive nerve here. Let's find out what is going on. Let's sit down with the secretary of defense, the attorney general, General Allen, whomever, and find out what the problems are."

Church turned in his chair in great annoyance. "We've already covered this ground several times," he said, exasperated.

"Sometimes it takes more guts to have a closed hearing," offered Tower. "The press is always hounding us for open hearings."

Morgan sat forward and said, "I don't agree with the chair that it is the re- sponsibility of the committee to reveal all wrongdoings."

Church was surfeited with debate on the NSA: "Let's vote on the Goldwa- ter motion to cancel any public hearings on the National Security Agency." Bill Miller called the committee roll and checked off the results on a pad: nays— Church, Mondale, Huddleston, Mathias, Schweiker; yeas—Tower, Goldwater, Morgan, G. Hart; absent—P. Hart (illness), Baker.

I was astounded: Gary Hart had supported the Goldwater position! The re- sult was almost a tie, but Tower properly declined to exercise Baker's proxy; the Goldwater motion would have excluded any public hearings on the NSA, whereas Baker had suggested that he might support a later hearing. It was a vic- tory for Church, but a hollow one, as he knew. The fact was that his committee stood badly divided—and in moments things would grow worse.

In light of the close vote, Church offered a suggestion: let the committee pro- ceed with a public hearing on the NSA watch list. The matter of NSA relation- ships with private businesses in the communications field (known by the code name Shamrock) could be deferred.

Senator Mathias, though, was unwilling to forget his own alternative. On the one hand, he rejected Goldwater's all-or-nothing motion; on the other, he was disinclined to go ahead with public hearings, even with Church's compromise.

"Let me repeat," said Mathias, "I believe we ought to defer *any* hearings on the NSA until we've had further meetings. I believe I have a motion to that effect."

"What have we been doing but meeting day after day!" replied Church an- grily. "I offer a substitute to your motion: that we defer SHAMROCK and hold hearings on the watch list."

"We'll lose our leverage if we accept this substitute," Mathias warned, but Church asked Miller to call the roll. Those in favor of Church's substitute watch list hearing were Church, Mondale, Huddleston, and Schweiker; voting for Mathias's motion to delay were Tower, Goldwater, Baker (proxy), Mathias, Mor- gan, and G. Hart.

Fritz Schwarz's words came back to me: "The chairman is losing his commit- tee," he had said, when the Democrats sided with the Republicans against the release of the assassination report by committee action. Now Church had lost his committee, at least for the time being. He was visibly shaken.

Immediately following the vote, Mondale asked for the floor and apologized for his "carelessness" in the Ohio speech. Quietly angry, Gary Hart told the mem- bers that the committee was losing its good name; if it could not contain itself for the duration of the inquiry, he refused to be a part of it. Church and Mondale made their amends, and the committee agreed to renew its self-discipline.

On the way back to the auditorium, I asked Rick Inderfurth about Hart's surprising vote. He said that Hart was deeply troubled by the indiscretions over the weekend. The committee leaders seemed unable to keep the secrecy understanding on the assassination report; what would happen if this carelessness extended to the delicate operations of the NSA? A public hearing on the NSA, Hart feared, might just invite further unnecessary disclosures. In disgust with the apparent inability of some senators to hold their tongues (including Goldwater, who was now openly talking to the press about committee "soft-pedaling" on the involvement of President Kennedy in assassination plots),[3] Hart had decided to vote against NSA public hearings. According to Inderfurth, the senator was not immovable in his opposition but needed to be assured that the committee really could stay within agreed-upon boundaries during an open session.

It was an unfortunate turn of events. Gary Hart had been a reliable ally for the chairman; now they had parted company. Losing the support of another Democrat—Morgan—was a blow too. All around, it had been a singularly bad day for Church. If the objective of the administration was to slow or halt the committee's work (as seemed to be the case more and more each week), it was succeeding admirably.

At Sea

Two days later, on 9 October, the committee reconvened to discuss possible hearings for October and November. The meeting began with the staff briefing, which centered on CIA covert action.

"What about proprietaries?" asked Huddleston after the briefing. "Let's explore them." Proprietaries were intelligence agency fronts—usually real or phony ("notional") businesses—behind which an agency concealed its espionage operations.

"I agree!" seconded Schweiker enthusiastically.

"We need to concentrate on the CIA–FBI interface," said Baker, using a bit of popular Washington jargon.

"We're in our ninth month and we've only held seven hearings," said Church gloomily.

"Maybe we need to break down into panels or subcommittees, with groups of us concentrating on specific subjects," suggested Mathias. Usually this is not the kind of suggestion a chairman likes to hear, for it implies a dispersion of control and authority. Church's face remained expressionless; he let the suggestion drop and turned to the staff of the FBI Task Force, asking for their proposed schedule of hearings.

The executive sessions, the staff suggested, would concentrate on FBI counterintelligence. The open sessions would begin with a probe of an FBI project to discredit Martin Luther King Jr.; move to the subject of COINTELPRO (the Bureau's covert action program directed against domestic and foreign groups within the United States from the mid-1950s until 1971); and end with a series of hearings on related FBI operations (such as the use of informants).

Baker responded first; he was worried about the King case. "Let's have a balance," he said, "not just focus on King. Perhaps a session on FBI infiltration of the KKK, too." Goldwater also expressed his concern about the King investigation; he feared that a public hearing might incite further racial unrest.

Silence and tension filled the room. Finally, Mondale offered a proposal: "Let's don't start off with the King case. Let's do COINTELPRO first." Baker agreed, endorsing COINTELPRO for the first hearing, then one day on King, and another day on the Klan or some other group.

Church brought up the Mathias proposal for further negotiations with the executive branch on the NSA, then assigned Mathias and Huddleston to discuss the public hearing controversy with the White House.

After lunch, the committee gathered again to hear testimony from a few tail-end witnesses on the assassination issue. Here it was October, and we were still taking testimony on assassination plots. The committee, lamented Bill Miller, continued to follow the assassination scent "like a pack of beagles."[4]

Back at the staff offices, I asked Walter Ricks, the young attorney who served as Senator Morgan's designee, why Morgan had voted against NSA public hearings. He replied that Morgan saw no need to have open hearings on every agency; he indicated that Morgan might be persuaded otherwise in the case of the NSA, though, if Church would take the time to explain his views personally to Morgan. I asked Ricks if Morgan and Church had gotten together privately since the beginning of the investigation, and he said no. Morgan, in fact, had wondered aloud to Ricks why the chairman had been so distant from the committee members.

I mentioned this to Schwarz later in the day. "Yes, I know," he said. "As the British say, Church keeps himself to himself."

The sense of drift permeating the Senate committee was noted by Miller in early October. Part of the problem derived from the "natural clash of egos and ambition," he wrote, especially as a result of the "large group of aggressive litigators who are seeking in part glory and are prone to the phototropism of televised hearings."[5] Another difficulty—the "hardest task" in Miller's words—was "to obtain the trust of those we have been investigating. It has come slowly, but it is succeeding."

Reporters sensed the lull and the frustration, too. "Congressional investigators seem adrift in a sea of information, stunned by the magnitude of the task, and less sure of their objectives than when they started," wrote Nicholas Horrock in the *New York Times* on 10 October. The analysis was painfully accurate.

At this time, a perceptible change occurred in the degree of executive branch resistance to the congressional inquiries. A steady breeze of opposition had been evident from the beginning, but in October its intensity increased dramatically. By the end of the year, the winds would reach gale force and completely change the direction of the House and Senate investigations.

The indications were easy to find; the parade of witnesses from the executive branch testifying against NSA public hearings, coupled with telephone calls from the president himself, were clear signs. Whether the Church committee technique of patient "conversations" (negotiations) with the administration would continue to be successful was open to doubt.

Nor was the NSA the sole impediment. On 9 October, the Senate committee received a letter from the president flatly opposing publication of the assassination report, on the grounds that it would reflect badly on the United States and provide the Soviet Union with an unparalleled propaganda weapon. This letter went to the chairman; then, on 31 October, each member of the committee received a more strongly worded message from the president (see chapter 9). The struggle had shifted from the acquisition of documents to their use in hearings (on the NSA) and in reports (on assassination).

On the House side, executive resistance was rising too. In fact, Pike introduced a motion before his committee to initiate a contempt of Congress proceeding against Henry Kissinger for his failure to produce a requested document. The motion was rejected by an eight-to-five vote; instead, the House committee elected to summon Kissinger for a personal appearance on 30 October to explain his position in a public forum. Following his defeat by a coalition of four Democrats and four Republicans, a dispirited Pike said sarcastically, "It was my opinion that we should proceed against Dr. Kissinger as we would against an ordinary mortal."[6]

In Senator Church's view, his committee had avoided some of the confrontation experienced by the Pike committee in the struggle for documents because "we got an early start and we had time to enter into negotiations with the White House."[7] In contrast, as a result of its late start, according to one scholarly observer, the Pike committee was "in a hurry." Its troubles derived, too, in the same scholar's opinion, from a greater inclination to ask "the tough questions"[8]—a conclusion open to doubt since the questions posed by the Church committee on the issue of assassination, and later on covert action and COINTELPRO, were as bruising as any asked by the House panel. Both committees were tough at different times on different issues, with the House committee emphasizing "quality of intelligence" failures.

The executive branch went beyond the mere construction of defenses; on 7 October, the president moved to the offensive. According to newspaper reports, President Ford would soon issue, in a major "shakeup," a new plan to revamp and improve control over intelligence agencies, and 80 percent of the plan was to be accomplished through executive order.[9] In short, a "knowledgeable White House official" implied, the president had the problem well in hand and the matter could be resolved without further congressional ado. The White House had launched a preemptive strike on intelligence reform.

Mail-Opening Hearings

While the committee seemed to drift as its members pondered the NSA imbroglio and reviewed the assassination report, the staff maintained a high level of frenzy in its research on COINTELPRO, covert actions abroad, CIA and FBI mail openings, and a host of other subjects scheduled for public hearings later in the year.

The FBI Task Force attorneys in charge of the mail-opening hearings had done a superlative job in marshaling the evidence. Everything seemed to be in good order except for one missing ingredient: the interest of committee members. "We've been over and over and over that," an irritated executive branch official told the *New York Times*.[10] Privately, several committee members were inclined to agree; at least, though, here was a topic they could settle on to air publicly.

The chairman's lack of interest was apparent on the opening day of the hearings. For the first time, rather than starting the questioning himself, he allowed the junior senators to begin. His attention wandered throughout the interrogation, and I could understand why. In the first place, he was locked in a wrestling grip with the Ford administration over an acceptable format for the NSA hearing. Pressure was building daily, and not just from the executive branch. The press was steadily nibbling away at the NSA story, revealing in piecemeal fashion the very facts the Ford administration had feared might be exposed through the Church committee hearings. Moreover, rumors buzzed around the auditorium that either the Pike committee or a House subcommittee chaired by Bella Abzug (D-NY) would go public with the NSA story any day.

The chairman had reason to worry, too, about new signs that his control over the committee might fragment further. The divisive NSA votes had been troubling enough; then, on 12 October, Senator Schweiker (who, with Gary Hart, chaired an ad hoc subcommittee established by Church to examine the adequacy of FBI and CIA investigations into the murder of John F. Kennedy) publicly called for an inquiry into the Warren Commission's findings on the president's death. Just the day before, the *Washington Post* had carried a long article on the CIA plot against Lumumba, with information that could have come only from the closed committee meeting with the CIA scientist who concocted the poison intended to kill the African leader. Together, these stories gave the impression, first, that the committee members (even the most junior ones) were now speaking out as individuals instead of through the chairman (as in the past), and, second, that the panel had sprung a serious leak. Would the whole assassination story, like the NSA findings, begin to dribble out before the report was published? This prospect cast a dark shadow across Church's countenance.

Nor did sharp criticism of the Senate inquiry in the *Washington Post* cheer the chairman. The congressional hearings "have barely scratched the surface," concluded reporter George Lardner Jr.[11] In his view, the few public sessions held by the Church committee had been "sporadic . . . exasperating, tedious, and inadequate." These "hurried glimpses" had been "good enough for a headline but little more. None of these issues was explored in depth." Furthermore, the committee staff had exhibited "no great detective work . . . or investigative ability" that Lardner could discern.

These conclusions were painful to most staffers, and even to the thicker-skinned, more experienced senators. For Church, flogged by dissension within his committee and vituperation from the executive branch, this salt stung all the more. So he sat at the mail-opening hearings with more on his mind than the art of steaming open envelopes.

The witnesses on mail opening included Richard Helms, back again from Teheran and as vague as usual. He told the committee that he was unable to remember whether the four presidents had been told about the mail-opening program during its two decades of operation, but he "thought" he had told Lyndon Johnson. Various postmasters general also either had amnesia on the subject or said they had never been told about the operation. Helms declared that he had informed Attorney General Mitchell, but Mitchell responded that Helms had told him only about a surveillance program involving the examination of the outside of envelopes (a legal activity often referred to as "mail cover"). The committee had reentered the wilderness of mirrors.[12]

At lunch, I talked about the mail openings with an experienced consultant working with the committee. "Well, in the 1950s anyone writing letters to the Soviet Union couldn't be all that good," he replied.

Perhaps so, but certainly the procedures had been all wrong. If the program had been so necessary and proper, the attorneys general and the presidents should have known about it and approved it more formally, in writing; otherwise, control became so much sand slipping through the fingers of those placed in positions of accountability.

I wondered if the elusiveness of authority we had seen in the assassination plots and the subjects of our public hearings would extend to CIA covert actions abroad—the committee's next focus.

9

Bombarded

Once the senators were seated on 23 October, William Colby and his aides were ushered into S407 by our security personnel. Finally, the committee would begin its cross-examination of CIA officials on the subject of covert action other than the assassination plots—the form of secret "intervention" that had occupied our attention for many months.

In 1947, a directive passed at the first meeting of the then newly created National Security Council authorized the CIA to engage in covert action in order to diminish and discredit the influence of international communism. As Henry Kissinger once described the rationale, "We need an intelligence community that, in certain complicated situations, can defend the American national interest in the gray areas where military operations are not suitable and diplomacy cannot operate."[1]

The Quiet Option

While the range of activities falling under the heading of covert action (CA) is wide, four categories have been predominant: election support; propaganda; paramilitary (that is, warlike) operations; and support for various anticommunist organizations.[2] Probably the greatest controversy has surrounded allegations regarding CIA paramilitary (PM) operations. The Agency's most publicized disaster—the Bay of Pigs—had been a PM CA, and charges had been leveled against the CIA for conducting other "secret wars" around the world, including a protracted intervention in Laos.[3] PM operations may include financial support for insurgents, the dispatch of "advisers" to training fields and battlegrounds, and the supply of weapons and ammunition.

Colby started with a history lesson, tracing the origins of CA back to the early days of the American Revolution. "Benjamin Franklin established the first covert proprietary, which was called the Hortalez Company," he began—and was abruptly interrupted by Senator Tower.

"The Hortalez Company was actually formed by the French government. It was a cover-up of the French activity. And it was first established by one Beaumarchais, who was the librettist of the *Barber of Seville*." Tower said all this so quickly and assuredly that his colleagues spontaneously gave him a round of applause (an unusual accolade on Capitol Hill).

Slightly embarrassed by this correction of his statement, Colby stammered and then complimented the former political science professor on his memory. The CIA director continued his presentation, looking at Tower occasionally to see if further amendments were forthcoming. Tower rested quietly in his chair, his fingers forming a teepee below his chin.

"When does the CIA decide to resort to covert actions?" Church asked, after the formal statement.

Colby had a rough checklist of procedures that he said the Agency considered before turning to this so-called quiet option. The situation had to be sufficiently important to the interests of the United States that extraordinary measures became acceptable. The risk of exposure had to be reasonably low. The cost, in terms of money and manpower, had to be within reason. Above all, the consequences of exposure, should it occur, could not be so politically dire as to cause grave damage to our interests. If the Agency, the 40 Committee, or the president had serious reservations on the grounds of any of these criteria, said Colby, the CA proposal would be turned down.

Senator Church's expression during Colby's discourse revealed skepticism. Finally, he could contain himself no longer. "The kind of intervention you are discussing has destroyed the moral leadership of our country throughout the world," he said. "Resistance, hostility, and hatred toward the United States— much of it stems from our covert actions. It has been 'counterproductive,' in that favorite Washington term." Church argued in favor of overt, not covert, assistance overseas on behalf of groups and ideals compatible with our own beliefs. "In the 1840s and 1850s we openly supported resistance movements in Latin America," he said.

"Our overt aid is frequently misused by the government we give it to," responded Colby. "And giving aid to governments doesn't reach to the activities beneath the governments. Moreover, Mr. Chairman, not all of these covert activities are exposed by any means."

"The only times when a covert action might be in order," continued Church, "are in a national emergency or in cases where intervention is clearly in tune with our traditional principles, as was true with our overt and covert aid to our allies in Western Europe following World War II." The chairman did not oppose CA per se, but rather its excessive and indiscriminate use.

"What we are really talking about here," Colby said, "is policy, not covert action." It was a fair point. Since the middle of the Vietnam War, Church had opposed executive branch policies that permitted or even encouraged American intervention abroad. CA was just one form—the most invisible—of such intervention. If Church could persuade presidents and their aides to adopt a more noninterventionist stance, then a decline in CA presumably would follow, but as long as our government aimed to mold events abroad, CA would remain one arrow in its quiver. For Church to attack CA missed the point, Colby implied, because its use flowed from broad policies set by several administrations.

After this hearing, the air in the staff offices was abuzz once more with talk of public hearings on the National Security Agency, stirred by a fresh spate of newspaper stories carrying allegations of NSA spying on American citizens. Feeding this interest were hearings in the House held by Congresswoman Abzug. Witnesses before her subcommittee testified that the NSA was obtaining cable traffic from major American communications corporations—precisely the "top secret" information (Operation Shamrock) the administration had been urging the Church committee to suppress. Meanwhile, the results of months of research on the NSA compiled by our committee in preparation for hearings lay dormant in thick briefing books, awaiting a decision from the senators. The staff of the Military Intelligence Task Force was in anguish.

Spurred by the bumper crop of revelations in the press (plus internal pressures from the staff), Senator Church decided to confront the committee again with a proposal for public hearings on the NSA. Colby was scheduled to visit the committee on 28 October for a second executive session on CA; Church would raise the subject of NSA hearings following the Colby interrogation.

On 28 October, Colby arrived again at S407 and spent the next two hours describing the efforts of the CIA, during the Nixon administration, to undercut the Allende regime in Chile. His testimony was a startling story of the use of bribery, propaganda, and the secret organization of groups to oppose the Allende regime. "Covert action is most successful," said Colby, "when you want to help someone who wants the help and doesn't have the means to succeed without it." Political factions of the right and the center in Chile wanted and needed the help; American corporations with investments in the country, a CIA CA bureaucracy eager to use its talents, and an administration fearful of another Cuba-like communist beachhead in Latin America were happy to provide it.[4] Once more, a phobia about communism seemed to lie at the heart of our compulsion to interfere in the political processes of supposedly sovereign states—even democracies. Concluding his remarks, Colby urged the committee not to hold public hearings on CA in Chile.

When the CIA director had left the room, the committee members turned toward Church. "Before we vote on public hearings on Chile," Church said, "we need to find out whether the executive branch will send witnesses if we do." Staff conjecture on Capitol Hill was that Kissinger—who appeared to have been a key figure in the anti-Allende schemes—would refuse to testify publicly on the question of CA. The committee could schedule a hearing and invite the central witnesses, but what if they refused to come? The committee could serve subpoenas, but what if they were ignored? The committee could introduce a motion of contempt on the floor of the Senate, but what if the chamber refused to vote against the popular secretary of state?

"But there is a decision we ought to make right now," Church went on, "and that is whether to hold public hearings on the National Security Agency. As you know, I believe we should, and I hope this committee will approve these hearings. I see no good reason why we can't have an open session tomorrow morning." The NSA debate was on again.

Church forcefully presented the arguments the staff had reviewed with him that morning; as suspected, a hearing on Operation Shamrock continued to draw strong opposition from committee members, with a majority still unprepared to approve. The senators, however, did accept Church's request for a carefully controlled review of the NSA watch list—although Baker thought the committee was still inadequately prepared. (Tower and Goldwater, the chief opponents of NSA public hearings, were absent from the meeting, though Goldwater had left a proxy with Baker to be cast against any sort of NSA hearing.) The discussion made it clear that a majority of those present favored having the NSA director read a statement on the watch list in public session the next day; neither the chairman nor Baker requested a formal vote. Rather than push the Shamrock issue to the breaking point at this meeting, Church settled for half a loaf.

Minaret and Shamrock

When I entered the caucus room with Church and Schwarz the next morning, a large crowd awaited the beginning of the NSA hearing. In his opening remarks, Church emphasized that the committee had proceeded cautiously: "Once the decision was made to hold public hearings on the NSA, the committee worked diligently with the agency to draw legitimate boundaries for the public discussion that will preserve the technical secrets of NSA and also allow a thorough airing of agency practices affecting American citizens."

I glanced over at senators Tower and Goldwater sitting to Church's left along the lengthy hearing table. Tower smoked his cigarette and stared with a pained expression at the green baize surface before him. Goldwater scowled as he watched Church.

"The discussions that will be held this morning," continued Church, "are efforts to identify, publicly, certain activities undertaken by the NSA that are of questionable propriety and dubious legality." Like the CIA and the IRS, the NSA had a watch list of over fifteen hundred American names. From 1967 to 1973, the communications of these individuals over international facilities were intercepted, analyzed, and distributed to the CIA, the FBI, and other intelligence agencies. While some of the individuals on the list, Church noted, might have posed a legitimate threat to order, their constitutional rights were inadequately considered. He reminded the audience that the NSA had been involved in the Huston Plan, an "illustration of how the NSA could be turned inward and against our own people."

Church asked Tower whether he wished to make an opening statement. "From the very beginning, I have opposed the concept of public hearings on the activities of the NSA," said Tower. The technology of this agency was "the most fragile weapon in our arsenal"—much too sensitive for public discussion. Moreover, the NSA was "the wrong target." The committee should have been focusing on the policy level: "It is more important to know why names were placed on a watch list than to know what the NSA did after being ordered to do so." Raising his voice and staring out into the crowd over his half-glasses, the vice chairman said, "There comes a point when the people's right to know must of necessity be subordinated to the people's right to be secure."

At the witness table, directly opposite Church and Tower, sat General Lew Allen with his chief aide, Bensen Buffham. Reading from a prepared statement, Allen told the committee that between 1966 and 1973, the NSA (in Operation Minaret) had intercepted the messages of 1,680 citizens and groups on behalf of six government agencies: the CIA, the FBI, the Secret Service, the DIA, army intelligence, and the old Bureau of Narcotics and Dangerous Drugs. He admitted that the NSA had failed to obtain court orders to authorize the electronic surveillance and had never received the explicit approval of incumbent presidents or attorneys general—though Allen's predecessor, Admiral Gayler, apparently had briefed attorneys general John Mitchell and Richard G. Kleindienst, as well as the secretary of defense, Melvin Laird, on the operation. Finally, on 1 October 1973, soon after becoming director, Allen received an order from the new attorney general, Elliot L. Richardson, to stop the Minaret program. Allen noted that intelligence from Minaret had helped the FBI avert a major terrorist plot in an American city and had led to the interdiction of several major narcotics shipments into the United States.

As Allen's responses to cautious questioning indicated, the technology of his agency was awesome; its machines had the capacity to grasp messages out of the ether, without the use of bugs or taps. Allen stressed, though, that the NSA had never conducted surveillance on strictly domestic United States communications; all of its intercepts had involved transmissions in which at least one terminal was on foreign soil.

During the questioning, Senator Mondale observed that one of the NSA intercepts was simply an invitation from a "peaceful" antiwar activist to a foreign singer, asking for a financial contribution to the anti–Vietnam War movement. The effect of this kind of spying, said Mondale, was to "discourage political dissent in this country."

Mondale, who lately had upstaged Senator Church during public hearings with a blend of incisive questioning and humor, asked Buffham what effect the Huston Plan would have had on Minaret. The deputy director replied that the watch list would probably have been increased.

"Were you concerned about its legality?" asked Mondale.

"That particular aspect didn't enter into the discussions," said Buffham, with a look of embarrassment.

Rather than asking questions, Senator Goldwater took his allotted time (each senator was allowed ten minutes in the first round) to state his opposition to the hearing. Any discussion of "classified information" was, in his view, a violation of Senate rules. Tower's wry sense of humor softened the tension only slightly.

> *Goldwater.* I just want to protect you and all of us.
> *Church.* All right, fine. Thank you, Senator Goldwater. I really appreciate that.
> *Tower.* I must say, Mr. Chairman, I am very touched by Senator Goldwater's concern for your safety.
> *Church.* I am, too, Senator.

Church excused Allen and Buffham, and said, "Now we have another matter." This was it: back to the debate over Shamrock hearings—only now in a crowded public forum.

Goldwater immediately objected to a Shamrock hearing, once again resting his case on his interpretation of the Senate rules. He believed that only the Senate as a whole could vote upon whether or not a committee could disclose classified materials in a public hearing. Church argued, however, that Senate Resolution 21 "gives the committee the power to pass such rules as it may deem necessary on disclosure."

The chairman explained to the public why the arguments against a Shamrock open hearing were insubstantial. These arguments said, first, that the disclosure of the identities of the companies would make other corporations hesitant in the future to cooperate with the intelligence community; and second, that disclosure would embarrass the three companies that had aided the government in the Shamrock program. In rebuttal, Senator Church observed, first, that corporations indeed should be hesitant to comply with government requests—at least long enough to assure themselves that such requests were lawful and ethical; that "fairness to the companies themselves requires that the facts be fully and fairly stated."

Moreover, the chairman continued, Shamrock deserved public scrutiny because it had perhaps violated Section 605 of the Federal Communications Act (protecting privacy) and the Fourth Amendment to the Constitution. Hearings would also assist public judgment on the need for an NSA legislative charter (instead of reliance solely upon executive orders), and they would encourage American companies in the future to be more circumspect about their relations with intelligence agencies. Finally, "the program" (Church never used the word Shamrock, since at the time it was still classified) involved neither ongoing activities nor technological secrets.

Tower remained unpersuaded. He agreed with Goldwater that no committee could disclose classified information under its own authority (the same question that had arisen with respect to the release of the assassination report). He read from an NSA document that said the Shamrock report written by the Church committee staff contained "secret" information. In the course of his reading, ironically, Tower spoke the forbidden word Shamrock; staff members looked at one another with mixed expressions of shock and amusement.

"President Truman decided that this matter should be kept secret," said Tower. "President Ford has personally and specifically requested of the committee that it be kept secret." He urged the committee to discuss the question further in a closed afternoon session.

Mondale came partially to Church's defense. He rejected the notion that the executive branch should govern what the committee decided to release to the public. "I don't think we can accept that definition for a moment," he said. "If we do, I think we are no longer a coequal branch of government." He was careful, however, to avoid the question of whether the committee could release classified information without first seeking permission from the full Senate.

Baker spoke up. He thought the Senate rules forbade unilateral committee action in this regard (the line of reasoning he had supported with regard to the assassination report). He said, too, that although he favored public hearings on everything—even assassination—more preparation was necessary on Shamrock.

Church's temper flared momentarily. "I thank the senator," he said in the accepted style of restrained Senate sarcasm. "I know his position on public hearings; but frequently, in executive session, he has voted against them on grounds that we were not adequately prepared."

With narrowing eyes, Baker denied opposing public hearings during the committee's closed meetings; instead, he said, he had on occasion "voted against declassifying or proceeding with a particular piece of information."

Senator Morgan also expressed reservations about a Shamrock hearing: President Truman "long, long ago was involved in this and gave his word" not to disclose the names of the corporations involved; therefore, Morgan was "awfully reluctant to go against the word of the president of the United States."

Once more it was obvious that this debate would remain unresolved. Lunch time had arrived. Church said the committee would take up the matter again in a closed meeting that afternoon.

The parallels between this debate on Shamrock and the debate on release of the assassination report (still in limbo) were close. Church had tried to persuade the committee to release the assassination report under its own authority and had lost; his colleagues wanted a full Senate review. Now he had argued a similar case with Shamrock. I wondered if the chairman would lose again.

The afternoon meeting in S407 produced echoes of the morning debate, reinforced with quotes and examples from classified documents. Church and Mondale led the charge in favor of Shamrock hearings, with the chairman stressing an "openness in a democracy" theme and Mondale emphasizing the prerogatives of Congress as a "coequal branch" to hold hearings on whatever it wished despite objections from the executive branch.

The leading voices of opposition were, as before, Tower ("It's too sensitive"), Baker ("We need more information"), Goldwater ("The Senate rules don't allow a committee to make a decision like this"), and—the lone Democrat—Morgan ("We should not undermine trust in the office of the president"). The debate soon bogged down in a parliamentary swamp; Goldwater and Baker interpreted the Senate rules differently from Church. As if Shamrock had become the stone of Sisyphus, the issue rolled back down the hill to await a clarification of the rules from the Senate parliamentarian. At least, though, Church obtained the permission of the committee to send the staff report on Shamrock directly by messenger to General Allen, requesting his judgment on its accuracy.

On Halloween Day, I accompanied Church to Room 224 in the Russell Building, the Armed Services Committee hearing room we had borrowed for the day to hear Colby's third installment on CA. This time the topic was PM operations.

Colby justified the PM option with three rationales: the commander in chief clause of the Constitution permitted presidential use of this option; the CIA kept the proper congressional committees informed of its use; and the appropriations committees of Congress legitimized the use of PM operations by funding the requisite arms and training programs. As in so many matters in which the CIA was culpable, Colby was right: some responsibility flowed back to Congress—and (though Colby did not say this) to its slack oversight of intelligence policy.

Valley

At the beginning of November, the White House dropped a couple of bombshells on the congressional inquiries. First, President Ford fired William Colby and Secretary of Defense Schlesinger in a major shuffling of national security officials (dubbed the "Saturday Massacre" by the press). Kissinger was asked to relinquish his position as national security adviser, retaining only the secretary of state slot. Early reports indicated that George Bush, chief of the American liaison mission in Peking, would replace Colby, and Donald H. Rumsfeld, White House chief of staff, would become the new secretary of defense.

The second bomb fell directly on the Church committee in the form of a letter from the president dated 31 October 1975. The strongly worded message went to each member of the committee, urging that the assassination report be kept secret. With three and a half pages of details, President Ford exhorted the committee members to take into account the grave harm publication would inflict upon national security.

"I am astonished that President Ford wants to suppress the committee's report on assassination and keep it concealed from the American people," responded Church in a statement to the press. "They have a right to know what their government has done." Stating that he would adamantly oppose Ford's request at the next committee meeting, Church noted that "the president himself asked the committee to investigate these charges. For months he has known of the committee's intent to publish its findings in the form of a special report."

On 3 November, a knot of reporters stood waiting in front of S407. CBS correspondent Daniel Schorr stopped Church when he arrived and asked for his views about the firing of Colby. As Church stood before several microphones, he trembled with anger. "There is no question in my mind but that concealment is the new order of the day," he said, his voice quavering. "Hiding evil is the trademark of a totalitarian government."

"I've never seen you so upset," said Schorr. No doubt Church's disposition had been further soured by a call on the Senate floor, in a speech by Goldwater, to end the investigation. "I can attest to the fact that we are turning up no new material that could assist anyone in drafting legislation for a more ethical intelligence operation," Goldwater had said.[5] (Three of his GOP colleagues on the committee—Baker, Mathias, and Schweiker—all disagreed with Goldwater at a subsequent press conference. "Once you get on that tiger," said Baker, "you need to ride it out.")

Inside the committee room, Church calmed down, and the members turned toward a review of last-minute changes in the draft of the assassination report. When the draft had been accepted unanimously, Church turned to the next item on the agenda for that day: the president's letter asking the committee to keep the assassination report bottled up. For what seemed a millennium, the members debated the meaning of various Senate and committee rules regarding the release of classified information. Even Senator Mathias, who had supported the assassination inquiry all along, was chary about the panel's prerogatives in this area.

"We must avoid becoming a rogue committee," Mathias said, only half joking.

"What we have here are some rogue rules," offered Schweiker with his boyish grin.

Church listened for a while longer, then suddenly tossed a document on the bench before him in a gesture of disgust. "I will have to reconsider my chairmanship of this committee," he said.

A silence fell over the room. No one had seen Church so utterly dejected. The committee had experienced many frustrating moments during the course of this inquiry, but at 4 o'clock on 3 November 3 1975, the chairman seemed to have hit rock bottom. The implication was clear: if the committee bowed to the president and kept the assassination findings secret, the chairman would resign.

The tense silence lasted several minutes, broken finally by the slow and soothing voice of the Kentucky senator, "Dee" Huddleston. He spoke eloquently of the hard work the committee had put into the report, the leadership and dedication of the chairman, and the right of the American people to know the facts about assassination plots. Each of the Democratic senators followed suit with briefer supporting expressions in favor of releasing the report. Even Morgan said he would endorse disclosure, though he remained concerned about the various and contradictory interpretations of the Senate rules.

As his party colleagues came to his aid, Church's spirits began to lift. He called for a vote to deliver the five-hundred-page report to the Senate before Thanksgiving, along with a request that it be released to the public. The committee would ask the Senate to convene in a rare secret session to vote on the release—a key concession made by Church to Baker and others who all along had disputed the committee's authority to release the document. The roll was called, and everyone voted "aye" with the exception of Tower, who abstained by answering "present."

The chairman, at long last, had gotten a committee decision on the release of the assassination report. Only one obstacle remained: a debate before the full Senate. Before adjourning, the committee—in another rebuff to the president—gave a tentative green light to Church (by a vote of seven to three, with Tower, Goldwater, and Baker opposed, and Philip Hart still ill and absent) to issue the Shamrock report, provided that he first made sure the Senate rules did not forbid the release. Why Shamrock but not the assassination report could be disclosed by the committee alone was a sleeping dog Church let lie.

The day had been one of decision, and Church looked pleased as he left the room. In one afternoon he had gone from the depths of the valley to high up the mountainside.

The newspapers the next day confirmed the replacement of Colby with Bush and Schlesinger with Rumsfeld. According to one experienced reporter, Colby had been ousted for "not doing a good job containing the congressional investigations"; George Bush, a new face, "would be able to go to Congress and ask for a grace period before pressing their investigations further."[6]

For Church, these personnel changes—called by some "the Halloween Massacre"—were part of an ominous pattern. "First," he told reporters, "came the very determined administration effort to prevent any revelations concerning NSA, their stonewalling of public hearings. Then came the president's letter. Now comes the firing of Colby, Mr. Schlesinger, and the general belief that Secretary Kissinger is behind these latest developments." He believed that "clearly a pattern has emerged now to try and disrupt this investigation." The chairman's face hardened. "As far as I'm concerned, it won't be disrupted."

10

Orwellian Nightmares

Senator Church turned to the main issue before the committee on 5 November. "Bill," he said to the staff director, "please read the decision of the parliamentarian concerning Shamrock."

Miller reported that no Senate rules prohibited the committee from presenting a statement on Shamrock at a hearing scheduled for the next day. This declaration from the office of the Senate parliamentarian crushed the central argument upon which Tower, Goldwater, and Baker had rested their case; the three men sat silent. So the committee would have its hearing on Operation Shamrock—though it would be carefully focused, with Church reading the report that General Allen had reviewed.

The group turned next to the assassination report to tie up loose ends before the review by a secret session of the Senate. Morgan expressed his reservations once more about public disclosure of the report; sitting near Church, I sensed the chairman's struggle to hold back anger. Morgan did not push his point, though, and the committee turned to the mechanics of final preparations.

Arriving back at the committee offices, I found a note on my desk: "Call Church." I telephoned the chairman and he said he wanted to review the draft of a speech I was preparing for him on the CIA. I went to his main office in the Russell Building. It was a folksy Idaho-oriented office, replete with a mountain scene on the walls and a largely rural, homegrown staff. Church joined me on his wide couch and we talked about the speech.

The nomination of George Bush to succeed Colby disturbed him, and he wanted to wind up the speech by opposing the nomination. I was sorry to hear this. The speech was designed to be a balanced critique of the Agency's performance as an intelligence gatherer; now it would become political. I thought Bush ought to be the subject of separate remarks. But I was the speechwriter, not the speech giver, and was charged with grafting on a new ending that stated Church's opposition to the Bush nomination. He hoped to influence Senate opinion on the nomination on the eve of Armed Services Committee hearings to confirm Bush.

I rapidly jotted down notes as Church discussed the lines he would like to take against the nomination. "Once they used to give former national party chairmen [as Bush had been under President Nixon] postmaster generalships—the most political and least sensitive jobs—in government," he said. "Now they have given this former party chairman the most sensitive and least political agency." Church wanted me to stress how Bush "might compromise the independence of the CIA—the agency could be politicized."

Within a day or two, the Colby–Bush affair took a peculiar turn. Just dismissed by President Ford, Colby was soon asked by him to stay on until Bush had been confirmed—a process that could take months. Although packed and ready to depart CIA headquarters, Colby gallantly agreed. Washington speculation settled on the theory that, in a rash moment, Ford had fired Colby without considering the fact that Bush could not simply pack his suitcase and show up the next day. China was far away; several diplomatic matters had to be tied up first; and, of course, Bush had to be confirmed by the Senate. When the White House staff explained these fine points to Ford, he had to go back to Colby—somewhat sheepishly, one imagines—and ask him to remain temporarily.

"The committee will please come to order," said Church to the press and the public in the caucus room on the morning of the Shamrock hearings. He explained that the committee had voted to release its statement on Shamrock, and then he read the report into the record. It outlined the cooperation between the NSA and the communications companies that allowed the Agency to read international telegrams from Americans for almost thirty years, from 1947 to 15 May 1975 (that is, just when Congress appeared ready to investigate the program). At first the telegram messages were sorted out by hand, according to names on the NSA watch list; then, in the 1960s, advanced technology made the task simpler. As Church explained:

> RCA, Global, and ITT World Communications began to store their international paid message traffic on magnetic tapes, and these were turned over to NSA. Thereafter, the telegrams were selected in precisely the same way in which NSA selects its information from other sources. This meant, for example, that telegrams to or from, or even mentioning, US citizens whose names appeared on the watch list in the late sixties and early seventies would have been sent to NSA analysts, and many would subsequently be disseminated to other agencies.

When Church finished the Shamrock statement, Tower spoke: "I must state my firm opposition to this unilateral release of classified information."

Seconding this view, Goldwater said: "The fact that the other body, the House, seems to be irresponsible in its treatment of the subject is no reason, in my opinion, for the Senate to try to use that as an excuse for disseminating secret material."

Joining in the fracas were Huddleston, Gary Hart, Mathias, and Schweiker, all speaking with Church in favor of the Shamrock disclosure.

"I do not see how you can pass legislation in a vacuum," said Huddleston. "I believe that there has to be a certain amount of knowledge made available to the public and made available to the Congress before reasonable and meaningful legislation can be processed."

"I happened to decide this issue on the basis that the public's right to know outweighs any danger that might exist to the government," said the peppery Schweiker, adding that "silence is consent."

Goldwater suggested that the senators were no more holy than the Shamrock participants.

Goldwater. I guess a lot of us are guilty of operations like this because many of us censored letters during World War II, reading those letters. So I think I would have to join the guilty as you would have to, also.

Church. I think that we should recognize the distinction between war and peace. It poses the question whether this country in peacetime wants to live always under the customs of war. This was a peacetime operation.

Mathias. The law provided—in fact, the law compelled us to read those letters to make the appropriate changes that were required, and it is the law that I think is important here. I think that the law does not extend to the activities of the NSA. The law must be made to extend to the NSA.

Tower. I think that we cannot draw this in strict terms of war and peace, in terms of whether or not the United States is actually at war. We are in effect in a war of sorts. That is a war of the preservation of the climate in this world where national integrity will be respected.

The lines had been drawn. Tower and Goldwater stood and departed (Baker never appeared) as Church turned to Attorney General Levi, the morning's witness, for his statement.

As one might have expected from the former dean of the University of Chicago School of Law, Levi gave a masterful presentation on the Fourth Amendment. He returned in the afternoon to answer questions. The exchange resembled a law school seminar and illuminated the views of the Justice Department in this tangled legal thicket. The attorney general seemed to believe that when it came to electronic surveillance, the executive branch could work out appropriate Fourth Amendment protections. In contrast, Professor Philip B. Heymann of the Harvard Law School, the next witness, placed the burden on Congress "to pass a statute that sets forth standards and then requires a warrant from a court," with monitoring by the courts or a legislative oversight committee.

Cheered by having Shamrock off his chest and by these spirited legal exchanges, Church walked with a new spring in his step after the hearing. As we strode down the corridors toward his car, I told him about the voluminous information the staff had assembled for subsequent hearings and asked him how he wished to absorb this material: through a series of oral briefings from Miller, Schwarz, and other key staffers? from summaries of the huge briefing books? the full briefing books themselves? some combination?

"Just walk me over to the hearings, and we can discuss the issues on the way," he said. "That's the best."

I was flabbergasted by this response. All the weeks that were poured into the production of these briefing books, and the chairman simply wanted a quick review as he walked to each hearing! I searched his face for a hint of humor. None could be found; he was serious. The two or three snippets of information that could be imparted in a peripatetic briefing would become, presumably, concise cues for the direction of the hearing. I thought of Stephen Spender's remark about the novelist Henry James; the committee staff, like James, had become a "great lonely giant mountain giving birth to a brood of mice."

Ups and Downs

"Beautiful rotunda, isn't it?" said Church the next day as he walked briskly through the main corridor of the Capitol. The vast dome three hundred feet above us was breathtaking in its splendor, but at the moment David Aaron and I were out of breath for another reason—the chairman was racing along at a near jog. He was headed for the next committee meeting with a buoyancy I had not seen for weeks.

The meeting was a closed session on the use of secret agents (as opposed to machines, such as sensors, radio scanners, and reconnaissance planes) to gather intelligence—usually referred to in the trade as "human intelligence" or, simply, "humint." With Church's request in mind ("Just walk me to the hearing"), I had asked Aaron to come along, since he had been studying this subject. The "briefing" turned out to be about what I expected: between standing in elevators, striding down hallways, sitting in the Senate subway car, and admiring the rotunda—all crowded by tourists and other noncommittee people—Aaron had about eight minutes to convey, in hushed tones, some information about the hearing as we rushed along toward S407.

Inside the hearing room, Church listened with uneven attention as a CIA official presented a series of charts. They illustrated persuasively that technical collection systems alone were insufficient to solve our intelligence problems. In the age of technology, the human spy remained of great importance; he could, among other things, help gauge enemy motivations.

Church departed within the hour. As we neared his Russell Building office, he shook his head in disgust: "When will this country stop being so uptight about the world? The foundations of the Republic will not crumble away if someone we don't like takes over in Chad."

Inside Church's office I was introduced to Jeff Shields. Later I asked a friend on the staff about this new face. "Haven't you heard?" he answered. "Shields is supposed to be helping put together a presidential campaign."

At lunch time I happened to come across Shields again, waiting for the light to change at a crosswalk by the Dirksen Building. A cold wind was blowing hard, and his longish hair danced across his forehead. He was in his early thirties and had a handsome, boyish face.

"How's the campaign?" I asked with a wink.

"The important thing is to get the investigation over with and send Church out into the primaries," he replied, as the wind helped blow us across the street. "When do you think you'll be through?"

It was a question I would hear almost weekly from Shields for three months, each time a little more frantically. I shrugged my shoulders and smiled. Church had been invited to appear on the *Face the Nation* television show the next Sunday (9 November), and as we parted, Shields reminded me that I was among a small group of staffers expected to meet with Church at 3 o'clock to help him prepare for the program.

At that hour, four staff aides gathered in Church's Russell office: Shields, myself, Bill Hall (a press aide), and Jerry Levinson (Church's top aide on the Multinational Subcommittee). The objective was to simulate a national news interview, with each of us posing as reporters. We hammered away at Church with the toughest and most likely questions we thought he would be asked on television. If someone didn't like his response, we'd stop and make suggestions for improvement. My job was to cover the investigation; others posed more political questions. It was a rehearsal for Church, giving him a chance to be tested on the issues beforehand in a format similar to the one he would face Sunday.

The Bush nomination was apt to receive attention on the show, since the lines had been quickly drawn on the issue, and camps on both sides were already exchanging volleys. George Herbert Walker Bush was far from an ideal foe. If we had to join in a confirmation fight, why couldn't it be against someone mean, venal, and repugnant? Instead, here was a former war hero, baseball star, and Big Man On Campus at Yale, a rich, handsome, well-connected former member of Congress (R-TX) who was hard not to like, someone who exuded charm and class with the ease of a Cary Grant. And to top things off, his father (Prescott Bush) had served in the US Senate with honor, representing Connecticut.

George Bush had faced some setbacks in his aristocratic life, losing two bids for a Senate seat from Texas, but not enough to dampen his cheerful disposition and wide popularity in Washington. His experience for the CIA directorship, however, seemed minimal. His foreign policy experience was limited to a stint as ambassador to the United Nations and then chief of the American liaison office in Peking. But President Ford, by all accounts, was less interested in specific qualifications than in establishing his own team.

A team player Bush surely was, serving as chairman of the Republican National Committee during the GOP's darkest hour—trying as best he could (all too hard, some critics suggested) to put the best possible face on the Watergate situation. "These are my guys," said the president proudly as the names Rumsfeld and Bush were announced for the new appointments. Loyalty was perhaps a qualification for the job more comforting to Ford than Colby's expertise. And not only might Bush be more protective of the White House's (and Kissinger's) interests than Colby, but he might be able—with his political ties and great charm—to woo Congress into a less belligerent mood. Nothing like placing a former member of Congress at an agency's helm to smooth rough waters with the legislative branch. As a *Washington Star* headline put it: CIA NEEDS BUSH'S PR TALENT. However correct Church's principle might be against placing a political person in charge of the CIA, the defeat of Bush would be difficult.

On Sunday, when CBS correspondent George Herman fired the first question at Church, it was indeed about George Bush: Would Church exclude anyone with political experience from heading the CIA in the future?

"I think that whoever is chosen should be one who has demonstrated a capacity for independence," replied Church, "who has shown that he can stand up to the many pressures, whether they come from the Pentagon or from the White House." He suggested Elliot Richardson, who resigned as attorney general during the Watergate crisis, as an example. In contrast, said Church, "a man whose background is as partisan as a past chairman of the Republican Party does serious damage to the agency and its intended purposes."

Two other topics dominated the news show discussion: the assassination report and the approaching presidential election. The Ford administration claimed that publication of the assassination report would threaten United States relations with Iran, observed Daniel Schorr (apparently because Richard Helms, our ambassador there, was implicated in the murder plots described in the document). This drew an emotional response, sending Church forward in his chair: "What are we talking about here? Agencies of the government that are licensed to undertake murder. . . . Is the president of the United States going to be a glorified godfather?" Settling back, he said more quietly: "There are more important questions than who's to be the ambassador to Iran, for goodness sake."

Turning to the second topic, Herman asked a tough question. If Church wanted to disqualify Bush as CIA director on political grounds, then "should the investigation of the CIA and other intelligence agencies be headed by a man whose aides say he is 80 percent certain to enter politics and run for the presidency?"[1]

Church seemed to blanch, then replied that he had "done everything a man can do" to keep himself and the committee out of presidential politics. "I've said it again and again," he stressed, "that until the active investigation has ended, which will come sometime in December, I will not be a candidate."

I smiled at the phrase "active investigation." Church used to say "until the investigation has ended"; now an important modifier had been added, allowing him to enter the campaign after the final public hearings but long before any windup meetings or the writing of the final report had been completed.

David Martin asked a follow-up question: "What if you came across a whole new area of wrongdoing suddenly? Would you be willing to extend your investigation into next year, possibly at the jeopardy of your presidential ambitions?"

"Of course," said Church.

I've always said this investigation was too important to jeopardize for politics. We've already extended the life of the committee six months in order to do a thorough and penetrating job of the whole assassination question. And if some other issue comes up, I suppose the evidence from the past would suggest that this is an honest answer when I say we would extend the life of the committee as long as necessary. But when this committee started, both the president and I agreed that we should try to get the job done as quickly as possible because a protracted investigation into this sensitive area would not be good for the country, and that's why I'm trying to get the job done by the end of the year and to get a final report in early next year.

Senator Church was not the only committee member to be spoken of as a presidential candidate that weekend. "Senator Mathias May Run in Primaries" announced the *Washington Post* on 9 November. Critical of what he perceived to be a drift to the political right by President Ford and the Republican Party, Mathias indicated he might begin a campaign in March to win the Massachusetts primary.[2]

On 10 November, I was disappointed to find in the *New York Times* a negative progress report on the Church committee, written by Seymour Hersh. He peppered his critique with several unflattering quotations from officials within the CIA and on the committee staff. From the CIA: "Frank Church was the first TV show to close this fall."[3] "The Senate had the staff but it got too bogged down in the assassinations." "The House goes after the arteries [basic questions like the accuracy of CIA intelligence], while the Senate goes after the capillaries [dart guns and shellfish toxin]." And from the staff: "The Committee has not been willing to hang tough and fight the Administration [on access to documents]; it's frittered away the psychological and moral leverage you journalists gave them [early this year]—when everyone was afraid of a cover-up." "The photographs of Church holding high the CIA dart gun [is the essence of the Church approach]. . . . There was a way to do the job, but it wouldn't have gotten headlines."

Others told Hersh that the committee was "manhandled" by the CIA; it never subpoenaed or threatened to subpoena documents,[4] and it "didn't go beyond what was reported by journalists."

In response to these criticisms, Church conceded that his investigation had failed to arouse intense public interest, but he insisted that it was premature to evaluate the committee before it had issued its findings. The chairman also sharply rejected as "groundless" the allegations that he had been a publicity hound. "The assassination matter would have been unprecedented box office," he observed in a telephone interview with Hersh. "It would have made the most sensational hearings held in the country." Church reminded Hersh that he had stood against public hearings on assassination "because I thought it would have caused damage" to the country. "It's just unconscionable," he concluded, "to turn around and say that the committee is headline-grabbing."

Miller was interviewed too, and in defense of the committee he made the point forcefully that by necessity most of its good work had taken place in closed sessions. "It takes a lot of maturity and strength to realize that the way you get to the gut issues is to handle them in executive session," he stated. "We're trying to put intelligence within the constitutional framework. That's the major work of the committee, and it won't be seen until February."

On 11 November, I walked with Church to the Senate floor. On the way he was stopped by reporters who quizzed him about his first major speech on intelligence, which he was about to give. Also, for the hundredth time, one correspondent wished to know if Church still stood by his "earlier assessments that the CIA acted like a rogue elephant."

Without noticeable annoyance, Church replied:

Of course. When the assassination report comes out, you will find cases where that is true; you will find other cases where it is not true. You never can draw one line and say that that particular line characterizes all the activities of the agency through all of the years of its existence. We are looking in the assassination report at a period that covers four administrations. We're looking at various cases, and the facts with respect to each case are not all identical. But you will find, as I said originally, much evidence in certain cases that would suggest that higher authority was not fully advised in a timely way of the activities that were going on.

The Senate floor was virtually deserted—as usual, except during a vote—for most senators were at work in committee or conducting legislative business in their offices. "Our objective has never been to wreck the intelligence agencies, but to reform them where necessary," Church began, with his deep, rich voice. "As the weeds are pruned from the garden, so the garden flourishes."

He was widely recognized as one of the three or four best orators in the Senate, and I could understand why. His enunciation was immaculate, and he spoke with conviction, rarely glancing at the paragraphs that he had read aloud to himself in his office often enough to know them almost by heart—an investment of time few senators were willing to make for a speech.

The analytic portion of the remarks centered on the quality of National Intelligence Estimates, or NIEs—a subject the Pike committee was exploring. An estimate is a paper that assesses the current situation in some part of the world, often including a forecast or "shrewd guess" as to what may happen. Coordinated by the CIA and drawing upon expertise throughout the intelligence community, these judgments and predictions form the building blocks of national security policy, laying out and often ranking a range of possible outcomes from events that may either threaten the United States or offer the nation some opportunity.

"The ingredients of sound estimates," noted Church, "are the same as those for good congressional investigations: reliable data, carefully weighed premises, meticulous analysis, complete impartiality, and good sense."

He presented a batting average for past NIEs. The CIA had made several mistakes over the years. One estimate had predicted that the Soviet Union would never attempt to place nuclear-tipped missiles in Cuba (as, of course, had happened during the missile crisis of 1962). Others wide of the mark included misreadings of the Soviet invasions of Hungary in 1956 and Czechoslovakia in 1968; an overestimate of increases in the Soviet intercontinental ballistic missile (ICBM) forces during the 1950s and 1960s; and the failure to anticipate the Arab–Israeli War in 1973. Church commended the Pike committee for its good work in examining recent inaccurate NIEs.

Seeking a balanced perspective, Church next pointed out a long list of CIA successes in the difficult realm of prediction. Militarily, in the previous twenty-five years, no important new Soviet weapons system, from the H-bomb to recent missiles, had appeared without first being heralded in advance by NIEs. Economically, the CIA had successfully tracked the flow of petrodollars and accurately analyzed many of the positions taken by the oil cartel. Politically, the Agency had prepared valuable biographic profiles on political officials throughout the world, "many of whom," Church said, "would otherwise remain strangers concealed within their closed societies."

He then began a transition toward an attack on the Bush nomination. "It is imperative that we preserve the independent, civilian estimates produced by the CIA" he said, "as a balance against estimates from the military services";

Church saw the latter as biased by "the most dour view on enemy threat assessments." The challenge was "not only a matter of standing up to the Pentagon," he continued. "We need a CIA that can resist all the partisan pressures which can be brought to bear by various groups inside and outside the government—especially pressures from the White House itself."

Then the ax fell:

> This is why the appointment of Ambassador George Bush is so ill-advised. It is one thing to choose an individual who may have had political experience, and quite another to choose someone whose principal political role has been that of chairman of the Republican National Committee. There is no need to eliminate from consideration an individual simply because he or she may have held public office. But the line must be drawn somewhere, and a man of Mr. Bush's prolonged involvement in partisan activities at the highest party level surely passes over that line.

Church said he remained undecided whether it was appropriate for him, as chairman of the intelligence investigation, to lead a fight against the confirmation of Bush, "but these are the reasons," he asserted, "why I will certainly vote against his nomination." He had flung down the gauntlet.

Despair at the Top

The committee had faced another frustrating subject at its 5 November meeting: how to approach public hearings on covert action in Chile—and especially what to do about Henry Kissinger. Only days before, the secretary of state had refused to discuss covert action in public before the Pike committee; nevertheless, some of our staff continued to argue that Kissinger had to be called—and subpoenaed if necessary—as a witness for our public hearing on Chile.

Church was adamantly opposed, on practical grounds. "If Kissinger refuses to testify in public—as every indication suggests he will—this committee has no way to enforce a subpoena," Church said. "We are not going to get a contempt vote against him in the Senate just because he refuses to testify on covert action in public." Church considered Kissinger too popular for a majority of senators to vote a contempt of Congress charge against him; besides, most members might well agree with the secretary that covert action was too sensitive a topic for public discussion.

"Let's avoid the needless pyrotechnics of the House committee," Church concluded.

I could see Church's point ("You don't win by losing," he observed to me later, emphasizing the improbability of winning a full-Senate vote against Kissinger to enforce a subpoena), but I also thought some staffers presented a good case to the contrary: Kissinger might be refusing to testify on Chile in public just to conceal his own involvement, and if he was responsible, didn't the American people deserve a public accounting? Why should Kissinger be allowed to hide behind veils of secrecy? The issue was still unresolved when the committee adjourned for the day, as was the question of which (if any) names of intelligence officers and agents should appear in the assassination report.

Church was in a foul mood as he, Schwarz, and I left the Capitol. It was raining, so we took the subway to the Russell Building, where the corridors were lined with colorful umbrellas opened and left to dry. A mail boy pushed his four-wheel cart hard with one foot and rode down the hallways, as if skateboarding through this gay obstacle course.

The rainbow colors seemed to do little to raise the chairman's spirits. He complained about the staff ("Too many people are dragging their feet") and the schedule ("We've *got* to speed things up!"). He wanted public television encouraged to bring their cameras back to our hearings. When we reached Church's office, he sat at his desk and asked gruffly how the schedule for subsequent hearings was shaping up. Schwarz told him that, unfortunately, there would be further delays; the investigative work on COINTELPRO and other cases was insufficiently developed yet.

Church clenched the arms of his chair. "Why do you do this to me?" he said, a mixture of anger and frustration in his voice. "No one listens to me. They get locked in, and they go ahead and do what they want. We'll *never* get all our work done. We've only got a month to go." Schwarz and I winced, stared at our shoes, and wished we were somewhere else.

"The assassination report is the only thing we've accomplished," Church concluded plaintively. "The rest of the staff has been spinning its wheels."

This indictment was patently unfair, born of despair and a detachment from the multitude of projects unrelated to assassination plots that had engaged the staff for several months. The next day I accompanied a group of FBI Task Force staffers to Church's office for a briefing about plans for a hearing on domestic intelligence abuses. Church took the opportunity to vent his spleen once more.

"The only public hearing we've been prepared for was on the shellfish toxin," he said scornfully, then looked at me and added, "and the Huston Plan." The last phrase was so obviously an afterthought that I drew little comfort from it. He ordered the staff to reduce the number of days planned for the FBI hearings, and urged us again to do whatever we could to bring public television coverage back to the proceedings.

Cynics viewed this last request as a further indication of presidential publicity seeking. A more charitable interpretation was that Church strongly believed reform would come only through public pressure, and public pressure would arise only if stimulated by extensive media coverage of the committee's findings. I was reasonably sure that elements of both perspectives entered into the chairman's calculations in an alloy only he could assay with any certainty. As for reducing the number of FBI public hearings, this would, in his opinion, lessen the tedium of excessive detail as well as hasten the committee toward the issue of covert action abroad. It was hardly a decision designed to inspire rapture in the hearts of those staffers sitting before him who had toiled for months on various FBI cases.

The next afternoon the committee met to discuss again the feasibility of a public hearing on covert action in Chile. Nerves were on edge, since word had it that Tower would attempt to dissuade the committee from this notion. Indeed, Tower did immediately argue against a public hearing on grounds that disclosure would prove embarrassing to the United States. Mondale countered with the view that the public had a right to know about the excesses of American foreign policy in this instance. The discussion was surprisingly brief, and when the roll was called, not a single vote was registered against the public hearing. Tower himself chose to abstain; Goldwater was absent—as was more and more often the case.

Other important matters remained, however, chief among them the question of what witnesses should be called—and, if necessary, subpoenaed. On this subject, emotions continued to run high. In a memorandum distributed to senior staffers, Bill Bader contended that Kissinger, Richard Nixon, Richard Helms, David Phillips (a recently retired CIA officer), and possibly William Colby should be given "a formal invitation this week, and if the response is that they will not appear, the Committee should then move to subpoena them."[5] Bader was aware of the possible consequences. "It should be appreciated, however, and fully understood," continued the memo, "that any refusal to honor the subpoena would put the Committee in the position of either acquiescing in this rebuff or initiating contempt proceedings."

Bader did not stand alone. In another memorandum to senior staffers, Aaron wrote:

I can understand the Chairman's reluctance to go the subpoena route and all the legal hassles that might entail. I do not believe we have to go that far in order for the Administration to take a hard look at its present position. On the other hand, I don't think that we should publicly eschew the possibility of a subpoena for the simple fact that this possibility is one that the Administration would probably like to avoid as well, and we shouldn't throw away any possible leverage we have to get them to favorably consider the possibility of participating in open hearings.

My bottom line on the question of Administration witnesses, CIA, perhaps Dr. Kissinger, is that without such witnesses the hearings may be either unpersuasive or worse, a dud.

We ought to think carefully about what our public posture is on Chile and the question of CIA and other current Administration witnesses. We will need a convincing rationale as to why we (a) did not call them, or (b) did not work hard to insure that they showed up.[6]

It was a warning that could not be easily ignored. Something had to be done to show that the committee had at least tried to have the majordomos in the Chilean case appear.

As was so often the outcome in controversial matters, the committee once more decided not to decide the ultimate question of subpoenas, but the members agreed without objection that Kissinger and the CIA would be invited to testify. (Nixon represented a more tangled problem, which was shelved.) Exactly who would be the witnesses remained uncertain, but at any rate, public hearings on covert action would be held.

The next day, 14 November, the Pike committee proved to be of a far firmer mind with respect to Kissinger. Charging the secretary of state with failure to turn over documents it had requested, the Pike panel issued three contempt of Congress citations against him that the committee fully intended to forward to the House for approval by the plenary membership.

"I profoundly regret," responded Kissinger, "that the Committee saw fit to cite in contempt a Secretary of State, raising serious questions all over the world [about] what this country is doing to itself and what the necessity is to torment ourselves like this month after month."[7]

On grounds of executive privilege, Kissinger had refused to surrender Department of State documents discussing covert action. As White House counsel Philip Buchan put it, Kissinger had the right to withhold these papers because "they do reveal to an unacceptable degree the consultation process involving advice to previous Presidents Kennedy, Johnson, and Nixon made to them directly or to a committee composed of their closest aides and advisers."[8] (In December, the Pike committee withdrew its contempt recommendation after Kissinger agreed to provide most of the documents requested and, more importantly, when the committee discovered little support in the full House to vote a contempt citation against the popular secretary of state.)

Staring out at me from the *Washington Post* on the morning of 16 November was one of the committee's most tightly held secrets: Laurence Stern reported that President Kennedy had once had a close friendship with a woman who was at the same time a girlfriend of crime boss Sam Giancana, the murdered Mafia figure linked to CIA assassination plots against Fidel Castro. Judith Campbell, a 1960 Kennedy campaign volunteer, had sometimes telephoned the president at the White House from Oak Park, Illinois, the residence of Giancana, and occasionally visited the president for what appeared to be sexual liaisons. Eventually, on 11 March 1962, J. Edgar Hoover personally warned the president of Campbell's potentially embarrassing background; thereafter, the calls apparently were no longer accepted at the White House.[9]

Such a personal relationship ordinarily would not have been the subject of a congressional inquiry; however, the possibility existed that the president may have known about the assassination plots and even used the Mafia moll as a go-between. This linkage was discounted, though, when Campbell gave the committee a sworn deposition that she had never heard of the plots, let alone discussed them with the president, and a thorough investigation by GOP staffers on the committee found no evidence to refute her statement.

The committee had thus been left with awkward information of no use to its assassination inquiry. What should be done with the discovery? It was finally decided that the situation could not be ignored completely in the assassination report, or else charges of cover-up would be inevitable; but the senators also agreed that since no evidence tied Kennedy into knowledge of the plots through Campbell, good taste recommended only the briefest of references to the episode. In the report, therefore, Judith Campbell was relegated to a footnote, which referred to her only as "a close friend" of the president who had "frequent contact" with him while at the same time being "a close friend" of Sam Giancana and John Roselli.

Stern's story, however, now made Campbell a subject for the front pages of the nation's newspapers. More important, the committee faced its first significant breach of security. (The earlier leak on the Lumumba plot, we were reasonably sure, had come from the CIA scientist involved or his attorney, who had, we knew, been talking with the press.) Someone among the senators or the staff had flouted the basic security rules and spoken to a reporter about sensitive information.

On 17 November, the committee gathered to discuss the impending FBI hearings. As he had made painfully clear to the FBI Task Force a few days earlier, Church wanted only two bureau hearings; but key members of the task force had an ace up their sleeve in response: Walter Mondale. They had adopted him as a mentor, since they liked him and agreed with him politically, but most of all because he showed more interest than anyone else in their work (thanks in part to skillful lobbying by a couple of the staffers). Now, Mondale was asked to push Church for more public hearings on the FBI, and he succeeded: five days were scheduled.

Between segments of a lengthy staff briefing, committee members brought up other problems. Church raised the Campbell case. He explained that a full internal investigation of the leak would be conducted; every staff member (but no senator) would have to sign an affidavit attesting to his or her innocence. What eventually happened was nothing. Catching a leaker is like trying to discover who put gum under the desktop. The incident did provide critics of the committee a few lines for their columns, however. Patrick Buchanan claimed, inaccurately, that "Chairman Frank Church wanted to strap a polygraph on anyone who had come within 50 yards of committee files."[10]

COINTELPRO

On the morning of 18 November, members of the FBI Task Force joined Church in his office shortly before the first FBI hearing. He had consented to a last-minute briefing there—a modest improvement over the theory of peripatetic summaries. We then walked to the Russell Caucus Room, which was brightly lighted and filled with spectators. Even public television had returned to record the proceedings; the horrors of COINTELPRO and FBI attacks on Martin Luther King Jr. apparently struck the fancy of ratings-conscious producers more than IRS abuses had done.

At long last the committee was turning toward the domestic side of its investigation. Until now, what the committee had done in public (and practically everything in private, too) had dealt with foreign intelligence—namely, the CIA and the NSA—the single day of IRS hearings and portions of the Huston Plan hearings being the only exceptions. While some observers on and off the committee had grumbled at the lopsided attention given the CIA and the NSA, most staffers on the FBI Task Force had been quietly pleased: they needed the time to pry more documents loose from the Bureau; time to understand and organize the truckload of papers they slowly obtained; time to prepare their briefs and investigate gaps in various cases; and time to persuade key members on the committee of the importance of their findings and to prepare these men to confront—knowledgeably and thoroughly—Bureau witnesses during public hearings.

Throughout the inquiry, the FBI Task Force, in the words of its leader, had experienced mainly "benign neglect" from Miller, Schwarz, and the senators.[11] The order of the day had been assassination plots, shellfish toxin and dart guns, Minaret and Shamrock, Kissinger and covert action. Meanwhile, the task force had gone about its work carefully and methodically, sifting through thousands of Bureau papers on COINTELPRO, King, and a dozen other cases.

"The assassination inquiry helped tremendously," remembers Elliff, "because the FBI was not in the headlines. The CIA was"[12]—which gave the task force an opportunity to build bridges of trust to the Bureau, out of the limelight. The assassination probe also gave the committee a reputation for trustworthiness,

Elliff adds; the senators and staff demonstrated they could deal with highly classified information in a responsible manner. This made the FBI more willing to believe their documents would not be given to the committee one day and appear in the newspapers the next.

Fritz Schwarz remembers that he hadn't paid much attention to the FBI Task Force until early fall; he was simply too busy with the assassination report, attendance at committee business sessions, involvement in hearings, and a dozen other chores. To gain a better feeling for what the group was doing, Schwarz brought in his own man—Paul Michel, an attorney, of course—to work as a special assistant and give "organizational direction to the excellent work and spirit of the task force."[13]

Michel had been working with the Justice Department in the office of the special prosecutor assigned to examine the question of financial corruption involving Richard Nixon. He was a bright, young, but experienced investigator who immediately proceeded to alienate the entire FBI Task Force. What did he know about the research they had been involved in for months, they grumbled privately in the green maze of the auditorium. They were the specialists; he, the interloper.

In essence, Michel was there to stop the research—which might have gone on indefinitely—and package the available findings for public presentation. This caused some dismay among a few consummate investigators who thought Michel wanted to move too fast, closing an investigation before all the facts were in. "It was like holding back a horse," one critic on the staff remembers.[14] Gradually, though, Michel was accepted and respected; his fairness, pleasantness, great energy, and quick intellect converted most foes into friends.

The FBI hearings began on 18 November—ten months after the creation of the Church committee. "The committee has adopted a different procedure for this hearing," said Senator Church to the packed audience. He explained how the majority and minority counsels would first present a report on the committee's investigation of FBI domestic intelligence operations. The two staffers sat at the witness table, bathed in the hot lights required for television.

"Today, in a sense, the select committee comes home," said Tower in his introductory remarks. "For today, the select committee begins hearings designed to shed light upon the nation's domestic intelligence activities. . . . Our charter is to reassess current activities. To this end, the staff's presentation will touch upon such controversial topics as warrants, disruptive techniques, 'black bag' jobs, COINTELPRO, and subversive activities."

And so it did, with senators walking in and out from votes on the Senate floor, the tourist tide ebbing and flowing, staff aides poised to set up and take down charts during the presentation, and a steady stream of information on the FBI pouring from the mouths of Schwarz and Smothers alternately.

A bleak history of FBI excesses emerged from these first two days of hearings. In one appalling operation after another, the Bureau had attempted to destroy various dissenting groups by discrediting their leaders and members. A primary target had been Dr. Martin Luther King Jr. In what was interpreted as an attempt to force King to commit suicide, the FBI had sent him (at his headquarters in Atlanta) a tape recording and a note from an anonymous source. The tape, obtained from electronic listening devices placed by the Bureau in various hotel rooms across the country where King had stayed, apparently contained sounds of King in moments of amour outside the confines of matrimony. The package was mailed in November 1964, thirty-four days before King was to receive the Nobel Peace Prize. The note inside read: "King, there is only one thing left for you to do. You know what it is. You have just 34 days in which to do it. (This exact number has been selected for a specific reason.) It has a definite practical significance. You are done. There is but one way out for you. You better take it before your filthy, abnormal fraudulent self is bared to the nation." A month later, the Bureau sent a copy of the tape to Mrs. King, who joined her husband in rejecting the FBI blackmail attempt.

This incredible scheme was but one of many directed against King by the Bureau. As Schwarz documented, the FBI undertook a concerted program designed (in the words of one Bureau document) to knock King "off his pedestal." Bureau officials were forced by J. Edgar Hoover, at the risk of losing their jobs, to rewrite reports on the civil rights leader, falsely charging him as a national security risk. Agents traveled across the country to urge clergymen and university officials to have nothing to do with him, spreading lies and innuendo to smear his character. At the 1964 Democratic Convention, and on many other occasions, King's hotel suite was bugged by the Bureau—this time to keep the Johnson White House apprised of political tactics planned by black political figures attending the party's nominating conference. The Kennedy administration had approved the use of electronic surveillance against King too.

Hounding King until his death, the FBI conceived of a plan to dishonor him among his own people by leaking stories to the Southern press that King preferred the greater comforts of hotels owned by whites in the South to those owned by blacks. Whether or not as a result of such stories, King lodged his group in the black-owned Lorraine Hotel in Memphis, where on 4 April 1968 he was murdered on the balcony by a bullet fired from across the street.[15]

Ultimately, the FBI had wanted to select and groom its own choice of a "safe" black leader in America. Smothers, the committee's black minority counsel, noted during the presentation that Hoover had never even hired a black person to serve as a true FBI agent, giving only the nominal title of agent to five of the Bureau's black chauffeurs so he could claim to President Kennedy that, yes indeed, he had several black agents. "This is the FBI that was presumptuous enough to decide it could determine who should be a national Negro leader," said Smothers in disgust.

It was not only the high and mighty who had been targets of FBI smear campaigns. In thousands of operations conducted by the Bureau from 1956 to 1971, various organizations and individuals felt the heavy hand of FBI harassment. One lowly placed white woman in a black activist movement in St. Louis inspired the propaganda skills of an anonymous FBI letter writer. The woman's husband was sent a Bureau letter, signed "A Soul Sister," alleging that she was having a sexual relationship with black men in the political group. "Like all she wants to integrate is the bedroom," read the letter, "and us black sisters ain't gonna take no second best from our men." Shortly after the letter was mailed, the couple separated. The St. Louis FBI division reported proudly to headquarters: "While the letter . . . was probably not the sole cause of this separation, it certainly contributed very strongly."

Black organizations were but one target. Antiwar protesters, women's liberation movements, socialists, the New Left, white hate groups—anyone Hoover or his advisers disliked went on the list. Another letter charging adultery was sent to the wife of a Ku Klux Klan member, using local slang to make it appear genuine and signed as though written by the wife of a fellow Klan member.

These and over two thousand similar cases across the country were the work of the infamous COINTELPRO, designed to smother the voices of dissent. Schwarz estimated that hundreds of thousands of Americans had been the subjects of Bureau surveillance at one time or another. Most of the COINTELPRO efforts failed to have any effect, and some were completely ludicrous (as when the Bureau infiltrated one benign women's group whose purpose was to "free women from their humdrum existence"). While many of the operations were comical, others—like those against King—stunned the audience during the public hearing and aroused the emotions of the senators.

"How can we fight crime when this is going on?" Church asked.

Ignoring the buzzers calling senators to the floor for a vote, Mondale sank his teeth into the Bureau witnesses like an angry bulldog—refusing to let go until he had fully expressed his outrage. He concluded that the FBI had acted little differently from the KGB.

Most gripping were the remarks made by Philip Hart. The session on COINTELPRO was the first public hearing that his failing health allowed him to attend. A complete silence fell over the crowded room as he slowly began his questioning in a soft voice that revealed his weakened physical condition.

He told a story of how his family of political activists had complained to him during the Vietnam War protests in Michigan that the FBI appeared to be trying to discredit dissent. He had discounted their arguments, attributing them to the frustration and paranoia of a protest movement. Now, he said, in a broken and emotional voice, he saw that his family had been right all along, and he had been wrong in defending the FBI.

"I've been told for years by, among others, members of my own family that this is what the bureau has been doing all this time," Hart said, summarizing the evidence presented by Schwarz and Smothers. "As a result of my superior wisdom in high office, I assured them that they were on pot—it just wasn't true. They [the FBI] just wouldn't do it." Hart paused and cleared his throat. Not a person stirred in the caucus room. "What you have described is a series of illegal actions intended to deny certain citizens their First Amendment rights—just like my children said."

"I had tears in my eyes," remembers Elliff. He was not alone. Most staffers were on the edge of their seats, listening raptly, reliving their initial shock at these abuses through Hart, who, having missed the briefings, was now hearing them for the first time. I had never seen an audience so quiet and deeply affected during a congressional hearing. It was, in the opinion of many observers, the committee's finest moment.

Several of the Democrats, plus Schweiker, seemed prepared to question the Bureau witnesses at great length. Church, though, failed to return at all on the second day after leaving for a vote in the middle of the hearing; and Tower, taking his place as chairman, grew steadily more impatient and asked Mondale in a whisper to "wrap it up." The gavel soon came down on this sad tale of what can happen even within a vibrant democracy.

The hearings, at least in the staff's view, were a success. "They showed that the greatest abuses in the intelligence community were perpetrated by the FBI," Frederick Baron reflects. "The bureau went whole hog."[16]

"If we had been ready to start [in September] with that *great day* [the Philip Hart day]," recalls Fritz Schwarz, "it would have been just the right way to go. We weren't ready to go on this, but Senator Church—for whatever reason—felt it necessary to begin right away [with the Cave of Bugs hearings]."[17]

With the first FBI hearings behind us, the committee now faced what many on the staff were referring to as D-Day. On 20 November, the full Senate would convene in an extraordinary secret session to examine—or at least receive—the assassination report.

11

Resistance

The assassination report had been ready for over a week and required only one last-minute change. United States district court judge Gerhard Gesell had agreed with Church committee attorneys that the name of the CIA scientist in charge of the shellfish toxin (as well as the poison for Lumumba) should appear in the report. He acknowledged that this might place the scientist's life in danger, as the CIA counsel had argued, but he concluded that "the public interest outweighs any private interest of the individual." In his decision, Gesell added that "a former government official has no right of privacy vis-à-vis the Congress when his personal conduct is undergoing review."

The CIA attorneys immediately appealed the decision to the United States circuit court of appeals, but through fear of further delays, the committee (at Church's direction) decided to do an abrupt about-face on the scientist's name so as not to jeopardize the plans to release the report on 20 November. Any delay would have postponed the release of the report until December, since the Thanksgiving recess was about to begin. The choice between holding out for one name and possible postponement was easy for the chairman, whose least favorite word had become "delay." The Massachusetts primary was only fifteen weeks away, and "Draft Church" groups had already formed in twenty-seven districts. Here was a state where Church's anti–Vietnam War credentials stood him in good stead. "I might throw my hat in the ring in Massachusetts," he told a *Boston Globe* reporter, "if there is any more room in the ring."[1]

The entire exercise over the scientist's name was something of a charade, since his name had already been mentioned in various newspaper stories. For whatever it was worth, though, it was stricken from the official report at the last minute.

The committee had already deleted twenty of the thirty names that the CIA had asked us to remove. As Church said repeatedly, only those names would remain that were "inseparably involved in the decisions that led to the involvement of our government in assassination attempts."[2] Colby nonetheless remained adamant to the last: the committee should expunge the remaining names as well. Calling a formal press conference on 19 November (only the second in the history of the CIA), he attacked the report because of the inclusion of the ten names. These individuals, he said, could be subjected to "extralegal retaliation" by terrorists and "unstable or extremist groups."

Yet Church stood firm. "We feel we have acted judiciously and properly," he replied on behalf of the committee. The members had taken this matter seriously, spending hours in research and discussion of the issue and finally deciding it would serve no good purpose to remove the remaining names—unless, of course, the full Senate voted to omit them (or to block the entire report!) on 20 November.

Behind Closed Doors

The secret session, along with the "Philip Hart Day" on the FBI, represented the emotional peaks of the investigation. We came to the Senate on the morning of 20 November with nervousness and excitement over the fate of the controversial report.

Only a dozen secret sessions had taken place in the Senate since World War II. At 9 o'clock, the heavy doors of the Senate chamber swung shut. Inside was a rare scene: almost one hundred senators had arrived simultaneously. Senator James B. Allen (D-AL) immediately asked for the floor: "Will the Senate be given an opportunity to express itself during the session on the advisability of releasing the names of CIA agents who may have been involved in assassination plots?" he asked. Colby had provided good ammunition for those senators opposed to the work of the committee. Minority Whip Robert P. Griffin (R-MI) said he too wished "to have a discussion on that particular question."

Clearly, this would be no rubber-stamp session, despite the urging of Stuart Symington (D-MO) that the senators "not chase windmills." Obeying the Senate custom of deference to the work of a committee, Symington declared that "whatever the committee thinks should be done with this report, I am going to be for."

Church asked that his committee be allowed to summarize its findings before the debate began, and one by one—starting with Church and Tower—the committee members presented their views on the report. Opening with the proposition that "the public is entitled to know what the instrumentalities of their government have done," Church outlined the sections of the report and emphasized that the plots were "aberrations" unreflective of "the real American character." To applause, he delivered his conclusion with strong feeling: "We must remain a people who confront our mistakes and resolve not to repeat them. If we do not, we will decline. But if we do, our future will be worthy of the best of our past."

As he had during the initial FBI hearing, Senator Tower wondered again, "At what point must the people's right to know be subordinated to the people's right to be secure?" Tower implied that while he could live with the report, he could live even better without it.

Senator Baker came directly to the major shortcoming of the research: "We do not know whether presidents authorized or did not authorize these assassination attempts." On balance, though, Baker figured it was more likely that presidents "did know and probably authorized the several activities than that they did not."

Senator Goldwater told the Senate that he had signed the report purely as "an act of gratitude for the hard work done by the committee and the staff." Publication of the report, however, was "an action which the Senate will come to regret." The exercise was a "spectacle of public self-flagellation" that would denigrate our reputation abroad and "tell the world we are retreating into isolationism." How a report critical of assassination signaled a retreat to isolation was unclear, but Goldwater's dislike for the report was plain enough.

Senator Morgan observed that "the next three months of the investigation" could be of greatest importance, for it would focus on domestic abuses. Morgan's references to the inquiry as though it were just gathering steam, at the same time that Church was increasingly referring to the approaching end of the "active phase," might have given pause to attentive listeners. Indeed, this contradiction would widen into a gaping chasm of disagreement within the committee.

When the last committee member completed his remarks, Church spoke about the key names in the report to illustrate how circumspect the committee had been. "At the eleventh hour, after the work of the committee had been done," he said, "any number of roadblocks were thrown up in an attempt to keep this report concealed. The very last of those roadblocks had to do with certain names contained in the report." The chairman sought to push aside this last barrier with a series of examples showing that the committee had acted "judiciously." The names of generals Viaux and Velenzuela, two key military figures with whom the CIA had contacts in Chile, were illustrative. Without their identification, the story of General Schneider's murder made no sense. Moreover, both names had already been revealed in the *New York Times*, and the Chilean military court had convicted the men for their involvement in the Schneider assassination.

The Senate had allowed the committee well over an hour to present its findings, but the floodgates of criticism could be restrained no longer. Senator Griffin was the first to come tumbling through. He immediately raised the question of Rule 36, the parliamentary bugbear that had haunted the committee. The minority whip was of the view that the rule denied the possibility for individual senators, or even committees, to release classified information given to the Senate by the executive branch; only the full Senate, by majority vote, could so act.

Griffin emphasized Section 5 of the rule to his colleagues:

Whenever, by the request of the Senate or any committee thereof any documents or papers shall be communicated to the Senate by the President or the head of any Department relating to any matter pending in the Senate the proceedings in regard to which are secret and confidential under the rules, said documents and papers shall be considered as confidential, and shall not be disclosed without leave of the Senate.[3]

He objected, too, that the senators had never seen the report before this morning, when a copy was placed on each legislator's desk. "I should think," he said, "that it would be the better part of wisdom to delay this decision until after the recess and to give senators an opportunity to be fully cognizant and aware of what they might be doing."

Church listened with color rising in his face, then said sharply, "We do not accept the proposition laid by the Senator from Michigan [regarding Rule 36], and we are prepared to refute it."

According to plan, Mondale rose from his desk to address Rule 36 on behalf of the committee. He told his colleagues, somewhat brazenly, that the Interim Assassination Report was "not here to be adopted or approved. It is here to be heard. That is the nature of this meeting." He advised the Senate, whose members had ceased milling about the chamber and were listening with uncommon attentiveness, that the parliamentarian had given the committee his views on Rule 36. This opinion, said Mondale, clarified that the rule applied only to "private communications" presented to "the Senate as a whole." In contrast, said Mondale, quoting the parliamentarian's ruling, "matters that go routinely before committees, which are often classified, can be released by those committees in their normal function."

Senator Pastore, well known for his sulfurous temper and scorching tongue, asked bitingly: "If you are not seeking the approbation of the Senate in what you are doing, why did we come here in secrecy to begin with?"

Unruffled, Mondale explained that the session had been called out of deference to the Senate, so that all interested members could be fully briefed on the report before its release. Since some questions might lead to classified material not in the report, the Senate had to meet privately. He pointed out further that the original resolution, which Pastore had introduced in January 1975, required the committee to issue whatever interim reports it felt were necessary in addition to a final report.

Finally, Mondale spelled out what the result would be if the Senate were required to affirm the release of any committee reports based in any way on classified information: "It will mean that whenever the executive branch wants to bottle something up they will take a stamp out of the lower left-hand drawer, stamp it 'top secret' and send it to you classified. It will be a new Official Secrets

Act of a kind we never had before. It will give the executive branch power they never had before, power binding not only upon the executive, but upon Congress itself. It will destroy Congress' power and responsibility of informing the public."

With this soliloquy, the wind beginning to fill Pastore's sails rushed out again. Speaking more softly, the Rhode Islander said simply that he "thought it would be a nice thing" to have a vote on the report. In this way, the public would know "that John Pastore and everybody else in the Senate are for the release of this publication." At this, the color receded temporarily from Church's cheeks.

Having dispensed with Pastore, Mondale now squared off with Griffin. He warned that unless released by the committee as planned, the report "will be leaked all over the town in the worst possible way. We are going to be charged with a cover-up."

Senator Mansfield agreed, adding that the report "will go out with or without action by the Senate this afternoon." Hubert Humphrey, Mondale's mentor, put it more strongly: The report, he said, "is going to appear in the *New York Times* and other publications. It is going to happen. It is printed. If we do not know that around here, then we are babes in the woods. We are blessed with a degree of innocence which an unborn child does not have."

Griffin, however, was persistent, leading the Senate into a protracted debate on Rule 36 and whether committees had the right over the full Senate to disclose classified information. He said he found the interpretation of the parliamentarian "incredible" (as had Senator Baker in our committee meetings), and wanted a roll-call vote on the opinion.

Church objected. In his view, any vote to be taken should be on the release of the report, not on complicated nuances in certain Senate rules. While an affirmative vote to release the report was unnecessary, he maintained, the Senate of course always possessed the right to reject a committee report or enjoin a committee from releasing a report. "We either vote it up or down," he insisted.

The chamber began to take on the characteristics of a large frying pan, with the senators so many Mexican jumping beans. As the debate on intractable Rule 36 heated up, the senators grew more and more perturbed, clamoring for the opportunity to speak, moving restlessly around the floor, thumbing through the thick report, and gesticulating with colleagues on debating points. "Question! Objection!" shouted various senators, as the scheduled review of the Interim Assassination Report degenerated into an emotional exchange on the meaning of Rule 36.

As individual senators were given the right to speak, a steady stream of criticism poured out.

Charles Percy [R-IL]. We are asked to approve something as a *fait accompli*, when we are told it cannot be kept secret anyway. . . . I cannot assume the responsibility against the judgment of the President of the United States without knowledge of what is in this report.

James L. Buckley [R-NY]. Frankly, I have been appalled, totally appalled and disturbed by the fact that we seem to be presented with a *fait accompli.* The distinguished senator from Minnesota [Mondale] and the distinguished majority leader have told us that we have to snap to because we have no choice, that it will be out in the streets.

Clifford P. Hansen [R-WY]. Every committee of the Senate is a creature of the Senate.

Allen. The committee has done a great job, but it ought to keep a great deal of this information within its breast. I think that therein lies the fault of the report. I do not feel that much of this information should be released.

Stennis. I think [the report] ought to be modified.

Clifford P. Case [R-NJ]. This is a matter which, because of its own nature as we all understand it now, ought to be handled by the full Senate, without prejudice to any other action by any other committee in any other circumstance.

The din in the chamber was terrific. "We are unable to hear the senator," said Senator Hansen at one point to Assistant Majority Leader Robert C. Byrd (D-WV). The Senate was, in a word, agitated—and time was running out fast. The hands on the clock had passed noon, and no resolution was in sight. Furthermore, most senators were clearly unprepared to vote on a thick report, filled with sensitive and controversial information, without an opportunity to study it. The packed chamber grew less crowded as members jumped out of the frying pan and disappeared into the cloakroom.

Efforts were made by Humphrey and Pastore to force a vote on the narrow proposition that the Senate "receive" the committee report and "concur" in its release, but each time, a call for yeas and nays was diverted by further objections, parliamentary inquiries, and extemporaneous breast-beating by individual orators.

Looking around the rapidly emptying room, Tower observed, "Obviously a number of people have decided that they do not want to vote on this issue." For this, the committee's vice chairman was "distressed and sorry." He announced that "since the Senate has not voted, I want now to publicly disassociate myself from public release of this report." Church wheeled away from Tower and stalked from the chamber.

One o'clock had come and gone. The assassination report had been laid before the Senate, and the Senate had taken no meaningful action on it (or on Rule 36). Now a congressional budget resolution pressed in on the schedule. A few lingering senators asked Edmund Muskie (D-ME), floor leader for the budget resolution, for more time on the report, and he grudgingly allowed a few minutes from his own limited schedule. Senators William Brock (R-TN), Jacob Javits (R-NY), and Sam Nunn (D-GA) lamented the fact that no vote had been taken. The impression was left, in Nunn's words, "that a committee may declassify information without the concurrence of the full Senate."

Senator James A. McClure (Republican), Church's fellow senator from Idaho, hoped that every member who voted in committee for the release of the report would not be expelled from the Senate, as he thought might be required by Rule 36. It was a touching—but hardly credible—expression of sympathy from a man who held no brief for Frank Church and would have happily provided the wheelbarrow to cart him out of the Senate if a chance of expulsion existed.

In the trailing moments of the Senate's attention, Baker and Huddleston best expressed the committee's dismay over the disturbing turn of events the day had brought.

"I think to have [the report] released by inaction casts credit on neither the Senate nor the committee, and I regret it," said Baker in a low voice. Huddleston echoed the frustration of each committee member who had supported the release of the report (that is, everyone but Tower and Goldwater) as he spoke with a heavy heart at the end of the debate:

> The whole purpose of coming before the Senate by the committee was simply to inform senators so they would not read about the report in the press before they had any knowledge of what it is all about. The unfortunate thing about this morning, of course, is that we spent nearly the entire time debating the question as to whether or not the Senate ought to vote or not vote on releasing the report. . . . We went through an entire morning without ever having an opportunity to answer one single question about the substance of the report. . . . It is unfortunate that the Senate today got hung up on these questions which were not even pertinent to the whole session today.

Huddleston and Baker left the Senate in a slow walk with unhappy faces.

The scene at the entrance of the Dirksen auditorium was one of bedlam. Reporters from all over the country and around the world crowded into the lobby, where harried committee secretaries were handing out copies of the report to a field of grasping hands. The minute the secret session ended at 1 o'clock, the committee staff had been instructed to give out copies to anyone with press credentials. It was a masterful tactic on Church's part, though one that failed to endear him to many of his colleagues, who—as the debate amply revealed—did not enjoy being on the receiving end of a fait accompli. Church was determined to issue the report. If the Senate so voted, fine; if it didn't vote at all, that was fine too. Only if the Senate had voted to delay or curb release would the chairman have been forced to hold it back—and even then, since it was already printed, the chances of a copy's "escape" to the press would have been high.

As I walked into the entrance area, a husky middle-aged man brushed by me and rushed up to the committee press officer. He had a copy of *Pravda* tucked under his arm. "Where is we getting report?" he asked, out of breath, in a thick accent. He might as well have had "KGB" printed on his hatband.

The release of the Interim Assassination Report provided a feast for the nation's editorial writers. Opinion ran from sharp condemnation of the CIA for engaging in murder plots to equally vociferous criticism of the Church committee for laundering the nation's dirty linen in public. The *Chicago Tribune* heralded the release of the report, "in spite of strenuous efforts to suppress it, as a crucial victory for this country. . . . There could hardly be better evidence of the health and recuperative powers of the American government."[4] In the *New York Times*, President Ford was chastised for being "party to a continuing cover-up of outrages"; the *Times* viewed the report "merely as a beginning of a new determination not to destroy the intelligence agencies but to put them on a short leash."[5] One scholar of the period would later call the report "one of the most chilling and important documents ever made public by a committee of Congress."[6]

Others saw the work of the committee in a different light. Columnist Charles Bartlett, for example, declared flatly that the report "should never have been published." While admitting that the committee "did its job thoroughly," Bartlett wrote, "The report holds the initiatives of an era in which the struggle was the main thing up to the judgments of an era in which political morality is everything." He concluded that "the danger of this act of penance may outweigh its fruits."[7]

Columnist Frank Starr agreed, and raised points that troubled professionals at the CIA and several committee staffers:

> While little old ladies in baroque European towns admire us over their tea for our courage in self-criticism, counter intelligence experts on Dzerzhinskii Square are getting a free primer on US covert operations. . . .
>
> Will Britain's Harold Wilson and Germany's Helmut Schmidt be eager to have their intelligence organizations cooperate with ours, knowing that if either should do anything questionable the superior US morality will make it all public?[8]

Only the passage of time, concluded Starr, would tell us which was the greater danger: our adversaries, or the possibility that we could have developed a police state of our own similar to theirs.

The most publicized criticism came from Secretary of State Kissinger. The time had come to end "the self-flagellation that has done so much harm to this nation's capacity to conduct foreign policy," he said in a speech to the Economic Club of Detroit.[9] The time had come, too, for an end to "the delusion that American intelligence activities are immoral . . . and the illusion that tranquility can be achieved by an abstract purity of motive for which history offers no example." As if this were the intention of Congress, Kissinger added that "we cannot allow the intelligence services of this country to be dismantled."

The administration had lost its battle to hold back the assassination report, but it was obviously continuing the war against the congressional investigations. The Kissinger statement was yet another jab in what one reporter called a new "policy of total non-cooperation with the Congressional intelligence inquiries."[10]

Reluctant Witnesses

Actually, the administration was still occasionally cooperative. When the Church committee was content to meet with executive branch officials in strictly private hearings, the administration was obliging. On 21 November, for instance, Kissinger came to testify on covert action—in particular, the clandestine involvement of the United States in Angola.

Without notes, and demonstrating an impressive mental sure-footedness, he related the story of the Angolan civil war.[11] Soviet interference in Angola was, in the secretary's view, incompatible with the canons of coexistence; it represented the largest influx of Soviet military influence anywhere outside the Middle East since 1960. The 40 Committee, therefore, recommended stepped-up covert intervention by the United States, and President Ford approved.

"This sounds like Vietnam all over again," said Church impatiently, after Kissinger had outlined the operation. "Here we go again with the belief that American vital interests require an increasing level of intervention."

"With all respect, Mr. Chairman . . ." said Kissinger, trying to regain control.

"What comes next when the covert action is insufficient?" Church continued, overriding the secretary of state. "Do you send in the Marines?" The chairman's voice had grown louder, and he was leaning far forward in his chair, his face a portrait of dismay.

"With all respect," Kissinger tried again, "there is a difference between Angola and Vietnam." In professorial tones, still unruffled, he proceeded to explain the difference to this recalcitrant pupil: Vietnam was, more or less, a civil war situation; in Angola, however, Soviets and Cubans were intervening to tip the balance among indigenous factions. Church sank back into his chair, as his expression changed from dismay to skepticism.

"Is it the spectacle of the Russians coming in and dictating the course of the government through force that worries?" asked Senator Mondale, dislodging a cigar from his mouth.

"That is it," said Kissinger. Other African states, he feared, would have to tilt to this new overwhelming force.

"But what about the force of nationalism?" Mondale continued. In his view, the proud nations of Africa would not long tolerate outside interference from Moscow or anywhere else.

Here was an argument Kissinger was disinclined to confront; he sidestepped it, taking great pains to clarify that the covert involvement of the United States in the Angolan civil war was being kept at a low and carefully controlled level.

Criticizing the CIA "secret war" in Laos during the 1960s, Kissinger advanced two principles of covert action. First, to fight "a jet-fighter war" as a covert war was unwise. As soon as it was no longer possible to keep a war carefully limited in scope, it was better to recognize the friendly forces officially and arm them overtly. The United States military should not be used covertly, he said, emphasizing that in Angola he would oppose sending in "our people" under any circumstances.

Second, Kissinger stressed that only those covert actions that supported a diplomatic "track" (objective) could be justified. In Angola, the covert action was designed to reestablish the balance of internal forces, which the arts of diplomacy could no longer achieve once the balance had been upset by the introduction of sophisticated Soviet arms on one side.

While providing few details (in part because the committee failed to push for them), Kissinger seemed to have assuaged the doubts of most members about the wisdom of American covert action in Angola (Church and Mondale excepted), at least for the moment. The secretary of state left S407 the same way he entered: with a smile on his face.

With letters dated 20 November, however, both Kissinger and Colby had declined the committee's invitation to testify in public on covert action in Chile. Colby noted that the administration was prohibiting present and past Agency employees from coming before the committee on this topic.

Kissinger wrote:

I believe it would be wholly inappropriate for an incumbent Secretary of State to appear in an open session to discuss, even on an unclassified basis, any real or purported covert operation of the United States Government. The very presence of the President's senior Cabinet officer at such a hearing would cast an implication which could have extremely serious international repercussions. The consequences of the presence of the secretary of state at such a session would, in my view, far outweigh whatever benefits there might be to the inquiry on which the Senate Select Committee is now embarked.

In response, Church announced on 26 November that the committee would go ahead with its hearings on covert action in Chile anyway, without the testimony of administration witnesses. On 4 December, the committee would take testimony from former State Department officials "who have the courage and the responsibility to see that the public interest will be served by speaking to the issues raised by the Chilean policy."

While Church was obviously intent on striking a tough posture by ridiculing the administration's stance, not everyone was impressed. Within the committee, key staffers continued to argue privately that subpoenas—not speeches—were the only remedy; outside the committee, the administration gave not the slightest sign of reconsidering its ban against testifying. Apparently the only witnesses we would have who had been intimately involved in Chilean affairs were former United States ambassadors Ralph Dungan and Edward M. Korry (appointees of Presidents Johnson and Nixon).

Korry was a dubious witness. Soon after the publication of the assassination report, he telephoned Greg Treverton, the committee investigator who had dealt with him most closely during the inquiry. His "conversation" with Treverton (more accurately a monologue) was rambling and inchoate. Treverton returned from the call visibly angry. Korry claimed that his views had been misrepresented in the assassination report, evoking an unfair image of villainy. "I didn't invent those cables he sent from Chile," said Treverton, exasperated.[12]

The struggles between the executive branch and the two congressional committees produced what James Reston referred to as "an air of confusion and even incoherence in our present national political debate."[13] An artificial truce settled over Washington as the gladiators on both sides of town laid down their weapons and left the arena for Thanksgiving celebrations around the country. But as the days crept closer to the 4 December hearings on Chile, dismay that neither Kissinger nor Colby would be witnesses grew more vocal on the committee staff and in the press. "Will Senator Frank Church and his committee really stand still for a new unilateral privilege allowing executive witnesses to decide when their appearance is 'appropriate'?" asked Anthony Lewis of the *New York Times*.[14] He urged that we subpoena Richard Nixon as well as Henry Kissinger: "[President Nixon] is subject to subpoena like anyone else. Is the Church committee afraid to issue one?"

Nixon's lawyer had a different view. "It is Mr. Nixon's position," he informed the committee, "that the separation of powers precluded Congress from requiring any President (or former President) from appearing before it for the purpose of investigating actions taken during his term in office. A President may, of course, voluntarily discuss such matters."[15]

"Kissinger's just too popular up here," Church said to me when I asked him again about a subpoena for the secretary of state. "Ultimately, a vote to hold him in contempt would fail."

More FBI Abuses

The staff had become accustomed to the bizarre during the investigation, but as we prepared for our next hearing, on additional FBI abuses, a ripple of curiosity moved across the Dirksen auditorium on the morning of 2 December. Schwarz had placed an intriguing note on our desks: "Gary Thomas Rowe, the Klan informant who will be one of our first witnesses this morning, will appear in a hood. He is doing this because he is now living under an assumed name in a new location and does not want his picture taken because he believes his life is in danger. Please advise your Senator so that he will not be surprised by the apparition."

Later in the morning, once the senators were seated for the next set of FBI hearings, the hooded witness was brought in. His white cloth hood flared out over puffy cheeks, revealing a large mouth and rolls of flesh sagging under his chin. Large, clumsily cut holes in the hood allowed him to see. His appearance created a low rumble of voices throughout the audience assembled in the caucus room. The second witness, unhooded, was an attractive young woman by the name of Mary Jo Cook. Both had been FBI informers, Rowe in the Ku Klux Klan (KKK) and Cook in the anti–Vietnam War movement.

The objective of these hearings was to help the committee develop new guidelines to govern FBI intelligence activities; on this morning, the use of informants was the topic explored. Rowe and Cook both had pitiful stories to tell. Rowe said he had participated (with Bureau condonation) in Klan acts of violence from 1960 to 1965 and, allegedly under FBI orders, had sown dissension within the Klan. "I was told to sleep with as many wives as I could to break up marriages," he testified.

Rowe also claimed that he had passed on important intelligence to the Bureau concerning a Klan scheme to attack freedom riders in Birmingham, Alabama, in 1961. As planned, the KKK charged the unarmed civil rights activists with baseball bats, clubs, chains, and pistols in a melee that lasted fifteen minutes. According to Rowe, the Birmingham police department had promised the Klan that its officers would stand by idly for fifteen minutes. When Rowe later asked the Bureau why it had done nothing to prevent this massacre, he said he was told: "Who in the hell were we going to report it to? The police department was involved." Yet, as Rowe testified, the Bureau had close ties to the Birmingham police and had been allowed unlimited access to the department's intelligence files on civil rights activists.

The second informant, Mary Jo Cook, was in some ways a more pathetic case than Rowe. One had a sense from listening to Rowe that his involvement in unsavory activities long predated his employment with the FBI; he seemed to have realized what he was getting into. Cook, in contrast, had slipped into her new identity more innocently. Her boyfriend had been a Bureau informant and urged her to pick up an extra $300 a month by being "a big sister" to disillusioned veterans in an organization called Vietnam Veterans Against the War (VVAW). All she had to do was tell the FBI what the group was doing. She was, in her words, "a vacuum cleaner for information" about the VVAW chapter in Buffalo, New York, in 1973 and 1974. "I became an informant," she testified, "not fully realizing what that meant."

Then, in July 1974, Cook traveled to Washington to witness a large antiwar demonstration. "I came and I saw people, people I had met in the course of my activities, with blood running down their heads," she remembered. Angered and alarmed that her information might have been used only to harm young critics of the war, with whom she had begun to sympathize, she complained to the FBI and resigned.

Responding for the FBI, Associate Deputy Director James B. Adams denied Rowe's allegations and testified that the Bureau never authorized him to disrupt the KKK by sexually engaging Klan wives, never condoned his involvement with violence, and always passed on to local police his reports about planned attacks on civil rights activists.

Adams acknowledged that this intelligence had little effect on the police, since some of them were sympathetic to the Klan; but, he said, "we had no authority in the absence of authority from the Department of Justice to make an arrest." (Eventually five hundred federal marshals were sent to make arrests designed to curb future Klan attacks.) In Adams's view, the Bureau's work against the KKK was "the FBI's finest hour." A balanced appraisal had failed to emerge from the hearings, he complained, because "of the necessity to zero in on abuses."[16] As for the use of informants, he emphasized that "it's been here throughout history, and there will always be informants. The thing we want to avoid is provocateurs, criminal activists, and to insure that we have safeguards that will prevent that."

The committee had no further questions, and John Tower, acting as chairman, brought the hearing to an end. (Church was absent from both this and the next day's session.) The following day, John Elliff summarized the research findings of his task force. This time the subject was presidential misuse of the Bureau from Franklin D. Roosevelt through Richard M. Nixon. Elliff revealed a startling portrait of FBI involvement in political operations at presidential behest. The

Bureau had given intelligence to President Johnson on seven newsmen, including David Brinkley (NBC), Peter Arnett (AP), and columnist Joseph Kraft. Both Roosevelt and Johnson had requested that the Bureau provide intelligence on several individuals who had written the White House in opposition to their foreign policy. For Johnson, the FBI conducted checks on Senator Goldwater's staff when the senator was the Republican opponent to Johnson in the 1964 presidential elections. Harry Truman, John Kennedy, and Richard Nixon also made use of the Bureau for political purposes. Only Dwight Eisenhower seemed to have clean hands. In Elliff's words, the "FBI intelligence system developed to a point where no one inside or outside the bureau was willing or able to tell the difference between legitimate national security or law enforcement information and purely political intelligence."

12

Covert Action

On the morning of 4 December, I drove with Church in his aged Mustang convertible to the Sheraton-Park Hotel in Washington, where he and Colby were speaking to an academic forum on covert action. The vast hotel auditorium was filled with people, and Colby was already on the stage, along with three men invited to evaluate the remarks of the two speakers.

Colby spoke first; the attentive audience applauded him stormily during and after his remarks. "In a number of instances," he said,

> some quiet assistance to democratic and friendly elements enabled them to resist hostile and authoritarian groups in an internal competition over the future direction of their countries. Postwar Western Europe resisted Communist political subversion, and Latin America rejected Cuban-stimulated insurgency. They thereby thwarted at the local level challenges that could have escalated to the international level.
>
> That there can be debate as to the wisdom of any individual activity of this nature is agreed. That such a potential must be available for use in situations truly important to our country and the cause of peace is equally obvious.

Colby acknowledged that "intelligence made some mistakes and did some misdeeds," but, he emphasized, "these were truly few and far between."

Church came to the podium next and spoke of covert action as the "swampland" of American foreign policy. He checked off a list of excessive operations conducted by the Agency: Guatemala, Indonesia, Iran, the Bay of Pigs, Laos, the assassination plots, and Chile. "The only plausible explanation for our intervention in Chile," he said, "is the persistence of the myth that Communism is a single, hydra-headed serpent, and that it remains our duty to cut off each ugly head, wherever and however it may appear."

The White House, Church complained, seemed to have the attitude that if use of the marines seemed too blatant, the United States could always send in the CIA. For him, it was a "fantasy that it lay within our power to control other countries through the covert manipulation of their affairs." Such intervention, he said, in a voice that had reached an emotional crescendo, had caused us to "lose—or grievously impair—the good name and reputation of the United States from which we once drew a unique capacity to exercise matchless moral leadership." The applause for Church was as frequent and enthusiastic as that which had punctuated Colby's remarks, though it came from different portions of the hall.

"Nevertheless," Church continued, "I do not draw the conclusion of those who now argue that all American covert actions must be banned in the future. I can conceive of a dire emergency when timely clandestine action on our part might avert a nuclear holocaust and save an entire civilization." He also endorsed "circumstances, such as those existing in Portugal today, where our discreet help to democratic political parties might avert a forcible takeover by a Communist minority, heavily subsidized by the Russians." In short, he favored those covert actions "consistent either with the imperative of national survival or with our traditional belief in free government."

This formula was the best we had been able to devise, but as I listened, I knew it was unsatisfactory. Our "traditional belief in free government" was a large part of what drew us into Vietnam—the kind of tragedy Church certainly wished to avoid in the future.

Church returned to his chair and listened to the other speakers. Charles Morgan, president of the American Civil Liberties Union (ACLU) chapter in Washington, DC, chastised Church for failing to go far enough in his criticism of covert action.

On the other side of the issue, Dr. Ray S. Cline, former CIA deputy director, complained that the congressional investigations were "destroying our intelligence service. We can no longer gather information abroad." He explained mockingly that covert action "is not a social disease, but a serious policy problem." Of course, the CIA may have made some mistakes, Cline allowed, tugging at his beard, "but I thought infallibility was reserved for another institution." He looked toward Church with a sly grin: "Of course, I was referring to the one on Capitol Hill."

Morgan, the angry man among the critics, spoke again, excoriating the CIA for its intrusion into Chile. His spirited attack evoked a sharp, emotional response from Church, who agreed with Morgan on this point. "The Western Hemisphere is not a colony of the United States," Church bellowed to the last row in the auditorium. "It is not the right of the US to decide what kind of governments they should have. We once knew that. Those were the days when we were the most respected country in the world. Let us get back to that." Applause broke out in "his" sections of the hall.

"Why not offer our assistance in the open?" argued former NSC staffer Morton Halperin, another panel participant.

As Church began a response ("We cannot show our hand in some circumstances . . ."), a winded young man came running up. "There's a cloture vote in the Senate," he said between gasps.

Church took a moment to point out that some speakers had accused him of handling the CIA with velvet gloves, while others said he had used a mailed fist. "So," he concluded, "I figure we must be doing just about right." We dashed for the underground parking, dodged through traffic on Rockcreek Parkway, and made the vote with one minute to spare.

Chile

Wending his way through the crowded caucus room later that day, Church took his place in the chairman's seat. "I spent the whole morning," he said, "publicly debating with Mr. Colby the covert operations that occurred in Chile during the period under investigation. And so it is not denied to him to discuss such matters publicly and before the assembled press at the Sheraton Park Hotel. It is denied him that he should come and testify here at the Capitol before this committee. I believe the position of the administration is completely unjustified." He berated Kissinger, too, for giving speeches in defense of covert action yet refusing to "answer questions before the Congress and the people of the country." Church said the committee was holding this hearing and releasing a report on Chile because "this committee and the American people cannot wait forever until the administration decides to honor the rights of the citizens of this nation to know the policies of their government."

In his own opening statement, Senator Tower disagreed completely with Church. "I have always clung to the view," said the vice chairman, "that information concerning the details of US covert operations should not be made public because of the possible hazards created for individuals and because the release of such information may jeopardize necessary activity." Senator Goldwater quickly agreed, saying, "It is a mistake that we are holding these hearings in public." In the absence of further comments, Church asked the staff director to begin the presentation. Miller gave a brief and highly critical account of covert actions, noting that they had been generally "successful against weak nations and far less so against our potential enemies." The CIA Task Force leader, Bader, led the committee a short way into the forest of details on the Chile case.[1] He noted that the United States had secretly spent over $13 million in opposition to Allende. In the 1964 election alone, the CIA spent $3 million, or about $1 per Chilean voter. The chairman seemed startled by the figures.

"Mr. Chairman, to get it into perspective," said Tower, attempting to play down the significance of these numbers, "I might say that I spent $2.7 million to run for election in 1972 in a state [Texas] with a population of eleven million."

("Yeah, but you needed it more," whispered a junior senator in an aside to Mondale.)

Church ignored Tower's interjection and pointed out that, comparing our population with Chile's, this $3 million would amount to $60 million in the United States, if a foreign power were to try to influence our elections in a comparable way.

"As a comparison," offered another staffer, Rick Inderfurth, "in [our] 1964 election President Johnson and Senator Goldwater combined spent $25 million."

Mondale, as was often the case, had the key question: what was "the threat that Mr. Allende [then president of Chile] posed to this country?"

Dead silence followed. The four staffers on the panel were looking at one another with long "after you" stares. Inderfurth looked at Miller; Treverton looked at Bader; Bader looked at Inderfurth; and Miller looked straight at the floor.

"What is this, a commercial break?" asked Mondale, staring at the television crews and back to the staff panel with a sardonic smile.

The silence became an embarrassment. Inderfurth waited no longer for Miller or Bader, the senior staffers, to speak up and offered this accurate—if now anticlimactic—answer: "I think the threats perceived by officials had to do with the presence of the Soviets in Chile and the question of subversion of other Latin American governments, using Chile as a base," he said. "There was a concern about a movement by Allende, despite the fact that he had been elected constitutionally, down the road toward a Marxist totalitarian state."

The two ambassadors testified next. Ralph Dungan, an intelligent and affable man who had been assigned to Chile from 1964 through 1967, acknowledged that our involvement in Chile was, "we now see with the amazing clarity of hindsight, a national disgrace." But, he added, the excesses "transpired under imprecise congressional mandates, haphazard oversight, and moneys provided by the Congress." Touché.

Ambassador Korry, angry from the beginning of his testimony, charged that Church and committee staff members had tried to prevent him from testifying. He decried "the suffocating national guilt that you, Mr. Chairman, have done so much in the past three years to propagate."

With remarkable calmness, Church pointed out that no one—Republican or Democrat—had asked for Korry to be called as a witness before now. As for the assassination report, over which Korry was most upset, Church explained that he had not been called as a witness because Korry had told the staff that he knew nothing of that activity.

Skipping over these fine points, Korry ripped into the assassination report. "Almost every page of the chapter dealing with Chile," he said, "contains a dishonesty, a distortion, or a doctrine." He was highly excited and plowed through seven major actions he said he had taken "to protect the United States from any complicity in Chilean military interventions." The assassination report, in his view,

> unconsciously falls in with a monstrous black-white mythology foisted on this country during the past three years, a morality fable in which American officials were all Nazi-like bully boys cuffing around decent Social Democrats, although Dr. Allende and his left Leninist Socialist Party had nothing but contempt for Social Democrats, and although Dr. Allende, as the Embassy had reported for many, many years, had personally been financed from foreign Communist enemies.

Korry said he had hoped to address the complex and serious questions properly raised by an inquiry into the intelligence community. Instead, he said, sitting on the edge of his chair and glaring at Church through thick-lensed glasses,

> you forced me today to try to expose what is wrong with government by headline. What happens when the public interest turns into a porno-flick, a sensate experience into a cynical careening from one superficial sensation— dart guns, poison, and all that—to another to divert the public from the complexity of reality; what happens to the civil rights of an individual—me in this case, but it can happen to anybody—to the quality of political life, to the national interest, to the truth, when moral fervor runs over into the moral absolutism that has now led to the desolation of Chile?

The committee was verbally whipped as never before. Church was prepared to concede only one point. "Yes," he replied, "I agree it has led to the desolation of Chile."

The next morning, the caucus room was again filled with a large crowd. The witness list consisted of Clark Clifford, former secretary of defense, and Cyrus Vance, former deputy secretary of defense, two of the best known and most highly regarded figures in government circles; David Phillips, a former high-ranking CIA officer with over two decades of firsthand experience with covert operations; and the ubiquitous critic of covert action, Morton Halperin.

Clifford spoke in a solemn and authoritative voice. "Our country may sustain some temporary reduction in the effectiveness of its intelligence operations [as a result of these hearings]," he said, "but I consider this temporary in nature, and an appropriate price to pay in preventing repetition of such abuses in the future." He was especially distressed by the looseness of internal control within the intelligence establishment:

On a number of occasions, a plan for covert action has been presented to the NSC and authority is requested for the CIA to proceed from point A to point B. The authority will be given, and the action will be launched. When point B is reached, the persons in charge feel that it is necessary to go to point C, and they assume that the original authorization gives them such a right. From point C, they go to D and possibly E, and even further. This has led to some bizarre results, and when an investigation is started, the excuse is blandly presented that authority was obtained from the NSC before the project was launched.

To establish proper control again, he recommended a five-point plan for reform: a new intelligence charter to replace the 1947 act (which he helped write) and draw clearer lines of authority; a joint House–Senate intelligence oversight committee; a new position of director general of intelligence; a rule that allowed only the new director general and the NSC to approve covert action (and then only when it "truly affects our national security"); and a regulation forbidding the CIA to undertake any domestic operations except to police its own employees.

Vance, destined to be secretary of state in another year, agreed with his patrician colleague that a joint intelligence oversight committee was desirable. Also in harmony with Clifford, Vance recommended that "it should be the policy of the United States to engage in covert actions only when they are absolutely essential to the national security."

Phillips, who was once in charge of CIA intelligence operations throughout Latin America, testified next. To my surprise, he recommended that the CIA leave the covert action business. The Agency was the best organization to carry out covert action, he maintained, but "effective and responsible accountability override practical operational considerations." To this end, he suggested the creation of a small agency with sixty people in support roles and forty operations officers to engage in the planning and execution of any properly authorized covert mission. In this way, "all US covert action eggs then would be in one small basket, a basket which could be watched very carefully." This new agency should be limited in its methodology. "It would not employ airlines or mercenaries or exotic paraphernalia," Phillips advised, "but would need the capability to provide friends with imaginative advice and what British intelligence officers have sometimes called 'King George's cavalry': money."

Last came Halperin, former NSC aide and the object of a lengthy and unproductive wiretap instigated against him by the Nixon administration. As he had made plain at the academic forum the day before, Halperin favored the abolition of covert action. "The possible benefits," he told the committee, "are far outweighed by the costs to our society of maintaining a capability for covert operations." In his view, covert action was "incompatible with our democratic institutions, with congressional and public control over foreign policy decisions, with our constitutional rights, and with the principles and ideals that this Republic stands for in the world."

On one point everyone seemed to agree: if a covert action might preclude the destruction of the United States by a nuclear holocaust, then that operation obviously would be justified. "The Constitution is not a suicide pact," acknowledged Halperin in support of this single exception to his position.

Church reiterated, however, that another kind of covert action might also be appropriate. Using Portugal as an example, he argued that American covert support would be legitimate to assist democratic parties in a struggle against a militant communist minority covertly supported by the USSR and attempting to impose a totalitarian regime against the express will of a majority of the people. In such a case, if the involvement of the United States were exposed, we could say, "Yes, we were there and we are proud of it, because what we tried to do clearly conformed with our traditional values as a nation. We stand for that."

Halperin agreed that we should help democratically oriented factions in Portugal and everywhere else, but strictly in an overt fashion. Let Portugal or any other country "choose between taking the aid openly or not taking it at all," said Halperin.

Church responded at some length:

Overt, open foreign interference in that struggle would probably be resented the way open, foreign interference in the political process in the United States would be resented. Doubtless it would backfire on the very groups we sought to help. Thus, I think that answer is too easy. It is too easy to say in such a situation, "Let it be overt, let it be open. Let them come to us and we will give them economic assistance or foreign aid," when that doesn't really address itself to the kind of situation that exists there. . . . I'm saying that there may be situations where the United States could act covertly, but would not be embarrassed later when it became known because our action was in line with our best traditions, helping people when they needed help to achieve free government. . . .

The problem I see with covert operations in the last twenty years is that they have been utterly directed toward the opposite objective, keeping all kinds of despotisms—corrupt, rotten regimes—in power all over the world. When we have been exposed in having done it, we have been severely damaged, and we have really lost our capacity for moral leadership.

Halperin remained unpersuaded: "If the situation is one in which the aid could only be given secretly," he argued, "I would think one would have to weigh how often you think it will occur, how important you think that will be against the consequences which we have seen in the past of having a covert capability, and whether you think you can correct it. But I agree that is a hard balance, and my view is that we can help those people enough in open ways that we should not take the course of having covert operations." The questioning continued on a high plane for the rest of the morning. The audience no doubt viewed these exchanges as less entertaining than Korry's vituperative language, but the committee found the insights provided by this set of witnesses enormously helpful for its own thinking on covert action. As Senator Mathias put it, during the hearing, "there are fewer skyrockets this morning but a lot more substance."

Church departed from the caucus room in high spirits. This session had captured his interest more than any other; indeed, in a sense, the Chile hearing represented his last hurrah on the committee. Preparation of the assassination report was the zenith of his personal involvement in the investigation; now this look at covert action had revived his flagging attention and stamina. But with his favorite foreign policy topics behind him and a presidential election before him, it became increasingly difficult to channel the chairman's efforts into the work of his committee.

The Lure of Politics

Immediately after the Chile hearings, Church boarded a plane for Massachusetts and addressed three hundred people at one meeting in Lincoln and another five hundred at Boston College—peculiar behavior, some observed, for a noncandidate. Speaking before the Los Angeles World Affairs Council a few days later, he struck a presidential stance. If he were president, he told the luncheon group of over five hundred people, he would take the covert operations wing out of the CIA, reduce its personnel by 90 percent, and place the remaining 10 percent in the Department of State, "where it would be subject to the overall policy considerations of our government in connection with the conduct of our foreign affairs."[2]

In a neat bit of semantic legerdemain, Church told reporters in Los Angeles that he was about to form an exploratory committee on the presidential race the next week, when the "investigative work" of the intelligence committee would be completed. This campaign committee was supposed to "determine whether it's possible to put together an organization and gather sufficient money to make it possible for so late an entrant to launch a campaign for the presidency."

"When the investigative work . . . would be completed"—this was the first time I'd heard that phrase. It was true that by the next week the public hearings would be over, culminating in three final days on the FBI. Church had ingeniously decided to call this the end of the investigative work, despite the fact that each of the task forces had several investigations underway (some in midstream), and some committee members strongly supported the completion of these various projects.

Visions of the White House danced in the heads of other committee members too. Later in the campaign season, Senator Schweiker would become the vice presidential candidate on the GOP ticket led by Ronald Reagan—a move that astonished most people because of the apparent ideological distance between the two men; and Howard Baker, by all accounts, longed for (and almost achieved) the vice presidential slot on the Ford ticket. After Church, though, the most audible presidential noises were those of Senator Mathias. He told a press conference in early December that he might run as a "third force" independent candidate.

This burst of overt presidential politicking by Church and Mathias was the first sign that a significant change had taken place in the investigation during the early days of December. The second sign came in a stream of memoranda that cascaded from the upper reaches of the staff hierarchy down to the desktops hidden here and there behind the green partitions of the Dirksen auditorium. We received schedules indicating when final staff reports were due (none later than 15 February); proposed outlines of our omnibus final report; notices to the designees urging them to forward the views of their senators on the final reports ("to insure the senators have an opportunity to make their input," said one memo); and finally, a cold announcement that our yellow Senate ID cards would expire on 31 December, and only a small group of people would be issued new cards for 1976.

A third sign was the dwindling attendance of senators at closed hearings. On 8 December, only two junior members appeared in S407, and they soon departed.

In memoranda to the chairman, Miller emphasized the work that still remained to be done; the list read "Counterintelligence, Defense Intelligence Agency, Military Intelligence in General, The Intelligence Budget Process, 'Wiseman' Hearings on the Future of Intelligence, Various FBI Cases." Miller suggested the desirability of a combined Church committee–executive branch working group for the development of "a consensus charter for the intelligence community."[3]

Last Public Hearings

While the Church committee was cooling down its activity, our sister committee on the other side of Capitol Hill seemed to be reaching a boiling point. On 8 December, Otis Pike filed contempt action in the House against Henry Kissinger for his failure to deliver subpoenaed documents on covert action, and he vowed to ask for a House vote in a few days, unless his committee opposed his position.[4]

As the full complement of the Pike panel gathered on 9 December for another war council on Kissinger, three members of the Church committee straggled into the Russell Caucus Room for the next round of hearings on the FBI. Senator Schweiker arrived first, bright-eyed and eager as ever; then came Gary Hart, cool and serious. They sat at their usual seats on opposite ends of the long hearing table. "The junior senators don't know enough yet to avoid boring hearings," whispered an aide seated next to me.

The two rookies sat waiting for the chairman, or some other elder, to enter and begin the proceedings. I was about to suggest to Hart that he begin when Church at last came through the caucus room doors. I could scarcely believe my eyes. The chairman's face was lined and heavy with fatigue; his eyes made him appear to be in a trance. The work of the committee had been wearing on him for months; clearly his campaign trips to the Northeast and to California had taken a further toll.

Church sat down, hunched his tired shoulders forward, and pushed the opening statement aside. In a dry, flat voice he told the crowd what he had rehearsed before the press in Los Angeles: "The hearing this morning marks a transition in the work of the committee. Heretofore we have been focusing on abuses, unlawful conduct, wrongdoing, which together have constituted the investigative phase of the committee's work. Today, and in future public hearings of the committee, we shall be concentrating on remedies." He skipped the formal opening statement altogether.

What a change from the first hearing in September, I thought to myself. Then Church had delivered a ringing fifteen-minute statement to a room bursting with people and television cameras, and with every senator in his chair. Now his opening remarks were three sentences long; rows of seats were empty; and only two members had bothered to join the chairman (Hart left within the hour).

The lackadaisical quality was accentuated by the sound of Christmas carols that came, not always on key, from a touring high school band playing in the Russell Building rotunda. Each time policemen opened the hearing room doors to usher in a few curious tourists, swells of Yuletide music poured in with them.

"The Bureau band no doubt!" said a note circulating through the staff seats.

Two of the morning's witnesses were former Justice Department officials who had served in the Nixon administration: William D. Ruckelshaus, once deputy attorney general, and Henry Peterson, a former assistant attorney general. The third witness was Norman Dorsen, a professor of law from New York University.

Ruckelshaus urged the passage of a new statute to limit the tenure of future FBI directors to eight or nine years; this would prevent the aggrandizement of power that J. Edgar Hoover had achieved in his long reign. The power Hoover amassed, said Ruckelshaus, who himself had served briefly as acting FBI director, "must never be permitted to again be possessed by one man in our history."

Peterson and Dorsen were chiefly critical of the Bureau's use of informants. These undercover spies, Dorsen observed, played a "vacuum cleaner" function in FBI investigations, sweeping in information about individuals and groups who might have had nothing to do with the original purpose of an investigation. He recommended that FBI informants be allowed to infiltrate groups only with the approval of the attorney general and a court warrant, since informants "are eavesdropping through human means." Peterson agreed with the need for greater control over the informer system but thought court approval would be impractical (presumably because of the large volume of informants used); Dorsen believed the technique should be tried, at least, to test its practicality.

On one point the witnesses and the senators agreed: for thirty years the Congress, the president, and the Justice Department had failed in their responsibilities to supervise the FBI closely. Moreover, legislative guidelines—particularly in the form of law—were even now conspicuous by their absence.

The next morning, we had a larger complement of senators, with Church, the two Harts, Mondale, and Huddleston on the Democratic side; and Baker, Goldwater, and Mathias on the Republican side. As a general rule, the better known the witness, the greater the attendance of committee members (a phenomenon related perhaps to the increased numbers of media representatives as well on such occasions). This time the witness was FBI director Clarence M. Kelley, in his only appearance before the Church committee (a frequency Colby and Helms must have envied). Church had rested a little, and the circles under his eyes had begun to fade; he read the full opening statement and turned the floor over to Kelley.

The problem of informants, introduced by Professor Dorsen on the preceding day, was picked up by Senator Philip Hart after Kelley's remarks. (Hart was allowed to begin the questioning, since he had to leave soon for a medical appointment; his illness, sadly, had been diagnosed as cancer, and he was undergoing treatments.) "Informants are the most pervasive type of eavesdropping device," he said, in a quiet and earnest voice. "It is a human device. An informant is really more intrusive on my privacy than a bug or a tap, because he can follow me anywhere. He can ask me questions to get information the government would like to have." Hart argued in favor of requiring court approval for the use of informants, as Dorsen had recommended the day before.

Stressing that the FBI informant system operated under careful controls already, Kelley said that requiring prior court approval would pose "a great many problems." How could the court monitor the use of informants? Would a separate approval be required for each use? He cautioned against requiring the judicial branch to "take over what historically have been executive-branch decisions." He appealed to the senators for a "clear and workable determination of our jurisdiction in the intelligence field."

The questioning that followed revealed that Mondale knew the briefing materials better than the other senators. He had done his homework; moreover, staff members on the FBI Task Force had taken a special liking to him, dropping by extra briefing materials and questions for his consideration. He had read and absorbed these materials and requested additional oral briefings. My efforts to encourage FBI specialists on the staff to aid Church in a similar fashion had evoked expressions of willingness but soon ran afoul of the chairman's increasingly frantic schedule. Church no longer had the time for, or—more fundamentally—Mondale's interest in, domestic intelligence subjects. Now, as Mondale stole the show, I watched the chairman's reaction; his facial expressions alternated between mild annoyance and acute irritation.

On the final day of these FBI hearings—the last that the Church committee would hold in public—Edward Levi, the attorney general, was again a witness. If Mondale's performance the day before had been spirited, on this day he was utterly aggressive. He had reason to be. The attorney general proposed to the committee, in his opening statement, an ill-defined set of guidelines for the FBI in the future. Among these proposals was one that would have allowed the Bureau to "obstruct or prevent" groups plotting to use violence or force that might threaten life or "interfere substantially" with the "essential functioning of government." In such cases, according to the proposal, the FBI could act legally against a group or individual before a crime was committed. Such authority was unprecedented.

When Mondale's turn for questioning came, he immediately struck out at the "vaguely defined" guidelines. Leaning forward on the edge of his chair and peering down on the attorney general, who sat primly at the witness table, Mondale said the guidelines failed completely to help the Bureau withstand orders from presidents or attorneys general intent on misconduct. Without the strength of law, he emphasized in a firm voice, the guidelines "would be swept away as quickly as a sand castle is overrun by a hurricane."

As Levi and Mondale traded opinions, their voices rose steadily and their exchanges came quicker. Levi's answers became retorts. The room quieted and the television cameras began to roll. The news sharks smelled blood.

The edge of tension appeared first when Mondale asked Levi if he had checked through the cases of past FBI abuses to see whether his proposed guidelines would prevent their recurrence. Did the Bureau have its list of "family jewels," like the CIA?

The attorney general skirted the issue for several minutes; clearly, he was unprepared for this line of questioning. He finally said that FBI director Kelley had asked his staff (as James Schlesinger had done at the CIA in 1973) to report any evidence of malfeasance in the Bureau, and some reports had been prepared in response. So there was an FBI "family jewels" list. Mondale then asked the inevitable question toward which he had been painstakingly building.

Mondale. Can we have those reports?

Levi. I do not think there are very many of them, but I assume you can have them. The only thing is that it is hard to . . . it is a continuing process, and there are . . . I would probably not think they would raise questions of misconduct but more be a matter of sensitive questions.

Mondale. Well, I would like to have the reports that came to Director Kelley in response.

Levi. Well, that I do not know about.

Mondale. I am asking you, as the head of the Justice Department, if we could get those reports.

Levi. Well, I do not know if you can or not, but we will certainly consider it.

Mondale. Why not?

Levi. Because I think that it is one thing to give reports of that kind in confidence to a committee of this kind and another thing to make them public.

Mondale. The CIA gave theirs to us. Why can't you?

Levi. Well, I am not in the CIA. I do not care to be. I do not wish to be.

Mondale. Do you consider that a good answer?

Levi. I—yes, I consider the answer as good as the question.

Mondale looked at Levi incredulously, then over at Church, "Well, I think that kind of arrogance is why we have trouble between the executive and the legislative branch. Thank you, Mr. Chairman." Mondale sank back in his chair in disgust.

Moments later, Levi said: "I apologize to Senator Mondale if I appeared arrogant. I thought that someone else was appearing arrogant, but I apologize."

In questioning by other members, the committee's dissatisfaction with these first-ever guidelines proposed by the Justice Department to control the FBI became increasingly obvious. They were "all very vague," observed Church at one point. Especially disturbing to some members was the concept of "preventive action." In certain circumstances (again ill defined), the Bureau would be allowed to take measures that might prevent violence. "The greater the danger or the more imminent the violence," read a proposed formula, "the more direct the preventive action allowed."

No one wished to see the FBI hamstrung in its efforts to prevent terrorist crimes or other calamities, but the imprecision regarding when, why, to what extent, and against whom the Bureau could take such action left the senators uneasy. The committee wanted guidelines that would allow the Bureau the flexibility it needed while guaranteeing the protection of individual civil rights. Despite eight months of preparation by Levi's staff, the proposals presented to the committee failed to strike this balance in any reassuring way, and the last of our public hearings ended on an ambiguous and disheartening note.

The FBI Task Force gathered its documents from the hearing table. Bulging briefing books had lain there for three hearings, untouched by most of the committee members. Question upon question written on three-by-five cards, yellow legal pads, and hastily torn scraps of paper were scattered where senators' elbows had rested. Placed there by staff, these suggestions for the most part perished on the green baize sea like so much disregarded flotsam. The senators were hesitant to ask staff questions when they themselves had failed to prepare thoroughly, uncertain where the dialogue might lead.

The result had been improvisation. The senators drew upon what they had seen in the newspapers, on television, or in a magazine; heard from a colleague or a staffer on the way to the hearing; or—reaching far back—remembered from an old law school lecture. Usually the outcome was short of ideal: a series of generalizations asked and received, interspersed with short speeches and perhaps a quotation from a founding father or other great American figure. For these last hearings, though, Mondale had come fully briefed, and the laurels went to him.

13

Tragedy

On 12 December, the day after its last public hearing, the committee convened in S407 for a business meeting. The objective was to decide upon an agenda to finish its work. Drawing on memoranda from Schwarz and Miller, Church presented a brief outline of how all the remaining tasks could be finished by February. His spirits were high, perhaps because we were finally discussing the end of the road, but this cheery countenance soon sank under a barrage of objections to his proposed schedule, coming (to his dismay) from his own party colleagues.

First, Gary Hart rejected Church's suggestion that it was pointless to continue the negotiations with former president Nixon over the ground rules for taking his deposition. "We have plenty of data already," argued the chairman. Hart, who had originally introduced the motion during the summer to obtain Nixon's testimony, disagreed and said the committee should pursue the matter further.

"Gary wants a free trip to California," observed Senator Tower, grinning.

"This testimony is not really essential," Church tried again. Hart, though, was immovable. Relenting, Church ordered Schwarz to talk with Nixon's attorney again.

Then came a more serious problem for the chairman. Senator Mondale asked for the floor and said that he did not think Church's plans to terminate the committee in February were realistic.

"You're not being arrogant again, are you, Fritz?" mocked Tower, who enjoyed the chance to have a little fun with the Democrats as they feuded among themselves. "What I object to is not your arrogance but your scene stealing," said Church to Mondale, with a joke releasing a grievance that had been building up within him all week. Laughter filled the room.

Mondale smiled, puffed expansively on a cigar, and went on to outline why he thought the committee still had several investigative tasks to complete before folding its tents. His primary interest was the staff research on the Martin Luther King Jr. case.

I sensed that Mondale was less than enraptured personally with extending the investigation but felt he owed the FBI Task Force staffers this favor for the special treatment they had given him. The result was a clash between a chairman who wished to disband his committee and, indirectly, staff investigators who wanted to pursue the trail of evidence still further. ("Some of those guys would be content to work on their cases for years," Church said to me in frustration after the meeting, fully realizing what lay behind Mondale's insistence. "This was never meant to be a permanent committee.")

Mondale concluded his remarks with the suggestion that the committee allow a couple of small groups to continue the investigative work on King and any other subjects that seemed to merit further scrutiny.

"I agree," said Senator Morgan, reversing his tendency to favor an early end to the inquiry. "The testimony of Attorney General Levi did more to scare me than comfort me."

After everyone had trooped back from a floor vote, Church spoke of how a new permanent committee could take up where we left off, drafting an FBI charter, setting a budget, and doing any further work on the King case. Mondale, however, was almost as resolute as Gary Hart had been on the Nixon matter, and he was clearly backed by Morgan as well as—through their silence at least—by the other Democrats. Schweiker also showed an interest in the further investigation of President Kennedy's death. The only allies Church could find were Tower, Goldwater, and Baker—an odd alliance, since on most occasions this trio had opposed him. His best pleading seemed to get him nowhere with his Democratic colleagues, and he put his head back and looked in despair at the low corrugated ceiling.

Tower took off on another tack, complaining that the staff was too large. "We've spent about $2,250,000 on this investigation already," he said. Between more floor votes, the committee fell into a prolonged discussion about setting a final deadline for its work. Typically, this issue would be resolved eventually through informal conversations and memoranda, rather than argumentation at a committee meeting.

As the senators filed out of S407, Church and Tower stepped before the press microphones. Church's responses were designed to encourage the press corps to turn the corner he himself had rounded in Los Angeles. The reporters dwelt upon Nixon, Kissinger, and the likelihood of more public hearings; Church hammered away at the fact that public hearings were behind the committee. "We're looking now to remedies," he said, three times in three minutes. "There is a sense that the committee wants to move with the moment." My recollection was that, fifteen minutes before, those who wanted to "move with the moment" were only Church, Tower, Baker, and Goldwater.

The chairman elaborated: "If we wait too long now after these revelations, and interest begins to dissipate, we may not be able to achieve our cardinal purpose, which is corrective legislation. And we feel it's terribly important not to let this moment pass. Therefore, we're putting our full emphasis on remedies and the completion of our report."

Then came the inevitable question: "What does all this have to do with your political plans?"

"Nothing," Church replied. "If I decide to get into the presidential race and the work of the committee has not then been completed, I would resign as chairman of the committee."

Here was a new wrinkle: Church would resign if the inquiry were prolonged and presidential fever had gripped him; this was the ultimate answer to Mondale, should he be successful in his efforts to stretch out the investigation. The following day, the "Church for President Committee" was officially formed.

Stormy Weather

On 15 December, George Bush appeared before the Senate Armed Services Committee for the first round of confirmation hearings. The small room was jammed with press, staff, and tourists. "We must not see the CIA dismantled," said Bush early in his statement. Few people would argue with that; I stood waiting for him to address what had become a more controversial point: whether he would close the door to presidential politics in 1976 if appointed CIA director.

Finally, at the end of his statement, Bush turned to this question: "When Secretary Rumsfeld was before this committee not so long ago, his name having been speculated on for vice president, he said, 'It is presumptuous of me to stand up and take myself out of consideration for something I am not in consideration for.' The committee accepted this answer then and I offer it now."

But what if Bush were asked by President Ford to be his running mate? Bush knew this question would be asked, and therefore he posed and answered it himself: "I cannot in all honesty tell you that I would not accept." The answer produced a rustle of movement through the press corps; eyebrows were raised, and pens scurried across yellow pads. "To my knowledge," Bush continued, "no one in the history of this Republic has ever been asked to renounce his political birthright as the price of confirmation for any office."

In apparent defiance of the law of physics that two bodies cannot occupy the same space, twice as many people seemed to crowd the hearing room the next day. Church soon took his place at the witness table. "So here we stand," he said, winding up his remarks, "in the wake of Watergate, and before us as the candidate for director of the CIA is a man with strong partisan, political background and a beckoning political future. I find the appointment astonishing. Now as never before, the director of the CIA must be completely above political suspicions." At the very least, added Church, Bush should choose between the CIA directorship and the possibility of a vice presidential nomination. "It is wrong for him to want both positions, even if it is a bicentennial year," he said wryly.

Senator Tower, a member of the Armed Services Committee, took this opportunity to needle his cochairman on the Intelligence Committee. "Would not our [intelligence] investigation have more credibility if you were to forswear any ambition to be president of the United States?" Tower asked, obviously savoring the discomfort this comparison brought to Church.

"If I become a candidate for president, I would step down from the chairmanship of the committee," Church responded sternly.

"Mr. Bush has said he would step down from the directorship of the CIA if he became a candidate for other office," Tower smoothly retorted.

With annoyance, Church snapped back: "If the situations are comparable in your mind, I can't persuade you."

With this kind of friendship between the two ranking members of the Intelligence Committee, I marveled that they had avoided throttling each other at some point during the long and stressful investigation.

On 19 December, President Ford disqualified Bush as a running mate, and sent a letter to the Armed Services Committee to this effect. The committee met after receipt of the letter and voted twelve to four in favor of the Bush appointment (with Gary Hart and three other Democrats in opposition).

The Bush issue was swept aside, for the moment at least, by other difficulties besetting the Church committee. First came a minor irritant in the form of columnist William Safire, followed by a problem of major proportions.

On 15 December, Safire fired his next in a series of salvos at our committee. The subject: Judith Campbell. The charge: cover-up. Safire disagreed with the committee's decision to exclude the details of the Kennedy–Campbell liaison from the assassination report.

"The private life of any public figure," wrote Safire, "is nobody's business but his own. . . . But when the nation's Chief Executive receives even a few calls from the *home telephone* of the leader of the Mafia in Chicago, that crosses the line into the public's business." There were, he said, "too many coincidences here. When Mafia leaders and a President share the same girl's attentions; when those two Mafiosi are chosen to make the hit on a foreign leader by our CIA; when the delivery of poison pellets is made to one of them on the weekend the President is with the girl in Florida; when the FBI is listening in, and cautioning the President—and when the President winds up murdered by a supporter of Castro, target of the aborted CIA assassination plot, the matter is worth a public examination." The final judgment was harsh and fully inaccurate in its reference to the committee: "The Church Committee has attempted a cover-up from the Government's end; the Mafia, by silencing Giancana forever, has clamped down the lid from its end."[1]

Angered by this accusation, Church repeated in an impromptu press conference that his committee had decided it would be inappropriate "to wade into the personal life of the president" in the course of its investigation, or to go "beyond the subject matter" allowed by the committee's mandate. "Had we had such evidence [tying Campbell to the assassination plots], we would have included it in the report," he said.

Tower agreed. The charges of a cover-up were "not sustainable on the facts," he told reporters. Having slapped Church on the cheek with his questions during the Bush hearing, the unpredictable vice chairman now patted him on the back: "I think Frank Church has bent over backward not to even give the appearance of covering-up. I think he has been totally fair and honest on this." He declared further that Church had never used the committee to promote his presidential aspirations.[2]

Bush, Safire, and Campbell, though, were all light breezes compared with the hurricane that struck Capitol Hill in December 1975. A Soviet–Cuban buildup in Angola had become public news, and some members of Congress quickly moved to curb American involvement in the African state. Beginning on 17 December, the Senate struggled for three days (in another rare secret session) over the cutoff of covert aid for Angola. On the third day, the senators voted, by a lopsided fifty-four to twenty-two, in favor of ending the aid; it remained to be seen whether the House would follow suit.[3]

The good ship *Church Committee* labored ahead sluggishly through these heavy December seas, tossed by powerful waves of opposition from the executive branch, plagued by internal dissension among the crew, its captain distracted by thoughts of buried treasure in the primary states, blown off course by strong crosswinds (like the Bush controversy), its sails torn by periodic blasts of cold air from critical journalists, and now caught up in the angry maelstrom of Hurricane Angola. Members and staff alike looked uneasily toward the lifeboats as the ship began to founder.

Fatigue was also becoming pervasive. By the end of December the committee had met more than 150 times, often for long hours. Other work was piling up in the in-boxes of members—most of it of greater interest to their constituents than the arcane details of CIA tradecraft; the price of corn had them worried, not the puzzles of counterintelligence. The perception that their constituents cared little about the committee further depleted energy and interest among the members. "I have almost no constituent mail on the investigation," one unnamed senator on the Church committee observed in mid-December, "nor do I get asked about it much."[4] Another said that the disclosures of FBI harassment of King represented the "high point of public interest"; the focus of the committee on foreign intelligence had drawn far less attention.[5] All of this led White House and intelligence officials to conclude by mid-December that, in the words of one, "the investigation is over and . . . there is little congressional support to continue it."[6]

Certainly the ship's captain was ready to lower the colors. "Now is the moment for reform," Church told a reporter in mid-December. "If we wait, the shock effect of the revelations we've made will wear away."[7] To another correspondent, he said: "You have to wrap it up some time. You're never going to get the whole truth; you're never going to be completely satisfied, and you've got to stop if you have any hope of reform."[8]

Some senators, however, privately voiced concern to reporters that the committee inquiry was being "wrapped up too quickly to meet Church's desires to run for the Presidency."[9] Staff aides, while admitting they had no "hard leads" to fresh abuses, told reporters anonymously that "large areas of domestic and foreign intelligence activities had been missed."[10]

So the ship continued to pitch about, uncertain of its course. Below decks, the crew worked on an oversight bill to create a permanent committee on intelligence and feverishly wrote chapters on various topics for possible inclusion in the final reports. Then, on 23 December 1975, the committee was struck by a bolt of lightning that, in essence, sheared off its mast and made further progress close to impossible.

The Welch Murder

Two days before Christmas, Richard S. Welch, CIA station chief in Athens, Greece, was gunned down in front of his home by masked assassins as he returned with his wife from a Christmas party. The murderers escaped, though one group calling itself "the November 17 Organization" later claimed credit for the ambush and said that the murder was a demonstration against the CIA and its imperialistic control over the Greek government. No evidence was ever obtained to establish the identity of the assassins.

Immediately, rumors and allegations arose that the Church committee was to blame for the death. "The assassination of the CIA Station Chief, Richard Welch, in Athens is a direct consequence of the stagey hearings of the Church Committee," wrote Charles Bartlett in the *Washington Star*. "Spies traditionally function in a gray world of immunity from such crudities. But the Committee's prolonged focus on CIA activities in Greece left agents there exposed to random vengeance."[11]

Nothing in the entire sixteen months of the Church investigation was more unfair than this and similar pronouncements. In fact, the committee had said nothing about Welch, or any other active CIA agent or officer, in any of its reports, press conferences, or other public statements; and we had never said a word about Greece.

The initial response of William Colby was to blame an underground newspaper called *Counterspy* for Welch's death. Published by a group of disaffected Vietnam veterans and former Defense Department intelligence officers, *Counterspy* had tried for three years on a shoestring budget to discredit the operations of the intelligence community overseas. Months previously, this newspaper had published the names of some CIA officers abroad, including Welch (wrongly stating that he was in Peru). In what Colby later attributed to a loss of temper, he said right after the killing that *Counterspy* was the cause.[12] The next day he moved away from this charge to speak more generally about a climate of hysteria regarding the CIA that had led to the assassination of Welch.

Only several weeks later did other reasons for Welch's murder emerge. He was apparently widely known as the station chief in Athens, and he lived in the same home that several of his predecessors had occupied. His house, as Welch wrote in a letter received by a colleague only four days before his murder, was "notorious" in Athens.[13] Moreover, he refused to be accompanied by a bodyguard, despite the fact that his name had also appeared in the Greek press as a CIA officer. In short, a major contribution to the loss of this fine officer (an erudite Hellenic scholar) was the inexcusably thin cover and protection provided by the Agency. In retrospect, however, Colby continued to attribute the death chiefly to the "sensational and hysterical way the CIA investigations had been handled and trumpeted around the world."[14] The implication was that Congress had no right to air the abuses of the CIA in public. Both our painstaking efforts to protect the names of intelligence officials and the serious problems of inadequate cover for CIA officers abroad were brushed aside with this sweeping hyperbole.

Colby's views were carried throughout the country, thanks largely to the unprecedented fanfare that accompanied the burial of the fallen intelligence officer. President Ford waived restrictions to allow the burial of Welch in Arlington National Cemetery. With the president and other dignitaries planning to attend the services, the laying to rest of Richard Welch became a national media event. As a member of Congress recalls, "The air transport plane carrying his body circled Andrews Air Force Base for three-quarters of an hour in order to land live on the 'Today Show.'"[15] Since the establishment of the Agency in 1947, thirty-one CIA officers had died before Welch in the service of their country, but his coffin was the first ever met by an air force color guard and many of the nation's highest officials.

Whether or not it was orchestrated in order to turn public opinion against the investigation, the ceremony surrounding the Welch burial had that effect. Though never without hate letters, the mail pouches received by the Church committee throughout 1975 had generally been filled with favorable responses to our investigation; now, however, they overflowed with hostility. One group, calling itself the Veterans Against Communist Sympathizers, vowed the deaths of Frank Church and Otis Pike.

The Welch funeral took place on 7 January with, according to the *Washington*

Post, "a show of pomp usually reserved for the nation's most renowned military heroes."[16] One editorialist who had followed the investigation closely wrote that the White House looked upon the Welch funeral as "a political device."[17] The ceremonies, he suggested, were "being manipulated in order to arouse a political backlash against legitimate criticism." Another noted that "only a few hours after the CIA's Athens station chief was gunned down in front of his home, the Agency began a subtle campaign intended to persuade Americans that his death was the indirect result of congressional investigations and the direct result of an article in an obscure magazine."[18]

Here, said a *Washington Star* headline, was "one CIA effort that worked."[19]

14

From Abuses to Reform

The chairman's authority over the Senate Intelligence Committee went into a steady slide toward decentralization as we moved into the writing of our final reports. No doubt much of this fission would have occurred even if Senator Church had tried to maintain a secure hold on every project and even if the committee staff had avoided the confusion of administrative control by two individuals, Miller and Schwarz, so different in style, temperament, and objectives. By virtue of this uneven leadership, though, the centrifugal forces almost always present in larger groups were given freer rein.

The reins in the chairman's hands became looser still in January when his campaign advisers opened Church for President headquarters on Capitol Hill. Now in communication with him daily, these advisers seemed to have greater sway over his schedule than the staff leaders of the investigative committee. The faces of Miller and Schwarz grew longer each week as they grumbled over Church's inattention. Miller was understandably anxious to have the chairman become involved in committee efforts to fashion an oversight bill.

Amidst the beehive of task forces, subcommittees, special teams, work groups, and individual entrepreneurs, two structures took on a dominance in the waning weeks of the investigation: the Foreign and Domestic Intelligence Subcommittees, headed (at Church's request) by senators Huddleston and Mondale. The Mondale Domestic Subcommittee exhibited high coherence and a strong sense of direction.[1] This was true in part because the staffers working under him were essentially the old FBI Task Force, plus Schwarz's team of lawyers. Also, Mondale involved himself in the staff work with uncommon attention and commitment.

The Huddleston Foreign Subcommittee lacked comparable coherence.[2] Its key staffers (Miller, Aaron, Bader, and Quanbeck) were by training and temperament more individualistic in their work habits—less accustomed to group writing efforts than the attorneys. Huddleston was also less ideally suited to his assignment than Mondale to his. He had no foreign policy background or expertise to speak of, having been chosen by Church because he was dependable, discreet, and the next ranking Democrat on the committee after Philip Hart (who was desperately ill) and Mondale. The upshot was a much more individualistic approach to the preparation of the foreign intelligence report.

A Shift in Focus

By January 1976, the limited cooperation that still existed between the Church committee and the executive branch centered on designing mutually acceptable legislative proposals for the reform of the intelligence community. The suggestion that representatives of the two branches work together on this objective had emerged initially in October 1975 during a luncheon attended by Bill Miller and CIA representatives. The idea germinated at the staff level and was finally proposed to Senator Church in a memo from Miller in December. Encouraged by Church, senior staff from our committee met with counterparts from the White House off and on during December and early January to discuss reform possibilities.[3]

For the most part, these initiatives were pursued enthusiastically by the committee staff. Though we had concocted several "bright ideas" on intelligence reform, how did they look to the men and women in the profession who would have to obey these laws—often in dangerous circumstances? For understanding their perspective, the dialogues were invaluable. Moreover, we needed to know what the White House would tolerate politically. As Miller said to me in December 1975, "We've got to keep the threat of a presidential veto in mind when we're spending all these long hours drafting reform legislation." So by January, the Church committee and the executive's intelligence experts had formed an uneasy alliance in the search for realistic reforms—an alliance that, unfortunately, would soon dissolve. In contrast to this limited cooperation we had nurtured with the executive branch, the Pike committee refused to participate in similar sessions with "the opposition." As its staff director told the press, the House committee wanted to prepare "its own proposals, independently, uncolored by influences of the executive branch."[4]

Discussions and decisions on the Church committee, then, were moving rapidly away from a focus on abuses to one on reform. The wisdom of including the executive branch in the reform dialectic (letting the fox into the henhouse, suggested cartoonist Herblock in a clever drawing) remained problematic. One thing, however, was clear. At the roots of the lingering distrust between the two branches lay an important political question: who would reap the benefits of whatever political capital might be gained with the American public by halting abuses and establishing safeguards against their repetition? In light of the Kilkenny catfight that had gone on between us periodically from the start, it seemed likely that one or another of the principals would lunge for the crown of champion reformer.

Just who would make the break was uncertain until 12 January. On this day, Spencer Davis, the committee's press officer, told me that Church had just called him about setting up a press conference for the next day. "I think he wants to present his priorities for change in the intelligence community," Davis said.

This seemed odd. Our final report was meant to be the vehicle for presenting these proposals, at which time each committee member would discuss his views at a special press conference. A unilateral statement from Church would be strongly resented by the other senators. I understood why Church was tempted in this direction: this would not only finesse Ford, Colby, and Pike but also generate a useful stream of publicity for the presidential campaign. I suspected that the campaign organizers were behind the ploy. ("Exposure, Johnson, exposure! That's the name of the game," one of them told me later that day.)

By midafternoon, Davis poked his Santa Claus countenance into my office and told me that Schwarz had laid out to Church the drawbacks of a solo press flight. Soon afterward, Tower let Church know in unambiguous terms that the Republicans—and, for that matter, the Democrats—would raise pluperfect hell over his press conference. The idea was quickly dropped, much to the chagrin of the busy beavers at campaign headquarters. Why the Intelligence Committee could not be more accommodating to the scheduling and image building of their candidate was beyond the understanding and patience of many in the rapidly mushrooming campaign hierarchy.

The press conference failed to stay canceled long, however. A few days later, Church requested that Davis gather the press corps after all. If he could not have a press conference without John Tower, he would have one with him.

Meanwhile, Miller had assumed top responsibility for the package of legislative reforms. The focal point for him and the other staffers on the "oversight group" (so called since their draft bill would establish a permanent committee to monitor, or oversee, intelligence activities) was 21 January 1976, when the Senate Committee on Government Operations (responsible for creating or abolishing committees) would begin six days of hearings on the proposal for a standing intelligence committee. Here would be the first major arena in the fight over a new permanent committee. Just as we had tried to reach out to the executive branch for its views on intelligence reform, now we reached toward the staff of the "Gov Ops" committee, chaired by Abraham Ribicoff (D-CT). This was a more pleasant experience: the members were on our side of town as well as on our side of the issue, and they had already given the matter a good deal of thought and preparation.

The Ribicoff committee staff had worked up an oversight bill of its own design, differing from ours on a few key provisions but generally moving in the same direction. Drafts of the Ribicoff legislation, like our own, had been shown to the executive branch for comment—a common practice in Congress. Ribicoff's aides could then review this collection of proposals, opinions, and recommendations from intelligence bureaucrats in search of solid substantive advice, and to test the political winds.

These negotiations over our bill and the Ribicoff bill were intricate and time-consuming, with countless meetings over shades of meaning and hues of interpretation. It is hard to say which is worse, a roomful of lawyers discussing a bill or a random gathering of bridge players on an ocean voyage; both quibble and fret beyond the endurance of any rational observer.

"Now let's go back to Section 13(a), Subsection (b)," one attorney would say. "Sure, why not, we've only been over it 120 times," another would respond with annoyance. "Hey, does Section 15(b) include the IRS?" a third would ask, sending everyone digging through his or her own Mount Blanc of papers in search of 15(b). This pattern repeated itself time and again as nuances were refined and polished. The sessions were maddening and soul destroying; they set the nerves on edge and numbed the mind. It was also the only way a sound bill could be constructed—one that various factions could live with, one that had a chance to pass.

For onlookers in the intelligence community and in the conservative press, though, these tedious meetings were anything but prosaic. Church committee staffers were telephoned continually by intelligence officers with anxious questions and vague fears about a monster oversight committee being created in the Dirksen laboratories; and columnists Rowland Evans and Robert Novak saw "an ominous new turn in the direction of super-oversight authority."[5] For them, "the anti-CIA orgy in Congress" was just "the latest example of the headlong rush by Congress to grasp new authority over traditional executive prerogatives, fueled by Congress' own failure for decades to make rigorous use of the oversight powers it has always had over US intelligence."

On 10 January, the off-again–on-again press conference was held. Church, Tower, and Miller, seated side by side in a small room of the Dirksen Building often used for this purpose, answered questions about the kinds of reforms the committee was considering. Miller noted that a bill from Ribicoff's committee to create a new Senate Committee on Intelligence was scheduled to come to the floor for debate and a vote on 24 February. The draft bill we were working on would serve mainly as a vehicle to influence the Ribicoff committee in its legislative drafting and, should that group reject language we felt was sound, to provide language for amendments Church or others on our committee might wish to introduce during the floor debate.

When I heard Miller announce the date for the oversight debate, I stepped into one of the telephone booths at the rear of the room and called campaign headquarters to see whether Church had anything scheduled for that day.

"What!" Carl Burke, the campaign manager, shrieked over the line. "He can't be there then! We have an important series of fund raisers in New York City that day—all day long."

Church had already departed, and Tower was speaking. I slipped a note to Miller explaining that Church might have to miss the oversight debate for a commitment in New York. His face turned red, and his head pivoted frantically from side to side. He bit his lips and scribbled back a note with a shaking hand: "He has two hours of debate on the bill. If he goes it is out of his control." I wasn't up to witnessing cardiac arrest that early in the morning. I left for the Dirksen auditorium.

Like it or not, Frank Church was the political equivalent of a busy surgeon in a large metropolitan hospital. He had dozens of patients to tend to. Our committee was one, and within it were senators and senior staffers who all wanted everything from having lunch to asking favors, large and small ("Frank, can we emphasize this point more in the final report?" "Senator Church, if you would only talk to Colby personally, we could get the document we need . . .").

Then there was the Church for President organization, comprising one manager and half a dozen would-be managers, each of whom seemed to view himself as the one properly in charge (perhaps because Burke was a newcomer to the national political scene). Naturally, each felt the need for a daily campaign strategy session with the candidate. Beneath them was a burgeoning corps of campaign volunteers of all ages who, in return for their efforts, reasonably hoped for a few words with the candidate—or at least an introduction.

On top of these demands came a mob of reporters from all parts of the country (and often from abroad), all wanting one-hour interviews with Church on intelligence issues, the campaign, or both.

Nor did the normal crush of Senate business politely cease in order to allow Church unfettered concentration on intelligence reform and presidential primaries. His Subcommittee on Multinational Corporations wanted him for hearings on what would soon become the Lockheed bribery scandal, or for planning sessions, or for signing letters. The Foreign Relations Committee had votes, hearings, and other meetings. His Energy Subcommittee of the Interior Committee had similar demands, as did the Committee on Aging, and there were also conference committees to attend.

And, always, there were constituents. Shaking hands with the folks from back home was money in the bank for vote-minded politicians; these visits, though, could consume large chunks of time. So could the barrage of foreign embassy officials in Washington, seeking appointments with Church in his capacity as a ranking member of the Foreign Relations Committee. The Washington social scene was a time stealer, too. Some invitations were hard to resist: White House balls, receptions for kings and queens, dinner parties for powerful officials, evenings of box seats and high culture at the Kennedy Center—the champagne bubbles rising above the coffee, smoke, and aspirin of day-to-day life along the Potomac.

Finally came the demands of the family, a social group that all too often came in second, third, or worse in the priorities of busy Washington officials. Church was better than many on this score, and occasionally the family would drive to Pennsylvania for a weekend at their cabin.

Little wonder senators seldom read books, let alone bulging briefing materials prepared by youthful aides. What did enter their sphere of attention tended to come on the run: cues from colleagues on the floor, in committee meetings, or on the subway headed for a vote; fragments from the newspapers over morning coffee; fifteen-minute briefings from aides (or five-minute ones striding down the hallway); snatches of news on the radio riding to work; an idea from a lobbyist or a constituent.

All of these forces swirled around Church as we approached the day of reckoning on whether the Congress—after more than two hundred attempts since 1947—would establish at last a permanent committee for intelligence matters. As the time grew nearer for this debate and for sending Church into the presidential primaries, the principal claimants for his attention on the committee and at campaign headquarters became increasingly frantic, each pulling the chairman candidate by an arm.

Attack and Counterattack

"The Agency has really been shattered," said one experienced CIA hand early in the new year. "We are going to need a lot of forthright executive support to recover."[6] President Ford could hardly have been more forthright than he was in his State of the Union address on 19 January. He turned to intelligence as he neared the end of his speech:

> As conflict and rivalries persist in the world, our United States intelligence capabilities must be the best in the world.
>
> The crippling of our foreign intelligence services increases the danger of American involvement in direct armed conflict. Our adversaries are encouraged to attempt new adventures, while our own ability to monitor events and to influence events short of military action is undermined.
>
> Without effective intelligence capability, the United States stands blindfolded and hobbled.
>
> In the near future, I will take actions to reform and strengthen our intelligence community. I ask for your positive cooperation. It is time to go beyond sensationalism and ensure an effective, responsible, and responsive intelligence capability.

The suggestion that the work of certain congressional committees was "crippling" our foreign intelligence capabilities came through loud and clear. The president was obviously continuing his efforts to stir up a public backlash against the investigations.

He was joined by former CIA directors and conservative editorialists around the country. John A. McCone, director from 1961 to 1965, wrote that the "tempest" over the intelligence community as a rogue elephant was unfounded. The CIA, he advised, was thoroughly supervised from the president on down. Though "a few" of the "recent accusations of wrongdoing [were] justified, some [were] imagined, others grossly overstated." The key objective now, he wrote, was "to extinguish, as much as possible, criticism" in order to "restore confidence and provide an on-going dynamic foreign intelligence service."[7] The most vicious remarks against the committee appeared on the editorial page of the widely distributed weekly, *TV Guide*. "A hundred KGB agents working overtime for the Kremlin would hardly have undermined the CIA as effectively as Senator Church's Committee did," the editor declared. "It was a shocking and immeasurably harmful blow to our national security."[8]

The committee suffered more than verbal assaults. We continued to have our familiar problems with documents. Throughout most of the inquiry, our headaches had come chiefly from trying to obtain papers from the executive branch; now the struggle shifted to reaching agreement on what papers could be published without detriment to the national security. As was often the case, the White House was even more intransigent than the intelligence agencies. We patiently entered into negotiations with the administration. Often these interbranch staff discussions were cordial and helpful to us, as errors in fact or interpretation were pointed out by intelligence agency representatives; at other times, they bogged down in what appeared to be intentional stonewalling and harassment of the committee in its efforts to finish its final reports.

Compared to events in the House of Representatives, however, our dialogues with the Ford administration were sweet reason. On 19 December, the Pike committee had voted, eight to four and seven to five, to release to the public its reports on covert action in Angola and Italy (a six-to-six tie buried the committee's study of United States support to Kurdish rebels in Iraq). In turn, President Ford flatly stated that release of these reports "would be detrimental to the national security" and, in a letter to Pike, said the reports would have to remain classified. The Pike panel was engaged once more in a constitutional crisis with the chief executive.

The Church committee was also unwilling to sit by idly while the executive branch regrouped its troops and rolled heavy artillery into place for the winter siege. At press conferences and luncheons, in television and radio news interviews and speaking engagements around the country, Church fought back at the committee's detractors.

On 14 January, on NBC's *Today* show, Church was asked about his critics—specifically those on his own committee.

Questioner. Senator, there's been some criticism from within your own committee that maybe the investigation didn't go far enough, that maybe it was prematurely cut back, and one of the reasons that's been suggested is your desire to get into politics to run for president.

Church. I really think that's unfounded, unfair really, because the committee has from the beginning had a limited life. . . . Now it's perfectly true, we haven't opened every door and examined every closet. It's not possible to do that in one year's time, but that wasn't our charge. Our charge was to make as adequate an investigation as possible, and nobody has suggested that the revelations we've made are insufficient upon which to ground valid recommendations. Then the constructive purpose of our work was to get those reforms written into the law, and we want to do that while we still have momentum. And that can be done. And that I regard as the reason for the investigation in the first place. Now, whatever is left to investigate can be taken up by the permanent oversight committee. So you see the argument is really without much merit.

Questioner. Well, some people say that your committee has gone too far and hurt the CIA. In fact, there has been some suggestion, only a suggestion, that somehow that's involved with the death of a CIA agent and disclosure of names. It's all part of one package. Is that true?

Church. Utterly untrue. And unworthy of a spokesman of the president even to permit such an innuendo. We took the precaution in the beginning of not even obtaining the names of agents currently on assignment overseas, because we didn't even want the possibility of an inadvertent disclosure that might imperil any agent that was actually on assignment in some foreign capital. There's no basis to that charge whatever. It's preposterous.

Continuing his counterattack, Church said that among the recommendations his panel would propose soon was one requiring the administration to provide notification to the Congress before launching a covert action. This position was aggressive, going beyond the practice (based on the Hughes–Ryan Act) of providing notification to Congress only in "a timely fashion"—that is, after the fact. The administration looked upon the Church proposal as an attempt to limit the constitutional prerogatives of the president and potentially to arm Congress with a possible veto over the covert action option.

Church refused to budge on this issue, and on the news show he rejected the administration's constitutional arguments: "There's no attempt to insert a veto power that would prevent the president from exercising his constitutional responsibilities as the chief architect of our foreign policy, but the Constitution provides that the Senate is both to advise and consent. Now this committee could not advise the president with respect to a significant new covert operation unless it had some information—unless it had word of that operation in advance." If push came to shove, Church warned, Congress could always "pull back on the purse strings" to halt unwarranted intelligence operations.

The next day Church called Kissinger a "compulsive interventionist" and criticized administration policy in Angola and Italy. He blamed the secretary of state directly for the misguided strategy favoring United States covert action in Angola, and he sharply criticized the rumored possibility (reported in the press) that the CIA was secretly funneling money to members of the Christian Democratic Party in Italy. "This is not a post-war situation in which the United States is trying to resurrect democracy from the ashes," Church told reporters. "If by now the system is so fragile and corrupt that it can't sustain itself with the support of the Italian people, then it is a futile exercise to try to prop it up with money."[9]

Whatever vigor the intelligence debate had lost while the nation mourned the murder of Richard Welch was being rapidly regained in the new year. Attack–counterattack between the Ford administration and the investigating committees was on again; nonetheless, there hung in the air a sense that the impetus of the investigations was fading quickly. Clearly, we had to make a strong case before the Ribicoff committee, complete our final report, and bring this acrimonious debate to an end. Whatever his motivations, Church was right; the time had come to close down the shop.

Closing down, however, continued to be infinitely more easily said than done. Few, if any, of us at the time had any comprehension of the major battles that lay ahead before the denouement.

15

Backlash

On 20 January, I walked into Fritz Schwarz's section of the auditorium. As he spoke into the telephone, he motioned me to sit down. As usual, his desk overflowed with papers, and on the floor a leather briefcase bulged at the seams as documents pushed out of its top. Crumpled yellow legal paper filled the trash can and spilled onto the floor. Schwarz sprawled in his chair, his long legs stretched out. Blue semicircles spread out under his tired eyes, and his pinstripe suit was rumpled. The chief counsel looked as if he had just detrained from the Trans-Siberian Express.

"What's new?" I asked as he hung up the receiver.

"Well, for one thing, I just informed Senator Church that we could not possibly finish the committee's work by February 29th," Schwarz replied. "Maybe by March 15th."

No wonder Schwarz looked battered. I could imagine how Church had taken that bit of news.

"What did he have to say?" I inquired.

"He was not pleased." Schwarz managed a grin.

I asked him what he thought of the staff work on oversight so far, since the next day the Ribicoff committee would begin its hearings on a proposal to establish a permanent oversight committee for intelligence policy. As Senator John Glenn (D-OH), a member of the Ribicoff panel, would put it during the hearings: "It is now the responsibility of the Committee on Government Operations to go forth with the recommendations and to try to solve problems brought to our attention by the Select Committee."[1]

Schwarz was unimpressed and uninterested in this aspect of the committee's work. "Oversight is overrated," he replied. "I fear that the creation of a new permanent intelligence committee will only serve to isolate intelligence in the Congress." He envisaged the eventual displacement of intelligence oversight responsibilities from other committees in the Senate (Appropriations, Foreign Relations, Armed Services, Judiciary) to a single new committee, which would then be highly vulnerable to manipulation and perhaps complete co-optation by the intelligence community. His prognosis was glum, but plausible. The old system of dispersed oversight authority, though, had failed to work very well.

The Ribicoff Hearings

Certainly, Senator Church strongly favored a permanent committee that could take over his unfinished agenda, and on 21 January, he presented his case in favor of a permanent intelligence committee. In a room filled with onlookers, Senator Ribicoff began the first of eight days of Government Operations Committee hearings on his oversight bill. He cited a recent opinion poll indicating that the public wanted closer monitoring of the intelligence agencies by the Congress and the White House (by a margin of 66 to 18 percent). "The nation is indebted to Senator Church and Senator Tower and the entire collective Senate committee and their staff," said Ribicoff, ending his statement. These words were a welcome ray of sunshine after the downpour of criticism that had soaked us intermittently over the previous couple of months.

Church recited before the Ribicoff panel the list of abuses we had documented, then emphasized that a new Senate Intelligence Committee should have broad jurisdiction to pass on annual authorizations for all the major intelligence agencies; a rotating membership (with senators serving a maximum of six years); prior notification of intended covert actions; and the right to make disclosures over the objection of the executive branch. He announced that within the week his committee would present the Ribicoff panel with its own draft of a bill to establish an oversight committee.

Senator Percy asked Church if he anticipated unanimous support from his committee in favor of his oversight bill.

"I had thought that there was a unanimous consensus of the committee," Church answered. "I am now told there may be some dissenting votes." He looked annoyed.

Percy turned to covert action, eliciting from Church a well-rehearsed criticism:

I think that covert activities in the past twenty years of the kind that we have engaged in have done this country much more harm than good.

Twenty-five years ago, this country had a matchless moral position from which it exercised immense leadership and influence in the world. Anything the United States stood for was automatically endorsed by three-quarters of the governments of the world.

Now we have had twenty-five years of manipulation by methods that were plainly copied from the KGB: coercion, false propaganda, bribery, abduction, attempted assassination, and where are we at the end of that twenty-five years?[2]

Percy replied icily that, in contrast to Church's perception, "some would say that these activities were not as apparent until the creation of the Senate select committee, and the publicity given in the last few months have far exceeded that of the last thirty years."

"That would not be true," said Church. "There are those who would say that, in fact, we are now the targets of what seems to me to be an apparently orchestrated effort to undercut the committee's recommendations."

Senator Tower spoke next. Within minutes it was plain that he had broken ranks with the Church committee majority. "I am not prepared to accept the legislation as drafted by the Select Committee," he said, "because I believe that serious analysis will reveal it to be both a premature and simplistic solution to an extremely complicated set of problems." Behind the hobgoblin of Tower's rhetoric emerged his abiding objection to a new oversight committee: jurisdiction. "Currently it is the Armed Services Committee [on which Tower served] that has the oversight responsibility of the CIA," he said, adding that "existing committees can and should perform required oversight."[3]

Tower next disagreed with Church's testimony favoring notification of Congress prior to the conduct of covert action. He quoted directly from the president's recent State of the Union address in which Ford rejected the idea of prior notification as an intrusion into traditional presidential powers: "The foreign relations of the United States can be conducted effectively only if there is strong central direction that allows flexibility of action. That responsibility clearly rests with the President."

Ribicoff asked Senator Baker to speak next. Baker was also a dissenter within the Church committee, though for reasons that differed from Tower's. (Goldwater, I later discovered, was the third dissenter, on grounds approximating those of Tower.) No wonder Church looked vexed: the loss of Baker's support would send a ripple across the Senate membership.

Baker said he strongly favored a new oversight committee—ideally, a separate committee in each chamber. Problems had occurred with oversight in part, said Baker, "because nobody was running the store." With a new committee whose jurisdiction was strictly intelligence, the members could be more watchful and less distracted by other chores; for example, intelligence was but a small portion of the Armed Services Committee's responsibilities.

Baker, though, stood foursquare with Tower on the issue of prior notification. I sensed, nonetheless, that he and Church were less far apart on this issue than each may have thought. Baker said he wanted language to guarantee that the new oversight committee was "fully and currently informed"—a phrase drawn from Section 202 of the Atomic Energy Act. The point on which most Church committee members seemed to agree was that Congress should know what was going on in the intelligence field, and not a week or a month after the fact. None of the phrases (even Church's "prior notification") asked the president to seek prior permission. Perhaps Church and Baker could reach an accommodation on this difference of opinion.

A second issue had caused Baker consternation for several months: the disclosure of information by a Senate committee. It was the old Rule 36 bugbear. Senator Church—and the Senate parliamentarian consulted by the committee—interpreted the rule to allow disclosure of classified information by a Senate committee over the objections of the executive branch. The parliamentarian's reading of the rule was wrong, in Baker's judgment. He believed that, ideally, declassification over the objection of a president should occur only through a "joint and concurrent [sic] resolution of the bodies of Congress."[4] At a minimum, he was convinced, Rule 36 meant that only a majority of the Senate membership could release a classified document to the public.

Three men from the Church committee had now testified before Gov Ops, and each had a different view on one or more key provisions of our oversight bill. "What bothers me," said Ribicoff, "as I listen to Senator Church, Senator Tower, and you, Senator Baker, is whether or not you can produce a bill within a week."

It was a good question, and one that obviously worried Church. Had he stayed to hear Tower and Baker, he would have been even more concerned. Tower had a troubling premonition: if the Ribicoff committee chose to submit a bill like the one envisioned by Church, "I predict that when we get to the Senate floor with a bill of this kind, you are probably going to run into all sorts of jurisdictional jealousies."

My jaw dropped when Tower testified that, unlike the KGB, the United States possessed no worldwide clandestine infrastructure of agents;[5] it dropped further still when he stated, in defense of the old oversight system, that the Church committee "did not come up with anything we had not already discovered in the Armed Services Committee."[6] Had the Armed Services Committee truly uncovered all the various illegalities we had come across? If the answer really was yes (as I doubted, since for one thing that committee had no access to FBI COINTELPRO files), it was even more astounding that Armed Services had failed to report these findings to the American people, or at least to the Justice Department.

For the next seven days, a long line of stars of various illuminations paraded before the Ribicoff committee to present their views on the merits of a new oversight committee: Dean Rusk, Nicholas Katzenbach, Colby, Helms, McCone, McGeorge Bundy, Clarence Kelley, Clark Clifford, Levi, and Kissinger, among others. While their views on specific points scattered in all directions like the traces of a Fourth of July skyrocket, the witnesses almost unanimously favored more vigorous oversight of the intelligence community through the establishment of a new intelligence committee. Only Senator Strom Thurmond (R-SC) joined Goldwater and Tower in opposition—all members of the Armed Services

Committee, whose turf was jeopardized by the establishment of an intelligence committee.

Dean Rusk emphasized that 1976 was hardly a "vintage year" to resolve controversial matters. Rather, they would require "very careful consultations over a period of time." We were in an election year, and as with each of our presidential contests, Rusk continued, the country would go through a "turbulent, tempestuous donneybrook."[7]

His testimony reinforced my growing sense that the Church committee could have a vital catalytic effect on intelligence reform, but others would have to carry the efforts forward: first, the Ribicoff committee, then the Rules Committee (which had twenty days to review and possibly modify—if not reject altogether—the Ribicoff request to establish a new standing committee), then the Senate itself, and finally, the permanent oversight committee. The road was long and perilous, with several opportunities for ambush by opponents.

Committee Wrangles

"Church isn't doing his homework," Miller said to me that morning. Schwarz echoed the complaint in the afternoon: "Church is trying to carry water on both shoulders. It won't work." Both staff leaders were unhappy about the campaign diversion.

At Church's office, I told him (without mentioning presidential politics) that "several of the staff think you are spreading yourself too thin."

He stopped writing long enough to look at me. "They'll just have to live with it," he said, with a quick flare of temper.

I pressed on: "There is considerable confusion over when you want various parts of the work completed." Regaining his composure, he replied that these matters would be settled at the next meeting of the committee.

The investigation was causing strain in others besides Church. The president was under fire too. On 22 January, the Pike committee voted nine to four to release its report to the public, despite efforts by the White House to block publication. It was "preposterous" and "outrageous," said one dissenter on the Pike committee, for his panel to obtain classified information from the executive under a nondisclosure agreement, then later publish this information.[8] The Pike committee majority, however, saw matters otherwise. As Les Aspin put it, the committee would set "a terrible, terrible precedent" if it concluded it had less right than the president to decide what information should be made public.[9]

Though displeased with the performance of the Pike committee, the *Chicago Tribune* saw one virtue in its progress as of January: its termination date was blissfully near. Now, said the *Tribune*, if only Senator Church who "has led the assault with a vengeance exceeding Mr. Pike's," would also regain his senses and "call off the bloodhounds."[10]

The Department of Justice was eager to see us go out of business, too, though for different reasons. Prosecutors in the criminal division of the Justice Department formally requested access to the secret testimony of witnesses who had appeared before the Church committee, hoping to find fresh leads that would advance several prosecutions they had launched as a result of allegations made by the Rockefeller Commission and the Congress.

This request was at the top of the agenda as the committee convened on 23 January, and confusion and uncertainty characterized the committee's response. On the one hand, the senators wished to see violations of the law dealt with by the government's attorneys; but on the other hand, the committee believed it had an obligation to protect the identities of those witnesses who had come to us in confidence.[11]

The principal target of the Justice Department's intelligence investigation was Richard Helms. The Rockefeller Commission had revealed CIA responsibility for a break-in into a photographic studio in Fairfax, Virginia, in 1971 (during Helm's tenure as director). The Agency had claimed to be searching for stolen classified documents (which it failed to find in the studio). The committee's vote on the Fairfax break-in was seven to four in favor of providing the relevant CIA documents in our possession to the Department of Justice. Morgan added his "no" to that of Tower, Baker, and Goldwater.

This same alignment held on the second vote, on CIA Chilean documents (which Justice Department attorneys wished to review in relation to possible charges of perjury stemming from testimony before the committee). The senators, however, proved unwilling to relinquish papers on illegal mail-opening operations; by the close vote of six to five, a motion was approved to table this request until the committee had completed its own inquiry.

Senator Goldwater tried unsuccessfully to return to the vote on the Chilean papers. Raising one of his favorite topics—maddening Rule 36—he argued that the committee alone had no authority to release classified documents to the Justice Department or to anyone else; only the full Senate could authorize this action. Moreover, he asked, with reference to Richard Helms, "Why hang a man who simply wanted to protect the office of the presidency?"

Senator Baker seemed less concerned with the fate of Helms than in having the committee take a "consistent" position on the release of documents to Justice. The turnaround on the mail-opening vote made Morgan and others wonder what rationale was guiding the group.

Baker moved that the committee honor either all or none of the Justice Department requests. The position seemed logical, but as Mondale emphasized, there were important distinctions between the various cases. If we had exhausted the materials ourselves (as we had yet to do on the mail opening), then Mondale felt we should turn them over. The Baker motion failed six to five.

Baker, as usual, was hard to deter. He next moved to refuse all the documents on Chile that had to do with the so-called Track II involvement—that is, plans to promote a military coup. The original coalition defeated this proposal seven to four. Tower was unsuccessful, though, in a subsequent voice vote to have all NSA documents held back, like the mail-opening documents, for the time being.

Three more Department of Justice requests were passed easily: to relinquish the CIA and FBI documents on Martin Luther King Jr. (by a vote of ten to one, with Goldwater the dissenter); on an alleged plot to assassinate columnist Jack Anderson (eleven to zero); and on the CIA scientist who had prepared assassination materials during the plot against Lumumba (by voice vote).

The second item on the agenda was the oversight bill, which immediately ran into a wall of jurisdictional jealousies. Members of the Church committee who sat on other committees in the habit of having access to intelligence information (Armed Forces and Judiciary) made it clear that these standing committees would refuse to give up their prerogatives; they would demand concurrent authority with any new permanent intelligence committee. Tower soon put his hand against his forehead and groaned, "We're going to get into a jurisdictional morass." Drawing back his sinking foot, Church adjourned the meeting.

The committee members who returned to S407 were in a better mood after lunch, full stomachs apparently having settled the impulse to debate. A cartoon by Oliphant circulated among them and brought a chorus of chuckles; it portrayed the Church committee scrambling for cover under tables, documents flying, as Frank Sinatra and three henchmen entered the door of the hearing room. The caption read: "The Church committee calls Frank Sinatra—er, on the other hand, if Mister Sinatra would rather not. . . ." The press had continued to speculate that the committee might call Sinatra in connection with the Judith Campbell matter, since he had reportedly introduced her to President Kennedy, but neither Democrats nor Republicans on the committee showed any interest. They had concluded, in Tower's words, that there was "not a scintilla of evidence" to suggest that a talk with Sinatra would be helpful. Besides, Church reminded the press later, "we are not authorized to investigate a president's love life."[12]

Schwarz informed the senators that former President Nixon had agreed (through his Washington lawyer) to answer, under oath, written questions from the committee. Without a formal vote, the seven members present quickly agreed. It was probably the best bargain we could strike in the waning days of our existence as a committee.

The members decided also that a letter should be written to the FBI inquiring about the status of its probe into the Sam Giancana murder. The committee remained uneasy about the circumstances of the mobster's death and wanted to make sure the slaying was thoroughly investigated by appropriate law enforcement officials.[13]

Finally, the committee returned to its morning debate on the oversight bill. Choosing now to ignore jurisdictional squabbles, the members voted seven to zero, with little debate, to accept the bill as drafted by the staff over several months (its differences from the bill drafted by the Ribicoff committee would have to be dealt with later). The afternoon absence of Tower and Goldwater, who steadfastly opposed the bill, facilitated quick passage. Apparently they (and perhaps Baker—also absent) had decided to fight this issue elsewhere.

As relations within the Church committee soured in the struggle over the oversight bill, they sweetened between Congress and the intelligence community. With the end of the inquiry near, the fighting spirit had gone from most members of the Church and Pike committees, and their colleagues warned privately against further bruising of the intelligence agencies. Colby told a reporter on 23 January that he thought the "friendlier" political atmosphere on the Hill was a result, in large measure, of the Welch assassination a month earlier.[14] It did seem evident that President Ford and the CIA had, in columnist Anthony Lewis's words, "won a warm public response when they dramatized the murder of a CIA agent in Athens and sought to blame it on leakers."[15] Despite this new mood, however, the "running battle" (Colby's phrase)[16] between Congress and the administration was not over yet. The next engagement was the floor debate on the nomination of George Bush as CIA director.

At 1 o'clock in the afternoon of 27 January, the Senate reconvened in closed session to finish the Bush debate. The vote would be taken at 3 o'clock sharp. The pro-Bush floor leader was Senator Thurmond, ranking Republican on the Armed Services Committee. The problem, as he saw it, was less Bush than the Church and Pike committees. "That is where the public concern lies, on disclosures which are tearing down the CIA," he said, "not upon the selection of this highly competent man to repair the damage of this over-exposure."[17]

Senators passed in and out of the chamber, listening to the speeches, quietly chatting with one another, or signing letters on their antique desks. At 3 o'clock, the clerk called the roll; when the voting was complete, the results were sixty-four to twenty-seven in favor of Bush. His foes had failed lamentably. Almost all the opposition came from liberal Democrats, with only a single Republican voting against Bush. The voting pattern within the Church committee, too, was sharply partisan: with the exception of Senator Schweiker (who was absent), the Republicans voted together, and all six committee Democrats were united in opposition.

Church may have been correct in principle, but Bush's status as a former member of the House, his father's position as a former member of the Senate, his own obvious charm and ability, and heavy White House lobbying had won the day. For better or worse, a politician would now head the intelligence community.

Turning Point

With Bush now confirmed, the time had come for William Colby's swan song. In his last public utterance as CIA chief, he blasted the Pike committee's classified final report, pronouncing it—at a press conference—"totally biased and a disservice to our nation."[18] It contained, he said, "outrageous statements designed to titillate and get a few headlines." The Ford administration and the Pike committee were close to "open political warfare," reported the *Washington Post*.[19]

One might have expected us to enjoy the fireworks from our vantage point on the other side of the Hill; after all, the more criticism the House got, the more responsible we looked. Yet while some self-congratulation was apparent on our side, the feeling was shallow; we fully realized we might join our House brothers in the same boiling caldron, with the CIA adding the salt, the White House bellowing the flames afresh, and the intelligence officials dancing around the fire in delight.

If Pike thought he had problems with the CIA and the White House, he discovered on 28 and 29 January what real trouble could be. Pike requested the unanimous consent of his committee to publish its final report. He asked, as well, for a two-week extension of the committee's life to polish the final recommendations. Objecting to an extension, Robert McClory (R-IL) forced Pike under the rules of the House to take the request for an extension to the Rules Committee. On 28 January, not only did the Rules Committee deny the extension, but also its members voted nine to seven to block publication of the final report altogether. They recommended that it be released only if the president had final authority over what secret information would be published. "The White House and the CIA," Pike said, "have jointly engineered the biggest cover-up since Watergate."[20]

A week prior to its confrontation with Rules, the Pike committee had received from the Ford administration a request for 250 deletions from the report on grounds of national security. The committee staff, in negotiations with intelligence community and White House spokesmen, had subsequently reached agreement: approximately seventy of the items in question would be deleted. But then a committee majority voted to overrule the administration's objections on the disputed passages of the report. "The majority conclusion of the committee was simply that we could not sweep the atrocious and horrendous things under the rug," Pike told the press. "We could not carry out our mandate if we said to the president—and that means saying to the CIA and the FBI—you can veto anything you want in our final report."[21]

The argument between Pike and the Rules Committee was sent to the full House for resolution on the evening of 28 January. The floor was crowded and noisy, a bustling, chaotic contrast to the smaller and more serene Senate chamber. The Speaker gaveled some 300 milling members to order, and the debate began.

The tension on the floor wafted up to the gallery. The speeches rang with emotion. The booming voice of Robert N. Giaimo (D-CT), a member of the Pike committee, filled the great hall: "If you think he is going to release anything that in his judgment would jeopardize the secrets of the United States," he said, pointing toward Pike, "then you are wrong."[22] Who did the House trust, he said, Mr. Pike or the CIA?

Congressman Morgan E. Murphy (D-IL), another Pike committee member, spoke with equal passion in favor of releasing the report as it was. "If we are not a coequal branch of this government, if we are not equal to the president and the Supreme Court," he said, "then let the president write this report, let the CIA write this report, and we ought to fold our tents and go home."

When Pike took the floor, he acknowledged that the report contained classified information but emphasized that none of it was "dangerous."

Opponents were no less impassioned in their views. McClory, the ranking Republican on the Pike committee, reminded the House that early in the investigation he and Pike had struck a bargain with the president: no classified information would be released by the committee until the president had certified that no harm would come to the national security by virtue of such a release.[23] To violate this agreement now would put the honor of the House in question, in McClory's opinion; it would be tantamount to double-crossing the nation's chief executive.

Otis Pike, however, had a different interpretation of the agreement. He retorted during the House debate that the original understanding "did not apply to our final report . . . I would not have agreed to it." Pike said it would be inappropriate to allow the CIA to "censor the report."

Dale Milford (D-TX), an ally of McClory's on the Pike committee, raised an argument close to one that had reverberated around S407 for half a year. "The issue is," he said, "can nine members of this House [the number of Pike committee members who voted for release of the final report] release information unilaterally?"—that is, without approval of the full House and over the strenuous objections of the president. It was the Goldwater–Baker theme song, "The Rule 36 Blues," all over again.

The debate revealed a widespread dissatisfaction with the Pike committee, especially over the multiple leaks that had come already from its report (whether or not the committee itself was actually responsible). In fact, the steady trickle of "inside information" about the Pike committee and its findings had become a ruptured dam. Observing this flood, the House members seemed more concerned about leaking than about the astonishing findings themselves.

When the last name was called, the House had voted against its own committee by a margin of 146 to 124; the executive branch would be allowed to censor the Pike committee's report. The president and the intelligence community had won their first major victory against Congress.

Dejected, Pike told reporters after the vote that the outcome had made "a complete travesty of the whole doctrine of separation of powers"; it made the work of his committee "entirely an exercise in futility."[24] He said he would have his committee vote the next week on whether to kill the report completely or accede to the president's red pen. He clearly favored the first alternative; the two thousand copies locked in the Pike committee rooms could turn to dust before he would bow to presidential censorship.

The next day proved eventful on the Senate side too: Howard Baker made it final that he was joining Tower and Goldwater in opposition to the Church committee's oversight bill. The names of the committee's senior Republicans were conspicuously missing from the top of the proposal as cosponsors, signaling throughout the Senate that key members of the investigating panel opposed its conception of a permanent committee for intelligence oversight.

All within two days, the House Intelligence Committee had ground to a halt, and the Senate Intelligence Committee had split asunder over the centerpiece of its recommendations. The White House must have rejoiced; the Welch death and leaks from the Pike committee report had produced, at last, a backlash against the congressional investigations.

16

The Big Leak

Senator Church introduced his committee's bill for a permanent Senate intelligence committee on 29 January 1976. The proposal, noted John Tower on the floor that day, was "hastily conceived and simplistic." Its distribution of responsibility was a "prescription for jurisdictional jealousy" within the Senate, and it unnecessarily proliferated the number of persons having access to sensitive information—"the very antithesis of keeping a secret." The proposal was, in short, said the vice chairman, "a legislative disaster."[1]

Undaunted by this lack of support, Church responded that "it might still be possible, as we work our way through the legislative process, to find a formulation that might enjoy the Senator's support." Church understood as well as anyone that the bill he had just introduced might be amended in a hundred ways before a majority coalition crystalized around it—if, in fact, one ever did.

Meanwhile, it was business as usual in the Dirksen auditorium. Bill Bader was stuffing the last pages into a large briefing book in preparation for yet another cross-examination of Richard Helms. I kidded him about the remote chances of getting the senators to absorb all the thorough research his CIA Task Force had prepared. "Yes," he agreed, "it's like trying to get a great tidal wave through the eye of a needle, if you'll pardon the malapropism."

The next day at CIA headquarters, a thousand high-level Agency employees gathered to see George Bush sworn in to replace William Colby. During the twenty-minute ceremony, President Ford described the intelligence community as the nation's first line of defense and said that appropriate gratitude to the intelligence corps was long overdue. "The abuses of the past have more than adequately been described," he said. "We cannot improve this Agency by destroying it." He thanked Colby for his "dedicated service" and the audience applauded loudly. Once Bush had been sworn in (politics would not "color" any CIA activities during his tenure, he promised in a brief speech), Colby escorted him and the president from the room and quietly slipped away. Another wave of hand clapping swept through the crowd as they noticed Colby's departure in his weather-beaten Buick. He waved back at the crowd—many of whom reportedly had tears in their eyes—and drove away in a late morning mist.[2]

The president's men soon let it be known that the White House was now concerned with only about 2 percent of the Pike committee report.[3] This represented a dramatic shift away from the president's earlier view that half the report ought to be shelved permanently.

The Pike committee nonetheless rejected these efforts at compromise and, on 3 February, by a vote of seven to four, decided it no longer had authority either to negotiate with the White House or even to distribute the report to other House members. The committee was prepared, though, to issue recommendations, which were voted upon on 3 and 4 February, and then released as a package on 10 February by a final vote of nine to five. The committee proposed to abolish the Defense Intelligence Agency; to create a six-man NSC subcommittee on covert actions; to give a permanent oversight committee the right to release any information or documents in its possession or control by a vote of a committee majority (the argument Church had made so often in S407 in defense of his interpretation of Senate Rule 36); and to provide the hoped-for oversight committee with full access to intelligence "sources and methods."[4]

The chances for achieving permanent oversight committees, however, remained problematic on the Senate side and downright bleak on the House side. The Pike committee's investigation had released deep emotions in the House. "Do something!" blurted Robert Kasten (R-WI) to Pike during a committee hearing, demanding a stop to leaks.

"What do you recommend? Lie detector tests?" replied the frustrated chairman. "I do not know where the leaks have come from."

"The air has gone out of the balloon," observed the thoughtful chairman of the Republican Policy Committee, John Anderson (Illinois). "There was too much blabbering from the Pike committee, and the House is now willing to relax and go back to its old ways."[5]

On the Church committee, John Tower offered a similar emphasis. In a letter to the *New York Times*, he wrote: "Reforms are clearly needed to prevent a recurrence of past abuses by our intelligence agencies. But what is needed most of all—as recent events have made clear—is a responsible, leak-proof means of Congressional oversight."[6]

The debate on intelligence had concentrated first on abuses, then on reforms, and now on leaks from Capitol Hill. Despondent, Church told *Washington Post* reporters that "the issue has become how to keep secrets rather than how to preserve freedom." No leaks had come from his committee, he emphasized, "only the administration's innuendos, which the press repeated." He was pleased about the stand the Pike committee had taken on the rights of a congressional committee to release classified information by majority vote: "If Congress permits itself to be gagged it ought to forfeit its oversight function."[7]

While the coals of opposition to further intelligence debate glowed brightly in the House, the administration, taking no chances, ordered the president's chief lobbyists to fan the fire. One correspondent reported at the time:

Late in January, when the House Select Committee prepared its report, the Administration began frantically lobbying to suppress it. "The pressure from the White House, the CIA, and the State Department has been astounding," one House member said at the time. "I've never seen anything like it." Administration lobbyists repeatedly invoked the name of Richard Welch, the head of the CIA station in Athens, who was murdered there last December. They charged that members of Congress who had earlier revealed CIA secrets were responsible for similar murders in the future. The implication of such charges was clear: members who voted to release the report would be vulnerable at election time this fall to accusations that they had jeopardized the nation's security.[8]

Appearing before the Ribicoff committee, Henry Kissinger "wrapped his reform package proposals in a running series of complaints about congressional leaks."[9]

Whether or not attributable to White House public relations work, by January 1976 the simple fact was that both of the congressional intelligence committees were less than highly regarded by the public. In December 1975, a Louis Harris survey had asked Americans how they would rate the job being done by the two committees. The results for the Church committee were 38 percent positive, 40 percent negative, and 22 percent unsure; for Pike, 36 percent positive, 40 percent negative, and 24 percent unsure.[10]

Even at that date, the image apparently held by the public was extremely disappointing. Our long hours and careful research to uncover and guard against abuses by the intelligence services seemed to go largely unappreciated or misunderstood. And to see ourselves rated virtually neck and neck with the House committee, even though we had avoided most of its pitfalls, was truly disheartening. Moreover, the image had no doubt grown worse, since the poll had been taken before the Welch murder and the presidential flag-waving at Arlington Cemetery.

Columnist Anthony Lewis concisely summed up the situation that confronted the Pike committee—and us: "There was a more basic reason for the House vote, however, than the Committee's performance. That was a backlash—a public backlash—against continuing exposure of secret operations. The members were hearing from back home that people were reluctant to hear about any more embarrassments on the American record."[11]

Capitol Hill watchers now believed that the investigating committees were in a state of "confusion and disarray";[12] that "enthusiasm for reform has cooled in the Senate";[13] and that "the year-long drive . . . has unquestionably faltered, especially in the House."[14] The *New York Times* was willing to concede that the Senate committee had "generally been more adroit in its dealings with the White House than the House Committee," but it predicted "even greater repercussions" against our report because of its expected greater detail.[15]

These dire forecasts made me feel as I had as a boy in Oklahoma, when reports of approaching tornadoes would send our family scurrying into a heavily fortified storm shelter in the back yard, where we would anxiously await the savage twisters. I had the same nervous expectation as I sat in S407 listening to James Schlesinger speak about reform. In the polemical storm over intelligence that had visited Washington, would a political twister sweep down and destroy us as it had our counterpart in the House? Church looked distracted too, and left in the middle of the executive session.

Regrouping

On the morning of 3 February, I received a call from Senator Church. "Come over," he said. "We need to have a strategy meeting on how to handle the White House counterattack."

The sky was thick with gray clouds as I walked across the street to the Russell Building. I looked down toward the White House, half expecting to see a twister (invoked by Henry Kissinger) ominously moving up Constitution Avenue.

In Church's office, he and Fritz Schwarz were discussing the expected White House campaign against our committee. The chairman posed the central question: "How do we handle the counteroffensive?"

We decided on a sequence of positive, reform-minded speeches by Church over the next few weeks, coupled with an accelerated effort to release individual staff reports on different topics. In this way, perhaps we could direct the attention of the press away from the problems of the Pike committee and the prospects of presidential reform, back to the deplorable abuses uncovered by our committee and proposals to prevent their recurrence.

This plan to regain the initiative would hardly solve all our problems, we fully understood, even if it worked; presidential opposition was only one of several thorns in our side. We also faced jurisdictional fights among existing committees (even Philip Hart, a champion of reform, was prepared to battle for the rights of the Judiciary Committee in the area of FBI oversight); apathetic or even hostile public opinion; waning legislative interest; a rapidly approaching committee expiration date; eroding support from conservative Republicans on the committee; and several knotty procedural and substantive issues—such as our old friend, Rule 36. Still, the tactics of the White House had to be confronted, and in some ways taking on the president might be a simpler task than resolving our other difficulties. At least Church had a lot of practice on this score; indeed, he had achieved a national reputation in his battles against presidents Johnson and Nixon over the Vietnam War.

Later in the day, Miller and I met Church on the second floor of the Capitol where he had a hideaway office, an island of tranquility just off a main corridor crowded with tourists. We sat on chairs with richly woven upholstery beneath an ornate mirror; a thick carpet and polished chandelier added to the elegance. Seniority had its rewards.

Miller was concerned primarily with the committee's oversight bill and urged Church to concentrate his energies on its passage. The opposition of Tower, Goldwater, and Baker especially troubled him; he asked Church to redouble his efforts to bring them back into the fold.

"I'll call Tower now," said Church. The telephone conversation began with the usual senatorial courtesies, but before Church had a chance to raise the subject of the oversight bill, Tower got down to business: he wanted to wind down the committee as rapidly as possible. Funds should be cut back immediately; designees were no longer needed; only a skeleton staff was necessary to complete the final task of putting the reports together. Church agreed to all this and, at last, was able to ask Tower about the bill. Within five minutes, the call was over.

"What did he say about the oversight bill?" I asked.

"He said, 'I'll take care of it,'" Church answered with a slightly dazed look, "whatever that means!"

Tower's evasive response, plus a press conference held by Goldwater later that afternoon, made me wonder if our worries about the White House were misdirected. Our major headache seemed to be less the president than our own conservative Republicans—if indeed a distinction could be drawn between the two. The Ford administration had a convenient fifth column within the committee.

The Goldwater press conference caught us by surprise.[16] He told reporters that he had known about CIA assassination plots against Castro for four years, having been briefed by the Agency in 1972. At the time, he said, he had been convinced that the plots had presidential backing. "I expressed no concern," he told the press. "If it was part of a presidential plan, I would assent." This was astounding. Not only had Goldwater never brought this up when we were involved in writing the Interim Assassination Report, but now he was admitting that he had kept the secret all those years—precisely the same sort of admission that had cost Lucien Nedzi (D-MI) the chairmanship of the House Intelligence Committee before Pike assumed that post.

Goldwater then raised again the charge that the committee staff had suppressed evidence showing the complicity of President Kennedy in the murder attempts: "We spent nine of the ten months trying to get Kennedy's name out of it." Yet one witness, he said, had told the committee in closed session that he had been asked in the Kennedy White House, "When are you going to get off your ass and do something about Cuba?" Apparently to Goldwater (and perhaps to the witness), this was shorthand for "Kill Castro." The senator stood before the press and motioned down toward the White House: "Everything points right down there."

It was one thing to have a columnist cry "cover-up" and quite another to have it come from a member of our own committee. The following day, several members expressed their displeasure. Goldwater's statement was "ridiculous," Senator Huddleston told a reporter. "[Goldwater] has suggested many times that he had information that the rest of us didn't, but never produced it. I assumed that if he knew anything that could contribute to the work of the committee, he'd come forward with it."[17] Not even Tower could stand still: "I don't know what Goldwater was talking about."[18]

The Goldwater jabs put Church in a foul mood. "Well, what bad news do you have for me today?" he asked when I came to his office on 4 February. Uncomfortable, I plowed ahead. Tower planned to introduce a resolution, I told him, designed to take the committee battle over Rule 36 to the floor. The vice chairman wanted a statute requiring a majority vote of the Senate before the release of any committee report over the objection of the president. The Church committee's proposed oversight bill had a similar provision, should the two branches disagree vehemently over the release of classified information; the committee's bill, however, applied to the procedures of the proposed permanent Intelligence Committee, whereas the Tower resolution was distinctly aimed at the final report of the Church committee itself.

"I believe Rule XXXVI of the Senate requires leave of the Senate before disclosing matters confidential or secret under the rules," stated Tower in a press release (dated 4 February). "To do less would make every one of the more than 300 committees and subcommittees of the Congress *de facto* equal of the executive." The Tower resolution smacked of a ploy to bottle up the work of the committee; perhaps the Ford administration could repeat on the Senate side its present victory in the House.

Church absorbed this news with an air of resignation, punctuated by slow shakes of his head. I asked if he wanted to make a rebuttal to Goldwater. "Yes," he said, with new life, "his remarks are a slur upon the committee. To say that former presidents—Eisenhower, Kennedy, Johnson—knew about the assassinations is a serious charge." He proposed that the committee vote to release all hearings and depositions related to the assassination investigation (following appropriate clearance by the CIA); then the public could see why the committee had reached a conclusion different from Goldwater's.

The White House, Tower, Goldwater, campaign fund raising—the weight pressed down on Church, and the strain grew more visible each day. I therefore hesitated before I dialed his home telephone number that evening. Scorned earlier as a messenger with perpetual bad tidings, I was reluctant to pass on more unhappy news. But five senior staff members, all from different factions on the committee, had stopped by my desk at different times that afternoon. Each carried the same warning: the staff was coming apart at the seams. Each was greatly alarmed by the disunity, the lack of clear leadership, the vagueness about how the reports were to be compiled and when, and the rumors that everyone was about to be sacked except for a small number of report editors. Each pleaded with me to have Church clarify the remaining schedule and organization of the work; "otherwise he faces imminent mass resignations," cautioned one.

How accurate these perceptions were, I was unsure, but they came from responsible individuals who spoke with conviction. So I related what I had been told, then braced myself for an acid response. Instead, the most mellow tones I had heard from Church in months came floating through the telephone. He told me not to worry and agreed to give the staff a pep talk. He went on to philosophize about the Senate.

"It's a cave of winds," he said. "No one ever listens to what happens there." He also lamented the "fickleness" of reporters in Washington. "They've gone from the abuses we've uncovered to the president's counterattack." He paused. "Now things are in the hands of Kismet."

The next day Church called for a special prosecutor to investigate evidence of CIA and FBI criminal activity. The Department of Justice seemed unsuited to lead a criminal inquiry into some of the abuses; the possibilities for conflict of interest were too great. (The CIA and the Department of Justice, for example, had once actually entered into a twenty-year secret agreement exempting the Agency from the usual requirement to report violations of the law committed by CIA employees.) "To avoid charges of a whitewash," said Church on the Senate floor, "it is in the best interests of the Justice Department to disqualify itself" in the prosecution of intelligence officials for past abuses.[19] The Department of Justice unequivocally rejected Church's recommendation. "I think it's a call for a second Attorney General," said Attorney General Levi; the recommendation was "destructive and debilitating," in his view.[20] The American Bar Association, though, supported the idea and adopted it as a measure to "depoliticize" federal law enforcement.[21]

The special prosecutor speech was the first of our cannon volleys to repel the charge from the White House. Our second shot was a statement from Church proposing a seven-year tenure-of-office limit for CIA directors. While hardly earthshaking, these recommendations did accomplish one of our purposes: they got Church back into the newspapers and reminded anyone who had forgotten that the Senate Intelligence Committee was still in business.

On the afternoon of 5 February, Church kept his promise to visit the committee staff. His remarks were a combined pep talk and explanation of remaining duties. The brief comments had a salutary effect—for four days. Then several of the designees came forth with a fresh grievance: Church was speaking out too much on the issues; apparently their senators were unhappy that the chairman was monopolizing the publicity. "If Church speaks out, so will my senator," said one designee. It looked as if the committee's findings might come cascading out in countless separate press releases—hardly an orderly or coherent way to present a year's work. Church's statements, designed to counter the White House advance, seemed to be having a different effect: they divided the committee further—even the Democratic majority, which had been cohesive on numerous controversial issues.

Enter Schorr

As we polished our reports, we also kept a close eye on the Pike committee. After the vote to release the group's package of twenty recommendations, Pike had announced on 10 February, "These proceedings are closed." The Pike committee's stormy six-month war with the White House had come to an end.

Or so it seemed. Within twenty-four hours, however, a version of the top-secret Pike report was on the nation's newsstands, and the committee was thrown back into controversy before the nameplate on its door had been removed.

The highly classified report was brought to the public through the pages of the *Village Voice*, a liberal weekly published in New York City. In bold red letters, the front page headlined: THE REPORT ON THE CIA THAT PRESIDENT FORD DOESN'T WANT YOU TO READ.[22] Within a few hours of publication, word of its availability swept through our offices, and the result was a mass exodus to Ann's, a newsstand housed in a small trailer across from the Dirksen Building. Soon every desk in the auditorium had a copy of the *Voice* opened to the Pike report.

In these pages, the American public could finally read for itself the scathing criticism of the intelligence community prepared by the House committee.[23] According to the report, the agencies had failed miserably to warn policy makers of the 1968 Tet offensive in Vietnam, the 1973 Yom Kippur War in the Middle East, and the 1974 coups in Portugal and Cyprus. The spending controls in the community were also said to be "inadequate," and covert actions were "irregularly approved, sloppily implemented." The list went on in great detail, usually with Kissinger portrayed as the archvillain. "Dr. Kissinger's comments [to the Pike committee] . . . are at variance with the facts," stated the report at one point. After reading these charges against the secretary of state, I could understand how the White House might wish to suppress it—above and beyond any arguments about the sacrosanctity of classified materials.

But how had the controversial document made its way to the *Village Voice*? This was now the primary issue in the House of Representatives, and within days—in a dramatic role reversal—the investigators on the Pike committee themselves became the subjects of a House investigation. Incensed by the publication of a report it had just voted to bury, the House once again showed itself to be more concerned with leaks than with the flaws in the intelligence community that the Pike committee findings had revealed.

The immediate reaction of Otis Pike was to blame the administration for leaking the document. "A copy was sent to the CIA," he reminded reporters. "It would be to their advantage to leak it to that publication."[24] The White House response was to denounce the substance of the report. "We are facing a new version of McCarthyism," said Kissinger.[25] The President offered the good offices of the FBI to track down the party (or parties) guilty of the leak.

The original source of the leak would remain unknown, despite months of investigation by the House Ethics Committee, but it was almost immediately apparent who had served as intermediary. Reporters William Claiborne and Laurence Stern of the *Washington Post* revealed that CBS newsman Daniel Schorr had been "instrumental in transmitting the report."[26] The well-known television correspondent, whose reporting a year before had stimulated our assassination inquiry, faced a contempt of Congress proceeding if he refused to give the Ethics Committee his source.

On 13 February, Schorr admitted his involvement as a middleman. He made the document available to the *Voice*, he explained, because he "could not be the one responsible for repressing the report."[27] Suddenly Schorr—not intelligence abuses—became the center of controversy in the Congress, the White House, the CIA, and the nation's major newspapers. For the first time in 106 years, the House initiated a formal investigation of a newsman. In launching its inquiry, the Ethics Committee asked for and received a half-dozen FBI agents to complement its own small staff, and Attorney General Levi subsequently ordered an FBI investigation.

As these probes gathered steam, Schorr lamented that as the target of a "secrecy backlash," he had been victimized by a new mood in the nation.[28] "There have always been in our country two great urges—one toward security, one toward liberty," he said. "The pendulum constantly swings between them. Security always comes back. And the pendulum appears to have started its return course. . . . I got hit by a swinging pendulum."[29]

The immediate effect on the Church committee of the *Voice* disclosure was to make us redouble our security precautions. Every briefcase and purse was checked, and the flow of paper within the Dirksen auditorium was traced minutely, with elaborate sign-out procedures for obtaining documents. All these measures evoked, according to one of our critics, the atmosphere of "a bunker under siege."[30]

17

White House Counteroffensive

Actually, the Dirksen Building seemed more like an oven than a bunker. As spring arrived prematurely, the Senate maintenance crew seemed unable to turn down the heaters—or perhaps they simply assumed that the warm spell would soon vanish. Instead, it lingered. The only solution for staffers was occasional escape.

One balmy afternoon in mid-February, Schwarz and I struck off in shirtsleeves for a quick walk. He was distressed with the Senate and with Frank Church. "Chaos! That's what this place is," he grumbled. We discussed the oversight bill. "Why is Church so unwilling to lobby other senators?" he asked rhetorically. "He seems to have an inability to relate to his colleagues." I suggested that he was a unique breed of legislator: a philosopher. His style was to make his position known; its wisdom should be persuasive enough.

"Damn!" said Schwarz, increasing the pace.

As we spoke, Church was out and around the country stumping for political support and campaign funds. Speaking in Chicago before the congregation of Reverend Jesse Jackson, he appealed for black support.

"I want to speak to you today as the spirit moves me," he said, leaving his written speech in his briefcase and taking a stab at "soul" oratory. I listened to a tape of the address later. In an emotional stream-of-consciousness performance, Church spoke movingly of equal justice under the law—that "star of destiny" which the United States still pursued. Accompanied by shouts of "yes" and "amen," Church the Orator took flight. He spoke of a president who had lied to the people and was forced to resign, of a vice president convicted of felonies, and of the "infection spreading down into the very agencies of government we had entrusted with great power."

The CIA had stopped remembering that it was supposed to spy on others and had begun to spy on the American people instead, said Church. We had found a CIA, he continued, that

> had forgotten we are a Christian nation and that was conspiring to murder foreign officials in little countries, like the Dominican Republic, and Cuba and the Congo, that couldn't possibly threaten the safety or security of this great nation. Latin leaders and black leaders. That's shame.
>
> And we found an agency that cannot learn that this is all contrary to

the charted course in the United States of America. That even now, within Angola, they're trying to determine who is going to run that little country. And that isn't our business, and that isn't the Russians' business. That's the business of the people of Angola. If anything should be clear from the recent history of Africa, from the long, long struggle of black Africa to be free, that lesson is that no independent African state—and particularly one that has suffered under the dictatorial control of the Portuguese for centuries—is going to long remain dominated by any foreign power, the Russians or anybody else.

So why don't we start living by our principles? Let the Angolans decide their destiny. They have a right to self-determination, and this country does not have to meddle in their affairs.

He spoke, too, of the FBI "vendetta" against Dr. Martin Luther King Jr. "If anything we have done this year needed doing more than anything else, it was bringing those facts out into public view."

End Run

While Church was traveling, I had lunch with James Angleton. The former CIA chief of counterintelligence became highly agitated as he discussed the congressional inquiries, comparing them to the pillaging of intelligence services in countries that had been overrun and occupied by a foreign power. "Only we have been occupied by the Congress," he said, "with our files rifled, our officials humiliated, and our agents exposed." This happened because of an "impotent executive" that failed to "carry out its constitutional responsibility to protect the nation's secrets."

I walked with Angleton from the Army–Navy Club to his car. "Let me tell you something," he said. "Washington is a jungle." His Mercedes eased into the slipstream of a Metrobus.

I had seen enough fur and feathers flying around the Dirksen auditorium— not to mention the tooth-and-claw struggles that had finally overwhelmed the Pike committee—to understand what Angleton meant. As he drove away, I wondered what dark threat might pounce from the bush upon our committee. I soon found out.

That same evening, 17 February, President Ford held a nationally televised press conference. "Tonight, I am announcing plans for the first major reorganization of the intelligence community since 1947," he said. The announcement, noted an observer, was "a pre-emptive end-run on the Congress."[1]

Here at last was the full force of the anticipated counteroffensive from the

Ford administration. The White House had peppered the battlefield with artillery for weeks, with repeated remarks from Kissinger and others to the effect that the United States was more endangered by "our domestic divisions" than by foreign adversaries.[2] Behind the scenes in the White House, the preparations for this presidential initiative had been underway for months.

According to an inside account, one faction within the White House had urged a counteroffensive as far back as Labor Day in September 1975—before the Church committee had held a single public hearing.[3] The proposal was to "take the initiative away from Congress by announcing that the Rockefeller recommendations had been implemented."[4] Others, who believed the Congress would never arrive at recommendations anyway, won the day with the argument "that therefore issuance of restrictions was in the long term an unnecessary limitation of foreign intelligence."[5]

Then, however, Congress had moved forward with widely reported hearings, putting the administration on the defensive. The White House realized by mid-November 1975 that a more sophisticated organization and better planning was necessary to deal effectively with the congressional investigations; the office of the White House counsel could no longer manage the task alone. Therefore, an Intelligence Coordinating Group was formed, led by presidential counselor James O. Marsh Jr. and made up of representatives from the major intelligence agencies, the NSC, and the Office of Management and Budget (OMB). From mid-November through mid-December, the group had met daily in the Old Executive Office Building to prepare a set of recommendations on intelligence reform for the president.

No new proposals were hewn out of hardwood; instead, ideas that had been floating around the intelligence community for years were picked out and packaged into options for presidential review. This "White Book" had accompanied President Ford on his 1975 Christmas trip to Vail, Colorado, where—with Secretary of Defense Rumsfeld—he spent long hours reading through the options. The president was not sure when it would be best to unveil his intelligence recommendations. Some advisers had urged him to improve his image of decisiveness by presenting them as part of the State of the Union message in January; others warned that doing so would only serve to antagonize Congress unnecessarily. At Vail, the decision was finally made "to go slow and work with Congress."[6]

On 10 January 1976, Marsh further briefed the president in the presence of the nation's intelligence chiefs (who themselves offered suggestions), and the alternatives were refined by a White House working group. By early February 1976, Ford had selected the options he wished to endorse. The strategy to "work with Congress" was junked. The Welch murder, periodic leaks of Pike committee findings, the House vote against its own committee, and—the last straw—the surfacing of the Pike report in the *Village Voice* spurred the president to announce his own intelligence plan—partially in the hope, no doubt, that he might turn retreat into rout on Capitol Hill.

As the time grew near for the announcement of the executive order, last-minute negotiations intensified between the intelligence chiefs and the White House staff, with special pleas for changes in the language coming from Attorney General Levi and others. "There has been strong disagreement on everything," a Ford aide told the press.[7] The disputes within the executive branch were said to be "sharp," the schisms "deep and emotional."[8]

Despite this internal bickering, the executive branch spoke with one voice on the night of 17 February (a feat rarely possible for the Congress). The administration at least appeared to have assumed a strong leadership role on intelligence issues. "The president had scooped the Congress," remembers a participant in the White House negotiations, "by announcing and initiating implementation of his decisions before the Senate even made its recommendations public."[9] The White House had found its legs and was off and running.

Holding up the straw man that he had presented on earlier occasions, the president told the nation in his television address, "I will not be a party to the dismantling of the CIA."[10] He presented a bureaucratic reshuffling of the intelligence community (the old Rockefeller Commission recommendations in new clothes) and something resembling a British Official Secrets Act to stop leaks.

The reshuffling took the form of a new part-time three-member Intelligence Oversight Board (IOB); a broadened membership and a name change for the 40 Committee, now labeled the Operations Advisory Group; and a new NSC Committee chaired by CIA director George Bush to give greater central coordination to the intelligence community. (That the average age of the men on the Oversight Board was just under seventy led columnist Carl Rowan to conclude that "Rip Van Winkle guards the CIA."[11])

The recommendations on abuses (Section 5) formed the heart—and the most controversial portion—of Executive Order No. 11905. Differing only slightly from the Rockefeller proposals of a year before, these recommendations drew both fire and praise. Anthony Lewis saw them as little more than "a blueprint for more secrecy, greater executive power, and less congressional oversight."[12] On the Hill, Pike said the order put emphasis "largely on preserving all of the secrets in the executive branch and very little on guaranteeing a lack of any further abuses."[13] Tower, in contrast, greeted the proposal as "positive and carefully planned."[14]

Several Democrats on the Church committee acknowledged the reforms as a positive step, but legislative remedies would still be required to build "a real consensus," as Mondale put it, for intelligence reform.[15] Church cast a more jaundiced eye. "I think the president reaches beyond his power," he said. "You cannot change law by executive order."[16] What the president really sought through this announcement, Church argued, was "clearly to give the CIA a bigger shield and a longer sword with which to stab about."[17] Despite his yearning to end the work of the committee, he called for hearings on the presidential decree and vowed that his panel would submit tough legislation to replace this cambric tea served by the White House.

On the staff, John Elliff immediately set to work on a critique of the executive order. He was uneasy with the authorization given to the FBI to detect and prevent various "subversive" activities. "Congress has never authorized the FBI to carry out 'preventive' functions," he noted in a memorandum.[18] Moreover, the term "subversion" as used in the order was replete with problems. Elliff cited the advice of Attorney General Robert Jackson, offered in 1940 and valid still: "Those who are in office are apt to regard as subversive the activities of any of those who would bring about a change of administration. Some of our soundest constitutional doctrines were once presented as subversive. We must not forget that it was not so long ago that both the terms 'Republican' and 'Democrat' were epithets with sinister meaning to denote persons of radical tendencies that were 'subversive' of the order of things then documented."[19]

The chief difficulty with the executive order, though, was that Section 5 on "restrictions" was silent altogether on the FBI. Either Levi or FBI director Kelley (or both) had lobbied effectively on behalf of the Bureau. In the question-and-answer period following the president's formal remarks at the 17 February press conference, a reporter asked about the omission.

"The attorney general is in the process right now of writing very strict guidelines involving the activities of the FBI," answered Ford. The Department of Justice apparently had run into several snags in its effort to draft language covering electronic surveillance; to allow Levi additional time, the department had been given permission by the White House to issue its own guidelines later.

As for CIA clandestine activities within the United States, the new order authorized the Agency to "conduct foreign counterintelligence activities . . . *in the United States*" (emphasis added). Abroad, the new authority of the CIA to spy on Americans was vague and open ended. Our intelligence agencies still had to obtain the approval of the attorney general for electronic surveillance and physical searches directed against American citizens traveling overseas, but virtually any other technique could be used if the citizen was "reasonably believed to be acting on behalf of a foreign power." This authority seemed sweeping to experts on the committee staff.

The only statute the president sought—and his most controversial proposal, resembling an Official Secrecy Act—was a provision to protect the secrecy of intelligence "sources and methods." "This legislation," Ford explained, "would make it a crime for a government employee who has access to certain highly classified information to reveal that information improperly." This sounded reasonable enough on the surface, but the precise implications were far reaching;

for example, it appeared to enable Justice Department prosecutors to require newspaper reporters to come before a grand jury and reveal their sources for articles containing classified information. The proposed law failed even to require proof that the person disclosing the information really knew it was classified. One Hill staffer observed, "It would be the final irony if all that resulted from this year of investigation is a new secrecy law."[20]

The emphasis on a secrecy statute made many people skeptical. After all, as historian Arthur M. Schlesinger Jr. pointed out, "the abuses have harmed the Republic considerably more than the leaks."[21] Even a former CIA deputy director properly suggested that President Ford had his priorities inverted. Instead of dwelling on a secrecy act, the president "should have proposed legislation establishing criminal penalties for persons at all levels who participate in activities which infringe on civil rights or violate the law."[22]

Three other aspects of the Ford intelligence plan were disturbing. First, other than a prohibition against "political assassination," hardly a word about covert action (or, in the administration euphemism, "special activity") was uttered in the thirty-six-page order—even though no other subject had so embroiled the CIA in controversy over the years. No doubt one of the plan's early drafters is correct: the existence and use of a covert action capability was simply "accepted gospel."[23] Covert action was raised obliquely in the president's message to Congress accompanying the executive order,[24] but only to call for a repeal of the Hughes–Ryan Act. I had not expected the president to renounce covert action, but it would have been appropriate for him to acknowledge its misuse in the past.

Second, the president's message left no doubt that he wanted solidified into law the "principle" that had emerged from the confrontation with the Pike committee: "No individual member, nor Committee, nor single House of Congress can overrule an act of the Executive."[25] It was Rule 36 again. The president's recommendation went even further than Tower's (whose bill permitted release by a vote of the Senate), let alone Church's (who preferred individual committee release except in extremely controversial cases, when a Senate vote might be necessary). The practical effect of the Ford proposal was, in the words of one critic, to make a committee "informed but impotent."[26]

Third, the president ignored what is probably the most important problem faced by any intelligence agency: how to improve the quality of its product. The great contribution of the Pike committee was its discussion of intelligence failures. The executive branch might have taken this opportunity to address past failures and subscribe to reforms on the collection-and-analysis side of the intelligence business.

In one respect, the executive order was a blessing to our committee. With deep fatigue setting in at all levels, we badly needed something to help stir our adrenaline and arouse us to dig in our spurs for one last charge at intelligence reform. An anonymous official speculated that Ford had "overstepped himself by offering such a limited program for reform and reorganization, provoking enough new debate to return the public's attention to the abuses rather than the leaks."[27] Correspondent Nicholas Horrock concluded: "President Ford, possibly more by accident than intent, appears to have rekindled the great debate on the future and control of the United States intelligence system."[28]

Continuing Skirmishes

On my desk the next day was a copy of a letter from the Department of Justice to Senator Church. In two sentences, an assistant attorney general wrote that he was responding to the committee's inquiry concerning the murder of Sam Giancana. "All the information which we have received through the present date," read the letter, "indicates that this was a gangland slaying intended to settle problems within the syndicate."[29] The response was hardly definitive; if that was the best the FBI and the Department of Justice could come up with, however, we had little alternative but to settle for it.

The next day we received more tidings from the Department of Justice: Richard Helms would not be prosecuted for his role in the 1971 break-in at a Fairfax, Virginia, photography studio. "It was impossible to prove he had intent to violate anyone's civil right," said one source involved in the decision.[30] The problem lay, as was so often the case, in the ambiguity of the 1947 National Security Act, which stated that "the director of central intelligence shall be responsible for protecting intelligence sources and methods from unauthorized disclosure." This language, concluded Justice Department attorneys, made it permissible for Helms to use extraordinary means (like the break-in) as required to honor his responsibility for the protection of classified information.

After the announcement, Helms's counsel—the famous Washington attorney Edward Bennett Williams—said that Helms himself thought the 1947 law should be changed to remove such powers from CIA directors.[31] (Though Helms was out of the woods in this case, he still faced a separate Justice Department investigation into possible perjury in his 1973 congressional testimony regarding CIA intervention in Chile.)

As our own investigation began to wind down, we encountered fierce resistance from the CIA in two areas that Bill Bader was pursuing: Agency relations with the press and with the nation's universities. The first sign of trouble came early in February 1976. Falling back on the same statutory provision upon which Helms had built his legal defense in the Fairfax case, the CIA refused to reveal to Church committee investigators the names of journalists or academics with whom it had established a relationship. To do so, argued the Agency, would transgress the responsibility "for protecting intelligence sources and methods from unauthorized disclosure"—again the language of the 1947 act.

Bader felt strongly about obtaining access to the names of journalists who had worked with the CIA. Without them, he believed, the committee could not hope to ascertain with any accuracy how extensively and at what level the CIA had "penetrated" the American media. It soon became a classic standoff. "We are not going to give them the names of sources," said the CIA publicly. "We're just at an impasse at the moment," countered Church, putting the best face possible on what appeared to be more than a temporary disagreement.[32]

Senator Huddleston seemed willing to take on the fight and scheduled a meeting with George Bush to hash it out face to face. "We are going to sit down and confront the issue," he told reporters.[33] On 17 February, Huddleston drove to CIA headquarters with Senator Mathias. The CIA was "not at liberty to reveal the names," Bush told them, and that included journalists and academics. The senators backed down; they agreed to Bush's proposition that the committee accept instead a batch of documents describing generally, without names, the Agency's association with scholars and reporters over the years. That, Huddleston announced publicly, was "all the information we need" to make an "accurate assessment" of the relationships; the names would not be sought further, he said, because "the name itself is not important to us."[34]

Several staff members on the committee, heatedly opposed to this "capitulation," approached Baker, Gary Hart, and Mondale with pleas to try again for access to the forbidden files. These senators made telephone calls to the Agency and met with Bush individually. Still Bush refused.

The intervention of a larger circle of senators, however, did seem to increase the quality and quantity of documents made available to the committee. The content of these summaries, though, remained far too general in the opinion of staffers working on the project, and they resolved to prod the senators again to request more detailed information.

As relations soured steadily between Church and Tower on the inside, and between the committee and the executive branch on the outside, we longed for some sign of good news. Finally, on 24 February, some came.

By the vote we had hoped for—twelve to zero—the Ribicoff committee reported out its bill to establish a permanent Senate Committee on Intelligence. The resolution still faced two hazardous obstacles on its journey through the legislative process: the Rules Committee and debate on the floor of the Senate. Still, a unanimous vote by a parent committee was often sufficient endorsement to convince a majority of the chamber to go along.

The vote was misleading, though, concealing divisions within the Ribicoff committee. During the three days of markup (19, 20, and 24 February), whereby a bill is drafted section by section in committee, debate was often heated and votes were divided. The discussion soon focused almost entirely on how to prevent leaks, not how to avoid abuses—just as had happened in the House debate over the Pike report.

Particularly contentious was the question of how many senators it should take to launch an investigation against a member alleged to have leaked classified material: six (that is, a majority of the proposed eleven-person oversight committee)? five? sixteen members of the Senate at large? The committee eventually settled on either five committee members or sixteen senators at large, though Jacob Javits (R-NY) was strongly opposed on the grounds that requiring so small a number could lead to inquisitions against unpopular members.

Despite these disagreements, Ribicoff managed to soothe the disputants and achieve his unanimous final vote. Much of his success rested on an assurance that I found foreboding: that this was only the first step, and members could refine the bill further in the subsequent forums of the Rules Committee and, of course, in full Senate debate. "There is no question in my mind," Ribicoff told his panel, "the Rules Committee will go over this with a magnifying glass."[35]

The president and the Ribicoff committee agreed (more or less) on one matter, rejecting Church's diction: in the Ribicoff bill, the phrase "prior notification" was abandoned. Its substitute, though, must have caused discomfort in the White House. The CIA, under the Ribicoff language, would have to keep the new committee "fully and currently informed with respect to intelligence activities, including any significant anticipated activities." When Church saw this, he told reporters he would be willing to "go along."[36] Our own staff analysis concluded that the addition of the phrase "anticipated activities" in the bill made it substantially synonymous with the intent of "prior notification," even though those two excitable words had been abandoned.[37]

Discrepancies among the Ribicoff, Church, and Ford approaches to intelligence reform hinted darkly at the possibility of a storm on the Senate floor, despite the surface unanimity of the Ribicoff committee. Nevertheless, we had moved one step closer to a permanent oversight committee. The twelve-to-zero vote was a better response to the White House counteroffensive than anything we had devised on the Church committee.

Also a step closer to completion were the various committee reports. The individual domestic staff reports had all been read by Schwarz and approved; they had also been approved by the senators and their designees, and then sent to the intelligence community reviewers for their comments (with a caveat: "The purpose of this review will be to ensure that the report does not inadvertently raise national security or classification problems"—not to arbitrate the committee's conclusions). One reporter expected the Church committee to have "less difficulty than the House Intelligence Committee did on the question of whether its report contains national security data . . . since it has worked closely with the White House and the intelligence agencies over the last two months to iron out questions on national security data in the report."[38]

Only the CIA reviewer drew exception to my Huston Plan report. While the study "reveals no problems" in "sources and methods," wrote the reviewer in his formal critique, "the title grates."[39] I had headed the document "Lawlessness and the Collection of Intelligence." During our discussion of the study, the CIA reviewer had commented sarcastically, "Pretty fancy title. Why don't you try 'criminality' or 'rogue elephant' somewhere in there, too?" I eventually relented on this point (even though the Huston Plan was a study of lawlessness), settling on the title "National Security, Civil Liberties, and the Collection of Intelligence"— hardly elegant, but evidentially less jarring.

More significant was the CIA's objection to my basic conclusion. "Huston's credibility is the gut issue of this draft," wrote the reviewer, and he was right. The committee found Huston's testimony credible and in harmony with the evidence; the reviewer obviously did not. "How innocent was Tom Charles Huston?" he asked rhetorically. "Did the wily old intelligence chiefs deceive the president or did they respond zealously to his requests?" He felt strongly that I had exonerated Huston too quickly and blamed the Agency excessively (though the study really traced the mischief to Sullivan's doorstep at the FBI as much as anywhere). "Is he to be blamed over Helms et al.?" the reviewer asked.

On 25 February, at the committee's first business meeting in a month, the senators agreed (without objection) to provide the Department of Justice with our files on CIA–FBI illegal mail opening, since we had finished our own work with these papers.

The committee soon hit its more usual rough sledding, though. Tower struck the first note of discord, bringing up the subject of personal correspondence between himself and Church several days earlier as to whether staff reports ought to be published one at a time under the authority of the committee or, as he wished, in a single package at the end of the investigations—preferably with clearance by a vote of the full Senate.[40]

"We certainly shouldn't let the staff issue its own reports, without approval of the committee," Baker said.

"Of course we'll have the committee approve these reports before each one is published," Church responded.

"I must object, Mr. Chairman," said Tower, his gold cufflinks reflecting light from the chandelier. "We cannot release reports as a committee. The Senate should be the final arbiter." A familiar refrain.

Baker introduced a motion that the White House be kept informed of all our reports, and the committee told of any objections by the administration before publication. Church's hopes to proceed with the publication of individual staff reports, beginning immediately with the COINTELPRO study, collapsed quickly through lack of support on the Democratic side.

Chagrined, the chairman suggested that the committee's recommendations should be marked up in public session; then they could be transmitted to the Senate as the committee's final judgments on the direction that oversight should take.

Tower balked quickly at the notion of a public markup. "Being shy," he said wryly, "I like to do my work in private. I object to the public session."

"My experience with this committee," said Church, "is that we only get it done when we begin to do it. We've got to get moving on these recommendations, and I think we should begin a public markup on March 8th." This time the sentiment seemed to be on the chairman's side; Tower shrugged and lit a cigarette. One never knew whether Tower had capitulated or merely retreated temporarily.

As March approached, the Church committee staff spent its time in endless meetings, hammering out report drafts and refining recommendations. Fatigue and frustration were our constant companions, and they sometimes accompanied the senators too. Church concealed his emotions from the public for the most part, revealing anxieties and discouragement through a grumpiness around the office.

On 2 March, Gary Hart let off his steam on the Senate floor. In a rebuttal to Goldwater's accusation that the Church committee had covered up the involvement of President Kennedy in murder plots against Fidel Castro, Hart called the claim "utter nonsense . . . the facts do not support that conclusion." It was "simply not true," he emphasized, that any effort had been made to protect the Kennedys.

As for the Judith Campbell situation, Hart said: "We could have interviewed Frank Sinatra, Howard Hughes—if there is a Howard Hughes—Lawrence Welk, and Captain Kangaroo, for that matter. All would have been equally irrelevant. Our purpose was not to stage a headline grabbing soap opera, but rather a probe of CIA assassination attempts. When the Campbell trial did not lead in this direction, the Committee saw no point in pursuing the irrelevant. Senator Goldwater certainly voiced no interest in handling the Campbell case in any other fashion."[41]

Hart reminded listeners of the committee's conclusion in the Interim Assassination Report (released in November 1975): the system of executive command and control was so ambiguous that no one could be certain at what level assassination activity was known and authorized. "This does not, however," he concluded, "give anyone the liberty to make wild accusations about presidential involvement—unless, of course, they are prepared to lay down the hard facts to support their claims. I invite Senator Goldwater to do so." The invitation was never accepted.

Most of the staff anxieties in March were focused on the Ribicoff oversight bill. This proposal, known officially as Senate Resolution 400, was reported to the Rules Committee, which in turn had to report it to the full Senate by 20 March. Then, after three working days, the Senate was scheduled to vote Senate Resolution 400 up or down. So before the end of the month, we would know whether our yearlong efforts to establish a permanent oversight committee for intelligence policy had succeeded. The existence of a new committee in itself, of course, would not indicate success. Emasculating amendments from the Rules Committee, or on the floor, could turn Senate Resolution 400 and the new committee into a paper tiger.

18

The Late, Late Strategy

On the evening of 2 March, Senator Church appeared before the American Newspaper Women's Club in Washington, DC, where he explained his "late, late strategy" for winning his party's nomination for the presidency. "This strategy," he said, "is based on the supposition that a number of candidates will knock themselves out of the race, and the opportunity will open up for a late entrant." Church listed the primaries he would contest, beginning with Nebraska in May, then Oregon, Idaho, Montana, and Rhode Island. (Massachusetts and other competitions Church had once eyed had been abandoned in favor of states where he had more time and a better chance to win.) Church noted that a strong showing in these primaries would provide "the kind of momentum which would count" at the Democratic National Convention. The formal announcement of his candidacy, he said, would take place on 18 March.

At the same time that Church became increasingly involved in presidential politics, the House of Representatives moved in earnest toward the investigation of the Pike report leak. The Ethics Committee requested $350,000 from the House to undertake a long and detailed inquiry—its first formal investigation in its nine years of existence. The entire Pike committee investigation had cost only $120,000 more than the Ethics Committee now wanted to spend to discover who leaked its findings.

As if Otis Pike had not gone through enough woes, it became known to the public on 5 March that the CIA had accused his committee of the loss of 232 Agency documents—some highly classified. Wherever the truth lay in this latest dispute between Pike and the CIA, Mary McGrory was no doubt correct: here was a "mismatch all the way." The CIA is an organization highly skilled in the arts of propaganda and manipulation—operations it has refined for three decades in countries around the world; by contrast, McGrory observed, the House is "a large, slow-witted, thin-skinned defensive composite that wants to stay out of trouble." If the CIA was fond of cloaks and daggers, the House had a "penchant for earmuffs and blinders."

McGrory accurately noted that when Richard Welch was murdered in December 1975, "the House went into a panic. It pulled down the curtains, bolted the doors, called for the smelling salts. What had it done? Actually neither the House nor the Senate Committee which also was investigating, had revealed the name of a single agent. The House was too terrified to notice." The House turned upon itself with a vengeance, largely forgetting the fact that the CIA had broken the law. "The CIA has scored its greatest domestic coup," concluded McGrory. "It has made the House go to war against itself."[1]

If the CIA had indeed manipulated the House of Representatives, that still only partially explained the troubles that beset the Pike committee and the Abzug subcommittee. Both appeared less interested in the time-honored method for obtaining sensitive information from the executive branch—that is, patient negotiation—than in a gloves-off slugfest. Whether driven by institutional pride, personal pique, partisan politics, individual ambition, or some other motive (one heard confirmation of each theory from different sources), the Pike and Abzug panels seemed unwilling to enter into dialogue with the administration over the boundaries of the public inquiry.

The Abzug subcommittee staff refused, for instance, even to attend an NSA briefing on interception technology. "I don't want to take part in some dog and pony show in their underground caves," said one key staffer. "Anything they want to tell us they can say at a public hearing."[2] One House Democrat echoed the views of many others: "[Abzug's] confrontation immaturity is what is destroying Congress's claim for equality with the executive branch."[3] In contrast to the Abzug panel, the Pike committee seemed to have had a large number of members committed to doing their homework, but like Abzug, they had been more inclined toward confrontation than compromise in dealing with the administration.

The Church committee refused to compromise, too, in confrontation with the Ford administration. Over White House objections, for example, we published the Interim Assassination Report; we held public hearings on the NSA and on covert action; and we reserved the right to make our own editorial decisions on what would appear in our final reports. We did, however, agree to remove some classified information from reports when the intelligence community made a persuasive case that we should; we did spend long hours listening to the views of the professional intelligence officers; we did recognize the futility of subpoenaing Henry Kissinger; we did try to operate in the spirit of bipartisanship (and usually succeeded); and for the most part we did avoid grandstanding.

On this last point, the dart-gun curtain raiser stands as a conspicuous exception. To demonstrate the validity of the generalization, though, recall that the Church committee also could have engaged in public pyrotechnics with Kissinger, held public hearings on assassination plots, subpoenaed Richard Nixon to testify on the Huston Plan and other matters, held sensational hearings on FBI harassment of Dr. Martin Luther King Jr., broadened the public hearings on the NSA, and more. Had we taken that attitude and approach, it might have destroyed our investigation, just as it did Pike's. Throughout his career, however,

Church had been a senator who preferred half a loaf to no loaf at all. Finding the middle ground, compromising except when he found compromise unconscionable (as in the question of withdrawal from Vietnam), had been a hallmark of his legislative career. As the eminent sociologist Max Weber put it, politics is a "strong and slow boring of hard boards";[4] Church had the requisite temperament and experience to realize this.

Yet even a person disposed toward negotiations and "reasonableness" has a fuse of finite length; Church's had grown short, and the rapidly approaching presidential primaries he hoped to enter increased his frustration.

Here a Leak, There a Leak

By 9 March, Miller and Schwarz had consulted with all the senators (or their designees) to schedule a review of the final drafts, the official markup of the final reports and recommendations. An unhappy chairman returned to the floor again to request an extension of the committee's life to 15 April.

While Church had been forced by Tower to abandon his plan to publish individual staff reports one after the other, he did order the committee staff to release, on 9 March, 996 pages of documents that had been used in our hearings and, over the months, negotiated to freedom. The papers, chiefly from the FBI and the CIA, illustrated how these agencies had sought expanded authority for the wiretapping of intelligence and counterintelligence targets within the United States, including various left-wing and "subversive" groups. Church desperately wanted something released by the committee after promising the press for months now that the reports would soon be finished, and this was the answer. These documents, however, were mere peanuts for meat-hungry lions.

The real news that day came from the attorney general's office. At a luncheon for newsmen, Levi revealed that he had provided copies of his new FBI guidelines to the Church committee and the House Subcommittee on Civil and Constitutional Rights. Levi had decided to prohibit the use of "preventive action" by the Bureau. Thus a major piece missing from the president's executive order slid into place. The Church committee had been preempted by the Ford administration, so it seemed, in every area of intelligence reform.

Only slightly daunted, we continued to spend most of our time working on our reports. A letter from Senator Mondale to the other committee members, dated 10 March, gives a sense of how these preparations were proceeding on the domestic intelligence front:

> On February 18, 1976, the Domestic Subcommittee adopted a procedure for review of Draft Reports on domestic topics. Essentially, the procedure was

for the reports to be reviewed by each Senator's designee, by senior staff members and by the minority counsel. We agreed to approve reports subject only to resolving issues which could not be resolved at the staff level. . . .

All agencies concerned with possible security problems as to any of these reports have reviewed the drafts and, in some cases, suggested changes on security grounds, all of which were incorporated into revisions. . . .

Suggestions were also made by the various agencies of an editorial nature and these have been incorporated, as appropriate.

On the day this letter was distributed, our committee was taken completely by surprise by the release to the press of former President Nixon's answers to the questions we had posed to him—many of which we considered top secret and based upon NSC documents. Nixon's lawyers had taken the answers to the White House to have them cleared on security grounds before offering them to the press. It seemed that every trick in the book was being used to prevent the Church committee's findings from appearing newsworthy. The committee was caught flat-footed, but in response we at least declassified our questions to place the answers in a more understandable context.

The answers themselves angered Church as much as the surprise release. Nixon referred to the presidency regally as "sovereign" and justified the president's right to break the law in certain circumstances. As examples, he served up Lincoln's Civil War use of US treasury funds without authorization from Congress, and Franklin Roosevelt's relocation of American citizens of Japanese descent during World War II—both of which were public decisions, unlike his own secret approval of the illegal options in the Huston Plan. He said, too, that his 1969 warrantless wiretapping of seventeen journalists and government employees was lawful "because of a Presidential determination that it was in the interests of national security."[5]

Nixon's advocacy of "the sovereign presidency," said Church, was a "pernicious and dangerous doctrine." For Church, "the lesson to be learned is not just that illegal actions were justified. Rather it is that once government officials start believing that they have the power and the right to act secretly outside the law, we have started down a long, slippery slope which culminates in a Watergate."[6]

Nixon's responses did more to evoke the image of a CIA out of control than anything our committee had uncovered. Time and again, contrary to the testimony of intelligence officials, the former president could not recall any specific directions he had given to foment a military coup against Allende. The rogue elephant had been rediscovered in San Clemente.

The whole question of the Pike report leak began to take on absurd dimensions as the month of March progressed. In the first place, it came to light that someone in the Department of the State had provided secret information on past

Middle East negotiations to a writer for the journal *Foreign Policy*, whose published article then portrayed Henry Kissinger as a brilliant negotiator who had skillfully maintained peace in the Middle East.

The implication for those who compared the Pike committee leak with the State Department leak was spelled out by columnist William Safire: "The criterion of classification has become intensely personal. What is embarrassing to Henry Kissinger is 'top secret,' and the leak must be plugged at all costs; but what makes the Secretary of State appear to be 'at the apogee of his genius'—no matter how secret—can be leaked with impunity." Safire referred to the Kissinger leak as "massive" and the Pike disclosure as "minor," and he urged the House Ethics Committee to "demand that the Secretary of State march up to the Hill to answer some questions."[7]

On top of this State Department leak came an amazing one from the CIA. At a briefing for Washington-area members of the American Institute of Aeronautics and Astronautics on 14 March, Agency officials disclosed intelligence that estimated Israel to have ten to twenty nuclear weapons "ready and available for use."[8] Earlier published estimates of Israeli nuclear capabilities had been based strictly on circumstantial evidence and taken lightly; now the CIA had revealed an estimate—presumably derived empirically—that went well beyond previous American judgments "both in quantity and state of readiness."[9] Here was a top candidate for leak of the year. I just hoped we could avoid a candidate of our own.

On 13 March, I wrapped up my duties as a committee staff member; Senator Church had asked me to join his personal staff as issues director. I left the Dirksen auditorium with mixed emotions. I knew I would miss the companionship of friends there, but I was pleased to leave behind the pressure-cooker atmosphere and the windowless green cubicle where I had sat for a year.

Within two hours, though, I longed for my niche in the auditorium. If his committee had been a pressure cooker, Church's personal office was a kitchen stove crowded with madly whistling teakettles. The suite of rooms in the Russell Building constituted a policy-planning office, constituency reception room, legislative strategy forum, ombudsman bureau, and media center all rolled into one, with Church's own office the single quiet spot—the eye of the storm. The 150 staffers who milled around the passageways of the Intelligence Committee's offices seemed, in contrast, as serene as Seurat's picnickers along the Seine.

Presidential Candidate

Senator Church's "late, late strategy" was hit directly by a mortar shell from the West Coast just about the time I began as issues director. In mid-March, Governor Jerry Brown of California casually informed reporters that he would run in his state's 8 June primary as a favorite-son candidate.

Brown's decision was a substantial setback. Church's entire strategy pivoted around his being the focal point in a last-ditch effort to stop Jimmy Carter of Georgia in the final few primaries. The climactic test, Church had calculated, could well occur in California, where—after first defeating Carter in Nebraska and the other primaries he had targeted—Church would sweep the Golden State triumphantly into his basket of victories. Carter would still have more delegates, but not enough to win on a first ballot; on a second ballot, Church's impressive string of successes—despite a seemingly hopeless late entry—might swing the convention delegates his way.

That was the theory—or the dream. The thirty-six year-old governor of California gave it a severe jolt. "Once Brown entered the race," Church said after the election, "I had to be content with small victories, and I certainly didn't have the undivided attention of the press."[10] Moreover, Carter was doing far better than we had expected and apparently was in the race to stay.

Despite these jolts, Church had to select a primary to enter in early May; he could hardly be considered a serious candidate if he waited until the 25 May western primaries. He needed to demonstrate some ability to win outside his own backyard. Nebraska looked like the best possibility; as one staffer put it, "Nebraska is another Idaho—without mountains." The issues Church had studied for almost twenty years as an Idaho senator were, for the most part, those that also concerned Nebraskans, particularly farming and conservation.

The campaign plans remained sketchy, and everything began to turn on Church's success in Nebraska. That state, though, was the second step in this journey; the first was to announce Church's candidacy in his home state. On 17 March, the Church for President organization boarded a chartered 727 at Dulles International Airport for the trip to Boise, Idaho. The Church campaign was at last taking flight.

The next day, people from all over Idaho drove in buses and automobiles toward Idaho City (population 5,000), the announcement site Church had selected for sentimental reasons. His grandfather had journeyed to Idaho City right after the Civil War to raise his family in the wide-open spaces of the West. His father had been born in the mining town. Here, too, his father-in-law, Chase Clark, had launched a successful race for the governorship in 1940.

In anticipation of the swelling crowds, the mayor of Idaho City doubled the police force, from one officer to two. Both were busily directing traffic to special overflow parking lots. The four blocks of Main Street were muddy from melted snow. The window casements and doors of the shops were freshly painted, however, and all the panes were scrubbed clean to display souvenirs commemorating the day. The street was a sea of Church loyalists, curious onlookers, and members of a high school band. The final estimate was around 2,500 spectators, all packed into a small block.[11]

Most of the seats in front of the redbrick courthouse, where the speaker's platform was raised, were occupied by families huddled together in the chilly air, passing thermos bottles filled with steaming coffee. Teenagers and college students sat on store roofs, stood on the tops of pickup trucks, and clung to other unlikely perches.

To a standing ovation, Church approached the microphones. He assailed "a leadership of weakness and fear" that allowed "the most powerful agencies of our government—the CIA, the FBI, and the IRS—to systematically ignore the very laws intended to protect the liberties of the people," and he blasted President Ford's "cosmetic changes." He attacked the argument the Church committee had heard all year: that since the KGB sinned, we must too.

> In stark contrast with contemporary presidents, our founding fathers were a different breed. They acted on their faith, not their fear. They did not believe in fighting fire with fire; crime with crime; evil with evil; or delinquency by becoming delinquents.
>
> They set themselves against the terrors of a totalitarian state by a government that would obey the law. They knew that the only way to escape a closed society was to accept the risk of living in an open one.

The first priority, continued Church, "is the restoration of the federal government to legitimacy in the eyes of the people." Drawing again upon his experience as chairman of the investigating committee, he emphasized:

> Nobody—no matter how highly placed in the government—has the right to break the law; to open our mail; to photograph our cables; to spread false propaganda for the purpose of discrediting decent citizens in their own communities; to open tax investigations against persons not even suspected of tax delinquency but targeted for political harassment, instead. These illegal and indecent practices must stop! Runaway bureaucracy must be harnessed once more to the reins of the law. For let it be remembered that in America the people are sovereign, and the government is their servant still!

Finally, Church addressed the argument that his entry was hopelessly late:

> There are those, I know, who say it is too late to enter the race for the presidency. But I had a difficult assignment to discharge first—the completion of the Senate's investigation of our intelligence agencies. It

would not have commended me to the American people to have abandoned that task in order to run for higher office. So, to those who say it is too late, I reply that it's never too late—nor are the odds ever too great—to try.

In that spirit the West was won, and in that spirit I now declare my candidacy for president of the United States.

Church was officially in the presidential race; the Senate Select Committee on Intelligence seemed far, far away.

The chances of winning the presidency were remote. At least, though, the fundamental assumption of the campaign scenario remained intact. "We were hoping for a confused result in the early primaries with no candidate breaking away," observed Bill Hall, Church's press aide. "And that's what happened."[12]

Who could tell for sure what might still happen? Church had successfully dodged enemy bullets in China during World War II, whipped a cancer diagnosed as terminal, and turned a 12,000-vote defeat for the Idaho state legislature in 1952 into a 46,315-vote victory for the United States Senate four years later. Maybe he had a corner on the most useful human quality of all: luck. He often remarked that his fight against cancer had changed his philosophy about life. "Before, I was a cautious man," he once said. "Afterward, I was prepared to take great chances."[13] While the *New York Times* saw Church's candidacy as a "high-risk strategy,"[14] the candidate himself looked upon the prospects with a certain amount of whimsy. As he told one reporter, if things went according to plan, "then it will be said, 'Well, Frank Church was the only one who figured it out this year, against the conventional wisdom of entering early primaries.' If it doesn't, then I'll be able to say back, 'As everybody figured, it was too late.'"[15]

Church's speaking schedule took shape; financial contributions steadily trickled in; citizens groups formed in Nebraska, Oregon, and elsewhere; mass mailing lists were almost ready; campaign brochures were printed; issues statements were drafted—Church, in short, was in business and ready to take on the world. But was the world ready for him?

The *Chicago Tribune*, for one, was unimpressed. Its editorial pages advised readers they could "relax now . . . Sen. Frank Church of Idaho has ended a period of truly bearable suspense: He finally announced his candidacy for the Democratic presidential nomination. The excitement of this long wait can be compared only to watching an ice cube melt. . . the suspense—what there was of it—is ended. We no longer have to wait for Sen. Church to drop the other sock."[16]

How widely this sentiment was held—particularly in Nebraska—was a worrisome matter. The editors of the *Boston Globe*, moreover, raised a point that I found more troubling still: "One fears that the candidacy [of Frank Church] will prove a complication minimizing the prospects for substantial reform of the CIA and the rest of the intelligence community."[17]

The Nebraska primary and the creation of a permanent Intelligence Committee stood like towering mountains before Church—Mount Everest and K2, both of which he would try to conquer in the same spring. The odds seemed long ("super long," said one commentator, with reference to the campaign),[18] but the challenge roused a spirited determination among those in his camp as they prepared for the ascents.

19

The Committee Reports

Soon after the announcement in Idaho City, Church appeared on NBC's *Today* show. "We've recommended the establishment of a permanent oversight committee," he stressed. "That's moving through the Senate now, and the last of our recommendations will soon be issued."[1] The proposal for a new oversight committee was, in truth, moving through the Senate, but with about the same ease and confidence as pioneers once passed through Comanche territory.

The fundamental problem remained the ancient question of turf—the territorial imperative. What jurisdictions belonged to which senators? The oversight resolution that emerged from the Ribicoff committee in February stripped the Judiciary Committee of its previous authority over FBI intelligence operations; similarly, the Foreign Relations Committee would have to relinquish authority over Department of State intelligence. The Armed Services Committee was hit less hard by the resolution but was expected nonetheless to share its control of military intelligence with the new oversight committee—an arrangement that Tower and Goldwater, among others, found impractical, unnecessary, and undesirable.

The argument over jurisdiction went beyond individual or committee pride. At stake was access to information—the lifeblood of the powerful in Washington. Without accurate information, legislators are cast adrift in a world of uncertainty; with it, they can exercise power with increased confidence. Primary sources of information for Congress are the executive agencies, with their thousands of trained data collators and analysts. In theory, this information is available to all members of Congress; in reality, the bureaucrats serve with greatest care those who authorize and appropriate their budgets at the committee and subcommittee level. So to reduce a committee's jurisdiction is to reduce its access to information and therefore its power. An aide on the Senate Foreign Relations Committee expressed his dismay over the desire of the Ribicoff panel to confine intelligence prerogatives within the boundaries of the proposed new committee: "We don't want to have some bureaucrats or the White House telling us CIA or the State Department does not have to come and talk about intelligence matters."[2]

Growing from this uneasiness over jurisdiction, a new feeling surfaced in the Senate in late March: maybe the country could do without a new intelligence oversight committee after all. In light of the Welch killing, the Schorr disclosure, and the attacks and counterattacks in the press, perhaps the time had come to lay this issue to rest as quickly as possible. "Hysteria has subsided and Congress is taking a more objective view," observed James B. Allen, a member of the Senate Rules Committee. This was so, he said, because the public feared that "Congress is out to destroy the intelligence agencies."[3]

Faced by these objections, the Rules Committee chairman, Howard W. Cannon (D-NV), indicated on the last day of March that he would seek a delay in the timetable for the Ribicoff resolution; instead of reporting the resolution to the floor on 8 April, he would ask the party leadership for a 30 April deadline. (As a ranking member of the Armed Services Committee, too, Cannon was no doubt feeling the heat from Chairman Stennis, not to mention Tower and Goldwater.)

Jurisdictional squabbles within the Senate were only part of our concern. The executive branch continued to pull the rug out from under the Church committee by publicizing initiatives the president planned to take toward intelligence reform. It could happen that by the time we were prepared to issue our final reports and recommendations, the Ford administration—through executive orders, press conferences, and the like—would already have said everything one could say on the subject. Our reports might read like last month's news.

Several instances of this effective administration tactic occurred soon after Senator Church's return from Idaho City. On 23 March, for example, the White House made public its support for an electronic surveillance bill that would require a special court warrant for national security wiretaps within the United States. A similar idea was an essential component of our FBI recommendations. As one newspaper observed, "The Administration has apparently proposed the measure in anticipation of a recommendation on the same subject by the Senate Select Committee on Intelligence."[4]

In late March, the press reported on Department of Justice plans to mail individual apologies to victims of the FBI COINTELPRO operation, revealing the tactics that had been used against them.[5]

In another decision, Attorney General Levi ordered the FBI to destroy its ill-begotten file on columnist Joseph Kraft, a subject of Bureau electronic and physical surveillance in Paris during the 1969 Vietnam War negotiations. (The file reportedly misidentified a telephone conversation between Kraft and Jean Monnet, a distinguished elder statesman well known for his role in the creation of Europe's Common Market, and not—contrary to a befuddled FBI agent's report—a "mysterious French woman."[6])

Even Robert Byrd, the Democratic whip and expert parliamentarian who had helped us during the secret session on the assassination report, offered little succor this time. His solution to the impasse was what appeared to be an emasculating compromise designed to allow the establishment of a permanent new committee, but one void of budgetary control over the intelligence community. "We may achieve the desired objective," Byrd said on 1 April during an appearance by Church before the Rules Committee, "by providing the new committee with subpoena powers and leaving the rest where it lies"—namely, in the Armed Services, Judiciary, and Foreign Relations Committees. A creature of compromise and conciliation, as all party leaders must be, Byrd sought to smooth the rough waters of jurisdictional strife.

Church, however, thought the compromise too lopsided in favor of the status quo. "The power of the purse is the ultimate authority," he emphasized to the Rules Committee; without it, oversight would be ineffective, because the agencies would take seriously only those committees that provided their life support through annual funding. He sought refuge instead in the obvious shelter: overlapping, or concurrent, jurisdiction between the new committee and the old ones. This, Church said, was the "traditional" solution in the Senate "where the interests of two committees . . . is strong." Byrd warned that he feared "the resolution will be subjected to unlimited debate," implying that if Church and Ribicoff failed to accept his compromise, they might lose their new committee altogether in a flood of endless verbiage—a filibuster—by opponents on the Senate floor.

Comity

During his Rules Committee appearance, Church was also taken to task on the ticklish issue of how the new committee would handle classified material. Some members of the Rules Committee agreed with CIA director Bush that the proposed committee should not have the authority to release classified information over a presidential objection.

The committees of Congress, retorted Church, could be trusted to deal with sensitive information with at least as much care and integrity as the executive branch. He reminded the Rules Committee that his investigative committee had produced no national security leaks. This was true, but the specter of the Pike committee sat silently in the room. Church had evidence beyond the record of his own investigation, however; he pointed to the CIA leak on Israeli nuclear weapons. This indiscretion represented, Church told the Rules Committee, "the greatest breach of security" he had ever known of in Washington, adding that he had "never even heard anyone was reprimanded."

I thought back to the conversation we had had the day after the incident, when he was even more outraged. "Can you imagine," he said, "how a leak of that kind would have been treated if it had come out of the Congress of the United States!" It could have destroyed our committee.

Church's argument, though, failed to answer the immediate question of the new oversight committee's authority to release classified information. The fundamental issue was the appropriate balance between national security on the one hand and the right of elected representatives to inform the people about government policies on the other. No end-all formula, regardless how complex, could be devised to solve the problem; disputes would have to be settled on a case-by-case basis, with both branches working in (as constitutional scholars like to say) "a spirit of comity." Despite strong disagreements on some matters, the Church committee and the Ford administration had demonstrated that the two branches could effectively negotiate differences of opinion on the public release of sensitive information. According to a *Washington Post* editorial at the time of the Rules Committee embroilment, the actual operation of the Church committee "has tended to soften these tensions, and . . . it has done so not by finding some magical formula to balance off interests in conflict, but rather by setting a procedural example of back-and-forth consultation to work out disagreements. The result is that there have been neither leaks nor impasses, an achievement for which chairman Frank Church and all of the members deserve major credit."[7]

This kind of consultation was clearly in evidence in the Dirksen auditorium during the latter days of March and early April, as committee staffers and intelligence agency representatives huddled together to negotiate points of dispute in the final report drafts. On 27 and 28 March, for example, the senior staff spent over twelve hours with CIA officials reviewing the committee findings on foreign intelligence. The CIA raised several objections to the report language: the committee's "vital national interest" standard for launching a covert action was considered "too restrictive"; curbs on recruiting foreign students within the United States were "unreasonable"; Angola should not be considered a covert action failure because the operation "was not allowed to reach its conclusion"; the committee figure on the number of covert action operations since 1947 was "too high"; ties with repugnant regimes were sometimes necessary and should be tolerated; various adjectives were considered too "pejorative." Nevertheless, as Bill Miller noted in a memorandum for the record, "in most areas there is basic agreement."[8] A few adjectives were toned down, but on its key findings and recommendations the committee stood its ground.

Some individuals looked upon these negotiations with profound displeasure. Within the Church committees, staffers on various hierarchical perches complained that the chairman was too compliant. Some hinted at open rebellion against what they viewed as a "lack of will" in completing certain areas of the investigation. The two topics that most made their blood boil continued to be CIA–media and CIA–academic relations.

No one could doubt that the CIA was prepared to stand firmly against any efforts by the committee to determine which journalists or scholars had been (or perhaps still were) employed by the Agency. As one staffer put it: "Church and some of the other members were much more interested in making headlines than in doing serious, thorough investigating. The Agency pretended to be giving up a lot whenever it was asked about the flashy stuff—assassinations and secret weapons and James Bond operations. Then, when it came to things that they didn't want to give away, that were much more important to the Agency, Colby in particular called in his chits. And the Committee bought it."[9]

The reason most frequently advanced to explain this failure of will was Church's haste to hit the campaign trail. By far the more important explanation, though, was the looming expiration date of the inquiry and the political backlash felt by the members after the Welch and Schorr incidents. "I had a great compulsion to press the point but it was too late," one anonymous committee member recalls. "If we had demanded [access to the names of journalists and scholars], they [the CIA] would have gone the legal route to fight it."[10] Church, Huddleston, and others were also wary that a committee demand for lists of journalists and academics could take on overtones of a witch hunt—conjuring up painful comparisons with Senator Joe McCarthy's techniques in the 1950s.[11]

The end result of this controversy was a brief section in the committee's final report summarizing some key issues without including details or names. "It hardly reflects what we found," Gary Hart has stated. "There was a prolonged and elaborate negotiation [with the CIA] over what would be said."[12] While the Church committee failed to treat these subjects more than superficially, the chairman certainly did not try to "bury" the preliminary findings or keep them away from other members (as one critic has charged[13]). Every senator's designee was aware of this matter, and any senator could have made an issue of the decision to forgo names if he wished; none did, presumably for one or more of the reasons I have suggested. As time ran out, the topic remained one of several left in limbo. The Church committee had nonetheless identified the problem for the first time in a government document, and other committees in subsequent sessions of Congress would follow the scent.[14]

The internal bickering within the committee over how to handle negotiations with the executive branch on such issues persistently raised the question of how tough we should be. Inevitably, the baseline for comparison was the Pike committee. As journalist Taylor Branch saw it, the Church committee seemed most interested in demonstrating it could handle national secrets responsibly, while the Pike committee wanted nothing less than to "impale" the CIA for its abuses. "The object of the exercise," according to a Church committee staffer cited by Branch, "was to prove that we were not Pike." But the result, according to Branch, was that "when the Church Committee cooperated, the Administration tended to see it as a sign of weakness and felt freer to hold back on information."[15]

This conclusion is hard to support. As a comparison of the multivolume final report of the Church committee with the Pike report (as leaked to the *Village Voice*) illustrates, the Senate committee gathered a massive amount of detailed information on the intelligence community, dwarfing anything any other government agency had ever produced. In Branch's own words, the committee's report on Chile, "while abstract and incomplete . . . is the most comprehensive account of a CIA covert action yet written."[16] Branch (among other critics) thought the Church committee should have subpoenaed at least Kissinger and Colby (as did the Pike committee, to no avail) when they refused to attend a public hearing on covert action. Though admittedly it would have been emotionally and symbolically satisfying to slap Kissinger and Colby with subpoenas, the Church panel knew what the outcome would be: the witnesses would have stayed home, and the committee would have looked foolish and impotent.

In place of pyrotechnics, the Church committee concentrated on procedures. John Elliff, the FBI Task Force leader, has commented on the value of this approach:

> When responses [from the executive] were tardy or materials delivered with major deletions, the senators did not move to open confrontation but held lengthy meetings with high executive officials to insist upon their specific requirements. The Committee did not waver in its adherence to the constitutional principle that Congress had the right to whatever information it needed; however, it was willing to tailor access procedures to the particular concerns of the executive. Sometimes this meant examining documents in the first instance at the agencies to determine their relevance, restricting access to the senators themselves and specifically designated staff, or assuring the executive an opportunity to review Committee reports before publication and state the case for secrecy.[17]

Nor did the executive branch relinquish its constitutional prerogatives in this process, occasionally asserting the doctrine of executive privilege. Still, the committee obtained most of the documents it requested. "The Committee's access to types of materials rarely, if ever, provided to Congress," Elliff concludes, "was not so much a victory for the absolute principle of the congressional right to information as it was a triumph for the process of accommodation and the constitutional concept of 'comity' between the branches." The tensions on the staff arose from the fact that one man's accommodation was sometimes another man's surrender.

An essential difference between Pike and Church was an apparent greater sensitivity on the part of Church regarding the importance of maintaining as cohesive a committee as possible. Church also seemed to remember better that the investigating committees would have to go to the parent chamber eventually to convert reform proposals into law; therefore, he wanted his committee to remain in favor with the Senate leadership and a majority of the members. This meant proceeding in a "responsible" manner: no unnecessary clashes with people like Kissinger, no leaks, no committee resignations, and the like.

In contrast, Pike seemed less concerned with in-house diplomacy and subsequent steps in the legislative process than in pillorying obstinate executive branch officials. While the Senate was now at least debating intelligence reform in the Rules Committee (if not enthusiastically endorsing the Church committee proposals), the House had abandoned the question of reform altogether in favor of an inquiry into how television reporter Daniel Schorr had obtained the Pike report. For various reasons—disharmony within its own ranks, leaks, unsuccessful negotiations with the Ford administration, occasional histrionics from its chairman, and the Schorr fiasco—the Pike committee had lost the support of the House, and in so doing had lost everything.

Turf

On the morning of 1 April, the Senate Democratic Conference (all the Democrats in the Senate) met—an infrequent occurrence—to discuss intelligence reform. Mansfield and Byrd immediately realized that their party was in disarray on this issue, particularly over whether to create a permanent Intelligence Committee and, if so, how to draw its jurisdictional boundaries. A thirty-day extension to the Rules Committee, decided the party leaders, would provide time to think about the problem further, seek the necessary amendments to satisfy various factions (if possible), and generally defuse what had become an emotionally charged issue.

The extension for the Rules Committee was less to prolong its hearings (which were completed by 5 April) than to give that committee a few weeks to mark up its own version of an intelligence reform bill. The approach to intelligence reform illustrated in classic fashion the fragmentation of the Senate. The Church committee had its favorite version of a bill, which, happily, was similar to Ribicoff's Government Operations version. The Judiciary, Foreign Relations, and Armed Services committees each had major amendments. And now the Rules Committee would spend a month (after the Church committee had just spent several months) preparing its version—which, if one trusted the rumors floating around the Russell and Dirksen buildings, would resemble the positions of the Church and Ribicoff committees as Dr. Jekyll resembled Mr. Hyde.

Moreover, there was some question whether any version would be passed. On 5 April, Hugh Scott, the Republican leader in the Senate, noted the "many differences of opinion" as to "whether or not there should be a committee on general oversight and surveillance, or a committee which removes jurisdiction from other committees, a proposal which has run into very substantial resistance on the part of a number of distinguished witnesses."[18]

In late 1975 practically everyone on the Church committee had just assumed the Senate would approve the establishment of a permanent oversight committee; after all, if our investigation had demonstrated nothing else, it showed beyond the shadow of a doubt that past and present oversight arrangements had failed. In addition to jurisdictional jealousies, however, subsequent events had cast a different light on the subject of intelligence reform. As observers put it, "Six months ago, the creation of a standing committee on intelligence oversight seemed a foregone conclusion. But that was before the House debacle, the administration's concerted attack on 'leaks,' the murder of Richard Welch, and the drying up of the seemingly bottomless well of revelations that kept the public interested. Today, the mood in the country has changed perceptibly and no intelligence agency reform is guaranteed."[19]

Meanwhile, all the committee staff could do was continue to shepherd its reports through the final printing stage, prepare the senators for the press conference that would accompany the release of the reports, and hope the committee members would lobby their colleagues in favor of the new oversight bill (though, of course, a few of the Republican staffers—notably those associated with Tower and Goldwater—opposed this last objective).

"Where is Church when we need him?" was a plea I heard often during this period. It revealed, first, an ignorance of the many hours he did spend reading and commenting on the reports during late March and April (despite presidential politicking) and, second, a lack of appreciation for Church's style in the Senate—even if he had had nothing on his mind besides Senate Resolution 400. The Lyndon Baines Johnson School of Charm, Cajolery, and Threat was simply not Church's alma mater. He was a graduate of the School of High Principle—not so high as to prohibit some compromises while a bill was being hammered out, but high in the belief that a member should be allowed to weigh the merits of a proposal free from the pressure of colleagues.

Despite the public backlash against the investigation in some quarters, Church revealed with every campaign stop a passionate belief in the importance of intelligence reform. The abuses uncovered by the committee became the centerpiece of his campaign addresses. He was, in essence, carrying the findings of the committee from the hearing rooms of the Senate to public forums of American citizens around the country:

> I am concerned that we really bring an end to the attitudes of arrogance, the disregard for the law, the trampling on the liberties of people in ways which, if they are not checked soon, will erode away the foundations of the

free society in this country. That infection we thought was limited to the White House in the days of the Watergate scandal actually spreads deep, its roots run thick within these major bureaus of the government. (Sacramento, California, 19 March)

No agency of the government has the right to do the kind of thing that this investigation has disclosed . . . the first item in the political agenda of this country is . . . the election of a president who has looked into the abyss, who knows how far this corruption has spread. (Oregon Democratic Party dinner, 3 April)

The law has to be respected by the CIA, by the FBI, and by every other agency of the government. So wherever you have illegal conduct, wherever you have wrongdoing, it must be exposed. The people who say, "Oh, no, you mustn't do that," are people who have forgotten that it is the peculiar American strength to do that. That's what keeps this government honest or makes it honest again, and that's what keeps us free. If you had a local police force and you found out that some of the policemen were involved in burglarizing the homes of the people in the community, would you say, "Sweep that under the rug because it might discredit the police force?" You'd say expose it, and see to it that those policemen go to jail; and once that's done, then the public can regain confidence once more in the honesty of the police force. Well, the same thing applies in government. (Lincoln, Nebraska, 12 April)

It's a weak president who tells us we must imitate the Russians in our treatment of foreign peoples, that our CIA must be a carbon copy of the Russian KGB. When we stoop to the Communist level, we betray ourselves. And it's a weak president who fails to use the muscle of his office to punish powerful government agencies that break the law and bully the people . . . These are crimes against freedom. And they must stop! (Nationally televised fund-raiser, 19 April)

Political calculations seemed immaterial to Church; for him, this topic was vital. Of course, he spoke of many other things as well, as every presidential candidate is expected to do; he obliged with lengthy question-and-answer sessions at each stop. The heart of his campaign, however, lay in abiding interest in foreign policy and intelligence reform.

As Church worked the crowds in the primary states, the Intelligence Committee staff worked the reports along the path to completion. The painstaking negotiations between the committee and the intelligence community over practically every paragraph of every study was a process that seemed to satisfy the Republicans on the panel and in the White House. No thunder, or even gray clouds, of objection were noticeable throughout most of April.

Then, on 22 April, a letter arrived for Church from President Ford. It read in part: "It is my understanding that the Select Committee expects to publish in its final report the budget figure for the Intelligence Community. It is my belief that the net effect of such a disclosure could adversely affect our foreign intelligence efforts and therefore would not be in the public interest."

Was this the beginning of administration efforts to pick away at the reports? The committee had already voted in favor of releasing the aggregate intelligence budget for fiscal 1976; now it was being asked to reverse itself. On how many other matters would the president intervene? To avoid further delay in the progress of the reports, the staff prepared the budget section with the controversial figure deleted; if the senators decided to release the figure over the president's objection, it could be done through a committee press statement.

On the very morning that the final reports were to be released (at long last!), the committee convened to consider the budget question. The meeting began with a plea from CIA director Bush to keep the aggregate total secret. Typically elegant in an expensive pinstripe suit, Bush presented an elaboration of the message in President Ford's letter.

The arguments for and against release of the figure were well known by the senators; after Bush's departure, extended discussion was unnecessary, and Church called for a vote. By a tally of six to five, the committee reversed its earlier decision to publish the figure. (As was frequently the case when a question before the committee was cast in terms of presidential prerogatives, Senator Morgan left his Democratic colleagues to give President Ford at least a temporary victory.) Instead, members opted to forward the final decision on release of the aggregate figure to the full Senate. (The figure was never released.) Church looked annoyed, but at least the other findings of the committee would soon be made public. The senators left S407 and walked to the caucus room in the Russell Building.

Findings and Recommendations

Senators Tower and Goldwater were absent from the press briefing. The two senior Republicans had done their best in recent months to dissociate themselves from the work of the committee—especially its recommendation for a new permanent oversight panel—and this final act of boycott served as a capstone to their mounting criticisms. "This is a report that probably should never have been written," concluded Goldwater's dissenting statement; its publication "will cause severe embarrassment, if not grave harm, to the nation's foreign policy."

"Gentlemen!" said Spencer Davis, the press secretary, quieting down the crowd of reporters (drawing scowls from the few women journalists in the room). Three million dollars and fifteen months after the birth of the committee, its chairman held up the first volume of the final report for the press to photograph. With flashbulbs popping in a disorganized light show, Church began his summary. (Small turtles dotted his tie, a symbol of the presidential campaign with its hope that despite a slow start, Church would nonetheless win the race to the White House. At that moment the turtles made me think less of Church's presidential chances than of the agonizingly slow and painful journey the committee had endured.)

Of the report's six volumes, book 1, entitled *Foreign and Military Intelligence*, was now officially in the public domain. In a couple of days, book 2 would follow (and another press conference—an undisguised attempt to sustain press coverage of the findings): *Intelligence Activities and the Rights of Americans*, summarizing the domestic side of our research. Book 3 contained thirteen detailed staff reports on such topics as FBI surreptitious entry, the Huston Plan, COINTELPRO, NSA surveillance, and the like—a rich lode of information about the dark side of government heretofore concealed from the American people.

These core volumes joined the bookshelf of our earlier publications: the Interim Assassination Report and the Chile Covert Action Report. In May, the committee would release three more volumes that included additional staff studies (among them a history of the CIA) as well as the testimony and documents made part of the public record during our open hearings from September to December—all in all a stack of green-covered Senate publications standing over two feet high and numbering several thousand pages.

The primary flaw in the report arose in those passages, most numerous in book 1, that had been negotiated and renegotiated between the committee and the agencies so many times (to meet administration "security objections") that they had lost some of their original meaning. Senators Mondale and the two Harts were especially dissatisfied with the results of these negotiations; they had legitimate grounds for their grievances, since the executive agencies sometimes made ridiculous demands. As the three senators explained in a joint "additional statement" (part of the appendix in book 1), the CIA "wanted to delete reference to the Bay of Pigs as a paramilitary operation, they wanted to eliminate any reference to CIA activities in Laos, and they wanted to excise testimony given to the public before television cameras." While the committee had successfully dismissed these objections out of hand, in other instances it had yielded too much ground, in the opinion of these senators. They were most annoyed by the diluted passages concerning CIA relations with the media and with academe. The relationship "is no longer clear," they complained; Church and Huddleston had bargained too much away, read the message between the lines.

They also criticized the watered-down accounts of ongoing CIA activities within the United States (notably the duties of the shadowy Domestic Contact Division, once less euphemistically called the Domestic Operations Division), and the complete expurgation of several sections on "Cover," "Espionage," "Budgetary Oversight," and "Covert Action." These omissions, they said, were the result of CIA exploitation of the committee's phobia about following the Pike committee's disastrous path. The end result, concluded the trio, was a successful operation by the Agency "to alter the report to the point where some of its most important implications are either lost, or obscured in vague language."

The right wing of the committee had spoken through its conspicuous absence (as well as in its own barbed "Separate Views" in the book 1 appendix). Now the committee's left wing was having its say. For the former, the report went too far; for the latter, not far enough. This placed Church where he often found himself: somewhere in the middle—a broker and conciliator of ideas. To say that Church was conciliatory, however, is not to say that on some issues, about which he felt deeply, he would fail to take an aggressive stance. He had been, after all, one of the first three or four senators to oppose the Vietnam War. And among the members of the Intelligence Committee, he was by far the most critical of covert action. In fact, not to be outdone by the various "Additional Views," "Separate Views," and "Supplemental Views" of other senators in the appendix, Church, too, had a statement in which he criticized his own committee for failing to circumscribe more sharply the covert action capability of the CIA. So the role of broker was conducted within limits. Church had no interest in having his committee viewed as an obedient lapdog, content to jump through administration hoops.

He may have been too much of a broker for some liberals, too ready to set aside tough issues for the new committee to handle, too willing to negotiate with "the enemy"; but these critics often seemed to forget the tough battles the committee took on. It insisted resolutely on access to files on assassination plots, over Colby's strenuous objections; on public hearings on NSA surveillance, despite a battalion of administration officials predicting calamity for the nation; on publication of detailed reports on assassination plots and covert action in Chile in the face of a presidential request to seal the information. It fought innumerable small and large engagements over everything from access to a document to the inclusion of important single words in the reports.

Church sometimes stood firm—generally throughout 1975 and whenever the issue seemed crucial to him or to a majority on the committee. Sometimes he backed off—late in the inquiry, when the issue did not seem fundamental to our overall efforts, or held a definite risk of badly dividing the committee turning the full Senate against it. It was a balancing act, and critics judged the chairman's skills according to their own ideologies and opinions regarding intelligence policy, presidential prerogatives, congressional investigative authority, and a host of other filtering lenses.

However one viewed Church's approach to the intelligence investigation, the first volume of the final report was now on the table, and by week's end the rest would follow. The results of the inquiry were there in black and white for all to evaluate.

The most conspicuous figure in the tapestry woven by the committee reports was a blind and toothless congressional watchdog. Over the quarter century since the CIA's establishment, the overseers on Capitol Hill plainly had been unaware of (or unconcerned about) excesses committed by the intelligence agencies. In a political system based on checks and balances, Congress had provided too few checks and permitted a shift in balance from the overseers to the overzealous. The supervisors in the executive branch had failed to perform any better.

The results were shocking. The CIA program to open mail from or to selected American citizens produced a secret computer bank of 1.5 million names; the FBI intelligence unit developed files on well over a million Americans and carried out 500,000 investigations of "subversives" from 1960 to 1974 without a single court conviction; the NSA computers were fed every single cable sent overseas by Americans from 1947 until 1975; army intelligence units conducted investigations against 100,000 American citizens during the Vietnam War.

The tactics sometimes used were alien to the principles embraced by the Bill of Rights and the body of statutes that have evolved to protect civil liberties in the United States. They were, in fact, more reminiscent of the means resorted to by Hitler's SS and Beria's secret policy under the Stalin regime: drug experiments conducted by the CIA on unsuspecting subjects; assassination plots attempted against foreign leaders in peacetime; murder and other violence incited among blacks by anonymous FBI letters; the families and friendships of dissidents disrupted by concealed Bureau harassment; burglaries carried out in the homes and offices of suspected subversives; elections manipulated in democratic countries; tax information misused for political purposes; academic and religious groups infiltrated.

As I read these accounts of lawlessness in the newspaper summaries of our research, the words of various intelligence officers echoed a counterpoint in the back of my mind. "Only 0.001 percent of the US mail was opened by the CIA and the FBI" (Angleton); "we were naturally pragmatic . . . we did what we were expected to do" (Sullivan); "if the US is to survive, long-standing concepts of 'fair play' must be reconsidered" (report to the 1954 Hoover Commission).[20] But just how far could one go in this direction? A controversial fragment of Barry Goldwater's 1964 Republican nomination acceptance speech loosed its mooring somewhere in my memory and floated to join the other flashbacks: "Extremism in the defense of liberty is no vice! . . . Moderation in the pursuit of justice is no virtue!"

Surely some limits had to be honored. I thought of the boast sent to Bureau headquarters by an FBI office in southern California during the 1960s: "Shootings, beatings, and a high degree of unrest continues to prevail in the ghetto area of southeast San Diego," read the memo. "Although no specific counterintelligence action can be credited with contributing to this overall situation, it is felt that a substantial amount of the unrest is directly attributable to the [COINTELPRO] program."[21] If the philosophy behind such extreme use of secret government power were acceptable, then it seemed every conceivable intrusion into the rights of private citizens could be anticipated. "You move from the kid with the bomb . . . to the kid with the bumper sticker of the opposing candidate," a born-again Tom Charles Huston had testified. In book 1 of the final report, the committee acknowledged the threat of espionage directed against the United States by the Soviet Union and other unfriendly powers, but it firmly rejected any responses by our country that might "undermine the treasured values guaranteed in the Bill of Rights."

Beyond the startling statistics of letters opened, cables intercepted, telephones tapped, anonymous threats made, computer files established, and offices broken into stood several less quantifiable abuses, as well as numerous instances of questionable policy decisions and plain old mismanagement. While much of the committee's investigation (particularly by the Schwarz team) involved alleged illegalities, roughly half of the staff time (mainly that of the Miller team) was directed toward assessing the way in which intelligence was collected and produced, the wisdom of specific policies like covert action, and whether the country was getting the best intelligence possible for the large sums of money spent.

From a budgetary standpoint, the committee's report raised serious questions about wasteful spending practices. In the first place, the lack of central coordination led to duplication of efforts and major problems in monitoring the flow of dollars. The fact that about 80 percent of intelligence funding went to agencies affiliated with the Defense Department overemphasized the collection of information (the primary mission of NSA, the service intelligence units, and the technical collection programs) at the expense of analysis and the preparation of perceptive intelligence reports for the nation's leaders. The CIA, supposedly the major analytic arm of the intelligence community, received only 20 percent of the total funding, and they tended to spend more of that on exotic instruments and exciting covert actions than on producing better analysis. Certainly the CIA director, in his subordinacy to the secretary of defense, was in no position to ter significantly a division of funding that favored the military.[22] In light of th budget realities, the report concluded that the analytic phase had become "the stepchild of the intelligence community." The government was presently "inundated with raw intelligence," a condition the committee found "unacceptable."

A central target for criticism of profligate spending was the CIA program of covert action. From the findings emerged a picture of a worldwide network of agents often engaged in little more than busywork. Between 1961 and 1975, nine hundred separate operations were carried out by the CIA in what the committee found to be an "excessive, and at times, self-defeating use of covert action." During the press briefing on book 1, Senator Mondale observed that past covert actions had been characterized by "high political costs and generally meager benefits."

While the report carefully steered clear of the rogue elephant theory, it warned nevertheless that the policy of covert action seemed to have developed a "bureaucratic momentum of its own." Especially troublesome to the committee was its discovery of several covert actions void of any formal approval whatsoever outside the CIA itself. Moreover, few (if any) records were kept by the Agency that could pinpoint responsibility for the initiation and execution of these operations.

The report criticized, too, the efforts of the CIA to infiltrate or manipulate universities, publishing houses, newspapers, religious groups, and other organizations in the pursuit of intelligence collection and the recruitment of agents. What worried the committee was the possibility that the integrity of private American institutions—the notion of a free press, for example—might be undermined by close ties (particularly financial) with secret government agencies. The reputation of all academic researchers might be unfairly sullied, closing the doors of access to even the most innocent of them in their research overseas; the American public might fall victim to CIA propaganda through the writings of authors and journalists employed by the Agency; religious groups might find their bonds with kindred believers around the world severed by distrust.

From the long list of CIA shortcomings presented by the committee (and I have summarized here only a small portion of the findings), in some ways the most disturbing had to do with the essential mission of the CIA: the presentation to the president and his advisers of the most reliable information obtainable on world affairs. "Know the truth and the truth shall make you free," reads the CIA motto, borrowing the biblical injunction. Yet as the committee discovered, the truth had been twisted, deleted, or ignored by some Agency officials.

Richard Helms was accused of expunging for intelligence reports, under pressure from the Nixon administration, information that downgraded the potential first-strike capability of the Soviet nuclear arsenal—a position that ran counter to the views of Melvin R. Laird (then secretary of defense) and Henry Kissinger. And in April 1970, Helms decided against sending an intelligence report on Cambodia to the White House on the day before President Nixon ordered American combat troops into that country—apparently because of the impending invasion plans—even though it indicated that such an operation would fail to thwart North Vietnamese efforts to gain supremacy. These findings struck at the roots of the CIA's raison d'être: the unbiased collection and presentation of facts affecting American security.

The FBI was chastised also. In book 2 of the final report, the Bureau was taken to task both for the list of shameful abuses over the years and for the weaknesses in FBI reform offered by Attorney General Levi. Several senators on the committee found the Bureau violations much more alarming than those of the CIA: for the most part, the CIA committed its abuses overseas, where laws and ethical standards were frequently different from our own and the boundaries of rectitude obscure; the excesses of the FBI, however, were almost always directed against our own citizens and violated our own standards of propriety.

These abuses, one hoped, were in the past, but the committee also found flaws in the new Department of Justice guidelines for the Bureau. They were too vague, concluded the report; their use of the term "subversive," for example, was so open-ended "as to constitute a license to investigate almost any activity of practically any group that actively opposes the policies of the administration in power." And going beyond Levi's recommended standard of "reasonable suspicion" that a crime is being planned, the committee preferred to limit "preventive" investigations "to situations where information indicates that the prohibited activity will *soon* occur." In an attempt to prohibit the wide range of mischief that had sheltered under the code name COINTELPRO, the report was also more specific than the Department of Justice in its suggested guidelines for carrying out investigations.

The committee offered a total of ninety-seven recommendations to help set the CIA, the FBI, and the rest back on track. We knew as well as anyone that placing individuals of integrity in these agencies (Helms's "honorable men") would be as important as any new statutes and guidelines, but legislation would be valuable to make formal and amplify the correctives found necessary by Ford, Levi, and Congress. If nothing else, the message accompanying the jeremiad in books 1, 2, and 3 was the need to return to a healthy respect for the law in the conduct of our intelligence affairs.

20

The Oversight Bill

Ultimately, the purpose of all the investigations and seemingly endless hearings on intelligence reform in 1975–1976 was to develop a new legislative charter for the intelligence community: to recast the National Security Act of 1947 so that it would more clearly define the limitations of and prohibitions on intelligence agencies and, in the words of our report, "set forth the basic purposes of national intelligence activities." The committee urged that a new charter "be given the highest priority by the intelligence oversight committee of Congress, acting in consultation with the executive branch." The sine qua non for success—the vehicle for reaching this objective—was the establishment of the new oversight committee.

Whether the request for such a committee would be honored by the Senate, however, had fallen into increasing doubt. As the *Washington Post* noted, "Ironically, the findings [of the Church committee] come at a time when the impetus for reform appears to be only a shadow of what it was last year."[1]

Rules Committee Ambush

The major cause of deepening gloom was the astonishing outcome of the markup meetings of the Rules Committee, held on 27 and 28 April. As chairman of the committee, Senator Cannon recommended by way of a substitute for the entire Ribicoff bill (Senate Resolution 400 [S. Res. 400]) the establishment of a new standing intelligence committee, but one with only subpoena powers and no legislative or authorizing—that is, funding—jurisdiction. This "oversight" committee (a variant of Robert Byrd's April proposal) would spend fifteen months studying the intelligence agencies and the present jurisdictions of Senate committees over them; at that point, the Senate could decide whether to expand the powers of the new intelligence committee.

Fifteen months studying the intelligence agencies? I couldn't believe my ears. I thought we had just done that! Surely this measure was some kind of joke and would be so treated by the nine Rules Committee members.

The roll was called on the Cannon Amendment: among the Democrats, Howard W. Cannon (Nevada) voted yea; Claiborne Pell (Rhode Island), nay; Robert C.

Byrd (West Virginia), yea; James B. Allen (Alabama), yea; Harrison A. Williams Jr. (New Jersey), nay; and Dick Clark (Iowa), nay.

Incredibly, the Democratic vote was tied. The three Republican members now had the power to support a strong new intelligence committee with legislative and budgetary authority or, in essence, to recommend the postponement (and probable burial) of the decision for another fifteen months: Mark V. Hatfield (Oregon) voted nay; Hugh Scott (Pennsylvania), yea; and Robert P. Griffin (Michigan), yea.

I was stunned: by one vote, five to four, the wisdom of the Rules Committee favored launching the Senate on another inquiry.

In the "Minority Views" of the Rules Committee report on the Cannon substitute for S. Res. 400, Senators Clark, Hatfield, Pell, and Williams reminded the Senate that "what is needed is legislative action, not further study." When the matter came to the Senate floor, they declared, "we shall oppose the [Rules] Committee substitute and seek a final product which will incorporate these elements."

The vote in favor of the Cannon substitute represented a major victory for members of the Armed Services Committee, who were strongly opposed to relinquishing any portion of their traditional prerogatives as CIA overseers. Cannon had no apologies; he was convinced that the reforms of Church and Ribicoff went too far: "Is the solution to cut off a dog's head if he has done something wrong? I'm trying to solve the problem without taking the kinds of steps that might jeopardize the intelligence community."[2]

Clearly, we faced an uphill struggle. Criticism of the Church committee persisted. The *Reader's Digest* took out advertisements in newspapers around the country to plug its May 1976 issue, which contained an article by former secretary of defense Melvin Laird entitled "Let's Stop Undermining the CIA."[3] The widely heard radio commentator Paul Harvey reminded his listeners in May that "the Senate Intelligence Committee—the so-called Church Committee—is still sticking pins in the FBI" (a reference to book 3 of the final report). After enumerating a series of terrorist bombings and killings in the United States, Harvey concluded, "Meanwhile, the Senate Intelligence Committee, which should be on our side, preoccupies itself with accusing our FBI of playing too rough."

Some observers, though, greeted the Church committee's final report with enthusiasm. A *Washington Post* editorial for instance, concluded: "The House may have been unable to deal intelligently with intelligence. The Senate, by this report [book 1], has earned the public's confidence in its capacity to join in the shaping of national intelligence policy."[4] The vote on a permanent committee, however, would take place on the Senate floor, not in editorial offices. How could we encourage a majority of the senators to feel as positively toward intelligence reform as did the members of the Church and Ribicoff committees?

Part of the answer would be leadership, but how much time and energy would Church have for this last surge? The timing could hardly have been worse for him: the debate on intelligence reform was now expected to take place on 10 May—exactly one day before the Nebraska primary. In his efforts to hold the reins of these wild horses pulling him in opposite directions, Church shuttled between Lincoln, Nebraska, and Washington's National Airport with a frequency that even Henry Kissinger, the king of shuttle diplomacy, might have found dizzying. Still, he knew that if he divided his time between leading the floor fight and campaigning for the primary, he might well lose both.

Fortunately, he managed to convince Majority Leader Mansfield to postpone the intelligence debate until after the primary, and he began to spend longer periods in Nebraska as the day of reckoning there came nearer. Around the state, Church volunteers worked in a frenzy to turn out the vote for their candidate. When the results were announced on 11 May, Church—in a nerve-rattling close call—had defeated front-runner Jimmy Carter by about a thousand votes, 39 to 38 percent.

Jubilant, Church joined his campaign workers at the victory celebration. The outcome, he said, was "a political miracle." His campaign was for real; the people of Nebraska had authenticated it. Our ambush of Jimmy Carter had worked.

Only one thought tarnished the moment: the memory that we too had just been ambushed by the Rules Committee. Whether these wounds were mortal for Carter in the one instance or for intelligence reform in the other would soon be known.

While the Church campaign army decamped and prepared to march on Oregon, the candidate himself switched hats and returned to Washington, DC. The next battle on his agenda would take place on the Senate floor.

Four versions of S. Res. 400 had popped up at one time or another: the original Church committee version; the Government Operations Committee (or Ribicoff) version; a pale hybrid offered by Byrd and Griffin early in the Rules Committee markup; and the version finally reported by the Rules Committee, the Cannon Amendment calling for yet another study.

The Church proposal had been blended into the Ribicoff bill, for the most part, during the Government Operations Committee markup, and the Byrd–Griffin proposal had been superseded by the Cannon Amendment. So the debate on intelligence reform had come down to a clash between the Church–Ribicoff approach and the Cannon approach. Technically, the Cannon Amendment, once passed by the Rules Committee on 29 April, rendered all previous versions of S. Res. 400 "dead texts" and would itself be the bill introduced by the Rules Committee to begin the debate. The Church–Ribicoff language, however, continued to have many supporters who were determined to fight for it on the floor; in a political sense, their text was very much alive.

The struggle had another dimension: Mansfield, the majority leader and longtime advocate of a strong intelligence oversight committee, seemed to favor the Church–Ribicoff proposal, yet the second highest Democratic leader, Robert Byrd, had voted in committee for the Cannon Amendment. The party appeared to be badly split on this issue, and "the Senate was headed for a real battle," Senator Ribicoff has recalled.[5]

Ribicoff talked with members of his Government Operations Committee and with Walter Mondale on 10 May (while Church was campaigning in Nebraska). Together they decided to approach Mansfield, Byrd, and Cannon to arrange a compromise version of S. Res. 400 before the issue disrupted the Senate. Ribicoff reached Church by telephone before proceeding with the plan, and the two decided what issues were negotiable and where Ribicoff and Mondale should refuse any compromise.

On 11 May, Democrats Mansfield, Byrd, Alan Cranston (California; the majority whip and third in the party's Senate hierarchy), Cannon, Morgan, Ribicoff, Huddleston, Mondale, and Clark, plus Republicans Percy, Baker, Javits, Hatfield, Scott, and Lowell P. Weicker (Connecticut) gathered with a few staffers in Byrd's elegant Capitol offices to see whether the two sides could agree on a middle ground. From time to time a couple of other senators from the Rules and Gov Ops Committees wandered in to listen and offer suggestions. Mansfield and Byrd, as well as Ribicoff and Mondale, were prepared to bargain rather than completely lose all hope for intelligence reform. That Byrd was evidently willing to compromise probably spelled the difference between victory and defeat for the Church–Ribicoff side; continued intransigence by the assistant majority leader, a man widely respected in the Senate, would have prolonged the debate and quite possibly resulted in nothing more than a continuation of the status quo. Even Cannon, plied with patient reasoning by Mansfield and Byrd, seemed ready to barter.

This meeting—in essence yet another markup of S. Res. 400—lasted several hours. Progress was slow and hard, with tough negotiating on sentences and even single words. Eventually, though, the session began to produce a workable formula. Everyone realized that many disagreements would still have to be dealt with during the floor debate and, above all, hammered out on the anvil of experience by the new committee, but the most prominent points of dispute had been smoothed down. By day's end, a grand compromise was achieved.

The Ribicoff coalition got its permanent Intelligence Committee, fully equipped with the powers of authorization and annual budget review; in return, the Cannon coalition was assured of shared jurisdiction over military and FBI intelligence with the traditional standing committees. Only the CIA would fall solely within the jurisdiction of the new committee. Points that could not be resolved satisfactorily, such as the size and composition of the proposed committee's membership, were drafted tentatively with the understanding that they would be the prime subjects of debate on the Senate floor. The group agreed to discourage floor discussion that might jeopardize the careful negotiations they had just completed on key issues.

Whether this understanding would be acceptable to the rest of the Senate was uncertain. There was little comfort in the absence of John Stennis from these meetings; he might well try to bring down this house of cards in an effort to preserve exclusive prerogatives over military intelligence for his own Committee on Armed Services. And, of course, we still had to contend with Tower, Goldwater, and several other Republican opponents who had been left out of the meeting. The situation was nevertheless a vast improvement over that of the day before, when the Ribicoff and Cannon camps seemed prepared to storm down the mountainsides and make war in the valley of the Senate floor.

The Debate Begins

On May 12, Senator Cannon stood by his Senate desk as the legislative clerk droned out the next order of business: "A resolution (S. Res. 400) to establish a Standing Committee of the Senate on Intelligence Activities, and for other purposes."[6] Above, tourists flowed in and out of the galleries, pausing a few minutes and asking each other in whispers where all the senators were; a couple of bored-looking journalists sat in the press section, scratching perfunctorily on their pads with fountain pens. From the lack of interest shown by observers, the historic debate about to begin might as well have been on soybean futures as on the future of intelligence oversight.

Cannon's monotone delivery did nothing to enliven matters. He spoke first of the "representative" group of senators who had been meeting to come up with a new compromise bill on intelligence reform (just how representative this group was would be sharply questioned later). Then he reviewed the history of his own Rules Committee's substitute amendment. The reactions of several senators to that amendment had caused him to reconsider his position, he said, and persuaded him to enter into another drafting session with Senators Byrd, Ribicoff, and others. Now, he had come before the Senate to present a new compromise. He spoke favorably, though not enthusiastically, for the compromise and presented to the few senators who now milled around the floor an impressive list of twenty-eight cosponsors supporting the measure.

Only a small fraction of the Senate had been included in the eleventh-hour compromise sessions; the rest of the membership still had to be convinced that the compromise was acceptable. Ribicoff turned to this task. "The compromise substitute is the product of much hard work and a commendable spirit of compromise and accommodation," he said, peering over his glasses with a wise-owl expression. "It is a delicately balanced proposal that addresses the concerns of the intelligence community, the executive branch, the Senate, and more importantly, the public."

Senator Roman Hruska (R-NE) took a turn to speak. The senior Republican on the Judiciary Committee was obviously there to head off any efforts designed to rob his committee's "historic jurisdiction over the Department of Justice and the FBI." Hruska said he favored the original Cannon Amendment, not any new attempts to compromise away the jurisdictional rights of the Judiciary Committee; he wanted no FBI oversight whatsoever for the new committee—not even shared jurisdiction; in his view, to share would be to separate the intelligence activity of the FBI from the law enforcement mission of the Justice Department. That old hobgoblin, jurisdictional turf, was with us again.

With the exception of Hruska, it had been the Day of the Conciliators. The next day, I was sure, Hruska would return with company.

In the well of the Senate floor on 13 May stood Senator Weicker, an imposing figure.[7] As a member of the Watergate Committee, the Yale-educated freshman senator had already exhibited a strong interest in, and skepticism about, the intelligence agencies. Wealthy and independent, Weicker was neither bashful nor concerned about traditional mores encouraging reticence among younger members; his comments could be brash and colorful.

How did all the intelligence abuses happen, Weicker inquired rhetorically. "Nobody in the Congress was looking," he answered. "We have had weak sight, we have had blind sight, we have had hindsight, we have had short sight, but we have not had oversight." For him, it was insufficient to say "we remember these things and so they will not happen again. We are not a government of memories, we are a government of laws." Moreover, Weicker observed, with a barb directed toward the White House, "It is not enough to go ahead and issue an executive order. Here today, gone tomorrow. We are not a government of executive orders."

Goldwater walked slowly through the swinging doors of the chamber and stood by his desk, ready to follow Weicker. When he spoke, his words came quietly. He favored a Joint Intelligence Committee, he said, but if this was impossible, then he supported the version of S. Res. 400 produced by the Rules Committee—that is, the Cannon Amendment. This was the only "compromise" he was willing to accept.

Mondale came next. He spoke long and forcefully, tracing the abuses uncovered by the Church committee. "The intelligence agencies pursued a private foreign policy often based on violence without the authority or knowledge of Congress," he said, and reminded his colleagues that the transgressions had been plentiful at home too. The solution: a new form of oversight since the present one was the "worst possible system"—one badly "fragmented," lodged in committees that viewed intelligence oversight "as an adjunct to their principal business." He zeroed in on the heart of the opposing arguments: namely that a new oversight committee could do without legislative powers. "Congress has only two types of power," he said, "the power to disclose and the power to control money. For intelligence, disclosure cannot be the primary remedy. Annual budget authorization is crucial to effective oversight." At his desk nearby, Church nodded strong approval as Mondale emphasized that "subpoenas are no substitute for the power of the purse."

Throughout the preliminary remarks, those who had been involved in the fashioning of the Great Compromise lauded the results of the effort and urged others to accept, as Javits put it, this "middle-ground choice." Javits told of the pressures on Howard Cannon, who "felt very, very deeply about the substitute which the Rules Committee recommended, but in that spirit of knowing that we had to do something effectively in this particular field yielded many of the things he thought he would never yield in order to gain the greater objective, which is to bring about a strong congressional capability to deal with the intelligence community."

The strategy of the conciliators was clear: to make the compromise appear as something so carefully worked out, so arduously labored over, and involving so many painful concessions by key senators that to question the results now would be an unthinkable faux pas, a heresy in this small club of gentlemen.

The response of James Eastland (D-MI), chairman of the Judiciary Committee, punctured any illusions that the rest of the Senate would fall in line like so many sheep behind this strategy. "I strongly suggest," said this most senior of all the senators, "that the best approach is not by including the activities of the FBI with that of the CIA and the Defense Department." In short, compromise all you like; just stay away from my committee turf.

At Mansfield's request to "dig in," various senators began to send their pet amendments to the legislative clerk for introduction into the debate. Some were minor and uncontroversial improvements or clarifications; others commanded lively attention (table 2). The first amendment came from Percy and was designed simply to change the proposed years of service on the new committee from nine to eight for each member, on a rotating basis that theoretically would draw all senators into the committee over the years. The purpose was to avoid the interruption—inherent in an odd-numbered sequence—of any one Congress. The amendment was accepted rapidly after both Cannon and Ribicoff—the key gatekeepers for amendments to the compromise—gave their assent.

The next amendment came from Huddleston, Javits, and William Roth (R-DE). The Senate Ethics Committee (officially called the Select Committee on Standards and Conduct) would continue to have the duty to investigate leaks, but this amendment, said Huddleston, clarified that the ethics panel would also

Table 2. Key Amendments to Senate Resolution 400[a]

Amendment No.	Subject	Chief Sponsor	Date	Outcome
1	8-year committee membership rotation	Percy	May 13	Accepted (without challenge)
2	Tightened guidelines for investigation of unauthorized disclosures	Huddleston, Roth, Javits	May 13	Accepted (without challenge)
3	Decreased committee size (from 17 to 15)	Cannon	May 13	Accepted (75–17)
4	Increased committee disclosure powers	Abourezk	May 13	Rejected (77–13)
5	Protection of intelligence methods	Allen	May 17	Accepted (without challenge)
6	Discretionary public reporting	Taft	May 17	Accepted (without challenge)
7	Mandatory sequential jurisdiction	Taft	May 17	Accepted (without challenge)
8	Solitary "B" committee assignment	Taft	May 18	Rejected (50–39)
9	Decreased committee disclosure powers	Nunn	May 19	Accepted (without challenge)
10	Exclusion of defense intelligence	Stennis, Tower	May 19	Rejected (63–31)
11	Cannon Compromise	Cannon, Ribicoff, Church	May 19	Accepted (87–7)

[a] The resolution itself was passed on 19 May 1976, by a vote of seventy-two to twenty-two.

have "the flexibility, the discretion, to dismiss frivolous and unwarranted allegations." The purpose was to guard against the ruination of a senator's reputation by gossip, innuendo, or unfounded allegations raised, perhaps by a single member. The amendment passed without challenge.

Cannon himself offered the third amendment: to reduce the membership of the proposed oversight committee from seventeen to fifteen. Senator Morgan was the first to object. He pointed out that doing so would shift the balance of power on the proposed committee toward the older committees that once had sole authority over the intelligence agencies: Appropriations, Armed Services, Foreign Relations, and Judiciary. The compromise specified that these four committees would each be allowed to have two members on the new committee, for a total of eight, leaving nine positions for "outsiders"—senators who did not serve on the four established committees. Under Cannon's proposal, the outsiders would be limited to seven—a minority on the new committee. Morgan was dismayed: "If we are going to place all the responsibility right back in the hands of those where it has been through all the period of time when the abuses took place, I am not sure we will have accomplished very much."

Soothing words of assurance from Cannon and Ribicoff filled the Senate chamber. Senator Mansfield would faithfully take into account the makeup of the entire Senate when choosing new committee members, observed Ribicoff, so the panel would reflect the sectional diversity of the chamber as well as the differences in seniority, age, and the like. "I have the utmost confidence in the appointing discretion of Senator Mansfield and his wisdom and judgment," continued Ribicoff primly. Smothering under these pillows of praise for the leadership, Senator Morgan's resolve grew short of breath and soon expired. With a slight change in the wording of Cannon's amendment so that it no longer appeared to require that Senate leaders consult with the senior members of the four established committees before making appointments to the new committee (they would anyway, most likely), Morgan found the proposal "more acceptable." Like Lord Byron's Julia, Morgan, whispering "I will ne'er consent," consented.

Less easily mollified, however, was Lowell Weicker, who had just returned to the floor. "I must confess I am quite surprised at having to rush in here," he said, "and find that such a vital point, which is a key part of the negotiation, has just been blithely dealt off." Weicker seemed unable to believe that the Senate would turn over majority control of the new committee to members of the existing committees, whose "track record is an unmitigated disaster." Control should go instead, he stressed—his voice filling every corner of the high-vaulted chamber—to "those who have not participated previously in the oversight process."

The irrepressible Weicker soon dispelled any doubt that he took this issue seriously: "Mr. President, I ask for the yeas and nays on this matter." The first formal roll-call vote on S. Res. 400 was underway. The buzzers rang throughout the Senate side of the Capitol and on through the Russell and Dirksen buildings. Senators moved toward the floor from hearing rooms, late lunches, the cloak-room, the reading room, private offices, and sundry other locations within hearing range of the buzzers. The count demonstrated that few senators were willing to challenge the leaders on this portion of the reform bill: seventy-five voted for Cannon's reduction-of-size amendment, seventeen against.

If Weicker had become something of a thorn in the side of the leadership on this issue, he was a mild irritant compared to the sharp arrows that struck next. The archer was yet another upstart freshman: James G. Abourezk. Short, barrel-chested, aggressive, and also unimpressed by the hallowed traditions of the Senate or the vaunted reputations of his senior colleagues, Abourezk had quickly developed a reputation as a razor-tongued critic of the upper house. Some viewed him as a total misfit, a mistake made by the citizens of South Dakota that would have to be endured for six years—with luck, no more.

On this occasion, Abourezk's complaint had to do with the disclosure provision in Section 8 of the compromise. As it stood, he said, the provision gave too much power to the president; it was too ambiguous, providing that the committee "may" refer to the full Senate a dispute over the release of information. "I fear that the reading intended by the drafters is that referral to the Senate is the only procedure by which information can be disclosed," said Abourezk. The Senate seemed to be on the verge of surrendering its independent power to declassify sensitive information; this section might give to the president a formal procedure for vetoing committee action.

"I can only presume that the drafters of the compromise have more confidence in the judgment of the president than they do in the judgment of their own colleagues who will work on the new committee," said Abourezk, adding, in an observation that sounded precisely like Church's interpretation of Rule 36, "I would have thought that a hard-working committee that is well acquainted with the issues before it could be trusted to make responsible decisions without endangering the nation." Abourezk strongly shared the suspicion of presidential power characteristic of several freshman members of the Congress whose careers had begun during the revelations of Watergate.

The leadership, however, was hardly a passive target; it had bows and arrows, too, and more experience in the sport. Looking quite distressed, Mansfield reached into his quiver first, finding Abourezk's amendment for increased committee disclosure power "contrary to the compromise." In fact, the Democratic leader failed to see how Abourezk's contribution had "any place in this compromise, which a lot of us worked awfully hard to achieve and to bring about the greatest degree of unanimity therein."

Ribicoff aimed next: the language in Section 8 "was cleared with, we thought, almost every element involved in this entire problem, including Senator Church.

. . . I would be reluctant to see the [compromise] in jeopardy." (Ribicoff was correct about Church: he had abandoned his earlier theory of complete committee discretion over disclosures weeks before. Willing to do battle with Baker in S407 over this issue in 1975, Church was unprepared to take on the entire Government Operations Committee in March 1976.) Cannon sent the third arrow, declaring the Abourezk perspective "very controversial."

The skin of Senator Abourezk was thick, though; he felt no obligation, he said, to honor a bargain to which he was never a party. This section "compromises the power of the US Senate to the president," Abourezk reiterated, adding that "the folly of this language can be illustrated by the example of the Pike Committee Report." He reminded the Senate of what had recently transpired across the Hill: "By a parliamentary maneuver, [the Pike report] was brought to the floor of the House, and the members who had not read the report and did not know the contents of it, voted, under pressure by the executive to withhold the report from the public." The implication, of course, was that this sad performance could easily visit the Senate unless the new oversight committee was given greater discretionary powers. Abourezk wanted a formal vote; for the second time on S. Res. 400, the buzzers sounded and the Senate filled, the tide of senators rushing in for a few minutes and ebbing back out.

A freshman against the likes of Mansfield, Cannon, and Ribicoff was unlikely to fare well; the vote was seventy-seven favoring a motion by Cannon to table Abourezk's amendment, thirteen against.

With the pained expression of a lion whose tail had just been trod upon by a lowly beast, Mansfield paced in the well of the Senate chamber, grumbling to various senators about another attempt to undermine the compromise. This time it was a Stennis amendment (or Tower amendment, or Stennis–Tower amendment, or Stennis–Tower–Thurmond amendment, as it was called from time to time, since all three men plus Goldwater sponsored it and spoke strongly on its behalf). This banner behind which the forces of antireform were now gathering was designed to keep all legislative responsibility related to military intelligence—and thus control of about 80 percent of all the money spent on United States intelligence—within the Armed Services Committee, where it had resided all along. If the old relationship was to be preserved, the efforts toward intelligence reform would be sharply curtailed indeed.

That the Stennis–Tower group was less than happy with the compromise cabal, from which they had been excluded, was clear from the start in the remarks of Robert Taft Jr. (R-OH), son of Mr. Republican himself, grandson of President William Howard Taft, and (most important in May 1976) a junior member of the Senate Armed Services Committee behind Thurmond, Tower, and Goldwater. In view of his committee assignment and his generally conservative tendencies, it did not require the legendary vote-counting genius of Lyndon Johnson (Senate majority leader, 1954–1960) to calculate Taft's likely position. "The first time I saw this proposal [the compromise] was when I read it in the *Congressional Record* this morning," Taft complained, adding that he refused to be "tied in a straitjacket procedure by entering into a unanimous-consent agreement."

Tower was equally piqued. The Senate had "overreacted"; with the S. Res. 400 compromise, it had created "a Frankenstein monster that will come back to haunt us." If adopted, the result would be "more inhibitions on intelligence-gathering capability, more revelations of matters that for disclosure are inimical to the security of the United States; and this so-called compromise comes to us without any report, without any hearings, with very little chance for input on the part of those who have serious reservations about the concept of an omnibus oversight committee in the Senate." In a word, the measure would leave the Department of Defense "hamstrung."

While the outcome of the debate remained foggy, at least the date of resolution was plain. Mansfield had convinced floor managers Ribicoff and Percy, as well as Stennis and Tower, to agree on a time for a final vote: no later than 5 o'clock on the afternoon of the following Wednesday, 19 May. The Stennis–Tower forces had won from Mansfield several days to prepare their case. During the next week, longer knives would be drawn.

21

Victory—And Defeat

On 17 May, the Senate floor was practically empty of senators. Staff aides, though, crowded the few seats along the walls, and tourists filled the galleries.

The Stennis–Tower amendment would "go to the heart of breaking the compromise," Percy was saying. "Once we invade this area and break the compromise that has been so painstakingly worked out, would we not then establish a precedent to say, then, let us take everything else back into the other Committee?"[1]

Agreeing, Mondale forcefully checked off the central arguments against the Stennis–Tower amendment: first, the amendment would remove from the new committee's jurisdiction "the overwhelming proportion of the activities of this nation in the intelligence field"; second, the military had been responsible for some of the most egregious abuses and deserved as close a watch by new overseers as the CIA and the FBI. "Anything the CIA does or the FBI does, the military can do and has done," he said.

After Percy and Mondale had extolled the virtues of the compromise for an hour, I began to wonder if its critics had decided to give up the ghost. Then in walked Robert Taft.

Skirmishes

In his first amendment, Taft sought to change the language of two sections to ensure that the new committee would not be required to disseminate to the public either annual reports or information on intelligence funding. Percy found the amendment acceptable, but Ribicoff pointed out that since William Brock (R-TN) had initially drafted the requirement for public reports (in March during the Gov Ops Committee markup of S. Res. 400), he ought to be consulted before the Senate went further on Taft's proposal. A page scurried from the floor to find Brock.

In the meantime, Senator Allen, a Southern conservative ally of Stennis, had a brief, noncontroversial amendment that he had cleared in advance with the floor manager: he wished to add an item to the list of subjects upon which the new committee would not be expected to report publicly. Already the committee was prohibited, quite properly, from disclosing the names of intelligence officers or their sources of information. With Allen's proposal—quickly accepted—the prohibition extended to the intelligence methods used to obtain information.

Allen also supported the Taft suggestions. The intention, he observed, was not to prevent the new committee from ever saying anything publicly; instead, it was to make sure the reporting was at the discretion of the committee— barring presidential objections—rather than mandatory. (The committee was free to seek plenary Senate approval over a presidential objection to committee disclosure.) By this time, Brock had arrived in the chamber to clarify his reasons for initially seeking public reports. They had nothing to do with any classical democratic theory of keeping the citizens informed on broad intelligence policy; rather, he seemed to have in mind an exercise in propaganda—a glorification of the intelligence agencies. The CIA and the FBI, he said, "have come under massive assault in recent months—for some valid reasons on occasion, but generally the assault has exceeded the crime. . . . I was hoping that this report would afford the agencies an opportunity to present their side of the case to the American people." Brock was "disgusted, frankly, with some of the machinations with regard to this [Church committee] investigation . . . there clearly have been excesses in reporting those abuses."

This seemed an odd function for the United States Senate: releasing official reports presenting the views of an executive agency. Taft properly retorted: "If there is a report of that kind made, I think it ought to come from the president of the United States to the people of the United States."

Taft's basic idea of altering the compromise language to make public reporting discretionary was acceptable to those in the chamber; it simply required changing the verb from the mandatory "shall" to the permissive "may." The first Taft amendment was accepted.

Just as this legislative fine-tuning was growing tedious, in rolled the heavy artillery from the Stennis–Tower encampment: Strom Thurmond, another septuagenarian from the South. Born in 1902, Thurmond still looked fit enough to participate again in the Normandy invasion, as he had done three decades before, though some of the fire had gone out of his once Bryan-like oratory.

Thurmond obviously did not appreciate the surprise tactics of the compromisers. "This legislation was not written in the Government Operations Committee and has not had the benefit of hearings," he said. "Once again we are witnessing an effort to push through the Senate highly significant legislation without the benefit of the views of the executive departments involved or the president of the United States . . . if other senators were brought into the legislative process in the calm of a committee hearing and markup, we could come up with better legislation."

He had a point, though this was hardly the first time such "surprises" had occurred on the floor; the Southern senators themselves were notorious for their private caucusing to plot secret legislative tactics, especially on civil rights in the 1950s and 1960s. But the best hope of the opponents was to slow the process down, if not by a filibuster, then at least by the stall of recommitting S. Res. 400 to the Gov Ops Committee for hearings on the compromise. "Otherwise," drawled Thurmond, "we will be asked to approve a very important bill which most of us had not even seen before last Thursday."

Turning to the actual text of the compromise, Thurmond made several criticisms which would be repeated often during the debate: "The Soviets must be laughing at us and the rest of the world looking on with shocked amazement. . . . It will lead to our nation becoming No. 2. . . . The size of our intelligence budget will become public knowledge. . . . The real need is to concentrate oversight in a smaller portion of the membership, such as a subcommittee." Then the central point: "In conclusion, I would favor strengthening oversight through a permanent subcommittee with high [*sic*] qualified staffs in the four defense committees."

Taft was worried that the new intelligence committee would fail to refer legislation to the relevant standing committees (Armed Services, in his case), even though S. Res. 400 was now based (as a result of the compromise) on the principle of sequential referral. To guarantee referral, Taft's second amendment asked for mandatory language that would force the committee to send its information and legislative drafts to the other committees concerned with intelligence issues. Following a half-hour of sparring with Ribicoff, the Democratic floor manager finally relented to a slight change in the language of Section 8 to emphasize that the other committees would indeed receive, as Ribicoff put it in debate, "any matter of importance" involving their interests. Then the amendment was accepted.

The fourth day of debate (18 May) began, as scheduled, with yet another Taft amendment.[2] Now he was distressed about the proposed designation of the Intelligence Committee as a "B" committee, secondary in importance to the major standing committees. This designation did mean that every member would, no doubt, place an emphasis on the work of his or her major committee assignment (where membership did not rotate and there was a chance to become chairman one day by climbing the seniority ladder) over the work of the Intelligence Committee, where service was limited to eight years. This "inferior" status (if one chose to view it that way) was an inevitable part of the trade-off in adopting the rotational concept. To encourage members chosen for the new committee to take the assignment seriously and devote proper time to it, Taft's amendment required them to give up any other "B" committee they served on—a proposal unlikely to be popular, since some of these committees (like the Committee on Aging) were useful links to constituents back home, even if they were less important career posts than Armed Services, Appropriations, and the like. Few members would be willing to give them up, especially in exchange for a committee assignment they would have to relinquish in eight years. That is why the compromise drafters had looked upon the new intelligence committee as strictly an add-on assignment.

Taft, however, was insistent. He wanted at least to defer for three years the decision of how an intelligence committee assignment would affect other committee assignments, until the newly created ad hoc Select Committee on Committees had an opportunity to report its proposals for reform of the existing committee structure.

Ribicoff was openly annoyed; enough was enough. "I do not feel I could depart in this instance and change the basic compromise," he said firmly. Percy, too, drew the line. He wanted the senators who were asked to sit on the new intelligence committee to use "their conscience and their own judgment as to whether they can handle the load." Dissatisfied with this advice, Taft requested a formal vote. He received more support than I expected (thirty-nine yeas), but fifty senators opposed the amendment and it was rejected.

One of Tower's aides was sitting next to me; I asked him when Tower and Stennis were going to put *the* amendment before the Senate: the one to remove defense intelligence from the jurisdiction of the proposed oversight committee. "Tomorrow," he whispered back. So the climax to this debate would come, appropriately enough, on the last scheduled day.

Major Assault

The final day of the debate (19 May) was a moment the Church committee had been working toward for fifteen months.[3] Tower introduced the key amendments, sponsored by Stennis, Thurmond, Goldwater, and Tower himself. The language was straightforward: simply strike from S. Res. 400 all references to "the Defense Intelligence Agency, the National Security Agency, and other agencies and subdivisions of the Department of Defense."[4]

Previously during the debate, Mondale had drawn "lessons" from the Church Committee investigation: "If there is one lesson that our Committee felt above all must be learned from our study of the abuses which have been reported, it has been the crucial necessity of establishing a system of congressional oversight."[5] "If there is one thing we have learned from this long study, it is that we must be very concerned about how human nature works when we clothe people with secret power, particularly with great secret power. If we are not careful, it will almost inevitably lead to abuse."[6]

On 19 May, Tower presented a rather different conclusion:

As a result of the investigation conducted by the Senate Select Committee on Intelligence Activities, there is one inescapable lesson that we in the Senate should have learned about the intelligence community—that is, that the entire community is a complex, fragile, and essential asset to the security of the United States.

While the committee's investigation revealed many abuses that occurred over the years, it also showed that such abuses were the exception rather than the rule in our intelligence agencies, and that more often than not the abuses that did occur were initiated by politicians who had authority over the agencies rather than by the agencies themselves. While the results of the Select Committee's investigation makes it clear that changes should be made in the manner in which Congress monitors the activities of the intelligence agencies, I feel that creation of a Select Committee on Intelligence with legislative and authorization authority is the wrong way to do this.

The separation of defense intelligence from the Armed Services Committee would entail, said Tower, "grave risk."

The next opponent was Milton R. Young (R-ND), a powerful but obscure member of what many considered the most important committee in the Senate: Appropriations. The most senior Republican on this money committee, Young also ran its Subcommittee on Intelligence Operations (along with the full committee chairman, John McClellan, D-AR); over the years this panel had exercised funding authority for the CIA, NSA, DIA, and the rest. "My major reason for opposing this bill," said Young, "is the excessive number of members of the committee and the size of its staff." The latter was "almost unlimited," he complained; on his own subcommittee, only five senators and two staffers had access to sensitive information.

As for the congressional investigations, "far too much information has been publicized," he asserted—and then walked straight into a hornet's nest: "These disclosures have very adversely affected the operation of our intelligence system. They have seriously damaged our intelligence agencies in foreign countries. The best example is the disclosure that Richard Welch was our top CIA agent in Greece. Shortly after he was identified as a CIA agent, he was murdered."

The two members of the Church committee present, Mondale and Huddleston, stood up from their chairs. Weicker's antennae flared, and like a provoked wasp, he zoomed in on Young. Just who had revealed Welch's name, Weicker demanded; "I ask the question since this has become a focal point as to whether or not Congress can be trusted with this type of oversight function."

"I think it was directly associated with the investigation at that time," said Young, startled by the reaction he had incited.

"No, I am afraid I am not going to let that point go unanswered, because it was used, as I say, as a focal point to turn around this whole investigation," retorted Weicker. "It was not as the result of any information coming from the Congress of the United States. It was divulged by a foreign periodical. That is the very simple fact of the matter."

"That he was a member of the CIA was published at the time of the CIA hearing," said Young, his face reddening, "and I do not think the Senator would deny that through the investigations, most people know how these intelligence agencies operate now."

Mondale could no longer restrain himself:

Mondale. We never had Mr. Welch's name because we never wanted it. We never asked for any names of any foreign operatives, because it was not necessary to our investigation and we did not want it. In fact, the record discloses, as we looked into it later, that the CIA had urged Welch not to move into that house, because it had been known in the community that the house had been the residence of the previous head of the CIA in Greece. So when we look into the record, our committee and the House Committee had absolutely nothing to do with the tragedy concerning Mr. Welch.

Young. Did not the members of that committee and more than seventy staff members have access to all of this kind of information?

Mondale. No, because we were very careful never to ask that kind of information, because we had anticipated that kind of problem. . . . What we wanted to know were issues that went to the question of accountability and control.

Huddleston wanted in on this too: "This matter has been brought up several times and has been used to try to denigrate the activity of the committee and the need for the oversight committee. . . . It has never been established that the revelation of Welch's identity had anything at all to do with that unfortunate occurrence . . . which really had no relationship to what we are discussing here today." (Indeed, according to CIA director Bush in testimony before the Church committee a few weeks earlier,[7] the Agency had no evidence that the congressional inquiries had any adverse effect on Welch's cover or any relationship to his murder.)

Like a man with one rake and three rattlesnakes (as Lyndon Johnson might have described it), Young was ready to clear out. "I am pleased to know that the committee feels there was no such leak," he said, "but the point I am trying to make is that there is no possible way to have a large Intelligence Committee with a staff of sixty or seventy and not have very damaging leaks such as this."

Stennis stepped in to calm raw nerves. "I want to make clear," he said, "that I have nothing except compliments for the Select Committee, the members of the special Intelligence Committee who have been investigating these matters. I not only assume, but I believe they acted in good faith. There are no changes to be made, by inference or otherwise."

He went on, though, to speak at length against the compromise. It lacked the "essential threshold requirement," he stressed: namely, a parallel and coordinate system in the House of Representatives. "When we would go to the conference [committee] on the proposed authorization bill," said Stennis, "the other side is not bound by it anyway." Moreover, to put defense intelligence budget requests through the normal two-step authorization then appropriations process was foolhardy: "Information will get out. I do not accuse anyone of intentionally leaking or telling anything, but it will get out." Stennis urged his colleagues to "just say as a fact of life that [defense intelligence] cannot go through the ordinary process." Waxing more persuasive each moment, this Senate fixture pulled out all the stops: "I beg, beg even, because it is so important, that senators reconsider the matter. Let us put in this amendment so as to have a special category."

In his earlier remarks, Stennis had already depreciated the notion that defense intelligence agencies had violated their trust: "Not much . . . was attributed to the services . . . a very small percentage of wrongdoing . . . no dirty tricks . . . they just were not in on those matters, except in a slight degree, and that was under some special orders more or less from the presidents of the United States during unrest and turmoil and high uncertainty."

Ribicoff responded immediately to Stennis's "not much" supposition. His list of military intelligence misdeeds was extensive: the NSA Shamrock program; 100,000 Americans spied upon by the army in the 1960s; army dossiers on legislators; army spying on priests, youths, and mothers; army mail-opening programs; military involvement in the Huston Plan.

Ribicoff then shifted the argument to demonstrate that members of the Armed Services Committee had nothing to fear from the new committee: two of them would be assigned to it; the rules would require sequential referral; and no one wanted to pull the rug out from under Stennis's committee. "What puzzles the Senator from Connecticut," said Ribicoff of himself, "is the hesitancy by the Armed Services Committee to really trust the remainder of the Senate in this way."

Another member of Armed Services seemed as hard to convince as its chairman: Sam Nunn (D-GA). He grilled Ribicoff further on everything from public disclosure procedures to sequential referral. The Democratic floor manager responded patiently but finally suggested that "a lot of gray areas" remained in the legislation. Senators would have to exercise "comity" and "common sense"; it was "impossible to answer all the questions." All the relevant committees would have to work out appropriate procedures over time, through some trial and error. Ribicoff stressed again his belief that the fears of the Armed Services Committee were ungrounded; "I do not think we are going to be that jealous or that shortsighted in this body." Nunn smiled skeptically and sat down.

Ready as ever for attack, Weicker said the Stennis–Tower amendment was "absolutely unconstitutional" in its intent to exclude military intelligence from the normal authorization process. Tower attempted to deflect this argument with the shield of public opinion: "There is no public outcry for this oversight committee . . . outside of a fifty-mile radius of Washington, DC," he said—a response hardly germane to Weicker's point. Some senators, Tower continued, seemed to have the impression that "the American people are out there shivering in fear of the vast abuses of the intelligence-gathering community of the United States," and such a belief was "bunk."

Weicker tried to bring the argument back to the constitutional issue, but he too got lost along the way. The necessity for proper authorization was his key point initially, but now he spoke of the need to disclose the aggregate intelligence budget figure. Nunn reminded him that his point had "no bearing" on the virtues or flaws of the Stennis–Tower amendment, but Weicker remained obstinate: the Armed Services Committee, under the Stennis–Tower amendment, could so carefully bury the defense intelligence budget that the rest of the Senate might never see it whole.

In a bad turn of events for the compromisers, Cannon himself became so annoyed with Weicker that he spoke against him. "Either House can require secrecy as to this part of the budget or other items that may require secrecy," he said, resting his case on Article 1, Section 5, Clause 3 of the Constitution.[8] So much for the unity of the compromisers.

Percy stepped forward with soothing balm. The new committee would never tolerate unauthorized disclosures of the budget or anything else, he emphasized blandly. He did, however, take exception to Tower's theory of public opinion on intelligence, noting that the people of Illinois (his state) and of Indiana (where he had traveled recently) were deeply concerned about intelligence abuses. In fact, he declared, "the entire country is looking to Congress now to find a way to have effective oversight."

During his commanding efforts to put the compromisers on the offensive again, Percy made only one slip. Stennis caught it like a twenty-year-old shortstop. The faulty reference was to "concurrent jurisdiction," which, Percy wrongly suggested, applied in this instance to the Armed Services Committee. Did it, indeed, inquired Stennis; if so, this meant that his committee would be given intelligence, new legislative proposals, and the like simultaneously with the new committee. Percy had bailed out Weiker; now Ribicoff had to bail out Percy: the jurisdiction was sequential, not concurrent, corrected Ribicoff. Stennis saw a rent in the opposition and gave it a few more tugs until finally Senator Pastore intervened with the lament that the Senate had "drifted into the sensitive question of committee jurisdiction." He, Ribicoff, and Percy together brought the debate back quickly to acceptable generalities.

Signs were appearing everywhere that both sides had said just about all they could think of to say on the topic of the Stennis–Tower amendment. Weicker had reached the point where he wanted Stennis to state what the amendment would do, instead of what it would not do.

"I covered that when someone had distracted the attention of the senator in some way," said Stennis, even his courtly manners wearing a little thin.

Nunn, however, was not quite ready to go home. "I am going to submit an amendment," he told the floor. He was determined to define more precisely what would happen if the president objected to public disclosure of information and the committee voted for disclosure. Hello Rule 36! It refused to stay down, no matter how many times it was hit on the head. "The Committee shall not publicly disclose such information without leave of the US Senate," read the text of the Nunn amendment. Weary, Ribicoff accepted the proposal—even though it wiped out his own pending recommendation that the motion of at least two senators on the committee should be required to send a dispute to the floor. Nunn's language had the effect of allowing the president to decide when an issue would be taken out of committee and transferred to the floor. Ribicoff's formula was easy enough for a president; Nunn made it a cakewalk. But the amendment was included in the compromise. Baker's long crusade against the parliamentarian's interpretation of Rule 36 had ended in his favor, not with a bang but a whimper.

The air was growing heavy with the same arguments. I hoped Church or Mondale (both of whom had just entered the chamber) could breathe freshness back into the debate.

Church's misuse of the term "concurrent" (when he meant "sequential") jurisdiction in his opening sentences was not encouraging, but he improved as he went along, and certainly his style of oratory commanded more attention than that of earlier speakers. "Instead of a club, the adoption of this [Stennis–Tower] amendment would leave the oversight committee with nothing more than a small stick, and would gut the committee," Church said. "If the Stennis amendment is approved, we are right back to where we started from . . . that seamless web has been broken, and we are back to piecemeal jurisdiction distributed among several committees of Congress, no one of which can do the job."

As the second half of this one–two punch, Mondale warned that with the Stennis–Tower amendment "we will be creating a situation where, if they wanted to repeat what has happened in the past, they would simply shift these activities over into the defense intelligence agencies because these agencies can do and have done, as this record shows, precisely the things that we seek to prevent."

The floor had filled again with a score of senators as word spread that Church and Mondale were now the point men. The crowd and the presence of his old Church committee opponents brought out the fighting spirit in Tower. No one was against oversight, he said emphatically; the question was which could do the better job: a new committee, or, as he preferred, "the other committees having jurisdiction over various elements of the intelligence-gathering communities." He vigorously defended the earlier record of oversight on the Armed Services Committee: "If there has been any dereliction, then the entire US Senate and the House of Representatives must bear the responsibility because this was the accepted way of doing business for so many years. Then when abuses were brought to our attention, we reacted, and quite properly, in mandating a special investigation."

The new committee was a bad idea for several reasons, said Tower, all of which had been expressed on the floor already: it would proliferate sensitive information, undermine foreign confidence in the United States, and create problems for the intelligence agencies. As for the Church committee, Tower could not resist concluding that it "chose to disclose more than it should have."

Second in the one–two counterpunch, Stennis said he hoped "this little amendment—and it is small—for the protection of this part of the intelligence program will be passed." That more than 80 percent of the intelligence budget could be construed as "small" was hard to swallow.

A restlessness swept across the floor. The time had come to settle this argument one way or the other. The roll was called on the Stennis–Tower amendment: thirty-one yeas, sixty-three nays.

The main assault on the Cannon compromise had been thwarted—despite the defection of Howard Cannon himself! The Rules Committee chairman had decided that the compromise ought to be broad enough to accommodate the desires of Armed Services Committee members to keep all military intelligence within their jurisdiction—a broad interpretation indeed, shared by no one else who had participated in the drafting of the compromise a week before. He had found it "virtually impossible to separate military intelligence from the total military picture," Cannon observed subsequently.[9]

I suspected that Cannon had also done some hard thinking about his return, after this was all over, to his chair on the Armed Services Committee—with Stennis sitting on his left, Nunn on his right, and Thurmond, Tower, Goldwater, and Taft across the table. These were men he would have to work with day in and day out. More than anyone else in the Senate, Stennis was someone who could help or hinder Cannon's legislative objectives on the Armed Services Committee, and military projects were central to the well-being of the economy of Nevada, Cannon's home state. Here was another illustration of an ancient Washington adage: where one stands depends upon where one sits.

The rest of the Stennis–Towerites were chiefly Southern conservatives, closing ranks behind Stennis and the military, with a few conservatives from other parts of the country and a single moderate senator, Hugh Scott (the minority leader, who sat with Cannon on the Rules Committee).

The Stennis–Tower failure apparently dissuaded Eastland and Hruska from introducing an amendment to separate FBI intelligence from the compromise, but we were still without a new intelligence committee. Votes remained on the compromise itself and, finally, on S. Res. 400 (as amended by the compromise, if passed). These votes were expected to be perfunctory, though, now that the Stennis–Tower attack had been repelled.

Assistant Majority Leader Byrd took the floor. He acknowledged the difficulty of changing jurisdictions in the Senate, but change was necessary. As he put it, with customary tact, "it is not that our present committee structure did not want, or try, to prevent abuses in the intelligence community—the fact is that the intelligence activities of our government have grown so large and so complex that the substantive committees, with all of their other heavy responsibilities, could not hope to give the necessary time and develop the specialized expertise needed to constantly monitor and effectively control the intelligence community."

When a vote was called on the Cannon Compromise, only seven nays came forth, in contrast to an overwhelming eighty-seven yeas. The seven holdouts—all men whose voting records were among the most conservative in the Senate—were Allen, Carl T. Curtis (R-NE), Paul Fannin (R-AZ), Hruska, McClure, Taft, and Thurmond.

Now, the vote on Senate Resolution 400, as amended, was in order. Seventy-two voices rang out "yea." Their IOUs paid back to Cannon on the previous vote, most of the Stennis–Towerites now rejoined the seven holdouts to register their disapproval of the new committee—twenty-two nays in all against the new Senate Select Committee on Intelligence. Among these men—staunch conservatives one and all—stood Tower and Goldwater.

All that remained was celebration for the victors—and a word of caution from one of the most thoughtful members of the Senate, Gaylord Nelson (D-WI). Amid an air of jubilation on the floor among the reformers, and with handshaking and backslapping aplenty in the cloakroom, the leading proponents of S. Res. 400 acknowledged the "wise counsel" of several senators who made the compromise possible—especially Robert Byrd. The tributes went around the room as faces beamed and spirits lifted. But Nelson's sobering thoughts were the last words to be spoken on the Senate floor in this important debate.

Nelson reminded his colleagues that they had created an instrument far from perfect. He was troubled by the disclosure procedure (as Abourezk had been): if the president objected to disclosure, the dispute now would have to go to the floor even if the Intelligence Committee voted unanimously in favor of release. This language (the Nunn amendment) "undercut" the new committee, Nelson observed, and set the stage in the Senate for a repeat of the controversy in the House over the Pike report. Once again a congressional committee might be overridden by a legislature responding more to presidential pressure than to whether public information would be genuinely injurious to the nation's security. "We undermine our claim to be a coequal branch of the government," said Nelson in his calm, deliberate manner.

The issue that had haunted the Church committee throughout the investigation—Rule 36 and who could disclose what—was, I suppose, an appropriate note on which to conclude the debate; after all, the Congress never could seem to decide whether or not the major problem before it was how to curb intelligence abuses or how to maintain secrecy. Curbing abuses was the top priority, maintained Nelson emphatically, but a majority in the House (and no doubt many in the Senate) had obviously become more obsessed with secrecy.

Despite shortcomings in the newly established Intelligence Committee, it was nonetheless there; the central recommendation of the Church committee had been adopted. The new fifteen-member committee had exclusive jurisdiction over the CIA; it had legislative and budgetary control over all the intelligence agencies (sharing jurisdiction sequentially with the Armed Services and Judiciary Committees for military and FBI intelligence); and it had the power of the subpoena to gather information from the agencies.

As Nelson wisely noted in his closing remarks, the Senate was engaged in at least a three-stage process: the exposure of abuses, the creation of a strong oversight committee, and—the path ahead—the consideration and enactment of new legislative charters for the intelligence agencies, to replace old laws and executive orders. "There is no substitute for carefully drawn legislative guidelines and statutory prohibitions in certain practices," he stressed. "The tasks remaining for the new committee, then, and the Congress as a whole, are formidable."

Nelson said he hoped the new committee would discharge its responsibilities as well as the Church panel had done; in words that we ourselves might well have chosen for an epitaph, he concluded: "The committee deliberations were conducted in a bipartisan, thorough, deliberate manner in which the foremost commitment was to obtaining the truth. Despite the delicate nature of the task and the constant possibility of clashes with the executive over sensitive materials, the committee avoided confrontation, on the one hand, and 'leaks,' on the other, while managing to present a comprehensive report, documenting a stunning array of abuses."

With the passage of S. Res. 400 and the establishment of the Select Committee on Intelligence, the Senate had ushered in a new and promising era of intelligence oversight.

Shattered Dreams

After voting for S. Res. 400, Church departed quickly for Oregon, where, journalist David S. Broder recalls, he exhibited the "rhetorical, arm-waving" style of speech that had made him a "Claghorn performer who embarrassed himself as the Democratic Convention keynoter 16 years ago." Broder had expected this; what surprised him was "the cool, controlled, and highly effective Church who could be seen both on live interviews and in filmed ads on Oregon television last week. That Church won votes."[10]

With only a week left before primary day, Church shuttled around Oregon in a small propeller-driven airplane, visiting community after community and holding question-and-answer sessions with voters, all to advance his campaign of "substance over style." The results of this effort were more victories against Carter in Oregon and in Idaho. This time the margin of victory was considerable: an expected landslide in Idaho (home turf), but also a respectable 8 percent in Oregon.

In retrospect, the belief that Church might win the nomination may look foolish, but at the time—late May—even the best political observers had not counted Church out. "If Carter is stopped," wrote David Broder, "Church is a more 'brokerable' candidate than the other survivors of the primary trial." At worst, Broder concluded, Church's wins in Nebraska and Oregon established him as a "credible contender for future years and a plausible choice for Vice President in 1976."[11]

Church knew he would come in behind Jerry Brown in California, Brown's own state. A strong second there, however, coupled with wins elsewhere might be enough to bring the Carter bandwagon to a standstill. But how could anyone short of Clark Kent campaign effectively in California, Ohio, and New Jersey—all of which held their primaries on the same day (8 June)?

This question led to a major strategy session on 28 May at Church's home. The meeting had surrealistic overtones: a half-dozen staffers sitting around Church's living room trying to decide what to do about three major primaries—only eleven days before the balloting! Carter had been working Ohio for six months at least. Moreover, we had only about $100,000 left for all three states—perhaps one-fifth of what Carter reportedly had budgeted.

The planning session was a fiasco. Tempers flared throughout as various factions sought commitments from Church to concentrate on "their" state among the Big Three. The outcome was an attempt to please the pro-Ohio and pro-California factions; Church would try to campaign in both states and, in his spare time, for 1 June primaries in Rhode Island and Montana too! New Jersey was out, since Carter seemed to have that state well organized already. The campaign staff left Church's home, each dissatisfied to one degree or another, while the candidate—frustrated, grumpy, pulled by contending forces, knowing full well he needed eleven months to prepare for this ordeal rather than eleven days—departed with his wife, a staff aide, and the Secret Service to board a plane bound for Rhode Island.

With so little time left, why was Church, asked a puzzled-looking correspondent at a press conference in Boston, "making such a major effort in Rhode Island when you've got the big states of Ohio and California ahead of you?"

"I never had made a distinction between big states and small," Church replied. "I was especially grateful for the support that I received from half the Rhode Island delegation, which endorsed my candidacy from the first day back at the time when nobody thought I had a chance to win anything anywhere. . . . I want to get up there and campaign hard, and it would mean a great deal to me to win in Rhode Island."[12]

On 1 June, Church came in behind both an uncommitted slate of delegates in Rhode Island and Carter—though he did win in Montana. Then everything caved in—including, literally, a major dam in Idaho, causing widespread flooding, loss of life, and considerable damage to property. Church had to halt his campaigning in Ohio to return home.

Moreover, he had developed an influenza sufficiently acute to make public speaking impossible; his throat was scarlet red and sore, his ears were infected, and he ran a high fever. Key events had to be canceled so he could gain badly needed bed rest. Finally, California and Ohio, the Church campaigners learned, could never be conquered in a few days, even under the best of circumstances. Not even the CIA could have choreographed a covert action against Church that would have been this successful. He finished a distant third to Brown and Carter in California, and to Carter and Morris Udall in Ohio. Carter's sweep of Ohio and New Jersey gave him all the delegates he needed for the nomination; Church's grand total of delegates came to seventy-nine. On the following Monday, he endorsed Carter's candidacy.

One dream, however, soon replaced another. Why not Frank Church as Carter's running mate? Broder had already raised the possibility, and Mary McGrory found the two "made for each other": "Carter the southerner and Church the westerner; Carter the preacher, Church the teacher; Carter, anti-Washington and Church pro; Carter, the country boy in foreign policy and Church the spouting expert; Carter fuzzy and Church clear."[13] Church had thought about the possibility even before the California and Ohio contests. He told reporters on the campaign trail that he thought the vice presidential candidate should be someone who had been through the primaries—narrowing the field to himself and a few others. Would he like to be the choice? "It's like asking a man what he will do if he's struck by lightning," he coyly responded to a reporter. "I haven't been struck."[14]

Soon after the primaries were over, Carter announced that he would ch
his running mate from a list of five prominent people, all United States sena.....
Edmund Muskie (Maine), Adlai Stevenson (Illinois), John Glenn, Mondale—
and Church.

According to press reports, Carter would personally interview each of the
five and make a decision before the Democratic National Convention. In the
meantime, some Carter campaign people (led by Atlanta attorney and Carter
confidant Charles Kirbo) would poke around the Hill to find out what they could
about the five. As I was subsequently told by several congressional staffers and
Carter campaign aides, this was Church's demise. In making the rounds, these
"talent scouts" heard the same thing from many senators: Church is a loner, hard
to work with, too independent, not much of a club man on the Hill, unlikely to
be an asset to Carter in his relations with Congress. In contrast, the researchers
were told, Mondale was everything a president could want: a team player, easy-
going, less arrogant, less ambitious, more popular, and the like. Kirbo and the
others apparently came away from the Hill with a negative view of Church, a
positive view of Mondale, and a lukewarm view of the others.

Until the last day of the Democratic Convention, the final selection was the
best-kept secret of the summer. Hopes within the Church camp were raised by
a *Washington Post* poll in early July: Church was first choice among convention
delegates, with Stevenson and Mondale tied for second.[15] Maybe at last Church
would steal a scene from Mondale.

The primaries of 8 June had shattered the first campaign dream; an early
morning telephone call shattered the second. At seven-thirty on 15 July, the last
day of the convention, Jimmy Carter called Church in his hotel suite to inform
him of his choice for a running mate: the lightning had struck Walter Mondale.

22

Aftermath

The intelligence investigation of 1975 must surely rank as one of the most sig-nificant inquiries conducted by the United States Senate. It represented the first serious examination of the dark side of government since the establishment of the modern intelligence bureaucracy in 1947; it unearthed more information (much of it highly classified) from the executive branch than any previous con-gressional inquiry had done; it set in motion forces that would revolutionize the approach to intelligence policy on Capitol Hill and consequently within the in-telligence community.

As a result of the investigation, the public gained an awareness of an import-ant part of government too long hidden from its view—and, unchecked, too great a threat to its freedom. The intelligence community presumably gained a new awareness as well about what was permissible policy, in contrast to the vague statutes and guidelines that had steered it in the past. Further, the Con-gress seemed to have learned afresh the importance of "auxiliary precautions"[1] for the protection of our liberties; with the creation of a permanent Senate In-telligence Committee, a promising framework was put in place for the closer supervision of the intelligence agencies.

The centerpiece in this framework was Section 11 of Senate Resolution 400, the most finely negotiated and delicately balanced portion of the resolution. Its provisions, presented below, opened the door to genuine oversight by man-dating a freer flow of information from the intelligence agencies to their legis-lative overseers (appendix 3). Drafted by a bipartisan coalition of Republican and Democratic staffers on the Church committee in close consultation with the Ford administration, and accepted by Democrats as well as most Republicans on the Church committee, the Ribicoff committee, and among the Byrd–Cannon–Mansfield "compromisers," this vital language was considered "out of bounds" for further tampering during the May 1976 floor debate and was never attacked by the opponents of reform. In an annual report, the new Senate Intelligence Committee would refer to this section as "the heart of the Committee's present ability to carry out its oversight responsibilities."[2]

Though S. Res. 400 was a simple resolution, rather than a law binding on the executive branch, its strong wording was nonetheless taken seriously by intel-ligence bureaucrats; indeed, as part of the Miller working group on oversight, they had helped fashion the language. The resolution had done nothing less than usher in a significant new era of executive–legislative relations for intelligence policy.

The first (and longest) era of intelligence oversight had lasted from 1947 until December 1974 and may be called the Era of Trust. As summarized in chapter 1, the congressional attitude then was largely one of faith that officials within the intelligence service would carry out their duties without violations of law or propriety (at least at home). While most did, a few did not, and the *New York Times* exposés led to the Era of Skepticism (1974–1976). The new reformist mood in Congress produced the first statute to place controls over the CIA since its establishment: the Hughes–Ryan Amendment (appendix 3), signed into law by President Ford on 30 December 1974.[3] This significant legislation required the president to approve and report to Congress all "important" covert actions. During this second phase also came the Year of Intelligence (actually lasting sixteen months), with the Church, Pike, and Rockefeller investigations and long lists of proposed intelligence reforms. It was a time for the Socratics; members of Congress demanded explanations, not simply vague reassurances. The bold language of S. Res. 400, notably Section 11, along with the creation of the permanent Senate Intelligence Committee, opened up the present Era of Uneasy Partnership between the executive and legislative branches.

For the House of Representatives, this experiment in institutional partnership was delayed for over a year. Once burned (by the Pike report leak), twice shy, the House moved cautiously, waiting until 14 July 1977 to establish its own permanent intelligence committee. Even then, the House leadership chose to omit from its oversight guidelines (Rule 48 created by Resolution 658) the most potent language of S. Res. 400—that is, Section 11 (otherwise the two resolutions were almost identical). This appeared to be the price the leadership had to pay to achieve at least some form of genuine oversight from a wary membership, whose message was clear: no more fiascos. The new committee would have to stay in line; the honor of the House was at stake.

In its early days, then, the House committee set out to prove it was not Son of Pike: no leaks; no headline grabbing; no unnecessary battles with the executive branch. From the start, the committee's first chairman, Edward P. Boland (D-MA), held to one dictum: oversight, yes, but in moderation and—as much as possible—out of the public limelight. The highest priority was for the committee to establish its credibility. As Boland put it before the House at the time of his appointment as chairman, "After this body's recent experience with previous select committees on intelligence, we must first prove to the Senate, to the president, and to ourselves that we can handle the job."[4]

In contrast, during this nascent phase, the Senate Intelligence Committee was invariably more aggressive. With a staff twice the size of that of its House counterpart and numbering among its membership Senators Huddleston, Gary Hart, and Mathias—seasoned investigators from the Church committee (as were most of the senior staffers, led by Miller)—the Senate committee was prepared to probe any allegations of wrongdoing.

As the House Intelligence Committee worked out its procedures and gained self-confidence, however, it proved to be equally aggressive. Prodded by staff hired from the Church committee, Congressman Boland wrote to the CIA director in 1977 requesting the same responsiveness for his panel as S. Res. 400 required for the Senate committee.[5] Formal requests for cooperation were augmented in both committees by innumerable informal meetings of CIA officials, legislators, and staff. As rapport developed and negotiations proceeded, the CIA liaison office dealing with Congress soon treated both panels as equals, despite the stronger founding document enjoyed by the Senate committee.

The child of the Church committee in union with the intelligence bureaucracy, S. Res. 400 thus became the standard on Capitol Hill for the conduct of intelligence oversight. Along with Ford's executive order, this document and its weaker House counterpart (H. Res. 658, substantially buttressed by the Boland letter of 1977) formally guided executive–legislative relations for intelligence policy. Informally, all attempts at shaping policy were hammered out and tempered along the way as the new partnership matured during these formative years. Selected legislators and staff pressed intelligence officials for information they deemed necessary for meaningful oversight, and these officials responded or resisted (often abetted by allies within the committees) as their leaders saw fit.[6] Clearly, the new committees took their work seriously. They produced annual intelligence authorizations, made extensive field visitations, held regular hearings (and occasional investigations), and put through a new law on wiretapping.[7] As the legislators made plain, they were prepared for—even insistent upon—a larger role for Congress in the exercise of intelligence policy.

The ultimate goal of reformers in the first few years remained the charge passed on to them by the Church committee: a comprehensive legislative charter for the intelligence agencies to replace the brief and often ambiguous clauses on intelligence in the 1947 and 1949 national security statutes. The Senate committee took the lead in 1976. Despite the continuing climate of wariness on the Hill, senators and their aides on the new oversight committee pursued lengthy private negotiations with executive branch officials (begun during the final months of the Church inquiry) toward this objective. The task was abetted by a change in government in January of 1977, as the Ford administration—resistant to further intelligence reform—gave way to the more sympathetic Carter administration.

Jimmy Carter had made intelligence reform a conspicuous part of his presidential campaign platform. Moreover, like dandelion seeds scattered in a meadow, legislative reformers associated with the Church committee had spread throughout the new administration: most conspicuously Senator Mondale as vice president, but also key staffers in the NSC, the attorney general's office, and the Department of Defense intelligence administration. In 1978, this network of reformers successfully urged upon the president an executive order (EO 12036, issued on January 24) that went far beyond its modest forebear signed by President Ford.[8]

The new executive order projected a readiness to consider tough legislative proposals on intelligence oversight. President Carter called it "a basis for Congressional action on a charter to be written for the Intelligence Community,"[9] and his intelligence director, Admiral Stansfield Turner (1977–1981), saw it as a penultimate move toward the legislative codification of strengthened oversight. "The last step in the whole process," said Turner in February 1978, "will be the development of legislative charters by the committees of the Congress."[10]

The order itself tightened internal guidelines on intelligence activities that could infringe upon the rights and privacy of American citizens here and abroad; for example, it required warrants from the attorney general for various types of surveillance operations once conducted by the CIA abroad under its own authority. The order required the attorney general further to assure that any "intelligence activity within the United States or directed against any United States person is conducted by the least intrusive means possible" (Section 2-201[a]). Civil libertarians still found the new order too permissive; former intelligence officials, though, called it "crippling."[11] Whether too limited or too strong, EO 12036 signaled a willingness on the part of the White House and the intelligence bureaucrats to try an experiment in closer controls over intelligence policy. Legislative reformers decided the time was ripe to advance the charter that the Senate Intelligence Committee had been busily crafting.

A charter, however, represented to the intelligence establishment the threat of more enduring and substantial changes in its accustomed practices. As law, it would be much more difficult to alter (or ignore) than an executive order (which could be modified by the stroke of a pen—perhaps even in a secret addendum). Moreover, the proposed "omnibus" charter (S. 2525, introduced on 9 February 1978) was truly far-reaching, dwarfing EO 12036 in size and intent; by 1978 it had ballooned into more than two hundred pages of restraints. Among the many detailed provisions were, for example, guidelines prohibiting any covert action that entailed the following:

The support of international terrorist activities.
The mass destruction of property.
The creation of food or water shortages or floods.
The creation of epidemics of diseases.

The use of chemical, biological, or other weapons in violation of treaties or other international agreements to which the United States is a party.

The violent overthrow of the democratic government of any country.

The torture of individuals.

The support of any action, which violates human rights conducted by the police, foreign intelligence, or international security forces of any foreign country.[12]

For the executive branch (and even for most members of Congress), such detailed provisions seemed to move much too far into the realm of congressional "micromanagement."[13] The accommodation worked out between the branches through the framework of S. Res. 400, the new oversight committees, and EO 12036 represented too slender a reed to support this imposing edifice. The quest for the Great Charter failed.[14]

Two more years of negotiations, however, produced agreement on a small but consequential package of legislative reforms. Wrapped in ambiguous phraseology and comprising only three pages, the Accountability for Intelligence Activities Act (known less formally as the 1980 Intelligence Oversight Act)[15] represented nonetheless a long step, in law, toward the concept of a growing (if still uneasy) partnership between Congress and the executive in the making of intelligence policy (appendix 3). This two-branch agreement came only through long and arduous dialogue. As Bill Miller has recalled, the law was "the result of discussions, negotiations, give and take with two Administrations including the direct involvement of two Presidents, two Vice Presidents, four Directors of Central Intelligence, three Attorneys General, and a partridge in a pear tree."[16]

An executive order (EO 12333) signed by President Ronald Reagan on 4 December 1981, subsequently weakened Carter's EO 12036 by returning considerable discretion in surveillance operations to the CIA, authorizing the Agency to conduct covert operations domestically, and further weakening the already enfeebled Intelligence Oversight Board (IOB).[17] The 1980 Oversight Act, nevertheless, remained standing as a solid reminder of congressional determination to institute closer supervision over the intelligence agencies. Under that act, the executive branch had to contend with statutory reporting requirements on intelligence far more comprehensive than those of the Hughes–Ryan Amendment.

Objectives of Intelligence Reform

What have been the objectives of intelligence reformers over the years, and what effect did the Year of Intelligence have on these objectives? The most extreme proposal, the 1974 Abourezk amendment (preceding the investigations—see chapter 1), sought nothing less than the elimination of an entire policy option: covert action. Too radical, this proposal garnered limited support despite the unusual interest in intelligence reform at the time. In every other instance, however, the objective of reformers has been to gain greater access to information within the executive branch regarding the conduct of intelligence policy. Put simply, an increasing number of legislators have wanted to know what was going on. To know would place them in a position to advise—and perhaps to help avoid disasters like the Bay of Pigs and abuses like those uncovered by the *New York Times*.

The pursuit of enhanced congressional monitoring of intelligence policy required two ingredients for success: first and foremost, motivation of legislators to be genuine overseers sensitive to the importance of checks and balances; and second, access to information in the executive branch. As a result of the *Times* exposés and the subsequent investigations, motivation was present by 1976 and, at least among some key members of Congress, has persisted. The significance of motivation for effective oversight across the policy spectrum, and specifically for intelligence policy, has been amply documented.[18] Less well addressed has been the significance of the information side of the equation.

By definition, one monitors an agency by knowing what it is doing. The entire concept of a legislative check on the executive becomes a mockery without congressional information regarding executive programs and plans. Too much information, of course, can be as harmful as too little; it can result in system overload, with already harried representatives and their staffs going down for the third time in a sea of paper. (During the Church committee investigation, the Department of Defense sent truckloads of low-level intelligence documents to Congress; the result of this tactic was to overwhelm staff investigators, at least temporarily, with largely useless information.[19]) Nor is more staff likely to solve this problem, since the number of voting members remains fixed, and they can assimilate only so much information. Moreover, in the intelligence field, larger staffs run counter to the need for tight security. So in speaking of successful oversight, an emphasis must be placed on the quality and depth, rather than volume, of information received by legislators.

The late Harold D. Lass once well defined politics simply as "who gets what, when, [and] how."[20] Similar questions are implicit in any effort to evaluate the monitoring of public policy, and intelligence policy in particular, by legislatures: who on Capitol Hill gets what information about intelligence programs from whom in the executive, and when? The answers (coupled with an examination of member motivation) provide useful insight into the effectiveness of intelligence oversight over the years. The answers have varied markedly from each major era of intelligence oversight to the next (table 3), and these differences underscore the importance of changes wrought by the Church committee investigation, with its culmination in the passage of Senate Resolution 400.

Table 3.   Intelligence Oversight on Capitol Hill: Who Gets What Information from Whom, and When

	Era of Trust (1947–1974)	Era of Skepticism (1974–1976)	Era of Uneasy Partnership (1976–2001)
Who	Often only one legislator	Up to 63 members and staff[a]	About 37 members and staff[b]
What	Haphazard	Important covert action	All important operations; illegalities, improprieties, and (since 1980) intelligence failures
From whom	CIA (infrequently)	President/CIA[a]	All agencies
When	Discretion of CIA	In a timely fashion[a]	Prior notification

[a] For covert action operations only.
[b] Except in time of emergency, when only eight legislative leaders are notified in advance.

Who?

In the Era of Trust, Senator Richard Russell (as chairman of the Armed Services Subcommittee on CIA Oversight) was often the only legislator, if any, kept informed of intelligence matters. The controversy swirling around the CIA in late 1974, though, brought on the Era of Skepticism and encouraged the establishment of a wider circle of legislators to be informed about CIA operations—at least those dealing with covert action. The instrument used for drawing the circle wider was the Hughes–Ryan Act. Under this law, the number of people responsible for the review of CIA covert actions soared to some sixty individuals—the members and staff of eight congressional committees. Included were the House and Senate committees on appropriations, armed services, intelligence, and foreign affairs. The full intelligence committees were briefed; in the others, only subcommittees or sometimes the committee leaders and a single staffer were kept informed.[21] Some of these individuals proved to be uninterested in the careful examination of covert action operations; however, the two dozen or so who were concerned represented a marked increase over the Russell days.

From the CIA's point of view, this expanded "who" was far too great to guarantee appropriate security. The Agency undertook a lengthy lobbying campaign to revoke the Hughes–Ryan law, making appeals to the Church committee and, subsequently, during the Era of Uneasy Partnership, to the more permanent overseers on the embryonic Senate and House intelligence committees. These early appeals failed, but the CIA persevered. By 1980, it had convinced the committees to repeal this portion of Hughes–Ryan with new language in the Intelligence

Oversight Act: the congressional circle of individuals briefed on sensitive intelligence operations tightened to include only members (and a couple of staffers) of the Senate and House intelligence committees. This number totals not quite forty individuals, although again only a small number (about a dozen) keep close tabs on the details of covert action proposals. It is a circle still too wide for Agency tastes, but more manageable than eight different committees.[22] (Some of the Intelligence Committee members also serve on the other committees once briefed under Hughes–Ryan rules and, in theory at least, are now responsible for warning these committees about operations of possible concern to them.)

The 1980 act contains two ambiguities related to the "who" question that concerned legislative reformers and perhaps comforted the intelligence professionals somewhat. First, if the president declares a condition of "extraordinary circumstances affecting vital interests of the United States" (Section 501[a][l]), sensitive intelligence information may be limited to eight leaders of Congress for an unspecified but presumably brief period of time. (Under such circumstances the full Intelligence Committees are supposed to be briefed "in a timely fashion," at least on covert actions—the old Hughes–Ryan formula). This so-called Gang of Eight[23] includes the chairmen and ranking minority members of the Intelligence Committees, the speaker and minority leader of the House of Representatives, and the majority and minority leaders of the Senate.

Second, the vague preamble of Section 501(a) states that the executive branch shall keep the Congress informed only when doing so would not violate constitutional prerogatives or jeopardize the protection of "sources and methods"—an ambiguous opening potentially large enough for the entire intelligence establishment to slip through. This language could constrict the "who" circle to zero if the executive branch were to claim "sources and methods" improperly to conceal information Congress might legitimately have the right to know—despite an attempt in Section 501(e) to warn the intelligence community against such a ploy.[24]

The "who" of intelligence oversight on Capitol Hill, then, has gone from virtually one man to an arguably excessive number of participants for a brief period, to a reasonable balance between too few and too many congressional supervisors. While secret recourse to the slippery language could shift this balance toward zero, the costs of an operation that skirted the Congress only to fail and embarrass the nation would be high for the executive branch.

What?

The information provided by the intelligence community to the congressional oversight committees was haphazard during the Era of Trust, depending primarily upon what CIA directors chose to relay (and the admonition from key legislators that they did not want to know too much). During the Era of Skepticism, the Hughes–Ryan Act made it a statutory obligation for the CIA to report to Congress—though only on "important" covert actions (as determined by the CIA and the National Security Council).

When the Senate passed S. Res. 400, it boldly addressed the "what" question in two of four key positions that went far beyond the existing oversight standards for intelligence during the Era of Skepticism. Here were real teeth for the legislative watchdogs. The first provision—Section 11(c)—required the CIA director to report to the intelligence committees on all activities that constituted "violations of the constitutional rights of any person, violations of law or violations of Executive orders, Presidential directions, or departmental or agency rules or regulations."[25]

In 1973, incoming director James Schlesinger sent a similar order to his officers in the CIA, receiving in return the long list of alleged wrongdoings dubbed "the family jewels." The most egregious leaked to *Times* reporter Hersh and formed the backbone of his exposé in 1974. Now the Senate wanted to become the repository for any future family jewels from the intelligence community—an effective approach to legislative review, but one never before attempted.

A second provision—Section 11(b)—required that "any information" requested by the Senate Intelligence Committee be turned over by the CIA director. This was a frontal assault on the Agency's fortress of "sources and methods," which, according to a potentially contradictory section of the 1947 National Security Act (Section 102[d][3]), the director was expected to protect. The "any" stipulation, set against the 1947 act, invited the executive and legislative branches to a struggle over the sharing of information, though the 1947 statute clearly had precedence—at least legally—because S. Res. 400 was not a law.

With the subsequent passage of the 1980 Oversight Act, however, these two provisions in S. Res. 400 did become law (Section 501[a][3] and Section [a][2], respectively). Moreover, the 1980 act broadened the first provision by requiring reports not only on improper activities but on "significant intelligence failures" as well (Section 501[a][3]).

With the second provision on "any information," the CIA now faced the iron of new law set against the iron of old law, a sure prescription for a clash. The introductory passages of the 1980 act tilted in favor of the CIA by stating that the text of the new law had to be honored only "to the extent consistent with due regard for the protection . . . [of] intelligence sources and methods" (Section 501[a])—a reference to the 1947 statutory obligation. The last substantive section of the 1980 law (501[e]), though, tilted back toward the Congress, emphasizing that "nothing in this Act shall be construed as authority to withhold information from the intelligence committees on the grounds . . . [of] sources and methods."[26] This fog drifting between 501(a) and (e), like previous legal ambiguities touching on executive–legislative relations, will no doubt have to be cleared through interbranch negotiations.

From Whom?

In the Russell days, the CIA director was usually the only intelligence official who briefed selected members of Congress on sensitive operations (on those rare occasions when a briefing was deemed necessary). Hughes–Ryan made CIA briefings on covert action mandatory—although just how elaborate they were usually depended upon how constantly individual legislators prodded. In 1976, though, Section 11(a) of S. Res. 400—in a third key provision—required reports on sensitive operations from all the intelligence agencies. The 1980 act cemented this concept into law binding on the intelligence community. Since two dozen or so agencies are too many to monitor closely, however, the Intelligence Committees have exercised this statute meaningfully only with the larger ones: the CIA, the NSA, the military intelligence units, and the FBI. Even with these entities, the reporting has been highly uneven; the committees have tended to focus on CIA operations.

When?

During the Era of Trust, decisions on when to report to Congress were largely left to the discretion of the CIA director. In the subsequent Era of Skepticism, Congress demanded (through Hughes–Ryan) reports on important CIA covert actions "in a timely fashion." This vague temporal prescription came to be interpreted by the Agency to mean "within twenty-four hours." With S. Res. 400, a new standard emerged: in the fourth key provision, Section 11(a) required the intelligence community to keep the Senate Intelligence Committee "fully and currently informed" (a phrase borrowed from Section 202 of the 1949 Atomic Energy Act) of "any significant *anticipated* [intelligence] activities" (emphasis added). This language signaled a legislative interest in prior notification—even though Senator Church had been pressured by Senator Ribicoff to abandon the controversial word "prior" (the idea of prior approval was not an objective—yet; see Section 11[a]). In sharp contrast to the Russell era, Congress had taken a firm stand in favor of advance briefings on important intelligence operations—no more faits accompli.

With the 1980 act, the "anticipated" phrase of S. Res. 400 became law (Section 502[a][1]); the Congress even added the forbidden word "prior" to emphasize its seriousness about being informed in advance of an important operation. In cases of "extraordinary circumstances affecting vital interests of the United States," the Congress still demanded to have at least its leaders (the Gang of Eight) briefed in advance of an operation (Section 501[a][1]).

Routinely, then, both committees are now supposed to be briefed by the CIA on covert actions approved by the president within twenty-four hours and before their implementation.[27] Two known exceptions have occurred. The first happened when the executive branch informed Congress days after the fact that the CIA and the Canadian embassy in Iran had worked together in a covert action to spirit away six American diplomats at the time of the hostage taking in 1979.[28]

The second happened in 1984, when the CIA secretly mined harbors in Nicaragua. By this time, in a supreme historical irony, Barry Goldwater had assumed the chairmanship of the Senate Intelligence Committee by virtue of the seniority system and the election to the Senate of a Republican majority in 1980—the very committee whose creation he had opposed throughout the Year of Intelligence. The failure of the CIA to report adequately on the Nicaraguan covert mining was too blatant a transgression of the new rules, however, for even Senator Goldwater to disregard. In a letter to CIA director William J. Casey, Goldwater complained sharply about having "to apologize to the members of the Intelligence Committee because I did not know the facts on this." He threatened "to raise one hell of a lot of fuss about it in public" if anything like this ever happened again.[29] Senator Goldwater's approach to intelligence oversight seemed to consist of allowing free rein to the agencies, then pulling back hard when operations were revealed in public to have gone too far or turned awry.

In response to this incident, the ranking Democrat on the committee, Daniel Patrick Moynihan (New York), resigned his vice chairmanship in protest over "not [being] properly briefed"[30]—the first time an intelligence overseer had taken such a step. "In no event was the briefing 'full,' 'current,' or 'prior,' as required by the Intelligence Oversight Act of 1980, a measure I helped write," declared Moynihan.[31]

Moynihan resumed his vice chairmanship after an apology from the CIA; but the experiment in partnership had nonetheless received its most severe jolt since the investigations of 1975–1976. Still, during this shaky period, oversight remained more vigorous than in the pre-1947 era. Information flowing to the Senate Intelligence Committee was obviously imperfect (though some senators appeared to have been better informed than others), as was the motivation of panel members to ferret out a more complete record from the spotty reporting. The House Intelligence Committee, however, was apparently apprised of the mining operation in some detail, though the briefing on Nicaragua seems to have been ex post facto—indeed, a month or more after the operation was launched.[32] In sum, while even the Nicaraguan episode produced better reporting to Congress than witnessed during the Era of Trust, the reports fell far sh٬ of the statutory requirements established in 1980 and therefore represented a serious challenge to the new oversight.

To assert themselves more strongly, the intelligence committees have sometimes formally voted on covert actions, though the results are legally nonbinding. This was done with each proposal reported to the Senate committee during its early years, less consistently in the House.[33] "In several cases over the past two years," reported the Senate committee in 1979, "Committee action led to modification or termination of covert action projects."[34] Reporting on sensitive collection and counterintelligence operations has been far less systematic in timing and comprehensiveness.

As part of the New Partnership, then, with S. Res. 400 the Senate (and soon the House in practice) claimed the right—legally codified in 1980—to be told of all illegal or otherwise improper activities discovered by the intelligence community, to have access to any other information it wished, to receive reports from all intelligence agencies, and to be informed of significant intelligence operations before their implementation. Here, at least on paper, was legislative oversight of real significance.

The Effects of Intelligence Reform

The chief result of the Church committee inquiry and the reforms it sired has been to draw the Congress more deeply into the making of intelligence policy through the detailed review of budgets, the offering of policy suggestions (usually in executive hearings), and even votes on sensitive operations. While committee votes on covert actions have been only a show of "advice," they sometimes represent powerful political signals about what is permissible from the legislative viewpoint and have given the executive branch pause, or at least occasion to reconsider. In two rare secret sessions, the Congress voted as a whole on covert action, prohibiting further operations in Angola in 1976 and in Nicaragua in 1982.[35]

How one reacts to this new legislative involvement depends in large measure upon how one views the role of Congress in the policy process—a subject of debate for over two hundred years. In the modern era, officials in high positions have differed dramatically in their acceptance of a congressional role.

The Reagan administration demonstrated a reluctance to work in harness with Congress and appeared to prefer a new Era of Trust rather than an institutional partnership. Despite the formal Oversight Act of 1980, briefings on covert action (not to mention collection and counterintelligence) have apparently been less forthright than during the Bush–Turner years. "We are like mushrooms," reported Congressman Norman Mineta (D-CA), a charter member of the House Intelligence Committee. "They [the CIA] keep us in the dark and feed us a lot of manure." His Republican colleague on the committee, Congressman C. W. "Bill" Young (Florida), has been similarly displeased. "You are treating this Committee like it is something you would like to see go away," he complained to new CIA director Casey during hearings.[36]

Director Casey failed to consult with the intelligence committees on his key appointments (including the sensitive deputy director for operations), and he took steps to downgrade the Agency's Office of Legislative Counsel (the main point of contact with the committees) and the Office of Public Affairs (which under Director Turner had developed open ties with journalists, scholars, and others for the discussion of global events). This, coupled with President Reagan's executive order on intelligence (EO 12333) and loosened guidelines (March 1983) for FBI domestic security investigations,[37] represented a significant slide backward from the reforms that had been achieved. Among other things, the new executive order made it easier to gather intelligence on American citizens (Section 1.8). It also eliminated the yearly NSC review of CIA policies, as well as NSC clearance of important CIA intelligence collection operations (which, as the U-2 shoot-down in 1960 illustrates, can be as risky as covert actions).[38]

The old Era of Trust continues to have its supporters in Congress—legislators content to leave intelligence to the experts and to defer judgment to the presidency. "I don't even like to have an intelligence oversight committee," Barry Goldwater said in 1980. "I don't think it's any of our business." Soon after being named chairman, Goldwater observed, in the spirit of the earlier era, "There are many bits of [intelligence] information that I would just as soon not know."[39] One of his first decisions as chairman was to appoint as staff director John F. Blake, previously a high-ranking officer in the CIA and president of the Association of Former Intelligence Officers. With the chairman of the Senate Intelligence Committee holding the door, the fox suddenly found himself in the henhouse. The CIA had achieved one of its more notable penetrations.

On the other side of the ledger, however, have stood some officials—including CIA directors—who have supported the idea of partnership. In 1976, William Colby testified in favor of stronger legislative oversight;[40] in retirement, Admiral Turner has written of the "valuable perspective" provided by the intelligence committees and has even called for a renewed effort to legislate an intelligence charter.[41]

Senator Goldwater had his counterweights on Capitol Hill too. Congressmen Les Aspin, Norman Mineta, Bill Young, Wyche Fowler (D-GA), Lee Hamilton (D-IN), J. Kenneth Robinson (R-VA), and Albert Gore Jr. (D-TN) on the House Intelligence Committee, and Senators Huddleston, Moynihan, and Joe Biden (D-DE) on the Senate Intelligence Committee were among the few who demonstrated a dedication to the principle that close congressional supervision of the bureaucracy is necessary for the proper control of government. These legislators were prepared to devote long, wearisome hours to the scrutiny of Agency programs—beyond the sight of television cameras.

Even stalwart proponents and practitioners of intelligence oversight largely agree, though, that it must be conducted within limits, avoiding micromanagement. The kind of executive–legislative compact envisaged by Warren Christopher (undersecretary of state in the Carter administration) for foreign policy makes good sense for intelligence policy: "As a fundamental precept," writes Christopher, "the compact would call for restraint on the part of the Congress—for Congress to recognize and accept the responsibility of the Executive to conduct and manage foreign policy on a daily basis." As Christopher notes, the executive branch must be prepared to provide Congress "full information and consultation," and "broad policy should be jointly designed"; for its part, Congress should only rarely, in extreme circumstances, attempt "to dictate or overturn Executive decisions and actions."[42]

The Senate Intelligence Committee was vigorous in its early days under the leadership of, first, Senator Daniel Inouye (D-HI), and then Senator Birch Bayh (D-IN). While it (though not each of its members) seems to have recently abdicated a partnership role, the House Intelligence Committee has tried to establish a proper balance between trust and intrusion. Chairman Boland has cautioned his staff against overzealousness ("I don't want any adversary proceedings between this committee and the intelligence agencies," he warned in 1978),[43] and the House committee's approach has usually been one of quiet but serious review of Agency budgets and policies. Boland has been prepared, though, to oppose executive decisions on those infrequent occasions when his committee colleagues have expressed strong misgivings—when, for example, he sponsored the amendment in 1982 to prohibit the CIA or the Department of Defense from using appropriations "for the purpose of overthrowing the government of Nicaragua or provoking a military exchange between Nicaragua and Honduras."

Whether the initiatives advanced in Senate Resolution 400 and the 1980 Oversight Act will actually produce a useful compact for intelligence policy remains uncertain. The results so far have been mixed: of late, a chiefly quiescent Senate committee, a more inquisitive House committee, and an intelligence bureaucracy that has welcomed the former but remained willing to cooperate with the latter. Since the Year of Intelligence, however, interbranch comity and consultation have indisputably increased, despite periodic backsliding. In this sense, the legislative reforms have fostered—at least partially—their intended results: the freedoms enjoyed by Americans have been enhanced by this new vigilance exercised by legislators over our secret agencies.

~~23~~

Reflections

The Church committee investigation opened a new age in the conduct of intelligence policy, with Congress demanding an opportunity for closer supervision of our secret agencies. Above all else, the Year of Intelligence stands as a benchmark in the history of intelligence oversight.

Both the investigation and the new oversight have been scorned by some and praised by others.[1] From the perspective of six years, the *Wall Street Journal* summarily dismissed the Church and Pike inquiries as "witch-hunts."[2] "In the zeal of some to reform and others to expose," concluded former president Nixon, "we have come very near throwing the baby out with the bath water."[3] Former CIA chief of counterintelligence James Angleton deplored the "now shaky and harassed CIA" and "the straitjacket Senator Church and the Committee's staff have brazenly tailored for it."[4] Some scholars have also joined the attack.[5] For critics, the fashionable cry in the wake of the investigation was: "Unleash the CIA!"[6]

Retired intelligence officers have taken special pains to play down the significance of the investigative findings. The agencies "did engage in some illegal and ill-advised operations," admits Angleton, but he adds, "These were by no means altogether reprehensible when weighed in light of the national security considerations prevailing at the time."[7] Criticizing the bent for sensationalism in the press and on Capitol Hill, Colby declared, "The [CIA dart] gun was never used. Yet, that [presenting the gun at open hearings] was the end result of a six-month investigation. The same applies to all the tales of assassination plots. There were actually only two targets and nobody died."[8] For David Atlee Phillips, the CIA had been, at worst, a "rogue mouse."[9]

Protestations to the contrary notwithstanding, the inescapable fact remains that intelligence officials were responsible for unlawful mail openings, break-ins, wiretaps, assassination plots (which failed from ineptitude and bad luck rather than lack of serious intent), the interception of cables and telegrams, dubious covert actions, buggings, intelligence failures, and inefficiencies. The Church committee did not invent these sad events—horrors, in some instances. All too often some intelligence officials seemed to consider themselves above the law. In the view of historian Henry Steele Commager, "It is this indifference to constitutional restraints that is perhaps the most threatening of all the evidence that emerges from the findings of the Church Committee."[10] The most important service of the committee was to enhance public awareness of the threat—the foundation of subsequent measures taken by Congress and the executive branch to guard against a return to this unhappy history.[11]

William Colby acknowledged in February 1976 that the congressional investigations had actually strengthened the CIA and clarified the boundaries "within which it should, and should not, operate."[12] As CIA director, Admiral Stansfield Turner also spelled out the advantages of rigorous oversight in a message to every Agency office: "Oversight can be a bureaucratic impediment and a risk to security. It can also be a tremendous strength and benefit to us. It shares our responsibilities. It ensures against our becoming separated from the legal and ethical standards of our society. It prevents disharmony between our foreign policy and intelligence efforts. It helps us build a solid foundation for the future of our intelligence operations."[13]

The catalog of abuses brought to light during the investigations made the necessity for the probes self-evident, but were the investigations conducted in a proper manner? What lessons may be learned from a study of the way in which the Church committee carried out its assigned tasks?

Politics and Investigations

In Great Britain, government investigations into charges of alleged illegality or impropriety are usually the prerogative of royal commissions or other ad hoc committees of inquiry made up of distinguished citizens and renowned experts. These nonpoliticians, free from considerations of reelection and partisanship, have a better opportunity to achieve objectivity and fairness in their proceedings—or so advocates of this system would argue. The British method, however, has a mediocre record of accomplishment.[14] Their purpose (like most US presidential commissions) apparently has been to display the complexities of an issue and allow for an airing of grievances rather than effect resolutions. This is hardly surprising, since the commissioners—though prominent in their fields—are rarely also political decision makers in positions of authority.

In the United States, to have the investigators also the decision makers reduces the shadow between the idea and the reality, the conception and the creation. Following the 1975–1976 investigation, the permanent Senate Intelligence Committee owed its creation to members of the Church committee and their alliances with key senators—Byrd and Ribicoff, for example—who were able to apply influence within the chamber in ways impossible for a panel of outside experts.

I suspect, moreover, that the glare of the political spotlight on legislators is likely to increase the chances for a responsibly conducted investigation. As the infamous Dies committee and the antics of Joseph McCarthy well illustrate, just the opposite can happen;[15] I remain optimistic, however, that television will expose the misuse of investigative powers more swiftly and widely than was possible in an earlier era and will destroy legislators (as it did McCarthy) who fail to conduct their probes within the bounds of public acceptability. Whether or not this conclusion is unduly roseate, I prefer to put my faith in inquiries conducted by elected representatives (who may be held directly accountable for their deeds on election day) rather than in a panel of experts, no matter how distinguished.[16]

The degree of Senator Church's devotion to presidential politics during the inquiry was a matter of constant conjecture during the Year of Intelligence. Perhaps in the deepest recesses of the chairman's mind, this inquiry had for him only one motive force: a White House residency. But I find this unlikely for several reasons. First, Church's interest in the CIA investigation was a natural evolution of his earlier scrutiny of covert action in Chile in 1973 as a member of the Foreign Relations Committee. Second, he worked too hard on aspects of the investigation that were necessarily conducted behind closed doors—a waste of time for someone who could have been on the rubber-chicken circuit in the primary states. Third, he rejected some investigative options (such as sending Nixon a subpoena or holding public hearings on assassination plots) that could have generated heat—and headlines—for a prospective presidential candidate.

I suspect Church was torn between wanting the chairmanship of the intelligence investigation out of interest in the subject and a hope that it might provide the requisite national visibility needed to win a presidential nomination. Once appointed, he concentrated on his committee duties for most of 1975; it was not until mid-December that fatigue, restlessness, and pressures to enter the approaching primaries led to a sharp decline in his involvement with committee affairs. By then (as he was careful to emphasize at the time), the "active phase" of the investigation was finished: most findings were in, the public hearings were over, and the reports were on their way to completion.

In Colby's view, Church avoided using the investigation for presidential politicking.[17] I think this judgment is fundamentally correct. Church naturally hoped he might achieve a favorable national reputation from the experience, but for the most part, he shunned the temptation to turn the proceedings into a television extravaganza. The dart gun theatrics, the watch list revelations, and the purple "rogue elephant" phrase were often interpreted as political posturing, but I think these scenes more likely derived from a sense that the evidence needed to be dramatized in order to have an effect upon the public. Without a strong public response, the chairman believed, Congress might never create a permanent oversight panel.[18]

The rogue elephant concept, moreover, did have some foundation; the CIA, on occasion, had lacked proper external and internal controls. Among other examples, storage of shellfish toxin was a violation of presidential orders; CIA officer William Harvey apparently went beyond boundaries envisaged by his boss, Richard Helms; CIA counterintelligence chief James Angleton was unaware of Operation CHAOS; presidents were apparently uninformed about ongoing illegal mail intercepts; and presidents may have been unaware of the various assassination plots against foreign leaders.

During the investigation, some committee staffers complained, too, that Church might have managed his committee better without the distraction of campaign organizers. I doubt if this made much difference, since his leadership style was relatively passive anyway. Church may have been first among equals on the committee by virtue of his authority as chairman to schedule meetings, lead press conferences, and the like; by personality, though, he was far from a domineering leader intent on manipulating his committee toward a specific end. Only during the assassination phase of the inquiry did his unsurpassed investment of time and energy in the study of details provide him a certain preeminence in these proceedings (though insufficient to persuade his panel members to release the assassination report without a Senate review).

Because of his superior foreign policy experience and his sheer interest in the subject of covert action, he again stood out during the probe into the Chilean case. At other times, though, he was more like a chairman of the board, recognizing other members, stating his own views, occasionally arguing a position (without arm-twisting), content for the most part to let his "sovereign" colleagues draw their own conclusions.

When pressures mounted on Church to enter the presidential primaries, his loose control over the committee did slip further, it is true, as subcommittees formed, led by other senators. The disaggregation proceeded even more rapidly and carried farther within the staff as it divided into various groups of investigators. At both levels, senators and staff, the committee's structure was characterized by multiple centers of power.

That Church's political aspiration was an asset rather than a detriment to the investigation is a proposition that must be taken seriously. The mixture of presidential ambition and investigative duties encouraged Church, I think, to conduct his inquiry in a way that made him appear (he hoped) thoughtful, mature, and responsible—in a word, presidential. Stanley Kelley has emphasized the importance of campaigns as part of the governing process: "Campaigns are frequently discussed, both by political scientists and newspapermen, as if they were a silly interlude in the otherwise serious process of governing. To treat them in this way is to miss the point badly. . . . Men who govern must be concerned with the popularity of their actions—among members of political elites and among voters generally."[19] As Frederick Baron of the committee staff has suggested, Church's White House hopes may have been a vital energizer for the investigation. "Presidential politics was a plus," he recalls. "This roused Church to stand up and oppose the intelligence community, head on, in public. The two interests coincided."[20]

More significant than Church's relationship with the presidential election was his choice of tactics for dealing with the executive branch. Here those successes enjoyed by the committee were based on perseverance, negotiation after negotiation, a growing record of reliability (leakproofness), and the bipartisan belief that Congress had a constitutional right of access to information held by the executive branch.[21]

Within the executive branch, different individuals looked upon the committee's requests with varying degrees of distress. Among the major agencies, the CIA (under Colby) and the DIA were relatively cooperative (though Colby strongly opposed the assassination probe); the NSA less so; the FBI least of all. In most instances, the White House under President Ford joined—and often led—the ranks of those stalling the investigation (though it proved more cooperative than Colby on the assassination study).

No cooperation was forthcoming, however, without constant prodding by the committee. On key sticking points, full-blown negotiations were required between executive officials and the senators. These dogged negotiations usually resulted in access to the information sought, though sometimes the committee failed (the probe into ties between the CIA and the media is one example).

The executive branch was only as cooperative as it felt compelled to be (when our leads were incontrovertible or bipartisan political pressure from the members grew intense); then it tended to throw out some information and retreat behind new fortifications until we were able to gather our forces again.[22] As one reporter accurately observed at the time, the investigation was "less inquiry by classic standards and more year-long bargaining sessions."[23] By this process of attrition, the Church committee gathered more, and more sensitive, documents than the executive branch had ever yielded before.

Much of what the committee reported was in fact a compilation of abuses that the CIA itself had uncovered (the "family jewels") in its 1973 internal housecleaning. The CIA deserves more credit than it was given by the Congress for its own efforts to identify and correct abuses, months before the harsh articles appeared. The Church committee, however, went beyond the list of abuses compiled by the Agency, flushing out new facts (such as the internal disputes over CIA counterintelligence administration), discovering undisclosed operations (the Lumumba plot, for one), and opening whole new areas of investigation outside the CIA itself (Operation Shamrock, the IRS, and various FBI case studies, among others).[24]

For some critics of the Church committee, these tactics of negotiation and compromise were signs of weakness and vacillation—a surrender in the struggle with the executive branch over legislative prerogatives. Especially deplored was the committee's unwillingness to use its subpoena powers more aggressively, in the fashion of the Pike committee (what one scholar has called Pike's "subpoena and cite" strategy).[25]

The Church committee did use the subpoena in an effort to gain access to the papers of Richard Nixon and to order the presence of some witnesses. The members also voted, and seriously threatened (in a letter to the CIA), to serve additional subpoenas for access to documents on assassination. For the most part, though, Church and his colleagues remained convinced that negotiations would produce better access than subpoenas—especially since the full Senate might well have rejected the latter, particularly had Kissinger been the target. Moreover, subpoenas often mean court battles and lengthy delays—anathema to a temporary investigative panel. So the Church committee did relent on certain subpoenas and, as time ran out, did back away from some Gordian knots that seemed impossible to sever in the short time remaining—CIA–media relations, for instance.

On other occasions, though, the committee demonstrated a combativeness that belied efforts to portray it as a pussycat. It fought for assassination documents and other covert action records against formidable resistance; it published the assassination report over the strongest objections from the White House; and it held public hearings on the NSA as well as on covert action, despite the vigorous opposition of the executive branch.

Church found it advisable to negotiate his differences within the committee as well as with the executive branch—though more reluctantly. He would have preferred that members simply follow his lead; but on the wisdom of NSA public hearings and on the advisability of releasing reports under the committee's own authority, the members balked. In both instances, partisan and ideological lines were crossed as senators took stands based less on traditional distinctions than on varying degrees of uneasiness over the sensitivity of NSA technology and over the parliamentarian's interpretation of Rule 36. Ultimately, Church accepted compromise: a carefully circumscribed public hearing on the NSA and a presentation of the Interim Assassination Report (but none of the other committee reports) to the full Senate before release.

For the most part, Church succeeded in keeping the committee on a nonpartisan keel, avoiding the rankling that ripped through the Pike committee. Partisanship may have had an effect on Senator Tower, who refused to endorse the committee's final report under strong pressure from a Republican White House; Senator Goldwater also abandoned the final report, but this seemed a natural culmination of his long-standing opposition. In contrast to these defections, the three remaining Republicans on the committee supported the final report and (along with Tower) most of the other committee decisions.

The committee's chief responsibilities were charted by S. Res. 21, which launched the investigation and explicitly mandated a probe into the Huston Plan, Operation CHAOS, COINTELPRO, covert action, and a dozen other topics. In addition to these obligations, the committee's course was often shaped by influences completely unexpected and beyond its control. The assassination plots, Shamrock, and the shellfish toxin episodes are all examples. Like most organizations, we were frequently overwhelmed by surprise.[26]

Though the senators were obviously tardy in adopting an agenda, the committee did try to plan its future. That it had failed by November to resolve even the question of what hearings to hold is an unfortunate commentary on its lack of administrative leadership at the top. Here again, however, unanticipated events—Machiavelli's *fortuna*—intervened to upset the initial intention of completing the work by September: the assassination plots, the laborious research on COINTELPRO and other central cases, the slow responses by the executive branch that forced even the hares on the committee into a tortoiselike pace.

Though not a part of our statutory mandate, the allegation of CIA assassination plots against foreign leaders became the sharpest unexpected thorn in the committee's side—and one impossible to ignore. The issue was trumpeted in every newspaper in the country. Moreover, the White House defaulted on its own investigation of these charges, severely damaging the credibility of the Rockefeller Commission's report on intelligence. The Church committee would have lost credibility as a serious enterprise had it followed suit. While some observers believed these allegations were merely a red herring, offered by the CIA to draw the committee away from other issues, I find that interpretation unlikely. By all accounts, Colby tried strenuously to keep this item off our agenda, and, indisputably, the facts emerging from the case histories of the plots reflected poorly on the Agency.

The more significant supposition is that the committee devoted too much attention to the topic, which after all was but one (rarely tried) form of covert action. Once the decision was made to enter this thicket, however, it seemed imperative to conduct a thorough investigation. The standing of the committee depended, in large part, on how it handled its first test; the quality of our reputation for objectivity and responsibility would, we knew, affect our efforts in every subsequent phase of the investigation. A methodical study was essential, and that took time—especially with all the foot-dragging by the executive branch.

Added advantages to the committee of careful work here included a thorough self-education in the arcane field of covert action (preparing us for the Chilean case) and a purchase of more research time for other projects that could not be made ready for meaningful hearings until late fall. The fateful intervention of the assassination issue was both burden and blessing.

Circles within Circles

The lure of campaigns, struggles with the executive bureaucracy (whose "first principle in dealing with an unwanted congressional investigation is delay, delay, delay again," writes a former Hill investigator),[27] proud and independent colleagues, the rush of time and unexpected events—all would be enough to daze a committee chairman, even if he had only his investigation to worry about. Yet countless other pressures bore down on him.

The huge staff required for a major inquiry can bring with it a storehouse of headaches. The power of the staff—hardly negligible—comes from its responsibilities to suggest agenda items, propose witness lists, draft reports, brief legislators, advance lines of questioning, and the like.[28] While legislators rarely just parrot the advice of their aides, such recommendations can be a strong influence.

On the Church committee, a complicated web of relationships was spun between staffers (as individuals and in small coalitions) and member-patrons. Over the objections of the chairman, staffers often succeeded in lobbying their patrons to intercede on their behalf for time extensions on their pet projects. Generally, it would seem that the larger and more temporary the staff, the less strong its loyalties toward the chairman; moreover, major investigative committees are typically staffed by experts who are strangers to the chairmen.

At the staff level, conflicting personalities and disparate methodologies can create disruption more readily than at the member level, where codes of civility are better established. During the intelligence investigation, three prominent methodologies emerged, each a banner around which rallied the loyalties of a different group of staffers. One camp advocated the marshaling of legal evidence based chiefly on documents; another, the use of benign interviews; a third, the examination of Agency in-house histories in search of facts and leads. Each approach made a significant contribution, and the committee ultimately benefited from its strained multidisciplinary tolerance—despite occasional misunderstandings, barbs, and even shouting matches.

The overarching problem of the Church committee staff was actually less one of differing professional perspectives (though this led to a few serious disputes between lawyers and scholars) than of confusing dual leadership. The chairman, mistakenly, stayed above these administrative disputes; the result was uncertainty over lines of authority and committee priorities. Since Church elected to stress the abuse side of the inquiry, his chief counsel should have been placed more clearly in command. Another chairman might have stressed the quality-of-intelligence issue, for which an academic staff director would have been a more appropriate choice. A major investigation has a diversity of tasks and profits from an array of staff training and expertise, but divided staff authority is a prescription for disarray.

While Church the Philosopher had minimal administrative interests or skills, even the most capable chairman is hard pressed to find the necessary time. The legislator as harried individual has become a popular textbook cliché, but the truth of this characterization remains central to an understanding of Congress (and why its rate of voluntary retirement has increased dramatically). The list of distractions is well known: constituent demands, lobbyists, perpetual re-election campaigns, fund raising, staff meetings, roll-call votes, subcommittee markups, committee meetings, conferences, and the rest—without mentioning news shows, the Washington social whirl, and possible presidential ambitions. "There's no peace, and very little time to think," confides a senator.[29] An investigative committee represents yet one more demanding commitment for the already overcommitted.

The predictable result is that members are unable to devote the time required to assimilate the evidence compiled by committee investigators (at least as logically and thoroughly as these experts would like). These various distractions also aggravate the difficulty of bringing cohesion to a large operation with independent power centers and few previous ties of personal friendship or confidence. The staffs are often collections of strangers, the senators a world unto themselves. Into this confusion a determined minority can sow dissension, cause delay, and locate points of leverage for tilting an investigation this way or that.

Congressional investigations of any magnitude, then, are bound to be imperfect. The attention of committee members will be episodic, insufficient, colored by extraneous events; the findings and recommendations will be incomplete, unrefined. The best an investigative panel can hope for, through its hearings and published findings, is to inform the public as accurately as possible, to propose ameliorative legislation or other appropriate remedies for the correction of wrongdoing, and to establish an agenda for the proper standing committee to pursue (with the greater leverage over the bureaucracy given to it by permanence and the power of annual authorization).

Judged against such realities, the Church committee attained a high level of achievement. Its multivolume reports, S. Res. 400, the permanent intelligence committees, and the Intelligence Oversight Act of 1980 are all palpable testimonials to its success. The senators indeed were distracted, the staff divided, and events disruptive; personalities did hinder performance; the executive was expert at delay. But through it all, the mandate of S. Res. 21 was fulfilled.

The committee's prescription for achievement was the same as that of any successful inquiry: despite the distractions, enough members found enough time—snatched from other obligations, public and private—to concentrate on enough of the work to make a good mark. No single senator sustained the investigation; various members were catalysts at different intervals. But had these men as a group been less intelligent, less responsible, or less experienced, the best staff in the world would have been of limited use. Ultimately, the good done by government depends upon the goodness of the governors—their talents, energy, sense of duty. The Church committee, with all its human frailties, evinced an effective blend of these qualities.

An Oversight Agenda

For proponents of an executive–legislative compact for intelligence policy, passage of the 1980 Oversight Act (appendix 3) was gratifying. Despite its brevity, this statute captured much of the spirit, and at least some of the substance, that sustained reformers during the Year of Intelligence and produced S. Res. 400. Indeed, Senate Intelligence Committee Chairman Birch Bayh heralded the law as "the end of an effort begun five years ago."[30] The ambiguities and shortfalls in the legislation, however, will no doubt haunt overseers of serious intent.

The "who" in the statute, for instance, has been drawn too narrowly. Arguably, the chairmen of the Senate Foreign Relations and Armed Services Committees (and their House counterparts) warrant CIA briefings automatically on key operations. Arguably, even in time of emergency the full Intelligence Committees can be briefed immediately (following prior notice to the eight congressional leaders).

Another troubling aspect lies in Section 501(b), which seems to condone nonreporting of "activities intended solely for obtaining necessary intelligence"— that is, sensitive collection programs. If so, this clause subtracts significantly from the principle in an earlier provision calling for reports on "all intelligence activity." In a word, perplexing ambiguities suffuse the law—the price of passage in 1980.

The term "all agencies" in the act responds fully to the "from whom" problem. A word of caution is nonetheless in order: reporting requirements in other statutes have sometimes been ignored by agencies within the executive branch, as with the Case–Zablocki Act regulations for reporting to Congress on international agreements.[31]

Beyond these areas of possible improvement in the 1980 Oversight Act lies a still bolder initiative advanced by Wyche Fowler, current chairman of the Oversight Subcommittee in the House Intelligence Committee. In a two-part proposal, Fowler seeks to achieve closer legislative control over covert actions, particularly paramilitary (PM) operations—those secret warlike activities conducted usually by the CIA.

The first Fowler amendment, entitled the Intelligence Activities Oversight

Improvement Act, would tighten the decision and reporting criteria for the use of covert action and, more controversially, prohibit PM operations "unless specifically authorized" by Congress—presumably in secret sessions of both chambers.[32] The president is allowed one exception to this rule: the PM option may be used "in the case of a country or territory invaded, attacked, or occupied by the armed forces of another country" if the president determines that secret military intervention "is essential in order to meet extraordinary circumstances affecting the vital interests of the United States" (Section 2[b][8]).

Common garden-variety PM operations, then, would be subjected to a secret vote in Congress, with all the high probability for leaks that a debate among 535 individuals would entail. The emergency use of secret military force would continue to be a matter of executive discretion, though with higher standards of what is permissible from the legislative perspective. Since this authorization process would probably result in public revelations about a proposed PM operation, the likely end result of this provision would be to bar all paramilitary activities short of those absolutely essential—or lead to a devaluation of the word "essential" by the executive branch in order to bypass congressional debate.[33]

The second Fowler amendment, entitled the Intelligence Expenditures Oversight Act, aims directly at the CIA Contingency Reserve Fund, a storehouse of capital in the Agency appropriated for use in unanticipated circumstances—a substitute for supplemental appropriations made to other agencies.[34] The fund has a "large number of dollars" and is replenished every "couple of years," according to Boland, who along with Fowler is concerned about the lack of legislative control over covert actions "being funded originally [that is, without further legislative review] from the contingency appropriation."[35] In the past, covert financing has fueled PM operations without congressional awareness, as when Agency for International Development (AID) money for refugee programs was diverted in the 1960s for PM activity in Laos.[36] Specifically, this Fowler amendment would ban covert financing (from the Contingency Reserve Fund or through transfers) of amounts over $2 million for any activity during a fiscal year, as well as for paramilitary operations, unless approved by the two Intelligence Committees (Section 2 and Section 3). Whether this committee-veto approach to controlling covert financing breaches the Supreme Court's Chadha finding remains a matter of dispute among legal analysts.[37]

The Fowler amendments fall somewhere in the middle of a continuum between the strengthened reporting requirements of the 1980 act and outright statutory prohibitions against certain types of intelligence activities (as proposed in Senate Bill 2525, the Senate's effort to establish a new intelligence charter). Their objective is to insert Congress into the decision process for covert action—not simply to receive reports on these operations but to help determine in advance whether they should go forward. This is where Congress stands at present in the evolution of oversight for intelligence policy. Legislators must now decide whether to adopt the more active role advanced by the Fowler amendments (and perhaps even revive the charter quest) or content themselves with existing reporting requirements and informal responses to executive proposals.

Regardless of the outcome over the debates on statutory improvements, the attitudes of men and women in both branches toward the notion of oversight will continue to be most important. The unfinished agenda of intelligence reform calls for uncommon dedication. Beyond the improvement of existing laws, the challenge includes tackling the ongoing problem of intelligence failures; further defining the proper relationship between the intelligence agencies and citizen groups (journalists, scholars, missionaries, and the rest); straightening out the continuing tangle of CIA counterintelligence disputes; resolving more clearly the kinds of covert actions (if any) that are compatible with our interests and values; and solving the still woeful state of cover for intelligence officers abroad. This is not to mention the routine monitoring of business as usual through hearings, budget reviews, field trips, and the like—which is a more important form of oversight than the occasional shock effect of an investigation.

In Senator Mathias's words a few months after the passage of S. Res. 400, a major question was "whether the [new permanent Intelligence] Committee will have guts. Anyone standing on the brink of a moment in history can have courage, but the courage that matters is the courage to stand alone and blow the whistle day by day."[38] This agenda may well be too demanding, as well as devoid of an outside constituency, to stir members into a struggle against the strong forces in the executive—and within Congress itself—that resist change.

Epilogue

In 1979, Frank Church achieved his life ambition: chairmanship of the Senate Foreign Relations Committee. The prize was not his for long; in his bid for re-election to a fourth term in 1980, Church was defeated by some four thousand votes (less than 1 percent of the total). While several influences contributed to this loss, he was often thrown on the defensive during the campaign by (in his words) the "hit-and-run attack" against him by opponents of his intelligence investigation.[39] Conservative groups financed "speaking engagements" during the campaign, bringing to Idaho former intelligence officers, the irrepressible Edward Korry, and others who promised to discredit the investigation.

In 1984, at age fifty-nine, Church was diagnosed as having cancer of the pancreas; within weeks he passed away.

Cancer had also claimed the life of Philip Hart, in December of 1976. By the tenth anniversary of the intelligence investigation in 1985, only three of the

Church committee members remained in the Senate: Gary Hart (who narrowly won reelection in 1980), Goldwater, and Mathias. Mondale left the Senate in 1977 to assume his vice presidential duties (including major responsibilities for intelligence policy); the 1984 presidential election would find him and Gary Hart battling each other in the trenches of the primaries and caucuses for their party's nomination, with Mondale the eventual nominee—only to lose in a landslide to President Reagan. Morgan was defeated in his bid for reelection in 1980, as was Huddleston in his quest for a third term in 1984. Schweiker resigned from the Senate in 1981 and became secretary of health and human resources in the Reagan administration. Baker and Tower also voluntarily retired from the Senate in 1984, with Baker in pursuit of the presidency and Tower dividing his time between business interests and the teaching of political science in Texas.

Postscript to the 2015 Edition

The Church committee investigation in 1975–1976 represented the high-water mark for intelligence accountability in the United States. Occasionally thereafter members of Congress would exhibit a strong commitment to the review of spy programs, as with the Iran-Contra inquiry (1987); the search for explanations as to why the secret agencies failed to warn the public about the 9/11 attacks, and why their assessment that Iraq had weapons of mass destruction (WMDs) proved so wrong (2004–2005); and the probe into the use of torture by the CIA as a method of intelligence collection (2014). Yet none of these probes equaled the scope and depth of the Church committee inquiry, with its examination of a vast array of intelligence subjects during a sixteen-month period, with eleven lawmakers deeply engaged throughout most of this time and a staff of 150—some seeming to work around the clock—turning over stones across the intelligence community. It was indeed the Year of Intelligence.

This is not to slight the important reviews that have taken place since 1976. The Senate Selection Committee on Intelligence (SSCI), for example, displayed a rare and laudatory tenacity in its study of the CIA's use of torture against suspected terrorists in the wake of the 9/11 attacks—an extreme form of tradecraft which the Agency prefers to call "EITs" (enhanced interrogation techniques) or, in an earlier version of cosmetic labeling, "intelligence educement." Six members of the SSCI staff—all from the Democratic side of the aisle, when GOP leaders called their staff off the investigation—spent five years trying to determine the authorization for torture; the nature of the interrogation techniques (which ran from waterboarding to confinement in cramped coffinlike boxes, along with sleep deprivation lasting days); and whether these methods had elicited useful information that shielded the United States against further terrorist attacks. On this key question, the findings pointed overwhelmingly toward a "no" answer. The long-known principle that anyone being tortured will lie to prevent further pain could be seen at work again in these protracted interrogation sessions at Agency prisons abroad and at Guantánamo—the same point James Angleton, the chief of CIA counterintelligence for twenty years, made to me during the days of the Church committee when we discussed the long detention by the CIA of the Soviet defector Yuri Ivanovich Nosenko in the 1960s. Angleton had been close to Israeli intelligence, which tried many of these harsh techniques and confided to him that they were largely useless. In contrast to "abuse interrogation," winning over the detainee through a more civilized approach to questioning—"rapport interrogation"—has demonstrated, according to FBI counterterrorism experts, a better chance of success.

Even if torture may work in some isolated cases—and might have to be tried no matter what in the extreme (and unlikely) ticking bomb scenario—the question of its legitimacy remains a serious matter. Two personal illustrations come to mind. At the time of the Abu Ghaib torture sessions carried out by army intelligence officers against suspected terrorists in a Baghdad prison by that name in 2003, I was the only American at an intelligence conference in Oslo. During breaks between conference presentations, participants from all over Europe would come to me in the hallways to complain about the methods used at Abu Ghaib, as captured in photographs making their way around the Internet: naked victims in dank prison cells being hosed down with powerful sprays of cold water, subject to the snarling lunges of German shepherd dogs, and humiliated by their nakedness in front of taunting female intelligence personnel. "How could you do this?" a senior scholar from Sweden asked me in anguish.

Two years later, when I was teaching at Yale University, the best student in my undergraduate seminar on national security asked me if we could talk privately. He told me that he had applied to the Agency for employment and things were moving along well toward his acceptance, but that he had had a change of heart based on reports the CIA was involved in torturing detainees (a euphemism for prisoners). He seemed shattered that his earlier zeal for intelligence work and the clear career pathway before him were now in ruins. He sought counseling about other possible avenues to serve his country in the national security field. I reminded him that only a small component of the CIA had been involved in torture; that intelligence analysis, for example, remained an important Agency endeavor, with its intelligence directorate providing timely reports to the president and others that improved the quality of foreign policy decisions made by the United States. Yet, disheartened that torture evidently had the imprimatur of the Agency's leadership, the student had reached a point where he was dead set against an intelligence career, so I talked with him (as I do all my students) about the many other opportunities in Washington, from Capitol Hill to Foggy Bottom.

How many other talented young Americans across the country have been turned off of intelligence work by the CIA's excesses is anyone's guess. Suffice it to say that the moral goodness of one's actions matter—not only to Swedish professors and Yale undergraduates but also to people around the world. Soft power is real, even if discounted by some cynics who see the world largely in terms of military and economic power.

On an electronic mailing list to which I belong, one that boasts an impressive roster of leading lights in the academic world of international relations, an exchange on the effects of torture drew this comment from a prominent pillar of wisdom in the field: "Soft power is not worth a plug nickel." I think this is flat wrong. What America stands for does matter—a lot. Supreme Court justice William O. Douglas observed that people around the world—like the disappointed Swede who spoke to me—admired the United States not "so much for our B-52 bombers and for our atomic stockpile, but for the First Amendment and the freedom of people to speak and believe and to write, have fair trials." Here was the "great magnet" that attracted friends for the United States.[1] Were Douglas still alive, he would have been appalled by America's resort to methods more apt to occur in Lubyanka or cellars in Pyongyang than in the facilities of a US government agency. So would another vital voice also lost to the march of time: the former chairman of the Senate Foreign Relations Committee, J. William Fulbright (D-AR). "If America has a service to perform in the world—and I believe it has—," he said, "it is in large part the service of its own example."[2] Torture is not exactly the example he would have chosen.

So the Senate Intelligence Committee's torture investigation, while not matching the Church committee in scope, certainly stands as a significant example of serious intelligence accountability in recent years. It may not have answered every question—such as why SSCI members failed to halt the torture program in the first place, at least once some of them found out about it a few years after its initiation; but the report did place the topic of torture before the public, allowing a national debate about the value of this medieval approach to intelligence gathering. Valuable, as well, were the inquiries (moving backward in time) into the intelligence errors related to 9/11 and to the Iraqi WMD hypothesis. Thanks to these probes, we have learned critical lessons that should help the United States in the future. Among them are the need to take intelligence more seriously;[3] the need to improve CIA–FBI sharing of information about terrorists bound for the United States; and, with respect to Iraq WMDs, the need to double-check intelligence sources rather than rely excessively on foreign intelligence organizations to provide information to us, as happened during the second Bush administration with the German source known as Curveball who emphatically swore that Iraq had WMDs—all lies, it turned out.

The Iran-Contra inquiry was important, too, though—like all of these cases of scandal and failure—painful to the nation. Some have discounted this scandal as of little significance, perhaps most prominently former vice president Dick Cheney, who earlier served as a member of the Iran-Contra investigative panel (the Inouye–Hamilton Committee). He seems to think that the committee was a total waste of time because the executive branch should be given wide leeway in foreign affairs. Yet in reality this scandal revealed the CIA at its worst—or at least some important elements of the CIA. (One cannot fairly indict the entire Agency for the misdeeds of relatively few CIA officers—although, as in the torture example, those culpable included the organization's top leadership.) Just looking at the Contra side of the scandal alone, it involved bypassing the Congress and conducting a privately funded covert action against the Sandinista regime in Nicaragua, despite a clear law (the Boland Amendment of 1983) to curb such activities. Harvard University law professor Laurence H. Tribe has spelled out the chilling implications: "Congress's control over the purse would be rendered a nullity if the President's pocket could conceal a slush fund dedicated to purposes and projects prohibited by the laws of the United States."[4]

When lawmakers asked the Reagan administration's national security adviser, Vice Admiral John M. Poindexter, during investigative hearings why the administration had chosen to ignore the Congress, he offered this explanation: "We didn't want any outside interference."[5] Put another way, he didn't believe in the safeguards of intelligence accountability put into place just a few years earlier by the Church committee, supported by a bipartisan majority in both chambers of Congress.

If the Church committee is intelligence oversight at high tide, the Iran-Contra scandal is low tide. That scandal is hardly the only worrisome illustration of intelligence missteps, however. On a much smaller scale, but still disquieting, are the many examples of the secret agencies failing to keep the Congress informed of its activities, as required by the Intelligence Oversight acts of 1980 and 1991. All too often, instead of briefing SSCI and HPSCI in their full complement, intelligence managers have merely whispered into the ears of just a few members—say, the chairman and vice chairman of the committees—cautioning them not to discuss the "briefing" with anyone else, even their top intelligence staff aides. Sometimes there have been no briefings at all, even solitary whispers; instead, SSCI and HPSCI members find out what's going on in the newspapers. And sometimes, especially in the lead-up to the Iran-Contra investigation, lawmakers have simply been lied to by the intelligence agencies. All of these approaches make a mockery of the oversight reporting statutes.

Alarming, as well, is the CIA's caper in 2014 of breaking into computers used by the SSCI staff during the torture inquiry and otherwise harassing the Senate investigators—all deeds carried out with apparent impunity, despite a strong denouncement from the committee's chair, Diane Feinstein (D-CA). A CIA-appointed panel established to look into this case (with three CIA officers among its five members) decided that the whole episode was a "misunderstanding." The Agency absolved itself of any real blame. Stunning, too, is the disclosure that the two outside psychologists selected to set up a company and guide the brutal interrogations were paid $81 million to run this program for four years. According to the *New York Times*, the chief of the CIA division that supervised the torture program became the CEO of the company when he retired from the Agency.[6]

As valuable as a Church committee and other forms of investigative oversight can be, they are hardly the best approach to intelligence accountability. Such approaches occur ex post facto, coming after a failure or scandal has occurred, too late to close the barn door. Better is ante facto accountability, in which lawmakers steadily review intelligence programs in advance of their implementation—day in, day out—with an intent to improve America's secret agencies and their programs; to maintain the levels of privacy expected by citizens living in a democracy; and, as well as mere mortals can, to anticipate future intelligence needs.

Political scientists Matthew D. McCubbins and Thomas Schwartz have recommended a vivid metaphor that posits two models of congressional oversight behavior: "police-patrolling" and "firefighting"—what one might think of, respectively, as routine inspections by overseers, in contrast to their engagement in intensive investigations of failures and wrongdoing (the firefighting of investigative accountability).[7] When on police patrol, a member of Congress routinely but aggressively searches for program information and indications of wrongdoing or inefficiency—sniffing for fires by, say, questioning bureaucrats in hearings. The idea is not to wait until things go wrong but rather to ensure, through continuous questioning and observation, that the nation's laws and regulations are being honored by officials charged with implementing them. Alternatively, in the role of a firefighter, a lawmaker may have to jump on the hook-and-ladder truck to investigate a major mistake or scandal (an alarm). Police patrolling is a sustained, normal activity; firefighting is more episodic and event driven.

Since the Church committee inquiry, the Congress has had to respond to five major fire alarms in the world of intelligence accountability: Iran-Contra (1987); the treason of Aldrich H. Ames within the CIA (1994); the 9/11 failures (2001); the Iraqi WMD failures (2003); and the revelations in the *New York Times* that the NSA had bypassed the Foreign Intelligence Surveillance Act (FISA) of 1978 and its lawful warrant procedure for intelligence wiretaps (2005). Other flaps have been important too, such as the torture disclosures; but they have not risen to the same threshold of national concern and attention from both sides of the aisle as these Big Five. One can imagine in each of these cases how SSCI and HPSCI lawmakers, as dedicated police patrollers, might have warded off the conditions that eventually led to traumatizing fire alarms. With Iran-Contra, for instance, what if lawmakers had followed through—more energetically and with a strong dose of skepticism—on the rumors in Washington that the Boland Amendment was being secretly ignored? The chairmen of these two committees did question national security adviser Robert C. McFarlane and Iran-Contra point man Lieutenant Colonel Oliver L. North of the National Security Council staff about the rumors, but the chairmen too easily accepted their denials.

What if extensive hearings had been held by SSCI and HPSIC (behind closed doors) into counterintelligence before the Ames disaster? Perhaps that would have caused the Agency to take the question of ferreting out moles more seriously, resulting in double-checking the bank accounts of Ames and other top counterintelligence officers.

What if the intelligence committees had examined CIA–FBI liaison relations before the 9/11 attacks, a fairly obvious subject of interest for those hoping for an effective, coordinated response to terrorist threats? They would have discovered a fractured relationship, which would manifest itself tragically in September 2001, when these agencies failed to communicate effectively about the entry of the 9/11 terrorists into the United States (at least two of whom the CIA knew about). What if the committees had held hearings and looked more deeply into the Agency's Counterterrorism Center report on aerial terrorism in 1995? Might that have led to tighter airport security, sealed cockpit doors, and more sky marshals on board commercial airliners?

What if the committees had probed into the quality of the data for the Iraqi WMD hypothesis? Surely they would have raised some questions about its obvious softness. As it was, Congress—not to mention the Bush administration—did not even demand a National Intelligence Estimate (NIE) on Iraq until the eve of America's invasion into that country.

What if SSCI and HPSCI had conducted routine police patrolling hearings into the activities of the FIS court in the aftermath of the 9/11 attacks? They may have discovered—long before word seeped out in 2005—that the White House and the NSA were violating FISA.

These questions underscore how vital intelligence accountability can be. Dedicated police patrollers on SSCI and HPSCI can save the nation from much grief—even tragedy, as the casualties from the 9/11 attacks and the extended war in Iraq remind us—along with the costs and turmoil of major ex post facto inquiries.

Early into his inquiries, Frank Church pondered on a national television talk show whether the CIA had become "a rogue elephant." It was a line that had come to him from McGeorge Bundy, the former national security adviser during the Kennedy administration. Over breakfast that same day, the two men had been discussing in general terms the course of the intelligence inquiry. Church had complained to Bundy about the Huston Plan of 1970, a White House scheme that called upon the CIA and other secret agencies to spy on Vietnam War protesters; and about how the CIA had continued its domestic spying even when the plan had been rescinded a few months after its approval by President Nixon. The chairman was dismayed, too, by his committee's discovery of shellfish toxins and other highly poisonous substances still stored at the Agency and military facilities, even though they had been banned by an international treaty and supposedly destroyed by the Nixon administration. Bundy opined that the CIA seemed like "a rogue elephant on a rampage." When Senator Church then went on the TV show, he no doubt had in his mind as well the CIA's use of LSD against one of its own scientists as an experiment in 1953, without his knowledge. (The scientist committed suicide soon after.)

Despite these fragments of evidence about "roguish" Agency behavior, Church clearly spoke in public prematurely, before the committee had really dug into its research. His colleagues reprimanded him at the next committee meeting, and he would be hounded by this rash statement thereafter. Even in 2014, the normally reliable columnist David Ignatius wrote that the torture report "revives the notion of the CIA as a 'rogue elephant' that was propounded by Frank Church's committee in the 1970s but has been rebutted by many historians."[8] Ignatius thus shifted a Sunday morning talk-show slip by Senator Church onto the shoulders of the entire Church committee and its final report. In fact, closer to the mark is the rest of Ignatius's op-ed, which reaches a conclusion well documented by the Church committee reports: "The real story of intelligence abuses in the 1950s and '60s is that they were ordered by presidents or their henchmen, who didn't want to know the dirty details."

Nevertheless, the CIA and the other intelligence agencies have in fact displayed moments in which one can only wonder about how well they have been supervised. Several Agency witnesses have misled the Congress over the years since the Church committee inquiry, denying (for example) involvement in the Iran-Contra affairs—only later to come clean when presented with documentary evidence to the contrary; and the NSA has often played footloose with SSCI and HPSCI, misleading them on its bypassing of FISA and on the scope of its metadata program (revealed by leaker Edward J. Snowden in 2013). Questions about authority and supervision arise, too, regarding the implementation of torture techniques; the targeting procedures for killer drones, especially when aimed at American citizens; and what other dubious collection programs the NSA may have squirreled away besides the metadata grab bag. And why does "rogue" come to mind when thinking about the CIA's destruction of torture videotapes without congressional approval; or its search of SSCI computers, accompanied by threats to the Senate staff?

All of this is to argue that intelligence accountability should be taken more seriously—by lawmakers, presidents and their presidential aides, judges, and, most of all, the public—than has usually been the case since the Church committee investigation. The intelligence agencies are vital to the security of the United States; and intelligence officers are among the brightest and most dedicated of America's public servants; over one hundred have given their lives in the cause of shielding the United States from harm, including Johnny Michael "Mike" Spann, a CIA paramilitary officer and the first casualty in the post-9/11 hunt of Al Qaeda and Taliban terrorists in Afghanistan. We should respect their work and understand that the overwhelming majority has been patriotic, competent, and law-abiding. Yet one can hardly dismiss Operation CHAOS, COINTELPRO, Iran-Contra, lapses in counterintelligence (Ames for one, tracking the 9/11 terrorists for another), faulty analysis from time to time, and the gaming of Congress as if it were a foreign country to be manipulated rather than a valued partner in the nation's defense.

The original edition of *Season of Inquiry* ended with an expression of concern that intelligence accountability "may well be too demanding, as well as devoid of an outside constituency, to stir [lawmakers] into a struggle against the strong forces in the executive—and within Congress itself—that resist change." Often since 1976 lawmakers have indeed failed in their police patrolling duties for intelligence activities. Still, they have sometimes succeeded, and even today's sluggish approach by members of Congress to espionage accountability has been an improvement over the dark ages that preceded the Year of Intelligence. The core hope of the Church committee remains alive that the United States will find a satisfactory balance between security and liberty, and that SSCI and HPSCI members will decide to act consistently as dedicated police patrollers and not just firefighters.

Chronology

The Era of Trust (1947–1974)

1947	CIA established
1948–1960	Several successful covert actions (CAs)
1961	Bay of Pigs disaster
1967	National Student Association flap; Katzenbach Report
1973	"Family Jewels" (Schlesinger compilation)
1974	Watergate; Hersh exposés; Hughes–Ryan Amendment

The Era of Skepticism (1974–1976)

THE CHURCH COMMITTEE INVESTIGATION (AND RELATED EVENTS)

Phase 1: Discovery

1975		
January	4	Rockefeller Commission established
	27	Church committee established
February	6	Church committee staff director appointed
	19	House investigative panel (Nedzi committee) established
	26	Church committee chief counsel appointed; committee meets with Levi
	27	Committee meets with Colby
	28	Schorr reveals assassination plots
March	3	Staff begins "chronologies," discovery plans, and document requests
	5	Church and Tower visit President Ford
	11	Bader recommends search of CIA in-house histories
	12	Formal letters to Ford and Colby requesting documents
	19	*Glomar Explorer* story; letter to Levi requesting documents
	22	Phillips founds ARIO

April	1	Miller and Schwarz begin negotiation with executive branch
	9	First full meeting of committee to discuss agenda
	10	Ford's "State of the World" address
	23	Committee discouraged over limited access to documents
	24	Strong letters to Ford and Colby request more meaningful documents
May	8	Church and Tower visit Rockefeller; fail to obtain documents from his commission
	9	Committee decides on assassination plots as top priority, interviews as prime methodology; CIA insists on monitoring interviews
	11	Nedzi committee appoints staff director

Phase 2: Interrogation

May	15	First formal hearing (closed): Colby on CIA
	21–23	Colby on assassination plots (closed)
	25	Rockefeller Commission retreats from assassination probe
June	11	Rockefeller Commission Report released
	13	Helms on assassination plots (closed)
	19	Giancana murdered
	20	Colby on assassination plots (closed)
	24	Goldwater blames presidency for abuses
	26	Staff dissension surfaces: lawyers vs. non-lawyers
July	11	Colby on assassination plots (closed)
	16	Levi and Kelley testify (closed)
	17	Pike committee replaces Nedzi committee
	17–18	Helms on assassination plots (closed)
	19	Church uses "rogue elephant" phrase
	20	Schweiker discusses committee findings on TV
	21	Committee begins to polarize
	23	GOP committee members oppose interim assassination report
	30	Church again rebuffed on assassination report
August	1	Month-long congressional recess begins
	12	Committee issues subpoenas to White House
	19	Ford warns against "crippling" intelligence agencies
	25	CIA reports to committee on discovery of shellfish toxin cache
September	4	Church urges shellfish toxin hearing

Phase 3: Presentment

September	16–18	Shellfish toxin hearings (public)
	19	Church rebuffed by committee on public NSA hearings, turns to Huston Plan
	23–25	Huston Plan hearings (public)
	30	Committee addresses long-range agenda, plans IRS and mail-opening hearings; Church wins support for public NSA hearing
October	2	IRS hearing (public)
	4	Mondale discusses assassination findings in public (Denison speech)
	5	Church discusses Mondale's speech and assassination findings on TV
	7	Levi on NSA (closed); Church loses support for public NSA hearing; Church and Mondale criticized for public remarks; White House hints at impending intelligence reform plan
	9	Committee decides to hold hearings on COINTELPRO; Ford opposes release of assassination report
	21–22, 24	Mail-opening hearings (public)
	23	Colby on CA (closed)
	28	Colby on CA (closed); limited public NSA hearing approved
	29	NSA watch list hearing (public)
	30	Pike rebuffed by his committee on Kissinger contempt citation
	31	Ford intensifies opposition to assassination report; Colby testifies on paramilitary CA (closed)
November	1	Ford fires Colby
	3	Church threatens resignation; committee supports release of assassination report (if presented to the Senate first) and SHAMROCK public hearings (if the Senate parliamentarian endorses release of classified documents); Ford appoints Bush to replace Colby
	5	Parliamentarian authorizes release of SHAMROCK papers
	6	SHAMROCK hearing (public)
	9	Church states he may be a presidential candidate by December; Mathias, too, hints at presidential bid
	11	Church's first major intelligence speech: critique of CIA, criticism of Bush nomination
	13	Committee plans public hearings on CA in Chile

November	14	Pike committee votes contempt-of-Congress citations against Kissinger for failure to provide documents on CA (later withdrawn)
	15	White House forms Intelligence Coordinating Group to cope with investigations
	16	Judith Campbell story leaks
	17	Church orders internal investigation of Campbell leak
	18	Church announces interest in Massachusetts presidential primary
	18–19	COINTELPRO, hearings (public): "Philip Hart Day"
	20	Kissinger and Colby refuse to testify in public on CA; secret Senate session on assassination report; Interim Assassination Report released
	21	Kissinger on CA (closed)
December	2–3	Hearings on FBI informants (public)
	4	Colby and Church address a forum on covert action
	4–5	CA hearings (Chile, public)
	9–11	FBI hearings, Mondale-Levi exchange (public); Miller formally proposes executive-legislative work group for "consensus charter"
	12	Mondale seeks extension of committee timetable
	13	Church-for-President committee formed
	15–16	Bush confirmation hearings (public)
	17–19	Senate debates Angola policy (secret session)
	18	Committee publishes report on CA in Chile
	19	Armed Services Committee approves Bush nomination; Senate rejects covert aid to Angola; Pike panel votes to release reports on CA in Angola and Italy, Ford objects
	23	Welch murdered
1976		
January	7	State funeral for Welch

Phase 4: Reform

January	19	Church and Tower press conference on reform proposals; Ford's State of the Union address promises intelligence reforms
	21–28	Ribicoff hearings on intelligence reform (public)
	23	Pike committee votes to release its report over presidential objections; Church committee endorses oversight reform bill

	27	Senate confirms Bush
	28	House Rules Committee votes to block Pike report; floor majority backs Rules Committee
	29	Church introduces committee oversight bill
	30	Bush succeeds Colby as CIA director
February	3	Church plans counteroffensive against rising executive opposition to his committee
	3–4	Pike committee releases its reform proposals
	12	Top-secret Pike report hits newsstands
	17	Ford presents intelligence reform package (EO 11905); committee thwarted in CIA media probe
	24	Ribicoff committee reports its intelligence oversight bill (S. Res. 400)
March	9	Committee releases documents on intelligence activities; FBI releases intelligence guidelines
	10	Nixon releases responses to the committee's questions
	18	Church declares presidential candidacy
April	23, 26	Committee publishes final reports
	27, 28	Senate Rules Committee tries to block Church–Ribicoff oversight bills
May	11	Church wins Nebraska primary; Cannon Compromise fashioned
	12–13, 17–19	Senate debate on intelligence oversight bill; establishment of permanent oversight committee passes
	23	Church wins Oregon, Idaho primaries
June	1	Church wins Montana primary, finishes third in Rhode Island
	8	Church fades in California, Ohio, New Jersey primaries
July	15	Carter chooses Mondale as running mate

The Era of Uneasy Partnership (1976–)

1976 Senate Intelligence Committee conducts annual authorization
1977 House establishes Permanent Select Committee on Intelligence
1978 Omnibus charter fails; Foreign Intelligence Surveillance Act (FISA) passed; Carter Executive Order 12036
1980 Intelligence Oversight Act passed
1981 Reagan Executive Order 12333
1982 Agents Identities Protection Act passed; Boland Amendment (Nicaragua) passed

1983 Fowler Amendments proposed

1984 Senate Intelligence Committee members charge CIA with failure to report adequately on mining operations in Nicaraguan harbors; relations reach low point in Era of Uneasy Partnership, which then shatters with the Iran-Contra scandal in 1987

Updated Chronology

2015 EDITION

1987 Iran-Contra investigations (Congress, Tower Commission, special prosecutor)

1989 Inspector General Act (strengthening the IG at the CIA)

1991 Oversight Act (strengthening covert action accountability)

1996 Aspin–Brown Commission on Intelligence

1998 Intelligence Whistleblowers Protection Act

2001 9/11 intelligence failures; Patriot Act

2002 Iraqi WMD intelligence failures

2003 Joint House–Senate inquiry into 9/11

2004 Kean–Hamilton Commission on 9/11; ODNI created

2005 Silberman–Robb Commission on Iraqi WMD failures; *Times* disclosure of NSA warrantless wiretaps

2008 Oversight Act modifying FISA to provide wider NSA leeway in wiretapping

2013 Snowden leaks

2014 SSCI torture report

2015 Congress reforms NSA bulk data collection

Note: On the eras of intelligence accountability, see Loch K. Johnson, "Accountability and America's Secret Foreign Policy: Keeping a Legislative Eye on the CIA," *Foreign Policy Analysis* 1 (Spring 2005): 99–120.

APPENDIX 1

US Intelligence Leadership, 1947–2015

Directors, National Intelligence

2005–2007	John D. Necroponte
2007–2009	J. M. "Mike" McConnell
2009–2010	Dennis C. Blair
2010–	James R. Clapper Jr.

Directors, Central Intelligence

1947–1950	Rear Adm. Roscoe H. Hillenkoetter
1950–1953	Gen. Walter Bedell Smith
1953–1961	Allen W. Dulles
1961–1965	John A. McCone
1965–1966	Vice Adm. William F. Raborn Jr.
1966–1973	Richard Helms
1973	James R. Schlesinger
1973–1976	William E. Colby
1976–1977	George H. W. Bush
1977–1981	Adm. Stansfield Turner
1981–1987	William J. Casey
1987–1991	William H. Webster
1991–1993	Robert M. Gates
1993–1995	R. James Woolsey
1995–1997	John M. Deutch
1997–2004	George J. Tenet
2004–2005	Porter J. Goss [the last person to serve as DCI]

Chairs, Senate Select Committee on Intelligence

1976–1977	Daniel K. Inouye, D-HI
1977–1981	Birch Bayh, D-IN

1981–1985	Barry Goldwater, R-AZ
1985–1987	David Durenberger, R-MN
1987–1993	David L. Boren, D-OK
1993–1995	Dennis DeConcini, D-AZ
1995–1997	Arlan Specter, R-PA
1997–2001	Richard C. Shelby, R-AL
2001–2003	Bob Graham, D-FL
2003–2006	Pat Roberts, R-KS
2007–2008	John D. Rockefeller IV, D-WV
2009–2014	Dianne Feinstein, D-CA
2015–	Richard Burr, R-NC

Chairs, House Permanent Select Committee on Intelligence

1977–1985	Edward P. Boland, D-MA
1985–1987	Lee H. Hamilton, D-IN
1987–1989	Louis Stokes, D-OH
1989–1991	Anthony C. Beilenson, D-CA
1991–1993	Dave McCurdy, D-OK
1993–1995	Dan Glickman, D-KS
1995–1997	Larry Combest, R-TX
1997–2004	Porter J. Goss, R-FL
2004–2006	Peter Hoekstra, R-MI
2006–2011	Silvestre Reyes, D-TX
2011–2014	Mike Rogers, R-MI
2015–	Devin Nunes, R-CA

APPENDIX 2

Organization of the US Intelligence Community

2015

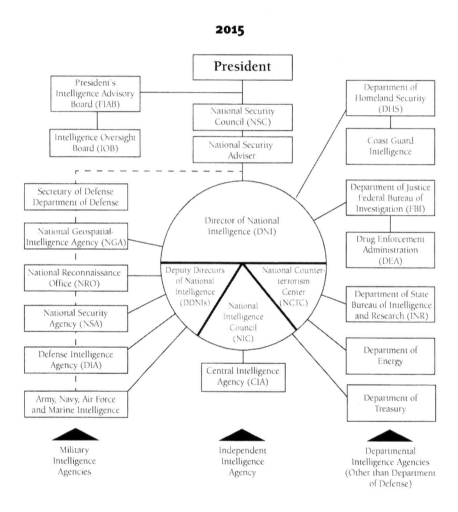

January 1975

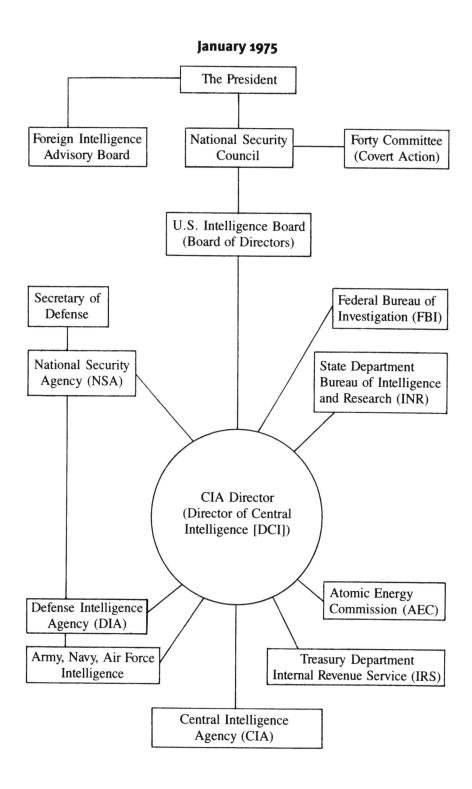

APPENDIX 3

Text of Relevant Intelligence Amendments and Acts

The Hughes–Ryan Amendment (Section 662 of the Foreign Assistance Act of 1974, 22 USC 2422)

Sec. 662. Limitation on Intelligence Activities.—No funds appropriated under the authority of this or any other Act may be expended by or on behalf of the Central Intelligence Agency for operations in foreign countries, other than activities intended solely for obtaining necessary intelligence, unless and until the President finds that each such operation is important to the national security of the United States and reports, in a timely fashion, a description and scope of each operation to the appropriate committees of Congress. . . .

S. Res. 400 from the 94th Congress

A RESOLUTION ESTABLISHING A SELECT COMMITTEE ON INTELLIGENCE

Sec. 11. (a) It is the sense of the Senate that the head of each department and agency of the United States should keep the select committee fully and currently informed with respect to intelligence activities, including any significant anticipated activities, which are the responsibility of or engaged in by such department or agency: *Provided*, That this does not constitute a condition precedent to the implementation of any such anticipated intelligence activity.

(b) It is the sense of the Senate that the head of any department or agency of the United States involved in any intelligence activities should furnish any information or documentation in the possession, custody, or control of the department or agency, or person paid by such department or agency, whenever requested by the select committee with respect to any matter within such committee's jurisdiction.

(c) It is the sense of the Senate that each department and agency of the

United States should report immediately upon discovery to the select committee any and all intelligence activities which constitute violations of the constitutional rights of any person, violations of law, or violations of Executive orders, Presidential directives, or departmental or agency rules or regulations; each department and agency should further report to such committee what actions have been taken or are expected to be taken by the departments or agencies with respect to such violations.

Accountability for Intelligence Activities (Title V of the National Security Act of 1947, 50 USC 413)*

CONGRESSIONAL OVERSIGHT

Sec. 501. (a) To the extent consistent with all applicable authorities and duties, including those conferred by the Constitution upon the executive and legislative branches of the Government, and to the extent consistent with due regard for the protection from unauthorized disclosure of classified information and information relating to intelligence sources and methods, the Director of Central Intelligence and the heads of all departments, agencies, and other entities of the United States involved in intelligence activities shall—

(1) keep the Select Committee on Intelligence of the Senate and the Permanent Select Committee on Intelligence of the House of Representatives (hereinafter in this section referred to as the "intelligence committees") fully and currently informed of all intelligence activities which are the responsibility of, are engaged in by, or are carried out for or on behalf of, any department, agency, or entity of the United States, including any significant anticipated intelligence activity, except that (A) the foregoing provision shall not require approval of the intelligence committees as a condition precedent to the initiation of any such anticipated intelligence activity, and (B) if the President determines it is essential to limit prior notice to meet extraordinary circumstances affecting vital interests of the United States, such notice shall be limited to the chairmen and ranking minority members of the intelligence committees, the Speaker and minority leader of the House of Representatives, and the majority and minority leaders of the Senate;

(2) furnish any information or material concerning intelligence activities which is in the possession, custody, or control of any department, agency, or entity of the United States and which is requested by either of the intelligence committees in order to carry out its authorized responsibilities; and

* Less formally known by government officials as the 1980 Intelligence Oversight Act.

(3) report in a timely fashion to the intelligence committees any illegal intelligence activity or significant intelligence failure and any corrective action that has been taken or is planned to be taken in connection with such illegal activity or failure.

(b) The President shall fully inform the intelligence committees in a timely fashion of intelligence operations in foreign countries, other than activities intended solely for obtaining necessary intelligence, for which prior notice was not given under subsection (a) and shall provide a statement of the reasons for not giving prior notice.

(c) The President and the intelligence committees shall each establish such procedures as may be necessary to carry out the provisions of subsections (a) and (b).

(d) The House of Representatives and the Senate, in consultation with the Director of Central Intelligence, shall each establish, by rule or resolution of such House, procedures to protect from unauthorized disclosure all classified information and all information relating to intelligence sources and the methods furnished to the intelligence committees or to Members of the Congress under this section. In accordance with such procedures, each of the intelligence committees shall promptly call to the attention of its respective House, or to any appropriate committee or committees of its respective House, any matter relating to intelligence activities requiring the attention of such House or such committee or committees.

(e) Nothing in this Act shall be construed as authority to withhold information from the intelligence committees on the grounds that providing the information to the intelligence committees would constitute the unauthorized disclosure of classified information or information relating to intelligence sources and methods.

Notes

Foreword

1. Paul Light, *Government by Investigation: Congress, Presidents, and the Search for Answers, 1945–2012* (Washington, DC: Brookings Institution Press, 2014), 193.

2. *Congressional Record*, 11 November 1975, 35786.

3. Robert M. Gates, *From the Shadows* (New York: Simon & Schuster, 1996), 559.

4. Anyone interested in a current intelligence bibliography may wish to consult my "Development of Intelligence Studies," in *Routledge Companion to Intelligence Studies*, edited by Robert Dover, Michael S. Goodman, and Claudia Hillebrand (New York: Routledge, 2014), 3–22.

Chapter 1. The End of an Affair

1. For an introduction to congressional oversight, see Morris S. Ogul, *Congress Oversees the Bureaucracy: Studies in Legislative Supervision* (Pittsburgh, PA: University of Pittsburgh Press, 1976); Joel D. Aberbach, "Changes in Congressional Oversight," *American Behavioral Scientist* 22 (May/June 1979): 493–515. On intelligence oversight, see Loch Johnson, "The US Congress and the CIA: Monitoring the Dark Side of Government," *Legislative Studies Quarterly* 5 (November 1980): 477–499; Anne Karalekas, "Intelligence Oversight: Has Anything Changed?" *Washington Quarterly* 6 (Summer 1983): 22–30; Thomas K. Latimer, "US Intelligence and the Congress," *Strategic Review* 7 (Summer 1979): 47–56; Harry Howe Ransom, "Congress and the Intelligence Agencies," *Proceedings of the Academy of Political Science* 32 (1975): 153–166; Stansfield Turner and Geoge Thibault, "Intelligence: The Right Rules," *Foreign Policy* 48 (Fall 1982): 122–138; House Permanent Select Committee on Intelligence, *Hearings on Congressional Oversight of Covert Activities*, 1984.

2. Senate Committee on Government Operations, *Hearings on Oversight of US Government Operations*, 3 February 1976, 362.

3. *Today*, NBC television, 10 June 1975.

4. Harry Howe Ransom, "Congress, Legitimacy and the Intelligence Community," paper presented at the Western Political Science Association Annual Convention, San Francisco, Calif., April 1976.

5. Quoted by Tom Braden, "What's Wrong with the CIA?" *Saturday Review* 2 (5 April 1975): 14.

6. Richard B. Russell Library, Oral History No. 86, taped by Hughes Cates (22 February 1977), University of Georgia, Athens.

7. Walter Norblad (R-OR), *Congressional Record*, 15 August 1963, 15086.

8. Jerrold L. Walden, "The CIA: A Study in the Arrogation of Administrative Powers," *George Washington Law Review* 39 (October 1970): 95.

9. *Congressional Record*, 9 April 1956, 5924.

10. Walden, "CIA," 96–97.

11. On the structure and budget of the intelligence community, see Harry F. Eustace, "Changing Intelligence Priorities," *Electronic Warfare/Defense Electronics* 28 (November 1978): 35–37. Eustace estimates that the American intelligence budget is just below $13 billion. On the budget, see also George Lardner Jr., "Missing Intelligence Charters," *Nation* 227 (2 September 1978): 169. On the organization of the intelligence community, see also Victor Marchetti and John D. Marks, *The CIA and the Cult of Intelligence* (New York: Knopf, 1974); Harry Howe Ransom, *The Intelligence Establishment* (Cambridge, MA: Harvard University Press, 1970); David Wise and Thomas B. Ross, *The Invisible Government* (New York: Random House, 1964), and *The Espionage Establishment* (New York: Random House, 1967); Frank Donner, "The Theory and Practice of American Political Intelligence," *New York Review of Books*, vol. 16, 22 April 1971, 27–39; Paul W. Blackstock, "The Intelligence Community under the Nixon Administration," *Armed Forces and Society* 1 (Winter 1975): 231–250; Tad Szulc, "Inside the American Intelligence Establishment," *Washingtonian*, 9 March 1974, 55–56, 99–106.

12. Leverett Saltonstall, *Congressional Record*, 9 April 1956, 5924. See also House Permanent Select Committee on Intelligence, *Hearings on Congressional Oversight of Covert Activities*, 3; Dean Rusk's testimony in Senate Committee on Government Operations, *Hearings on Oversight of US Government Intelligence Functions*, 22 January 1976, 75.

13. Cited by Marchetti and Marks, *CIA*, 122.

14. Quoted by Bob Wiedrich, "Can Congress Keep a Secret," *Chicago Tribune*, 3 February 1976.

15. Interview, Washington, DC, 21 November 1975.

16. On 14 April 1971, cited by Ransom, "Congress, Legitimacy and the Intelligence Community," 13.

17. William Colby and Peter Forbath, *Honorable Men: My Life in the CIA* (New York: Simon & Schuster, 1978).

18. Senate Committee on Foreign Relations, *Hearings on CIA Foreign and Domestic Activities*, 22 January 1975, 11.

19. 28 November 1961, cited by Wise and Ross, *Invisible Government*, 248.

20. David R. Mayhew, *Congress: The Electoral Connection* (New Haven, CT: Yale University Press, 1974), 125.

21. Following the Bay of Pigs debacle and the Cuban missile confrontation, the Senate critiqued the intelligence failures experienced during these crises; after the capture of the *Pueblo* spy ship by North Koreans in 1968, a House Armed Services Subcommittee focused on intelligence shortcomings reflected in this incident; and in 1970 a Senate Foreign Relations Subcommittee, under the leadership of Senator Stuart Symington (D-MO), revealed and criticized CIA paramilitary activity in Laos. Senate and House probes into CIA involvement in the Watergate scandal and the uncovering of secret CIA funding of Radio Free Europe (without congressional authorization) are other examples

of more energetic oversight efforts. See Ransom, "Congress and the Intelligence Agencies," 163–164.

22. Harry Howe Ransom, "Secret Intelligence Agencies and Congress," *Society* 12 (March/April 1975): 36.

23. See *Congressional Record*, 14 July 1966, 15673, cited in Walden, "CIA," 98.

24. On these votes, see *Congressional Record*, 11 April 1956, 6068; 14 July 1966, 15699; 2 October 1974, 33482.

25. See Sol Stern, "NSA and the CIA," *Ramparts* 5 (March 1967): 29–38.

26. The *Times* printed stories on the CIA practically every day from 22 December through 31 December. For the phrase "massive spying," see Seymour M. Hersh, "Underground for the CIA in New York: An Ex-Agent Tells of Spying on Students," *New York Times*, 29 December 1974. Among the other findings revealed by Hersh were these: over two dozen CIA agents were assigned to surveillance missions in New York City during antiwar protests at Columbia University; the CIA conducted telephone wiretaps and break-ins, and developed "psychological assessment" profiles of student leaders; a Domestic Operations Division within the CIA was responsible for infiltrating various ethnic and émigré groups in major cities throughout the United States; and the Agency ran a media operation known as Continental Press out of the National Press Building in Washington, and secretly funded American publishing houses (including the well-known Praeger Publishers in New York City).

27. See Colby and Forbath, *Honorable Men*, 394–395; Edward Jay Epstein, "The War within the CIA," *Commentary* 66 (August 1978): 35–39; William Colby, letter to the editor, *Washington Star*, 20 August 1978.

28. Interview with James Angleton, Washington, DC, 29 July 1975; see also Colby and Forbath, *Honorable Men*, 396.

29. Colby and Forbath, *Honorable Men*, 391.

30. *New York Times*, 31 December 1974.

31. Co-sponsored by Senator Harold E. Hughes (D-IA) and Congressman Leo J. Ryan (D-CA), the amendment became law on 30 December 1974 (22 USC 2422). See appendix 1.

32. See John T. Elliff, "Congress and Intelligence Community," in *Congress Reconsidered*, edited by Lawrence C. Dodd and Bruce I. Oppenheimer (New York: Praeger, 1977), 196. William Colby remembers that the Ford administration hoped its commission would "still the outcry and thus prevent a full investigation of intelligence from getting started." Colby and Forbath, *Honorable Men*, 398.

33. Colby and Forbath, *Honorable Men*, 402.

34. *New York Times*, 11 June 1975.

35. Colby and Forbath, *Honorable Men*, 391.

Chapter 2. A Committee Is Formed

1. For the debate on S. Res. 21, see *Congressional Record*, 21 January 1975, S524–S529; 27 January 1975, S967–S984 (the adopted resolution is at S983).

2. Ibid., 21 January 1975, 596F.

3. Ibid., 27 January 1975, S984. Two years earlier, Mansfield had sent a similar letter to federal agencies requesting them to preserve all their files related to the Watergate incident for the pending Ervin committee investigation. At that time, CIA director Richard Helms had his secretary destroy all the tapes of conversations in his office over his seven-year directorship—hardly a promising precedent for the intelligence investigation. See Commission on CIA Activities within the United States, *Report to the President*, June 1975, 204.

4. Interview with Frank Church, Washington, DC, 20 March 1979.

5. Cited in George Lardner Jr., "Frank Church Joins the Pack," *Nation* 222 (17 April 1976): 468.

6. Church interview, 20 March 1979.

7. *Washington Post*, 28 January 1975.

8. *Christian Science Monitor*, 3 February 1975.

9. CBS television, 1 February 1975.

10. *Congressional Record*, 21 January 1975, S968.

11. Senate Committee on Government Operations, *Hearings on Oversight of US Government Intelligence Functions*, 21 January 1976, 17–18.

12. Quoted by Albert R. Hunt of the *Wall Street Journal*, on *Washington Week in Review*, PBS television, 2 November 1979.

13. On the CIA–Watergate connection, see David Wise, *The American Police State* (New York: Random House, 1976), chap. 7, and the Commission on CIA Activities within the United States, *Report to the President*, June 1975, chap. 14.

14. Rowland Evans and Robert Novak, "Sen. Baker: Looking Ahead," *Washington Post*, 21 March 1975.

15. Interview with Mrs. Laura Church, Boise, Idaho, 18 March 1972.

16. George Lardner Jr., "Frank Church's Presidential Dreams," *Washington Post*, 18 April 1976.

17. Steve Leopold, interview with Frank Church, *Stanford Daily* (Stanford University), 20 February 1964.

18. Interview with attorney Bruce Bowler, Boise, Idaho, 17 March 1972.

19. Jack Anderson and Les Whitten, "Frank Church—A Study in Courage," *Washington Post*, 15 March 1976.

20. *Boise Journal*, 17 August 1956.

21. "An Apostle of Non-Interventionism," *Washington Post*, 10 May 1975.

22. See, e.g., sources cited in Gwen Gibson, "DC Wash," *New York News*, 28 May 1960; David S. Broder, "Frank Church: The Unbeaten Candidate," *Washington Post*, 30 May 1976; Lardner, "Frank Church Joins the Pack," 467–468.

23. See Mary Perot Nichols, "Frank Church: The Hottest Liberal Dark Horse," *Village Voice*, 2 June 1975; Anderson and Whitten, "Frank Church"; Lardner, "Frank Church Joins the Pack."

24. See Colman McCarthy, "Philip Hart: The Gentle Way Is the Effective Way," *Washington Post*, 2 February 1976.

25. See Connecticut Walker, "'Mac' Mathias: The Brightest GOP Senator Scouts a Third Party," *Parade*, 15 February 1976.

26. On this initial concern of Hart's, see Richard E. Cohen, "Freshmen in the Senate Being Seen—And Heard," *National Journal* 11 (17 March 1979): 440.

27. *New York Times*, 25 January 1976.

Chapter 3. Establishing an Agenda

1. Walter Pincus, "The 'Spying' Inquiry," *Washington Post*, 4 February 1975.

2. For the text of S. Res. 21, see *Congressional Record*, 27 January 1975, S983–S984.

3. Interview with F. A. O. Schwarz Jr., Katonah, New York, 8 June 1979.

4. Memorandum from William G. Miller to Frank Church, 31 January 1975.

5. Interview, Washington, DC, 12 June 1979.

6. "The Names in CIA Files: Some Belong, Some Don't," *Washington Post*, 2 February 1975.

7. 31 January 1975.

8. William G. Miller, Memorandum for the Record, 26 February 1975.

9. Ibid., 27 February 1975.

10. Schwarz, 8 June 1979.

11. Ibid.

12. Memorandum from William G. Miller to Frank Church, 4 March 1975.

13. This account of the White House meeting is drawn chiefly from William G. Miller, Memorandum of Conversation, 5 March 1975, and Church interview, 20 March 1979. See also *New York Times*, 9 March 1975, and *Congressional Quarterly Weekly Report*, 8 March 1975.

14. *Los Angeles Times*, 21 February 1975.

15. *Washington Post*, 16 March 1975.

16. *Washington Post*, 10 March 1975.

17. *Washington Post*, 11 March 1975.

18. *New York Times*, 16 March 1975.

19. *Washington Post*, 17 March 1975.

20. Throughout this week and the next, the nation's television networks and leading newspapers carried one story after another about possible CIA assassination activities.

21. *Washington Post*, 17 March 1975.

22. See, e.g., *Washington Post*, 28 March and 4 April 1975; *Newsweek*, 28 April 1975.

23. See *Washington Post*, 19, 20, 21, 23, and 30 March 1975; *New York Times*, 20 and 26 March 1975.

24. *Boston Globe*, 20 March 1975.

25. Ibid.

26. *Washington Post*, 22 April 1975.

27. *Washington Post*, 19 March 1975.

28. Memorandum from William B. Bader to William G. Miller and F. A. O. Schwarz Jr., 11 March 1975.

29. Schwarz interview, 8 June 1979.

30. Interview with William B. Bader, Washington, DC, 12 December 1978.

31. Interview with Frederick Baron, Washington, DC, 4 December 1978.

32. Schwarz interview, 8 June 1979.

33. Memorandum from William G. Miller to Frank Church, 31 March 1975.

34. Interview with William G. Miller, Washington, DC, 15 December 1978.

35. Schwarz interview, 8 June 1979.

36. Baron interview, 4 December 1978. The committee learned to appreciate the line, "To the innermost bit it is nothing but layers, smaller and smaller, nature's a joker!" (Henrik Ibsen, *Peer Gynt*, act 5, scene 5).

37. Interview, Washington, DC, 21 December 1978.

38. 7 April 1975.

39. William G. Miller, Memorandum for the Record, 1 April 1975.

40. Memorandum from William G. Miller to Frank Church, 3 April 1975.

41. *New York Times*, 9 April 1975.

42. On the establishment of ARIO, see *Washington Post*, 22 March and 10 May 1975. The organization is now called the Association of Former Intelligence Officers (AFIO).

43. *Washington Post*, 8 April 1975.

44. "CIA: Power and Arrogance," *Washington Post*, 27 April 1975.

45. Cited by Buckley, *Washington Star*, 23 March 1975.

46. In 1977, Helms entered a plea of *nolo contendere* to a charge of refusing to answer material questions before a Senate committee. He was chastised and fined by a DC district judge. See *Washington Post*, 5 November 1977.

47. William G. Miller, Memorandum for the Record, 14 April 1975.

48. Letter from Frank Church to William Colby, 16 April 1975.

49. Press briefing, Washington, DC, 24 April 1975.

50. *New York Times*, 24 April 1975. The reference was to Saigon, which was on the verge of collapse.

51. The letters, signed by Church, were dated 24 April 1975.

52. Memorandum from William G. Miller to Frank Church, 24 April 1975.

53. Memorandum for the Record, 29 April 1975.

54. Memorandum from William G. Miller to Frank Church, 30 April 1975.

55. William G. Miller, Memorandum of Conversation, 6 May 1975.

56. Quoted in Nichols, "Frank Church."

57. Schwarz interview, 8 June 1979.

58. *New York Times*, 10 May 1975.

59. Quoted in ibid.

60. *Washington Post*, 10 May 1975.

61. Quoted anonymously in *Washington Star*, 12 May 1975.

Chapter 4. Assassination Plots

1. *New York Times*, 15 May 1975.

2. 18 May 1975.

3. See Ward Just, *Boston Sunday Globe*, 1 October 1979; Thomas Powers, *The Man Who Kept the Secrets: Richard Helms and the CIA* (New York: Knopf, 1979), 7, 119.

4. See Colby and Forbath, *Honorable Men*, esp. chap. 13.

5. See Powers, *The Man Who Kept the Secrets*, 297.

6. Colby and Forbath, *Honorable Men*, 407.

7. Interview with William Colby, Washington, DC, 21 March 1979.

8. Ibid.

9. Ibid.

10. Letter from Frank Church to the Rockefeller Commission, 22 June 1975.

11. Baron interview, 4 December 1978.

12. Schwarz interview, 8 June 1979.

13. See Senate Select Committee to Study Governmental Operations with Respect to Intelligence Activities, *Alleged Assassination Plots Involving Foreign Leaders: An Interim Report*, 20 November 1975 (hereafter *Assassination Plots*), 181n.

14. Ibid., 41.

15. Ibid., 25.

16. Ibid., 142n2.

17. Ibid., 199.

18. See Daniel Schorr, *Clearing the Air* (Boston: Houghton Mifflin, 1977), 148.

19. *Washington Star*, 28 June 1975.

20. Press conference, following McCone's appearance before the Church committee, 6 June 1975. Speculates another, anonymous "veteran intelligence officer": "If Congress had been asked to vote on the assassination of Fidel Castro in the early 1960s, the measure would have passed by at least a two-to-one majority, and the person who introduced the bill would have been given a medal. Now Congress is indignant that such a plan was ever being considered." Quoted by Bonner Day, "The Battle over US Intelligence," *Air Force* 61 (May 1978): 13.

Chapter 5. Rogue Elephant

1. 9 June 1975.

2. Commission on CIA Activities within the United States, *Report to the President*, June 1975, quote from 10. One of the most repulsive findings of the commission was related to a CIA program in which the hallucinogenic drug LSD was dispensed to unsuspecting subjects. One case had led to a suicide, according to the commission's report. Soon after the release of the report, newspaper interviews with the family of the suicide victim uncovered the ugly details of the case. Along with four other scientists, the victim (Dr. Frank R. Olson, a civilian biochemist) had been given LSD by two CIA employees at a week-long conference in 1953. After drinking the drug, Olson and the others were told about the experiment and informed that their reactions would now be observed. Olson exhibited signs of imbalance at work during the next week and on 27 November was flown to New York City by the CIA to be examined by a psychiatrist. He and his Agency escort were booked into a room on the tenth floor of a hotel. At 1:30 in the morning, the escort heard a noise and awoke to see Olson leap from his bed and run full speed toward a drawn window shade. The CIA scientist plunged to the street below. Mrs. Olson and her three children

were told only that he "jumped or fell" to his death; nothing was said about the drug experiment. As they grew up, the Olson children lived with shame and doubt regarding the death of their father. "And we suddenly learn that for twenty-two years we were lied to, led to believe that Frank Olson had a fatal nervous breakdown," said the Olson family in an angry and moving statement to the press. See *Washington Post*, 10 July 1975. In a meeting with the family later in the year, President Ford called the experiments "illegal and unconscionable." *Washington Post*, 19 December 1975.

3. Nicholas M. Horrock, *New York Times*, 22 June 1975.

4. *Newsweek*, 16 June 1975, 19.

5. Interview with Burt Wides, Washington, DC, 20 December 1978.

6. Miller interview, 15 December 1978.

7. Interview, Washington, DC, 12 June 1978.

8. Taylor Branch, "The Trial of the CIA," *New York Times Magazine*, 12 September 1976, 115.

9. Church interview, 20 March 1979.

10. Schwarz interview, 8 June 1979.

11. Interview with Mark Gittenstein, Washington, DC, 22 December 1978.

12. Interview with Seymour Bolton, Washington, DC, 15 November 1979.

13. Memorandum from William G. Miller to Frank Church, 22 July 1975.

14. Schwarz interview, 8 June 1979.

15. According to one of the summaries, the Bureau's program of harassment against Chicago's Black Stone Rangers was an effort "to promote fraternal discord among black groups in Chicago." Only much later, when we obtained the actual COINTELPRO documents, did we learn that this operation was really designed to incite murder, blacks against blacks, through the use of anonymous letters. Here was a memorable object lesson in the importance of obtaining original documents, not summaries.

16. *New York Times*, 24 June 1975.

17. Reference to the Mondale meeting with the press was made by a reporter during the Church committee press conference of 23 June 1975.

18. *Newsweek*, 7 July 1975, 15.

19. The 40 Committee was a small NSC group that made sensitive intelligence recommendations to the president.

20. *Face the Nation*, CBS television, 20 July 1975.

21. Foreword to *Alleged Assassination Plots Involving Foreign Leaders*, the commercial edition of the Senate's *Assassination Plots* (New York: Norton, 1976), xxii.

22. *Assassination Plots*, 158.

23. Ibid.

24. Ibid., 149.

25. Ibid.

26. Ibid., 154.

27. Committee hearings, 9 June 1975.

28. Memorandum from Arthur M. Schlesinger Jr. to President John F. Kennedy, 5 September 1962.

29. *Assassination Plots*, 154.

30. Ibid., 151.

31. Ibid., 1.

32. Lardner, "Frank Church's Presidential Dreams."

33. Powers, *The Man Who Kept the Secrets*, 7.

34. Ward Just, *Boston Sunday Globe*, 1 October 1979.

35. Church interview, 20 March 1979.

Chapter 6. The Cave of Bugs

1. Schwarz interview, 8 June 1979.

2. From "Second Speech on Foot's Resolution," delivered in the Senate 26 January 1830, reprinted in *The Writings and Speeches of Daniel Webster*, vol. 6 (Boston: Little, Brown, 1903), 7.

3. *Chicago Tribune*, 4 August 1975.

4. *Washington Post*, 4 August 1975.

5. Ibid.

6. For a similar theme, see columnist Patrick Buchanan, *New York Times*, 8 August 1975.

7. *Washington Post*, 8 August 1975.

8. Cited in Carl Bernstein, "The CIA and the Media," *Rolling Stone*, 20 October 1977, 67.

9. Clark Clifford, former secretary of defense and one of the framers of the 1947 National Security Act, agreed with Church and earlier told the *Boston Globe* (24 July 1975), "For nearly 30 years, the CIA has wheeled and dealed without supervision."

10. *New York Times*, 20 August 1975.

11. *Panorama* (television news show), Washington, DC, 12 September 1975.

12. *New York Times*, 14 September 1975.

13. *New York Times*, 12 September 1975.

14. Later in the year, Colby disciplined the officer responsible for keeping the poisons, relieving him of further management responsibilities and reducing him in grade from GS-15 to GS-14. The poisons were given to research laboratories.

Chapter 7. Sinister Forces

1. *Washington Post*, 13 September 1975.

2. *Washington Post*, 17 September 1975.

3. *Washington Post*, 18 September 1975.

4. Anthony Lewis, "Only Congress Itself," *New York Times*, 18 September 1975.

5. Talking paper prepared by Tom Charles Huston for President Richard M. Nixon, 5 May 1970. For additional details on this meeting and other aspects of the Huston Plan case, see Loch K. Johnson, "National Security, Civil Liberties, and the Collection of Intelligence: A Report on the Huston Plan," in *Supplementary Detailed Staff Reports on Intelligence Activities and the Rights of Americans* (book 3 of *Final Reports of the Senate Select Committee to Study Governmental Operations with Respect to Intelligence Activities, 1975*), 921–986.

6. Theodore H. White, *Breach of Faith: The Fall of Richard Nixon* (New York: Atheneum, 1975), 133.

7. See *Supplementary Detailed Staff Reports on Intelligence Activities and the Rights of Americans*, 952. The memorandum was written sometime in July 1970.

8. Ibid., 960. The memorandum was dated 5 August 1970.

9. Apparently without an appreciation of the irony, on 7 October 1972 the Nixon administration appointed Huston to a Census Bureau Advisory Committee on Privacy and Confidentiality.

10. *Washington Post*, 26 September 1975.

11. Jay Shelledy, interview with James Angleton, *Lewiston* (Idaho) *Morning Tribune*, 6 June 1976.

12. Foreword to Alan Reitman, ed., *The Pulse of Freedom* (Norton: New York, 1975), 18.

13. See Hannah Arendt, *The Origins of Totalitarianism* (New York: Harcourt, Brace, 1951).

Chapter 8. Adrift

1. On 19 September 1975, David Aaron had written a memorandum to the White House staff, stressing bluntly that the committee wanted the National Intelligence Estimates on Chile after these "many, many weeks." On 22 September, Bill Miller wrote Seymour Bolton of the CIA liaison staff, warning him that the committee's patience was wearing thin, and that the members had voted unanimously to subpoena CIA documents but were willing to suspend the subpoena for a short time if the Agency showed immediate good faith.

2. After the investigation, another staffer recalled: "When the senators found out . . . that the hearings on the IRS didn't promise to be very 'sexy' they cancelled all but one day of the scheduled IRS hearings, and weeks of preparation by the staff went down the tube. It got rather frustrating." Larry Zelenak, interview with former FBI Task Force staffer Barbara Banoff, *Harvard Law Record* 63 (December 1976), 3.

3. See, e.g., *New York Times*, 6 October 1975.

4. Letter from William G. Miller to John Sherman Cooper (former senator, R-KY), 6 October 1975.

5. Ibid.

6. *Washington Star*, 22 October 1975.

7. Church interview, 20 March 1979.

8. J. Leiper Freeman, "Investigating the Executive Intelligence: The Fate of the Pike Committee," *Capitol Studies* 5 (Fall 1977): 109.

9. *Washington Post*, 1 October 1975; see also *Chicago Tribune*, 9 October 1975.

10. *New York Times*, 19 October 1975.

11. *Washington Post*, 19 October 1975.

12. The problem of amnesia among witnesses has plagued many a legislative investigation. See, e.g., Samuel Dash, *Chief Counsel: Inside the Ervin Committee—The Untold Story of Watergate* (New York: Random House, 1976), 194–195, 245.

Chapter 9. Bombarded

1. *NBC News*, 13 January 1978. For scholarly studies on covert action, see Emanual Alder, "Executive Command and Control in Foreign Policy: The CIA's Covert Activities," *Orbis* 23 (Fall 1979): 671–696; Loch Johnson, "The CIA: Controlling the Quiet Option," *Foreign Policy* 39 (Summer 1980): 143–153. See also *Covert Action*, vol. 7 of the *Hearings of the Senate Select Committee to Study Governmental Operations with Respect to Intelligence Activities*, 4 and 5 December 1975, 100–127.

2. See Harry Rositzke, *CIA's Secret Operations: Espionage, Counter Espionage, and Covert Action* (New York: Reader's Digest Press, 1977).

3. On the Bay of Pigs, see Peter Wyden, *Bay of Pigs: The Untold Story* (New York: Simon & Schuster, 1979); on Laos, see Marchetti and Marks, *CIA*, 235–236.

4. This summary of covert action in Chile is based on Church committee–published reports. See esp. *Covert Action*, 144–203.

5. *Congressional Record*, 4 November 1975, 34813.

6. Leslie H. Gelb, *New York Times*, 4 November 1975.

Chapter 10. Orwellian Nightmares

1. A few weeks earlier, Church's press secretary had offered this estimate to inquiring reporters.

2. Others perceived a rightward movement by Ford, too. The president's last-minute objections to the assassination report, e.g., were interpreted by *Newsweek* (10 November 1975) as partly "a desire not to alienate right-wing supporters by allowing further damage to the image of the CIA."

3. Indeed, public television had abandoned its coverage of our public hearings; the anticipated ennui of the IRS hearing, along with the uncertainty surrounding the rest of our agenda, was apparently too much for them.

4. In fact, it did threaten in a letter written by Miller on behalf of the committee (William G. Miller to Seymour Bolton, 22 September 1975). The threat seemed to loosen more documents from the CIA's tight grip.

5. Memorandum from William Bader to Bill Miller, 12 November 1975.

6. Memorandum from David Aaron to Bill Miller, 13 November 1975.

7. *Wall Street Journal*, 17 November 1975.

8. Ibid.

9. For this story from Campbell's vantage point, see Judith Exner, *My Story* (New York: Grove Press, 1977).

10. *Chicago Tribune,* 11 March 1976.

11. Interview with John T. Elliff, Washington, DC, 15 December 1978.

12. Ibid.

13. Schwarz interview, 8 June 1979.

14. Interview with FBI Task Force staffer, Washington, DC, December 1978.

15. A few of the committee staffers brooded darkly about the possibility of a setup by

the Bureau, whereby King was "encouraged" through FBI media leaks to abandon plans to stay in a white-owned hotel in Memphis and move to the less secure Lorraine; no evidence was ever discovered to corroborate this hypothesis, however. For the most recent evidence on the King murder, see House Select Committee on Assassinations, *Final Report*, 1979.

16. Baron interview, 4 December 1978.

17. Schwarz interview, 8 June 1979, original emphasis. For another example of strong pressures from committee members to rush forward with an investigation before the staff work was completed, see Samuel Dash's account of the Senate Watergate inquiry in *Chief Counsel: Inside the Ervin Committee—The Untold Story of Watergate* (New York: Random House, 1976), 53–54, 97.

Chapter 11. Resistance

1. 18 November 1975. Nine Democrats were already expected to enter the primary.

2. See, e.g., *Washington Post*, 20 November 1975.

3. See *Senate Manual*, Senate Doc. No. 91-1 (Washington, DC: Government Printing Office, 1969), 51.

4. *Chicago Tribune*, 24 November 1975.

5. *New York Times*, 22 November 1975.

6. Wise, *American Police State*, 213.

7. *Washington Star*, 24 November 1975.

8. *Chicago Tribune*, 24 November 1975.

9. *Washington Post*, 25 November 1975.

10. Anthony Lewis, *New York Times*, 21 November 1975.

11. For a historical perspective on the 1975 Angolan civil war, see David Ottaway, *Washington Post*, 18 May 1978; Gerald J. Bender, "Angola: Left, Right and Wrong," *Foreign Policy* 43 (Summer 1981): 53–69.

12. One of the most chilling passages in the assassination report consisted of quotations from cables sent to Kissinger by Korry. One cable indicated the kind of pressure Korry had brought upon the retiring president of Chile, Eduardo Frei, to join a coup against Allende. "Not a nut or a bolt will be allowed to reach Chile under Allende," he had warned Frei. "Once Allende comes to power we shall do all within our power to condemn Chile and the Chileans to utmost deprivation and poverty." See *Assassination Plots*, 231n2.

13. *New York Times*, 30 November 1975.

14. *New York Times*, 1 December 1975.

15. Letter from Herbert J. Miller Jr. to Senator Frank Church, 13 November 1975.

16. Reflecting back on the congressional investigations, former CIA director Colby concluded similarly that they lacked a "sense of proportion." Just as "television focuses on the one soldier out of step in a parade," Colby continued, "so did the investigators focus on the few abuses, leaving a false overall impression for the public." Interview with William Colby, Washington, DC, 27 February 1979.